Praise for *The Au*

"On the wave of the great peace movement that grew in the 1980s with the slogan 'For a Europe without missiles from the Atlantic to the Urals,' some communist parties, Italy's in particular, launched a dialog with certain social democratic parties whose leadership had in those years taken a similar position, and with the CPSU itself that Gorbachev had come to head, proposing a 'third way' for Europe outside of the blocs. Had the occasion been seized then to rediscover Austro-Marxism, which would have allowed a more profound reworking of the different political-strategic outlooks, the process would have been sturdier. This did not happen, and it was another lost opportunity.

"Even as a not very orthodox communist, it never occurred to me at the time to look into Austro-Marxism, since my generation harbored a strong suspicion that it involved opportunistic superficialities. It is only recently, largely thanks to Otto Bauer's *The Austrian Revolution*, that I have discovered the richness of the Austro-Marxist tradition and the many affinities between the writings of Bauer and of our Gramsci, especially on the question of hegemony.' To his credit, Togliatti legitimized Gramsci's analysis from the very first post-war years, but not enough to open the way to Austro-Marxism, which remained taboo for us. This excellent new English edition of Bauer's classic work will surely stimulate new interest in Italy and help fill this void in its Marxist culture."
—Luciana Castellina, cofounder of *Il Manifesto*

"The revolution in Central Europe in 1918–21 was a giant event that came closer to changing world history than most of us realize. For English speakers, this translation opens a challenging new window on the history of the Austrian workers' council movement and the role of the Entente powers in the counterrevolution that followed. Published in 1923, it stands unique as an analysis of the revolution's internal dynamics and the costs of defeat."
—Mike Davis, author of *Planet of Slums*

"Otto Bauer's book on the Austrian Revolution is one of the forgotten shining gems of the extraordinarily rich literature that Austro-Marxism has to offer. Thanks to this excellent new translation, this classical work is now available to the English reader in a complete version for the first time. Students of European socialism, of Marxism, and of European history will

be able to enjoy a first-rate theoretical and historical analysis of modern mass democracy by the leading theoretician of European social democracy during the interwar years and after. Otto Bauer's book, first published in 1923, caused quite a sensation in its time, and rightly so. It is one of the classics of Marxist political analysis, only comparable to Marx' *Eighteenth Brumaire of Louis Napoleon* or Trotsky's *History of the Russian Revolution*. Like Trotsky in Russia, Otto Bauer was one of the core protagonists of the Austrian Revolution of 1918–1919, which led to the establishment of the first republic in the part of the Habsburg Empire that became Austria. How does the character of a democratic republic based on universal suffrage change due to the shifting power relations between the major social classes? This is the problem Bauer scrutinizes in his seminal book. His findings—that the contents and the meanings of the republic can and do change even if the political forms established by a constitution remain the same—are still relevant today. Bauer's analysis, which exemplarily highlights the crucial difference between the form of the state and the form of governance, covers an exceptionally broad terrain: from parliamentary politics up to the first forms of proto-corporatism (dubbed 'functional democracy'). His book triggered a lively debate among leading political and legal theorists, notably Hans Kelsen, the father of the first Austrian republic's constitution, Bauer, Karl Renner, and Max Adler. Bauer's final reflections on modern democracy and its crises appear in his last major work, *Between Two World Wars?*, published in 1936."
—Michael R. Krätke, author of *Friedrich Engels*

"Red Vienna and the contributions of its protagonists like Otto Bauer are tragically overlooked on the contemporary left. Walter Baier and Eric Canepa have edited a thrilling work from Bauer with the aim of correcting that—and to chart a new course for those looking for alternatives to bankrupt social democratic parties and defeated Leninist ones."
—Bhaskar Sunkara, founding editor of *Jacobin*

THE AUSTRIAN REVOLUTION

OTTO BAUER

Edited by Eric Canepa and Walter Baier

Introduction by Walter Baier

Haymarket Books
Chicago, Illinois

Published in 2021 by
Haymarket Books
P.O. Box 180165
Chicago, IL 60618
773-583-7884
www.haymarketbooks.org
info@haymarketbooks.org

ISBN: 9781642591620

The translation, research and gathering of pictorial material for this book was funded by Transform Europe and partially financed through a subsidy from the European Parliament; its publication was made possible by the generous support of Lannan Foundation and the Wallace Action Fund.

Distributed to the trade the US through Consortium Book Sales and Distribution (www.cbsd.com) and internationally through Ingram Publisher Services International (www.ingramcontent.com).

Special discounts are available for bulk purchases by organizations and institutions. Please call 773-583-7884 or email info@haymarketbooks.org for more information.

Cover image of *Proclamation of the Republic in Front of the Parliament*, 1918, by Rudolf Konopa, Wien Museum, Vienna. Cover design by Rachel Cohen.

Printed in Canada by union labor.

Library of Congress Cataloging-in-Publication data is available.

10 9 8 7 6 5 4 3 2 1

CONTENTS

Part IV: The Equilibrium of Class Forces

Part V: The Restoration of the Bourgeoisie

ACKNOWLEDGEMENTS

We would like to thank transform! europe for its financial support of the translation, research, and the acquisition of pictorial material and Heidemarie Ambrosch of transform! europe for her coordination of this assistance. The Verein für Geschichte der ArbeiterInnenbewegung (Association for the History of the Labour Movement – VGA), Vienna, provided crucial support in supplying source materials and providing much detailed information and ongoing fact-checking; in this regard we thank in particular Georg Spitaler as well as Michaela Maier (director VGA), and, for making available the VGA's rich photographic archive, Elfriede Pokorny. For pictorial material we are also grateful to Manfred Mugrauer and Fini Seif of the Kommunistische Partei Österreichs-Bild-Archiv, Vienna, Nicola Fontana of the Museo della Guerra, Rovereto, Caterina Tomasi of the Fondazione Museo Storico del Trentino, Trento, Daniela Geist and Frauke Kreutler of the Wien Museum, Vienna, and Barbara Kramreither of the Heeresgeschichtliches Museum (Museum of the History of the Army), Vienna.

For further source material and source checking we would like to thank Klaus Zeleny of the Hans-Kelsen-Institut, Vienna, Lisa Kenny of the British Library's News Reference Team, and Zdenek Matušik and Lenka Válková of the National Library of the Czech Republic.

In New York thanks are due to Michael Lardner of the Marxist Education Project for his mediation in providing printed copy needed for proofreading.

Also in the United States, we thank Haymarket Books, in particular Ida Audeh and Janet Reed Blake for their painstaking proofreading of the text, Rachel Cohen for typesetting it, Nisha Bolsey for coordinating the whole project, and Duncan Thomas and Brekhna Aftab for their efforts in promoting the book in Europe.

And finally, we would like to thank Perry Bernstein of New York who went through the whole text suggesting countless, often crucial, substantive corrections.

Needless to say, all responsibility for errors and omissions rests solely with the editors.

—Walter Baier and Eric Canepa, Vienna, April 2021

INTRODUCTION

OTTO BAUER
AND AUSTRO-MARXISM

Walter Baier

In the future, the conditions under which the workers' parties of different countries will have to struggle will be more diverse than ever. Therefore their methods and ideologies also will differ fundamentally, which means that contemporary socialism needs to recognize the diversity of methods and ideologies of the different labor parties as the inevitable result of the diversity of the working class's economic and political conditions of struggle in the different countries—and, despite this diversity, to unite the labor parties within a community.
Otto Bauer, *Zwischen Zwei Weltkriegen?: Die Krise der Weltwirtschaft, der Demokratie und des Sozialismus* (1936)[1]

When people speak of European Marxism, they have in mind a division between an Eastern tradition oriented to Lenin and a Western one originating in Luxemburg and Gramsci. Too little is known about the Central European tradition, which is actually no less developed or rich and whose most important manifestation was Austro-Marxism. The municipal policies of Red Vienna in the 1920s and 1930s made Austro-Marxism famous worldwide. Of Austro-Marxism's theoretical legacy, Rudolf Hilferding's book *Finance Capital*—which Lenin cited in his famous study of imperialism—is still well known; and Karl Renner's and Otto Bauer's studies on nationalities policy are remembered, at least among specialists. But the

1

numerous Austro-Marxist contributions to state theory, to the theory of socialist transformation, and the theory of the developmental tendencies of political democracy have been generally forgotten, although their authors, as the German historian and political scientist Michael Krätke finds, constitute by far the most productive group of German-speaking Marxists.[2]

The Austro-Marxist School

Otto Bauer was born on September 5, 1881, into a well-to-do, liberal Jewish family. He attended gymnasium in Merano and Liberec (Reichenberg), where his father had settled for business reasons.

At the turn of the century he returned to Vienna and matriculated in the University's Law Faculty. The circle of Marxist theoreticians there who formed around him (later known as Austro-Marxists[3]) would occupy leading positions within Austrian Social Democracy.

In 1927 Bauer attributed the coining of the term "Austro-Marxism" to an unnamed US socialist.

> At that time the term "Austro-Marxists" designated a group of Austrian comrades who were active in the field of scholarship: Max Adler, Karl Renner, Rudolf Hilferding, Gustav Eckstein, Otto Bauer, Friedrich Adler, and others. What united them was not a specific political tendency but the distinctiveness of their scientific work. . . . While Marx and Engels were principally inspired by Hegel and the later generation of Marxists had accepted materialism, these more recent Marxists drew partly on Kant, partly on Mach. In Austrian universities they had to deal with the so-called Austrian school of political economy. . . . And, finally, in Old-Austria they were all shaken and politically socialized by the struggles of nationalities and had to learn how to apply the Marxist conception of history to complex phenomena, which did not permit a superficial application of Marxist method.[4]

In 1907 the 26-year-old Bauer published his first major work, *The Question of Nationalities and Social Democracy*, in which he tried to deal with the most difficult question that Social Democracy in Austria, united in 1889 into a party, faced: the complex national relations of the multinational state ruled by the Habsburgs.*

The Dual Monarchy—or to be more precise the Cisleithanian half of

---

* German-Austrians, Czechs, Slovaks, Slovenians, Croatians, Italians, Ruthenians (Ukrainians), Poles, and Hungarians were its principal ethnic components.

the Empire*—embarked on the path to capitalist development later than the other European great powers did. Its bourgeoisies grew in backward agrarian nations—*peoples without history*, as Friedrich Engels infelicitously called them[5]—who raised demands for national emancipation.

The problem was that the multinational state was a conglomerate of centuries-old dynastic acquisitions and conquests (crownlands) of the Habsburgs, which in turn were inhabited by nationally mixed populations. The dynamic of capitalist development provoked considerable migratory movement between the crownlands, which shifted the ethnic relations. "In Vienna in the last decade before the World War nearly a quarter of the city's two million people were migrants from Bohemia and Moravia . . . the unassimilated Czech population from Vienna hovered around a quarter of a million."[6]

Social Democracy was the only internationally organized party in the Empire.† It was thus predestined to put forward a program for the democratic reconstruction of the multinational state, the famous Brünn Nationalities Program,[7] which was based on studies by Renner who was a constitutional jurist.[8] In reconstructing the state he proposed combining two principles that would upturn it: the personality principle and the principle of national self-administration. The personality principle was to anchor national rights as rights of individuals without tying them to a specific national territory. A Czech worker in Vienna would be part of the Czech national community just as the German-speaking official in Prague would belong to the German-Austrian community. Self-administrative bodies of the national communities so formed were to replace the historic crownlands and regulate their cultural affairs in complete autonomy, while the state as a whole would be governed by a parliament elected by universal suffrage.

With this Nationalities Program, Social Democracy not only put forward a concept for salvaging the multinational state but also announced its readiness to govern that state.

---

* After Austria-Hungary was reconstructed as a Double Monarchy in 1867 in the framework of a state reform (the "Ausgleich" or Compromise) giving far-reaching autonomy to the Kingdom of Hungary, the northern and western parts of the Empire, which consisted of crownlands inhabited by German-speaking and Slav populations, were designated Cisleithania in contradistinction to Hungary (Transleithania), whose western border was defined by the river Leitha.

† In fact, the SDAP was informally referred to as the "Austrian International."

However, in the mid-1890s the Social Democratic Party, too, was seized by national disintegration. Initially, the workers, as the underdogs of the nations, kept away from the national strivings that came from the bourgeoisie. Later, however, when they affiliated to the national communities through their participation in the general struggle for universal suffrage, they were gripped by these strivings.[9]

In his book Bauer reacted to this phenomenon by giving Renner's constitutional-law proposals an ideological foundation. The book was amicably received by Czech intellectuals, even though they considered the proposals to be unrealizable.[10]

It is indeed legitimate to ask whether at this point the corrosion of the multilateral state had advanced so far that nationalism, which Social Democracy's program attempted to overcome, would inevitably spread to the party itself.

Theoreticians like Josef Strasser—whose unconditional internationalism, certainly insufficiently complex in comparison to Bauer's analysis,[11] was suspected of buttressing the dominant position of the German-speaking parts of the movement—were pushed to the margins of the debate, which was especially polarized in the Czech party.

When in 1911 Austrian Social Democracy dissolved into national parties, it finally fell victim to its most significant political success—the achievement of general suffrage, although still restricted to men.[12] Renner's finely chiseled plan for salvaging the multinational state became obsolete—at the very latest with the world war initiated by the Habsburgs. But this was not the case with Bauer's work whose central question—the relation between class struggle and nationalism—is still relevant today.

Best known is perhaps his definition of nations as "a community of character that has grown out of a community of fate."[13] Less known, but remarkable because of its closeness to today's social science methods,[14] is what he said in the Preface about his work: that "the focus of theory is not to be sought in the definition of nation but in the description of the integration process from which the modern nation emerged."[15]

The moment of truth for Social Democracy in Austria came on July 28, 1914, when Franz Joseph declared war on Serbia. The party executive as well as the national parties supported the war unleashed by the Emperor and the military caste. In August Bauer was drafted into the army and landed in a Russian prisoners-of-war camp from which he returned in 1917. As a leftist and opponent of war, which he had become under the influence of the Russian Revolution, he now distanced himself from Renner's position on nationalities policy, which continued to be oriented to the maintenance of the multinational state.

In January 1918 Bauer presented the Nationalities Program of the Left.[16] It unconditionally recognized the right of the peoples oppressed by the Habsburgs to national self-determination and the formation of their own states. When the party executive switched to this position, it was too late to transform the multinational state into a Central European federation of independent states; but it is Otto Bauer's achievement as Foreign Secretary of the newly proclaimed Republic of German-Austria that the disintegration of the Empire and formation of new states did not lead to a Central European war.

Bauer's achievement as a theoretician of the national question is overshadowed by his German nationalism. As Foreign Secretary recognizing the right to self-determination of all peoples of the Monarchy, he could not conceive of claiming this right for the German-speaking Austrians other than through annexation to Germany. When this was rejected by the victorious powers in the Paris peace negotiations, he resigned.

His German national convictions also influenced his attitude to the annexation forcibly accomplished by the Nazis in 1938. His anti-fascist convictions were of course impeccable, but he could not bring himself to defend Austria's national independence since he continued to think in a Pan-German context. "The German-Austrian working class can only be free if the whole German working class is free. The future of the German-Austrian working class is the future of the German Revolution," he wrote just a few weeks before his death in exile in Paris on July 5, 1938.[17]

Revolution and State in Otto Bauer

In November 1918 in Central Europe, a 400-year-old empire disappeared. From its ruins four new states arose: Hungary, Czechoslovakia, the Kingdom of Yugoslavia, and Poland. "And the rest is Austria," French prime minister Georges Clemenceau is supposed to have said. Out of "the rest" the German-Austrian Republic was formed; in it the power of the emperor, the nobility, and the military bureaucracy passed to the bourgeoisie.

The victory of the bourgeois revolution was not won on the barricades by an insurgent people but fell into their lap through the defeat of the Habsburgs in war. "The victory of the western powers over the central powers was the victory of bourgeois democracy over the oligarchic military monarchies. It was the biggest, bloodiest bourgeois revolution in world history."*

Within a few weeks Social Democracy—the only entity that maintained order—enacted women's suffrage, the eight-hour day, and state unemployment compensation. This was followed six months later by laws introducing factory councils and paid vacations as well as the socialization of large economic enterprises.

The subject of Bauer's *The Austrian Revolution* is the period from 1918 to 1922. His chronicle, which includes substantial nineteenth-century background of the Czech, Yugoslav, and Polish nationalist movements, begins with the dissolution of the Empire in the last months of the war, with accounts of the national revolutions in Central Europe, the founding of the German-Austrian Republic and its revolutionary convulsions, and the consolidation of bourgeois rule in the late fall of 1922.

Austria's victorious bourgeoisie at first walked on shaky ground. In contrast to the new nation-states, in which independence masked the underlying social antagonisms, the passive bourgeois revolution in Austria intensified class antagonisms and pressed toward social revolution.

In quick succession the political constellations changed: The initial hegemony of the socialist working class in the first weeks of the Revolution was followed by what Bauer called the *equilibrium of class forces*, in the context of a coalition government of Social Democrats and conservatives, and finally by the predominance of bourgeois forces and—by way of external economic and military pressure—the full restoration of bourgeois rule.

Bauer described this as the necessary succession of stages of a bourgeois revolution, but also as transitional stages to a new assault on the part of the working class—which appeared to him inevitably imminent—but this time toward a socialist revolution. This must have seemed all the more plausible after Social Democracy had emerged from the elections for the Constituent National Assembly in 1919 as the strongest force.

In that context Otto Bauer also became head of a parliamentary commission charged with preparing the socialization of large-scale industry and landholding. He explained the goals of socialization in a series of articles appearing in the *Arbeiter-Zeitung* in 1919, also published as pamphlets in Austria and Germany under the title *Der Weg zum Sozialismus* (The Path to Socialism).

"There is not one path to socialism but many," he wrote.[18] Democratic

---

* See pp. 167 in this volume.

socialism presupposed "the economic self-management of the whole people."[19] Inspired by English guild socialism, he envisaged the management of socialist branches of production occurring not through the state but through "bodies composed of representatives of the workers and employees working in these branches of production, of the representatives of consumers who need the products of these branches, and of state representatives."[20] It would be complemented by a democratic factory statute in which the elected workers' committees manage the plants together with the technicians and the administrations of the production branches.

Bauer envisaged the "expropriation of the expropriators" "not in the form of a brutal confiscation of capitalist and landed property"[21] but by means of compensation payment whose costs would be met by a wealth tax and thus borne by the owning classes themselves. At the time the articles were written, Bauer viewed the realization of socialism as an immediately practical task.[22] But as the revolutionary wave in Central Europe subsided and the soviet republic in neighboring Hungary collapsed, the Christian Social Party no longer felt pressured to compromise, and with the help of the Entente power, Italy, it torpedoed Bauer's plan to socialize heavy industry.* Finally, the coalition of Social Democrats and Christian Socials fell apart.

Under the changed relation of forces, the struggle for socialism could only be continued as a defensive war of position. This shift of strategy constitutes the real subject of Bauer's *The Austrian Revolution*.

During the whole of 1919, especially during the period of the Hungarian and Bavarian soviet republics, the Social Democrats were in sharp conflict with the Communists who wanted to establish a soviet government in Austria, which the Social Democratic majority of the Vienna Workers' Council rejected.[23]

The main arguments for this rejection, which were still disputed by Communists and Social Democrats decades later, are laid out in Bauer's book.† In this respect we should mention that the Communist historian Hans Hautmann, in his 1971 standard work on the early history of the Austrian Republic, grants the cogency of the Social Democrats' argument that in the event of the establishment of a proletarian dictatorship, the Entente would abandon the country to famine, considering it "more persuasive than the Communists' counter-argument that 'soviet Hungary will supply us with food.'"[24]

---

* See pp. 248–49 in this volume.

† See pp. 207 and 251–52 in this volume.

The defeat of the Hungarian Soviet Republic in August 1919 led to the marginalization of Austria's Communists. Nevertheless, the idea of councils/soviets and the Soviet Union remained popular, and therefore in 1920 Bauer felt the need to articulate a position on it in a small book entitled *Bolschewismus oder Sozialdemokratie* (Bolshevism or Social Democracy). With all of his criticism of the Bolsheviks' dictatorial and terrorist exercise of power, he did not dispute the socialist character of their regime. From the critical assessment of the Bolshevik experiment, he turned to the fundamental question for the socialism of his day of whether "Bolshevism is the only possible, the only expedient method for every proletarian revolution or is a method of the proletarian liberation struggle suited only to specific Russian conditions and not applicable to other countries."[25]

His arguments for the latter position referred to the weakness of the Russian bourgeoisie, the lack of a massive bourgeois intellectual stratum, and its peasantry's scant capacity for political articulation—quite the opposite of conditions in Western and Central Europe where these strata constituted the majority of the population, providing the bourgeoisie with a broad basis for its domination, against which it was impossible to govern by force. "Therefore," Bauer concluded, "one will have to also allow them influence over the social organism, over the state, even if only in the form of an opposition."[26] Or, expressed in general terms: "Force is the midwife of every old society pregnant with the new; but force cannot bring the new society to light before it has matured in the womb of the old society."[27]

Bauer pointed out that the democratic state, like any other state, also rests on force. But "it uses armed force only for the purpose of enforcing its statutes, ordinances, and regulations in the face of resistant minorities. The content of the statutes, ordinances, and regulations is not determined by force as such but exclusively by the social power of the classes. . . . Therefore the violation of the social factors of power can only be sustained as long as the contradiction between the legal and social division of power is not too great."[28]

And, finally, Bauer used a formulation, which, absorbed into the party program years later, was to develop an unexpected life of its own: Even if the proletariat is to conquer political power by means of democracy, he wrote, the bourgeoisie will defy its rule. If the bourgeoisie resorts to violence and economic sabotage, even a democratic parliament will arrogate to itself dictatorial instruments of power. "This can also be called dictatorship of the proletariat, but it is a completely different sort of dictatorship from Bolshevism.

It is not a dictatorship against democracy but a *dictatorship of democracy.*"[29]

The ensuing controversy over Marxian state theory, in which among others Hans Kelsen, founder of the pure theory of law, intervened,[30] is characteristic of the vibrant intellectual atmosphere of the young republic.[31]

Kelsen qualifies Bauer's concept of equilibrium of class forces as the attempt to bring the coalition policy of Social Democracy in 1919–20 into line with Marx's and Engels's theory for which the state is nothing other than an instrument of oppression in the hands of the ruling class, which would then be superfluous in a free society of the future.[32]

This theory, Kelsen maintained, enters a crisis as soon as "the proletariat—not least on the basis of a democratic constitution—has become a political force, which immediately confronts its party with the possibility, even the necessity, of taking over the government of a state—whether alone or in coalition with bourgeois parties—which its theory rejects as an exploitative organization destined to 'wither away.'"[33] Kelsen claimed that Renner (unlike Bauer) had correctly recognized that "the state is also a state of the proletarians," and the government only the political expression of the "social relation of forces long since having constituted the modern state."[34]

By this Kelsen meant that since every state, at every point of time, is the expression of a social relation of forces, there is a permanent contention for the state within the state, by no means only under the conditions Bauer described as episodes of equilibrium. If that was so, then the difference between a capitalist and a socialist state would shrink to nothing more than a quantitative relation in which both tendencies have an impact on the state. Since every state is a compromise struck on the basis of the relations of force between the classes, it is only a difference of degree that separates the current state from "a future one—a social construct that completely corresponds to the socialist ideal—a difference of degree consisting of purposeful reform, which cannot be elided by revolution."[35]

This leveling of the difference is something Bauer did not want to accept, and his answer appeared in an article in *Der Kampf*: Certainly, the working class was not completely powerless in the last years of the Monarchy. But when the state, shorn of its instruments of force by the revolution, could operate only through agreements with workers' organizations, a new quality of democracy emerged—a functional democracy. "In fact, the overturning of the entire functioning of the state in Austria was so complete because it involved not just a shift within an existing state but actually the founding of an entirely new kind of state."[36]

The debate's merit was that it went to the heart of the difference be-tween (Kelsen's) progressive liberalism and (Bauer's) revolutionary reform-ism. With the collapse of socialization, which removed the material basis of Bauer's concept of a socialist transformation of society, the state-theory debate had to be put on hold.

Renner, who returned to the issue in 1929 in a completely changed polit-ical situation, was able to argue on empirical grounds: "In any case, socializa-tion through the state, as long as one does not truly and lastingly control it, is unthinkable. . . . Politics as an instrument of the class is insufficient for reach-ing the goal." And cuttingly directed against Bauer: "*Politismus* is in crisis."[37]

To *politismus* (understood as a one-sided overestimating of the poten-tial of politics) Renner opposed his own concept of an economic democ-racy embodied in factory councils, trade unions, production and consumer cooperatives, and many other forms of democratic self-organization of the working class, not only as a strategy for surviving non-revolutionary pe-riods in which the working class, "due to the insufficient stage of devel-opment is barred from real economic power for years to come, but also as "a means of free association . . . a means of a *purely economic* nature, a means of revolutionizing the economy from within, thus not non-eco-nomic means but those *which can prepare the new economy in the womb of the old*."[38] To be clear, Renner, in his text, did not present proletarian self-organization on the basis of the economic, social, and cultural inter-ests of the class as a surrogate for the struggle for power in the state but as its completion, as the precondition for its success and sustainability. "The main practical problem in realizing socialism," he wrote, is "the judicious division of labor between political and economic democracy."[39]

Democracy or Dictatorship

For Michael Krätke, Austro-Marxism represents "the most elaborated vari-ant of an open Marxism to date."[40] If this is true, then it was due not only to the theorists themselves but also to the movement in which they partic-ipated. Between 80 and 90 percent of the working-class vote went to the Social Democratic Party. In contrast to Germany, Czechoslovakia, Italy, and France, the party succeeded in averting a split. In membership and number of organizations, the Social Democratic Party of German-Austria*

---

* Sozialdemokratische Arbeiterpartei Deutschösterreichs (SDAPDÖ; Social Democratic Workers' Party of German-Austria) was the name of the party between 1918 and 1934.

was the largest workers' party of its time. Through Red Vienna it materialized its countermodel to the conservative federal state. The backbone of the party's self-confidence was the *Republikanischer Schutzbund*, an 80,000-person-strong military self-defense organization, whose very existence, it was assumed, would deter any attempt at a reactionary coup d'état.

Ideologically, Austrian Social Democracy dissociated itself just as much from revisionism as it did from Third International dogmatism. This made it the leader of *centrism* in Europe's socialist movement. In 1921 the International Working Union of Socialist Parties* was founded in Vienna, which aimed (without success) at bringing about a reconciliation between the social democratic London International and the Communist International.

The Austro-Marxist party program (the Linz Program), ratified in 1926 and authored by Bauer, drew major international attention; it proclaimed a democratic transition to socialism. Complemented by an agrarian program and the loosening of the traditionally hostile attitude toward the Catholic Church, the program was to prepare the ground for achieving a parliamentary majority. Bauer wrote a pamphlet defending the new religion policy in the face of a skeptical membership.[41] The demand to treat religion not as an affair concerning the party but as a private matter was a practical necessity in view of a political opponent that called itself the Christian Social Party. But the initiative remained half-hearted. Bauer called for tolerance for religion but did not bring himself to appeal to democratic tendencies within the Catholic movement, and as a result the attempt failed to break through the demarcation line of religion.

Aimed at opening up the party, the Linz Program has paradoxically entered the annals of history as signaling the opposite of this. Certainly, Social Democracy was unhesitatingly committed to struggling for power with democratic means, but it added the following serious restriction: "If, however, the bourgeoisie will act against the social revolution, which it is the working class's task to undertake, and through systematic suppression of economic life defy it through violent insurgency and conspiracy with foreign counterrevolutionary powers—then the working class will be forced to break *the resistance of the bourgeoisie by means of dictatorship*."[42]

---

* Internationale Arbeitsgemeinschaft Sozialistischer Parteien.

The Defeat

It is not unfair to judge Otto Bauer's politics and theory in the light of their practical failure. It is a failure that has its origin in the foiling of socialization and which ended in the military defeat of February 1934. The use of the term *dictatorship of the proletariat*, although it was clearly conceived as a last resort against an aggressive counterrevolution, was used by Social Democracy's political opponent for a campaign accusing the party of fundamentally dictatorial goals.

Already by July 1927, when a spontaneous mass demonstration of the Viennese working class was brutally crushed by militarily armed police, it had become clear that major sectors in the state and the Christian Social Party were steering toward a reactionary dictatorship. Not ready to put up a militant resistance that would undoubtedly escalate into a civil war, the party leadership around Bauer also rejected offers of coalition made by the Christian Social Party in 1931 and 1932.

Clearly, the strategy developed in the Linz Program did not solve the problem that the bourgeoisie, which was pressing toward fascism, placed before the socialist movement. On the one hand, the dismantling of democracy occurred gradually, in well-calculated steps, so that the Social Democratic leadership did not resolve to use the force they regarded as the last resort; on the other hand, it could only conceive of a coalition under conditions favorable to itself, that is, on the basis of the famous "equilibrium of class forces." But the national and international relation of forces developed to its disadvantage; the advance of fascism expressed the predominance of the ruling class. A coalition with those parts of the bourgeoisie that rejected a reign of violence would have meant that Social Democracy was ready to declare for the defense of democracy and national independence and put aside the goal of socialism for the time being. Otto Bauer was prepared to accept this consequence only when the other side had already decided on a coup d'état and did not want to compromise.[43]

In spring of 1933 the Christian Social Party shut down the Parliament and governed through emergency decrees. This was followed by the paralysis of the Constitutional Court and the prohibition of the Communist Party and the Schutzbund. However, the Social Democratic Party's way of thinking prevented it from answering these unambiguous steps toward dictatorship by calling a general strike.

On February 12, 1934, when units of the government's executive branch wanted to occupy a worker's center in the Upper Austrian capital Linz, armed resistance broke out spontaneously, and in a few hours it spread to Vienna and other industrial centers. Only a few units of the Schutzbund were able to intervene in the battles and they found themselves in a hopeless position against the superior forces of the police, the Federal Army, and paramilitary units. The party failed to ensure a united leadership in the confrontations or to organize the general strike that it foresaw in the event of an emergency. After three days, the workers, reduced to a few nests of resistance, had to lay down their arms. The battles cost hundreds of lives, and nine Social Democratic leaders were convicted and executed. On the same day, the Social Democratic Party, the Free Trade Unions, and a thousand sports and cultural organizations connected to Social Democracy were prohibited, and the democratically elected Vienna city administration was removed from office.

February 12, 1934, marked the tragic end of the Austro-Marxist political experiment.

However, in contrast to Germany, the Austrian labor movement did not go down without a murmur but was defeated in a military confrontation. After this, thousands of Social Democrats joined the Communists who were already conducting their struggles underground. Others formed a new party, which they called the Revolutionary Socialists in order to convey their ideological distance from the collapsed mass party.[44] Josef Hindels, an icon of Austria's left socialism who as a Young Socialist took part in the armed clash, has indicated in his memoirs that both tendencies were motivated by the idea that the February battle was not only a defeat but also "a bright shining beacon of the struggle against fascism."[45]

The prophesy was fulfilled, which Bauer articulated at the end of a pamphlet he wrote in exile a few days after the battles, namely that the defeat of the Austrian labor movement opened the way to Hitler's eastward expansion and represented a step toward the next major European war: "Europe will yet experience what a key factor in European peace was destroyed with Austrian Social Democracy."[46]

However, the trauma of February 1934 also changed the mentality of broad layers of the working class, as Bruno Kreisky, who in 1970 was to become the first social democratic Prime Minister of Austria,[47] pointed out: "For the Austrian working class, the day on which it was liquidated and its resurrection postponed to the distant future was such a shattering blow that it considered the 12th of February as the great confrontation, more so than Hitler's entry four years later."[48]

Chaplain and General

Kreisky especially lamented the self-delusion of many intelligent Social Democrats based on the mere existence of the Schutzbund. In his memoirs he wrote: "The fact that in the end nothing of what was simulated in innumerable repeated exercises was ever put into practice was due to the attitude of the party leadership, which in the bottom of its heart rejected any civil war provoked by itself."[49] The well-known Social Democratic intellectual Norbert Leser attests to a "thoroughly illusionary character of Bauer's politics."[50] Like Kreisky, he considers the most important cause of the defeat to be the rejection of the Christian Socials' coalition offers, one of which was presented by Ignaz Seipel in 1931, at the height of the economic crisis.[51]

Conversely, the rebuke of left critics is that in his endeavor to avoid a civil war, Bauer increasingly retreated before an increasingly determined enemy. In his 1986 book with the indicative title *Der Austromarxismus. Eine Autopsie*, the then prominent Trotskyist Raimund Löw writes: "The only thing which the party leadership offered in opposition to the daily small defeats was the idea of the decisive battle of the future."[52] The Austrian Communist Party's leading theoretician of the period, Ernst Wimmer, formulated this more elegantly: "Otto Bauer was sublimely able to present every past defeat as inevitable and do the same in terms of the future, prophesying inevitable victories."[53]

Going beyond this approach, the historian Fritz Weber criticizes Austro-Marxists for being slow to respond to mass unemployment with a program for growth and employment. In fact, they combined the ideological prediction of the imminent collapse of the capitalist economy with a classic economic policy conception commensurate with the economic science of the day, according to which fighting inflation and balancing the budget took precedence[54]—which proved ineffective in view of the economic and financial crisis.[55] This criticism is not unjustified, but it once again points to the political problem. Even had the party decided early enough on an economic program that had aimed at public credit and boosting mass purchasing power (as the trade unions demanded[56]) instead of boosting exports and stabilizing the currency, it would, in order to put it into effect, have had to assume government responsibility, which it did not want to do for both political and ideological reasons.[57] This systemic relation between a policy for growth and employment and the readiness to enter into a coalition with the bourgeois parties underpinned the alliance between trade unionists and right-wing Social Democrats, introducing the rightward shift of the party after 1945.

It is true that the party's decision not to adopt the opposite strategy, that is, to use force to stand in the way of fascism, is to a considerable degree due to Bauer's personality. In a 1928 article in *Der Kampf*, Renner wrote: "The army would have been lost that wanted to make its chaplains into its generals."[58] Bauer's longtime fellow traveler and friend Julius Braunthal said this in a friendlier way: "The truth about Otto Bauer is probably that nature had not meant him to be a leader of battles. The deep source of his trepidation about taking a violent road, however he explained it tactically and theoretically when the question came up, was his innate abhorrence of violence. . . . This feature of human gentleness in Bauer's nature, which ennobled his personality, is admittedly a character trait of weakness when it comes to brutal power struggles."[59]

Legacy: Integral Socialism

In February 1934, when the Schutzbund's military position had become hopeless, Bauer was able to elude arrest by crossing the Czechoslovakian border. Just a week later he finished the pamphlet *Der Aufstand der öster-reichischen Arbeiter. Seine Ursachen und seine Wirkung* (The Uprising of Austrian Workers: Its Causes and Effect), in which he dedicated a chapter to the mistakes of the party he led.[60]

A week later, the *Arbeiter-Zeitung*, now a weekly rather than a daily, published its first issue under his direction. In contrast to the leaders of German Social Democracy, Bauer decided not to install a party leadership in exile but rather a Foreign Bureau of Austrian Social Democracy whose function was to support an illegal party to be built within the country. "It seemed wrong to us," he wrote in his posthumously published book *Die illegale Partei* "to burden the new party, which would have to be built on the ruins of the old one, with a leadership that bore heavy responsibility for the politics of the old party decimated in the February catastrophe."[61]

Die illegale Partei was published in 1939, one year after Bauer's death; it was the last, and unfinished, work by Bauer, a solid study, among other things, of historic and contemporary illegal parties, but also a significant contribution to general party theory.

His last book published in his lifetime, *Zwischen Zwei Weltkriegen? Die Krise der Weltwirtschaft, der Demokratie und des Sozialismus* (Between Two

World Wars? The Crisis of the World Economy, of Democracy, and of Socialism), appeared in 1936. It was dedicated to the Revolutionary Socialists working illegally within Austria. In it Bauer utilized the preparatory work for the intended but not completed second volume of his 1931 investigation of the development of capitalism and socialism after the First World War.[62] The fundamental new reality that he investigated was the Europe-wide advance of fascism. Remarkably, he did not see fascism as the last resort of a bourgeoisie that had been hard-pressed by the Revolution; rather, he showed that the fascist dictatorships in Italy, Germany, and Austria were established at moments when the labor movement had been weakened and put on the defensive. "The capitalist class and the large landowners have handed over state power to the fascist gangs not in order to protect themselves from the proletarian revolution but in order to depress wages, destroy the social achievements of the working class, and smash the trade unions and the working class' positions of political power; thus not to smash a revolutionary socialism but the achievements of reformist socialism."[63]

At the same time, the book documents a disillusionment with reformism. The reformist formula of reaching socialism through democracy is now inverted by Bauer: "Only a revolutionary dictatorship [can] create the social preconditions for democracy liberated from class domination."[64]

However, in reformism Bauer saw not only ideological degeneration. In contrast to Lenin, who identified the social base for reformism with a thin layer of a privileged *labor aristocracy*, Bauer recognized that it is "the large mass of workers of Western and Central Europe and of the United States of America" whose improved social conditions estrange them from the idea of revolution.[65] "Only in Russia, where the bourgeois revolution still lay ahead could socialism be revolutionary, as it had been in Western and Central Europe in the age of the bourgeois revolution."[66]

Thus, the contradiction between reformist and revolutionary strategy expresses an inherent tension that exists between the theoretical socialist goal of the labor movement and the necessities of its daily struggle under parliamentary conditions. It is not the existence of this contradiction but its absolutization, he felt, that facilitated the victory of fascism. From this Bauer derived the concept of a renewed, integral socialism.

"Integral socialism, which aims to absorb the two major orientations of the labor movement, cannot resolve the contradiction between the reformist labor movement and revolutionary socialism, which is grounded in the very conditions of existence of the working class. It can and must position revolutionary socialism in a relationship to the reformist labor movement, and the reformist labor movement in a relationship to revolutionary socialism, of a kind other than that of a polarized antagonism."[67]

The aim here is not the simple adding up of the existing movements, nor a political compromise reached between the two enemy internationals, but rather the transformation of both through a higher synthesis of a revolutionary social democracy and a democratized communism.

Zwischen Zwei Weltkriegen? represents Bauer's testament. It was made available to an Austrian readership only in 1975 by the Socialists' student organization in an abbreviated study edition (because of funding limitations). In the Preface, Josef Hindels wrote that the book deals with the need, and possibility, to transform labor parties and thus indicated the reason why socialist and communist publishers had for decades failed to bring out a new edition.[68]

Halted Reception

It has been said of Austrians that they confidently look to their past. Social Democracy would have had every reason to be proud of its cultural and intellectual heritage and hold its banner high. That it has not done so in the decades after the Second World War does it no credit.

To this important heritage belongs the *Marx-Studien* published by Max Adler and Rudolf Hilferding from 1904 to 1923, in whose numbers appeared, for example, *Die Sozialfunktion der Rechtsinstitute besonders des Eigentums* (The Social Function of Legal Institutions, in Particular of Property) by Karl Renner (under the pseudonym of Josef Karner); *Kausalität und Teleologie im Streite um die Wissenschaft* (Causality and Teleology in the Debate Over Science) by Max Adler; *The Question of Nationalities and Social Democracy* by Bauer; and Rudolf Hilferding's *Finance Capital*.

Part of this great cultural legacy is the theoretical journal founded by Otto Bauer, Adolf Braun, and Karl Renner, *Der Kampf*, which up to 1934 was, with its German counterpart *Neue Zeit*, the journal of reference for Marxist thinking in the interwar period.

Already by 1918–19 the Austro-Marxists tried to found an institute in Vienna for social science research in the tradition of scientific Marxism. "If their attempt had not foundered on the unwillingness of the official party leaderships . . . the first institutional home for the scientific confrontation with Marx's and Engels's heritage would have been located in Vienna rather than Frankfurt."[69]

Austro-Marxism had a considerable power of attraction in German Social Democracy as well, especially in its left wing. Programmatically, it was the militancy displayed in the Linz Program, its use of the threat of a dictatorship of the proletariat, which found an echo among the left German comrades, as at the political level they could remonstrate their own party leadership by holding up the model of the Austrians' refusal to enter a coalition with the bourgeois parties. In the domain of ideology it was the outsider of Austrian Social Democracy, Max Adler, who with his distance from Realpolitik and rapturous orientation to "the revolutionary spirit" and "the ultimate socialist goal," inspired the left of the German party and above all the Young Socialists.[70]

When, however, the events of July 1927 showed the limits of the politics practiced by the Austrians, a more critical discourse developed in the German party's left wing as well, which was further stimulated after the defeat of February 1934.[71]

After the liberation from fascism, it was almost natural that those political tendencies of Austrian Social Democracy prevailed, which in 1934 had developed "to the right" of Otto Bauer.[72]

In the post-war Austrian Social Democratic Party Otto Bauer's heritage could only have continued to exist as a theoretical and political platform of a left socialist tendency. There was no place either for democratic socialism or integral socialism in an Austria liberated by four powers and torn apart by the Cold War. Fritz Weber soberly assessed the situation: "The history of left socialism in the first years after 1945 is the history of a defeat."[73] And from the right-wing social democratic side, Norbert Leser's 1968 *Zwischen Reformismus und Bolschewismus* assigned responsibility to Otto Bauer for the defeat of February 1934.

A typical example of the assessment of Austro-Marxism on the part of Communist orthodoxy is the entry in the 1964 *Marxistisch-Leninistisches Wörterbuch der Philosophie* published in the German Democratic Republic. It speaks of a "variety of revisionism" whose "ideological point of departure was the narrow-minded, petty bourgeois outlook of the leaders of Social Democracy on the national question."[74]

Yet in Communism itself divergent tendencies developed after 1956. The Austrian Communist Party's theoretical journal, *Weg und Ziel*—in a special issue commemorating the fiftieth anniversary of the Russian October Revolution—published an article by the distinguished historian Herbert Steiner on Otto Bauer and Austro-Marxism, which ended with the noteworthy statement: "Even today the enemies of the labor movement are vilifying the rich contributions of Otto Bauer. Our generation, however, can learn much from him."[75]

When at the end of the 1960s the social democratic parties of Germany and Austria found themselves in the waiting rooms of power and the worldwide student movement opened up a new left discourse, a new interest in Austro-Marxism began to develop again.

Hans-Jörg Sandkühler's and Rafael de la Vega's 1970 anthology, *Austromarxismus*, published by Europa Verlag, is an odd book. In the Introduction the editors point to a renaissance of Austro-Marxism, which they wished to counter with a "documentation of errors" and by "making transparent the anti-communism that the catchword of democratic socialism barely conceals."[76] Yet their book presents a representative, intelligently selected collection of Austro-Marxist texts contributing, paradoxically, to their dissemination.

The last European boom of Austro-Marxism, at least from the present perspective, occurred at the end of the 1970s. In the social democratic parties of Germany and Austria, several left tendencies were articulated. In Italy the Communist Party was approaching the peak of its influence, and in France the Communist Party and Socialist Party were preparing to assume joint responsibility for government. In the search for a theory adequate to these challenges and in an effort to find a common language, Eurocommunists and left Socialists reflected on Austro-Marxism.

Between 1975 and 1979, the nine-volume edition of Otto Bauer's works was published (on the initiative of Bruno Kreisky, Federal Chancellor of Austria and chair of the Social Democratic Party); however, its price kept it from reaching a broad readership.

In 1978 and 1981 Austria's Social Democratic youth organizations mounted international symposia, with the approval of the party leadership, on the theme of Otto Bauer and his importance for the European left. The participants included Detlev Albers, Jean-Pierre Chevènement, Pietro Ingrao, Josef Hindels, Lucio Lombardo Radice, Giacomo Marramao, and Eduard März.[77] Due to the rhythm of the major party careers of the participating youth functionaries from Austria and with the collapse of Eurocommunist attempts in Italy and France, this interest, too, ebbed. And with the demise of state socialism, which removed party-organized communism's basis and legitimacy, the discussion of Austro-Marxism and integral socialism seemed finished. An attempt to take up the threads again was made in 2007 by transform!europe, the think tank of the Party of the European Left, together with the Rosa Luxemburg Foundation, in the form of an international symposium and accompanying conference volume.[78] A similar conference in 2018 broadened the theme of Austro-Marxism to the reconstruction of Marxism in Central and Eastern Europe.[79]

• • •

Today it looks as if history has left behind both tendencies of the traditional European labor movement, and thus Austro-Marxism. The great programmatic goal of ushering in socialism by peaceful means was not achieved. But the major contender of the socialist movement, that is, party-organized communism in all its varieties—Leninism, Trotskyism, Maoism, and so on—has fared no better at the beginning of the twenty-first century.

Can we do anything more than list the important contributions both tendencies made to European intellectual history, their advanced theoretical ideas, as well as their political errors and defeats, in order to consign them to a museum of failed experiments? We fundamentally disagree with such a fatalist outlook.

For one thing, the success and/or failure of past socialist experiments ought not to be judged only according to the self-affirming words written into programs, but rather mainly on the basis of concrete historical possibilities. In his Preface to the *Critique of Political Economy*, Marx wrote that "no social formation is ever destroyed before all the productive forces for which it is sufficient have been developed, and new superior relations of production never replace older ones before the material conditions for their existence have matured within the framework of the old society."[80] From this perspective, the trajectory of transition to a higher form of society was different and longer than the protagonists of the twentieth-century socialist movements had imagined.

However, we are publishing this classic work in the conviction that the questions it raises have not only remained topical but are more relevant today than ever and that a scientifically practiced, undogmatic Marxism must contribute to their answers.

Michael Krätke finds that the theoretical contributions of Austro-Marxists, especially to state and transformation theory, "are ahead of and superior to everything commonly offered in Marxism as political theory."[81]

Whether or not one shares this assessment, the intensity of the social and political confrontations in interwar Austria forced Austro-Marxism to pose the most important questions on a level fully the equal of the work of Lenin, Luxemburg, and Gramsci. It is time that it be appreciated accordingly.

Nothing could better illustrate these achievements than Otto Bauer's 1923 key work, *The Austrian Revolution*.

BIBLIOGRAPHY

Books by Otto Bauer

Der Weg zum Sozialismus. Vienna: Verlag Wiener Volksbuchhandlung, 1921.

Bolschewismus oder Sozialdemokratie. Vienna: Verlag Wiener Volksbuchhandlung, 1921.

Die österreichische Revolution. Vienna: Verlag Wiener Volksbuchhandlung, 1923.

Die Nationalitätenfrage und die Sozialdemokratie, in *Marx-Studien. Blätter zur Theorie und Politik des Wissenschaftlichen Sozialismus*, Max Adler and Rudolf Hilferding, eds. Vienna: Verlag Wiener Volksbuchhandlung, 1924. (*The Question of Nationalities and Social Democracy*, Joseph O'Donnell, transl. Minneapolis: University of Minnesota Press, 2000.)

Sozialdemokratie, Religion und Kirche. Vienna: Verlag Wiener Volksbuchhandlung, 1927.

Kapitalismus und Sozialismus nach dem Weltkrieg. Erster Band: Rationalisierung—Fehlrationalisierung. Vienna: Verlag Wiener Volksbuchhandlung, 1931.

Der Aufstand der österreichischen Arbeiter. Seine Ursachen und seine Wirkung. Prague: Verlag der Deutschen Sozialdemokratischen Arbeiterpartei, 1934; reprint, Vienna: Verlag Wiener Volksbuchhandlung, 1947.

Zwischen zwei Weltkriegen? Die Krise der Weltwirtschaft, der Demokratie und des Sozialismus. Bratislava: Prager, 1936.

Die illegale Partei. Paris: Édition "La Lutte Socialiste," 1939.

Essays and Articles by Otto Bauer

(under pseudonym Karl Mann) "Das Selbstbestimmungsrecht der österreichischen Nationen" in *Der Kampf* XII, 4 (April 1918).

"Das Weltbild des Kapitalismus." In *Otto Bauer: Eine Auswahl aus seinem Lebenswerk. Mit einem Lebensbild Otto Bauer von Julius Braunthal*. Vienna: Verlag Wiener Volksbuchhandlung, 1961, 102–40.

"Die Geschichte eines Buches." In *Otto Bauer: Eine Auswahl aus seinem Lebenswerk. Mit einem Lebensbild Otto Bauer von Julius Braunthal*.

Vienna: Verlag Wiener Volksbuchhandlung, 1961, 182–94.

"Die Verwirklichung der nationalen Kulturgemeinschaft." In *Otto Bauer: Eine Auswahl aus seinem Lebenswerk. Mit einem Lebensbild Otto Bauer von Julius Braunthal.* Vienna: Verlag Wiener Volksbuchhandlung, 1961, 156–65.

"Marx und Darwin." In *Otto Bauer: Eine Auswahl aus seinem Lebenswerk. Mit einem Lebensbild Otto Bauer von Julius Braunthal.* Vienna: Verlag Wiener Volksbuchhandlung, 1961, 194–205.

"Ignaz Seipel." In *Austromarxismus*, Hans-Jörg Sandühler and Rafael de la Vega, eds. Frankfurt a.m.: Europäische Verlagsanstalt and Vienna: Europa Verlag, 1970, 228–37.

"Wir Bolschewiken." In *Otto Bauer: Eine Auswahl aus seinem Lebenswerk. Mit einem Lebensbild Otto Bauer von Julius Braunthal.* Vienna: Verlag Wiener Volksbuchhandlung, 1961, 306–11.

"Austromarxismus." In *Austromarxismus*, Hans-Jörg Sandühler and Rafael de la Vega, eds. Frankfurt a.m.: Europäische Verlagsanstalt and Vienna: Europa Verlag, 1970, 49–55.

"Das Gleichgewicht der Klassenkräfte." In *Austromarxismus*, Hans-Jörg Sandühler and Rafael de la Vega, eds. Frankfurt a.m.: Europäische Verlagsanstalt and Vienna: Europa Verlag, 1970, 79–98.

"Demokratie und Sozialismus." In *Austromarxismus*, Hans-Jörg Sandühler and Rafael de la Vega, eds. Frankfurt a.M.: Europäische Verlagsanstalt and Vienna: Europa Verlag, 1970, 98–120.

Programmatic Documents

Das Brünner Nationalitätenprogramm, https://de.wikipedia.org/wiki/Br%C3%BCnner_Programm.

"Das Nationalitätenprogramm der Linken" in Otto Bauer, *Werke*, vol. VIII. Vienna: Europa Verlag, 1980.

"Sozialdemokratische Arbeiterpartei Deutschösterreichs," *Das Linzer Programme* (November 3, 1926), http://www.otto-bauer.net/linzer_programm.pdf.

Books and Articles by Contemporaries and Predecessors

Adler, Max. "Die Beziehungen des Marxismus zur klassischen deutschen Philosophie." In *Austromarxismus*, Hans-Jörg Sandühler and Rafael de la Vega, eds. Frankfurt a.M.: Europäische Verlagsanstalt and Vienna: Europa Verlag, 1970, 155–91.

———. "Gesellschaftsordnung und Zwangsordnung." In *Austromarxismus*, Hans-Jörg Sandühler and Rafael de la Vega, eds. Frankfurt a.M.: Europäische Verlagsanstalt and Vienna: Europa Verlag, 1970, 191–205.

———. *Kausalität und Teleologie im Streite um die Wissenschaft*, Vienna: I. Brand [Verlag der Wiener Volksbuchhandlung]. 1904.

———. "Der Klassenkampfgedanke bei Marx." In *Austromarxismus*, Hans-Jörg Sandühler and Rafael de la Vega, eds. Frankfurt a.M.: Europäische Verlagsanstalt and Vienna: Europa Verlag, 1970, 140–55.

———. "Linkssozialismus. Notwendige Betrachtungen über Reformismus und revolutionären Sozialismus." In *Austromarxismus*, Hans-Jörg Sandühler and Rafael de la Vega, eds., Frankfurt a.M.: Europäische Verlagsanstalt and Vienna: Europa Verlag, 1970, 206–63.

Engels, Friedrich. "Democratic Pan-Slavism" (*Neue Rheinische Zeitung* No. 222 and 223, February 15 and 16, 1849), MECW, vol. 8, 362–78.

Hilferding, Rudolf. *Finance Capital: A Study of the Latest Phase of Capitalist Development*, T. B. Bottomore, ed. London: Routledge & Kegan Paul, 1981; original edition, *Das Finanzkapital*, Vienna, 1910.

Kelsen, Hans. "Democracy and Socialism." The Law School of the University of Chicago, Conference on Jurisprudence and Politics, April 30, 1954, 63–87; in German, Hans Kelsen, *Demokratie und Sozialismus. Ausgewählte Aufsätze*, edited and introduced by Norbert Leser. Vienna: Verlag der Wiener Volksbuchhandlung, 1967.

———. *The Political Theory of Bolshevism: A Critical Analysis*. Berkeley: University of California Press, 1948.

Kreisky, Bruno. *Zwischen den Zeiten. Erinnerungen aus fünf Jahrzehnten*. Vienna: Siedler/Kremayr & Scheriau, 1986.

Renner, Karl. *Das Selbstbestimmungsrecht der Nationen in besonderer Anwendung auf Österreich*. Leipzig: Franz Deuticke, 1918.

———. "Probleme des Marxismus." In *Austromarxismus*, Hans-Jörg Sandühler and Rafael de la Vega, eds. Frankfurt a.M.: Europäische Verlagsanstalt and Vienna: Europa Verlag, 1970, 263–302.

———. "Was ist Klassenkampf." In *Austromarxismus*, Hans-Jörg Sandühler and Rafael de la Vega, eds. Frankfurt a.M.: Europäische Verlagsanstalt and Vienna: Europa Verlag, 1970, 302–29.

————. *Wege der Verwirklichung. Betrachtungen über politische Demokratie, Wirtschaftsdemokratie und Sozialismus, insbesondere über die Aufgaben der Genossenschaften und der Gewerkschaften.* Berlin: Dietz, 1929.

Strasser, Josef. *Der Arbeiter und Nation.* Reichenberg: Runge & Co, 1912.

Secondary Literature

Albers, Detlev, Josef Cap, Pietro Ingrao, and Didier Montchane, eds. *Perspektiven der Eurolinken.* Frankfurt a.M.: Campus Verlag, 1981.

Albers, Detlev, Josef Hindels, and Lucio Lombardo Radice, eds. *Otto Bauer und der "dritte Weg." Die Widerentdeckung des Austromarxismus durch Linkssozialisten und Eurokommunisten.* Frankfurt a.M.: Campus Verlag, 1979.

Baier, Walter, Lisbeth N. Trallori, and Derek Weber, eds. *Otto Bauer und der Austromarxismus. "Integraler Sozialismus" und die heutige Linke.* Berlin: Karl Dietz Verlag, 2008.

Beneš, Jakub S. *Workers and Nationalism: Czech and German Social Democracy in Habsburg Austria, 1890–1918.* New York: Oxford University Press, 2017.

Braunthal, Julius. "Otto Bauer: Eine Auswahl aus seinem Lebenswerk." In *Otto Bauer: Eine Auswahl aus seinem Lebenswerk. Mit einem Lebensbild Otto Bauer von Julius Braunthal.* Vienna: Verlag Wiener Volksbuchhandlung, 1961.

Buttinger, Joseph. *Am Beispiel Österreichs. Ein geschichtlicher Beitrag zur Krise der sozialistischen Bewegung.* Cologne: Verlag für Politik und Wirtschaft, 1953.

Fuchs, Albert. *Geistige Strömungen in Österreich 1867–1918.* Vienna: Löcker, 1984.

Hautmann, Hans. *Die verlorene Räterepublik. Am Beispiel der Kommunistischen Partei Österreichs.* Vienna: Europa Verlag, 1971.

Hindels, Josef. *Erinnerungen eines linken Sozialisten.* Vienna: Dokumentationsarchiv des Österreichischen Widerstands, 1996.

————. Preface to Otto Bauer, *Zwischen zwei Weltkriegen?* Vienna: Verband Sozialistischer Studenten Österreichs (VSSTÖ), 1975.

Hobsbawm, Eric J. *Nations and Nationalism Since 1780: Programme, Myth, Reality,* 2d ed. Cambridge: Cambridge University Press, 1992.

Kardelj, Edvard. *Die Vierteilung Nationale Frage und Slowenen.* Vienna: Europa Verlag, 1971.

Klaus, Georg, and Manfred Buhr, eds. *Marxistisch-Leninistisches Wörterbuch der Philosophie*. Hamburg: Rowohlt Taschenbuch Verlag, 1972.

Krätke, Michael. "Austromarxismus und Kritische Theorie." In *Handbuch Kritische Theorie*, Uwe Bittligmayer, Alex Demirovic, and Tatjana Freytag, eds. Wiesbaden: Springer Verlag, 2018.

———. "Die Vernichtung des Austromarxismus. Der jüngste Akt eines alten Trauerspiels." *Sozialistische Politik und Wirtschaft* 7 (June 1980), 73–87.

Kroll, Thomas. *Kommunistische Intellektuelle in Westeuropa. Frankreich, Österreich, Italien und Grossbritannien im Vergleich (1945–1956)*. Cologne: Böhlau Verlag, 2007.

Leser, Norbert. *Zwischen Reformismus und Bolschewismus. Der Austromarxismus als Theorie und Praxis*. Vienna: Europa Verlag, 1968.

Löw, Raimund, Siegfried Mattl, and Alfred Pfabigan. *Der Austromarxismus—eine Autopsie. Drei Studien*. Frankfurt a.M.: isp-Verlag, 1986.

Mommsen, Hans. *Die Sozialdemokratie und die Nationalitätenfrage im Habsburgischen Vielvölkerstaat: Vol. I: Das Ringen um die supranationale Integration der zisleithanischen Arbeiterbewegung: 1867–1907. Veröffentlichungen der Arbeitsgemeinschaft für Geschichte der Arbeiterbewegung in Österreich*, Vol. I. Vienna: Europa Verlag, 1963.

Sandkühler, Hans-Jörg, and Rafael de la Vega, eds. *Austromarxismus. Texte zu "Ideologie und Klassenkampf."* Frankfurt a.M.: Europäische Verlagsanstalt and Vienna: Europa Verlag, 1970.

Sandner, Günther. "Austromarxismus und Multikulturalismus. Karl Renner und Otto Bauer zur nationalen Frage im Habsburgerstaat." In *Kakanien Revisited*, http://www.kakanien.ac.at/beitr/fallstudie/GSandner1.pdf.

Steiner, Herbert. "Am Beispiel Otto Bauers–die Oktoberrevolution und der Austromarxismus." *Weg und Ziel*, Sondernummer, July 1967.

Storm, Gerd, and Franz Walter. *Weimarer Linkssozialismus und Asutromarxismus. Historische Vorbilder für einen "Dritten Weg" zum Sozialismus?* Berlin: Verlag Europäische Perspektiven, 1984.

Weber, Fritz. "Der Kalte Krieg in der SPÖ. Koalitionswächter, Pragmatiker und revolutionäre Sozialisten 1945–1950." *Österreichische Texte zur Gesellschaftskritik*, vol. 25. Vienna: Verlag für Gesellschaftskritik, 2011.

Wimmer, Ernst. "Otto Bauers zwei Seiten (Zum 100. Geburtstag Otto Bauers)." *Weg und Ziel*, no. 9, 1981.

———. "Rückgriffe auf den Austromarxismus." *Weg und Ziel*, no. 2, 1980.

PREFACE

I dedicate this book to the representatives of the Austrian working class: to the thousands who bravely stood up to bloodthirsty military authority during the war; to the thousands whose intelligence, whose sense of responsibility, whose courage in the revolutionary years repeatedly saved the Austrian working class from the temptations that arise from famine, despair, and illusions in one's own ranks; to the thousands tenaciously struggling today as they defend themselves against an uncomprehending, hate-filled enemy. May this book help these thousands of people to understand the broad historical context of the running battle they have waged, each in their factories, municipalities, and in their organizations, and may they draw new insight, new strength, and new confidence from this understanding for the approaching battles.

I dedicate this book to the comrades in the Austrian army—to the Social Democratic officers, noncommissioned officers, and soldiers. They now have to face the most difficult battle: a battle that will put their convictions, their tenacity, their sagacity to the severest test. May this book tell them that the goal of the struggle is worth the sacrifice of battle.

I dedicate this book to the Austrian intellectuals, the engineers, physicians, teachers, especially the young students, who want to understand the emancipatory struggle of the working class. May it help them to rip apart the net in which they are entangled, a net of persuasion that inculcates class prejudice, class hatred, and class lies by means of innumerable newspaper pages and professorial chairs.

And I dare to dedicate this book to the school of Marx throughout the world, for the book also has something to say to them.

Scientific socialism arose from the contemplation of two great experiences: the experience of the Industrial Revolution of the nineteenth century and the experience of the political revolutions from 1789 to 1871. The world that Marx and Engels analyzed has been completely upturned by war and revolution. Only by digesting the wealth of new experiences that we have accumulated in the war and the revolution can scientific socialism adapt to the changed environment. Only by working through these new experiences scientifically can twentieth-century socialism evolve. This book hopes to offer a small contribution to that enormous project. The interactions between the national and the social revolution; the transformations of the state, of democracy, of the relations of the working class to the state and the nation that are occurring in and through the revolution; the development of special types of state in a phase in which class forces are in equilibrium; the function of temporary class cooperation within class struggles; the interactions of the economy, power, and intellect in the development of revolutionary class struggle—these are problems of the greatest general interest, which I hope the history of the Austrian Revolution can help clarify.

Otto Bauer
Vienna, May 6, 1923

PART I

WAR AND
REVOLUTION

PART I

CHAPTER 1

THE SOUTHERN SLAVS
AND THE WAR

Austria-Hungary's ultimatum to Serbia precipitated the World War. Its immediate cause was the collision of the Habsburg Empire with the aspirations to freedom and unity of the Southern Slav people.

In the course of the nineteenth century, the Southern Slav bourgeoisie developed from Southern Slav peasant tribes. Under the leadership of the bourgeoisie, these tribes struggled against the foreign domination and national fragmentation that were features of feudalism in Yugoslavia. This struggle was the bourgeois revolution of the Yugoslavs; its goal was the liquidation of the feudal relations of domination on Southern Slav soil; and this national revolution of the Yugoslavs was the war's point of departure. It ushered in the national revolution that brought down the Habsburg Monarchy.

Already in the ninth century the Slovenes—the northwestern tribe of the Southern Slav people—had succumbed to German domination. The Slav peasants in all of Slovenia became bound to German landlords through corvée and interest payments. The manor was German, while the peasant village was Slovene. German landlords were followed by German burghers who founded towns in Wend regions; the towns were German but the villages remained Wendish.* Class and national divides coincided here. In the nineteenth century the Carniolan poet France Pešeren still complained:

---

* Wend (*windisch*, adjective): A German term originally designating Sorbs but traditionally used in the Austrian Empire to refer to Slovenes. *Windische Mark* is the equivalent of *slovenska krajina*.

> As a rule German is spoken in this country by the lords and ladies, who issue orders; And Slovenian by those who are in the servant class.

For a millennium the Slovene language was a mere peasant vernacular and the Slovene people a nation without a history. A Slovene school system could not emerge because schools were only for the sons of German landlords and burghers, not for Slav farmers. A Slovene literature could not develop, for who would want to write in a language that only ignorant, illiterate peasants spoke? When, in the turbulent days of the Reformation, Protestant preachers tried to preach the Gospel to peasants, one of them, Primož Trubar, observed that "there was not a single letter or register, still less a book, written in our Wendish language, because it was thought so rude and barbaric that it could be neither written nor read." Trubar and Juri Dalmatin, who translated the Bible into the Slavic peasant language, had to borrow hundreds of words from foreign languages since Slovenian only had designations for concepts relevant to peasant life. The bloody Habsburg Counter-Reformation put a swift end to these first attempts to create a Slovene literary language; Trubar's heretical writings were burned, and for two more centuries the Slovene language again disappeared from literature.

And just as the Slovene peasants had no part in any aspect of higher cultural life for a thousand years, so they also had no part in any aspect of state life; only the landlord class, not the peasants, were participants in the life of the state. With subjection to the German landlords, the Slovene peasants fell under the dominion of the German Duchy of Carantania; along with the lands into which the Duchy was divided, it became part of German-Austria. It was through the seignories in which the Slovene peasants labored for the German feudal lords that the political domination of German-Austria was established over the Slovene tribe.

Five hundred years after this destiny befell the northwestern branch of the Yugoslav people, the same happened to the southeastern branch. After the defeat at Kosovo (1389), the Serb princes became vassals of Turkish magnates; after the catastrophe of Varna (1444) Serb lands became Turkish provinces. The Serb people became a subjugated, exploited *rayah*.* The towns became Turkish castles, with only the villages remaining Serb, and Turkish *sipahis*† and Greek priests ruled over the Serb peasants. Only in Bosnia did a

---

* *Rayah* denotes subject non-Muslim people in Turkish-ruled Balkan territory.
† The fief-holding *timarli sipahi* were a light cavalry order of the Ottoman army.

part of the national nobility assert itself; but it could assert its possession and title only at the cost of accepting Islam and thus becoming part of the ruling Ottoman system. And so the Serb people also fell under foreign domination.

Only at the center of the Southern Slav area of settlement, in Croatia, could a national political system assert itself. Only there did the people live under the dominion of a national rather than foreign nobility. But there, too, fierce clashes resulted in the continual loss of pieces of national independence. Threatened by the Turks, the Triune Kingdom of Croatia was not in a position to protect Dalmatia from the Venetians, and so this Slav country came under foreign Italian domination. Croatia itself, however, at first threw the Turkish menace into the lap of the Habsburgs. Then, after the Turks had been driven back, the Croatian nobility, whose privileges were threatened by Habsburg absolutism, threw itself into the arms of Hungary in order to defend its feudal rights by uniting with the more powerful Magyar nobility, even at the price of state independence. In this way, between the Turks and Venetians, between Austria and Hungary, the Croatian nobility lost national and state independence. Many noble families were eradicated in the Ottoman Wars. Others ended on Austrian gallows during the Kuruc Wars. German, Magyar, and Italian feudal lords inherited the latifundia of the Croatian magnates. The rest of the Croatian high nobility succumbed to the powerful force of attraction of Viennese court customs; while Latin was the lingua franca of the Sabor* and the official language of the authorities, the educated nobility used German or Italian in daily life. Only the uneducated peasant nobility, the *Zwetschkenjunker,*† still spoke Croatian. The Croatian nobility, however, relinquished Croatia's special state rights and united with the Magyar nobility as *una eademque nobilitas*‡ to defy Habsburg absolutism: When Joseph II abolished serfdom in Hungary and Croatia, the Croatian Sabor transferred its fiscal and military conscription authority to the Hungarian parliament, hoping the latter would protect it against the emancipation of the peasants. And so Croatia became a mere territory affiliated with Hungary, and the Croatian nobility then was no longer a vehicle for national culture and national independence.

Feudalism thus left the Yugoslav peoples a terrible legacy; their territory was divided by Austria, Hungary, Venice, and Turkey. Over the local Slav serfs there were German lords in Slovenia, Italian lords in Dalmatia,

---

* Croatian parliament.
† Literally "plum Junkers."
‡ "One and the same nobility."

Magyar ones in the Banat* and Bačka, Turkish sipahis in Serbia, and Muslim beys† in Bosnia. Everywhere the Yugoslavs became a peasantry without a history, dependent tenants of foreign lords; even in Croatia the national nobility was estranged from its ethnicity. The only bearer of national life was the peasant. But the horizon of the poor uneducated peasant hardly extended beyond the boundaries of the manor. The Wendish peasants of Carinthia regarded the Carniolans as foreigners, and the Catholic peasants in Croatia hated their Greek Orthodox neighbors as infidels. There was no consciousness of the national commonality of Yugoslav peoples. It took a long succession of violent upheavals to lead the Yugoslav people up from this condition of servitude, fragmentation, and lack of history.

The war that Joseph II and Catherine II launched in 1788 against Turkey was the turning point in Serbian history. Austria now called the Serb rayah into battle against Turkish domination. This call found its strongest echo in the small split-off from the Serb people that had settled in Hungary a century earlier under the leadership of the fugitive patriarch of Ipek. Many of the Serb colonists earned their living from commerce, as uprooted, transplanted peoples are wont to do; and in this way a mercantile Serb bourgeoisie developed, some of whose sons found their way to German universities and there fell under the influence of eighteenth-century Enlightenment literature, experiencing the shift from Church Latin to German that was occurring at the time within the sciences. At this point lively movement began to occur among Hungarian Serbs. Schools and church communities were founded: Dositej Obradović and Vuk Karadžić substituted the Church Slavonic school language with the vernacular, "just as it is spoken in the market place and is sung in round dances," and in so doing created the new Serbian written language and the beginnings of Serbian literature. However, at the same time the clash of weapons also roused the rayah on the other bank of the Sava. Irregular Serb voluntary corps fought under Austrian command against the Turks. And if Austria surrendered the Serb rayah to the Turks once again, as the terrifying news about the beginnings of the Great French Revolution drew the attention of the Viennese Court toward the west, the military feats in which they had just been involved strongly reinforced the self-confidence of Serbs. "What have you made of our rayah?" the Turks then complained.

---

* Banat is a historic region in southeastern Europe, covering parts of Romania, Serbia, and a small corner of Hungary.
† Provincial governors in the Ottoman Empire.

The war had revealed the weakness of the Turkish feudal state in the face of modern absolutism. Realizing this, Sultan Selim III attempted a reform of the military and the political system on the European model. The Janissaries rose up against these attempted reforms. The governor of the Belgrade Pashalik, Hadji Mustafa Pasha, even mobilized the Serb peasants against the rebellious Dahia.* Thus in 1804 the Serbs revolted, led by Kara Djordje. But as soon as they subdued the Dahia the rebelling rayah aimed its weapons against Turkish domination altogether. This was the beginning of the great liberation struggle of the Serb peasants against Turkish feudalism. Promptly instrumentalized by Russia and Austria, and just as promptly betrayed by the Tsar and the Emperor, at bottom the Serb peasants were fighting for their freedom. The first uprising brought autonomy to the Serbs: the Treaty of Adrianople (1829) established state autonomy and the Treaty of San Stefano (1878) the recognition of independence from Turkey. And with the growth of the state the nation emerged; the state created the Serbian school system and the Serbian bureaucracy whose sons brought back European ideas from foreign universities. Slowly and gradually a bourgeoisie began to separate from the peasantry and became the vehicle of the emerging national culture. And so in the course of a century a nation grew out of the rayah.

What the 1788 Ottoman War was for the Serbs, the War of the Fifth Coalition in 1809 was for Croatia. The Kingdom of Illyria, founded by Napoleon, united Slovenia, Croatia, and Dalmatia for the first time into a state; it liberated the peasants from corvée and patrimonial jurisdiction; it introduced Slovenian as the language of primary schools. To be sure, by 1813 Austria reestablished the old regime; however, once the impulse was there its effect continued. Croatian students in the universities of Vienna and Pest now dreamt of "Illyrian" freedom, of the national unity of all Southern Slav peoples. The national liberation struggles of Germans and Italians, of Poles and Magyars, were their models. They eagerly took up the then nascent Slavonic Studies. This was at first only a movement of a few young enthusiasts, but it soon gained historical significance. Ljudevit Gaj, the first to have established a standard spelling for Croatian, was the leader of the Illyrian movement; striving for the national unity of the three "Illyrian" peoples, he based his orthography on the same Shtokavian dialect from which Vuk Karadžić had formed the Serbian literary language. Thus, Croats and Serbs arrived at a common written language. And this literary

---

* The leaders of the auxiliary Janissary troops of the Ottoman Empire.

movement became a historically effective force when the Croatian nobility began to embrace it.

After the 1830 July Revolution in France, the struggle of Hungary's parliament against the Viennese Court assumed a revolutionary character. The reactionary Croat nobility came into conflict with the Magyar reform movement, putting up resistance when the Hungarian parliament wanted to impose equal rights for Protestants in Croatia, too. It was furious when demands to abolish the peonage of the peasants began to be raised in Pressburg* and Pest. When Hungary replaced official Latin with Hungarian, the Sabor resisted its introduction into Croatia. In this case it availed itself of the Illyrian cultural movement and introduced Croatian as the state language. Threatened by revolutionary Hungary, the Viennese Court took the side of the Croatians. In 1848, when Hungary's revolutionary movement led to full-fledged revolution, Jellačić's Croatian contingent subdued revolutionary Hungary and revolutionary Vienna for the Habsburgs, while at the same time the Serbs of the Banat struck at the Hungarian Revolution from behind. But the Yugoslavs soon became acquainted with the "gratitude of the House of Austria." To be sure, triumphant absolutism severed Croatia and Serbo-Hungarian Vojvodina† from Hungary, only to subject them to the same brutal tyranny to which Hungary was subjected. And after 1859 and 1866, the Habsburgs concluded their peace with the Magyar nobility at the expense of the Southern Slavs. Vojvodina was once again handed over to Hungary. Dalmatia remained in Austria, and it was refused annexation to Croatia, while the Austro-Hungarian Compromise of 1867 was imposed on Croatia itself. The vestige of its old constitutional independence, which the compromise allowed Croatia, became a mere semblance. The bans‡ were appointed by the Hungarian government. The state parliament was based on elections in which, thanks to the narrowly configured census suffrage, officials made up the majority of voters; since the right to vote had to be exercised publicly, no official could dare vote against the government. As a result, the bans appointed by the Hungarian government could put together the state parliament as they pleased. In essence, Croatia became a Magyar pashalik ruled with brutal force and cynical corruption. The twin hatred for the Viennese Court, which had betrayed it after 1848,

---

* Old-Austrian name for Bratislava. See Glossary for the German names of other cities.
† See Glossary.
‡ *Ban* is a noble title in South Slav areas, used under the Habsburgs and Kingdom of Hungary for chief government officials.

and the Magyar ruling class, which had oppressed it since 1868, filled the soul of the Croatian people.

With this twin hatred, the Croats grew into a modern nation. However much Magyar foreign domination aimed at disadvantaging the country, its nineteenth-century economic development nevertheless broadened the urban bourgeoisie. However small the vestige of constitutional independence the Compromise of 1867 wanted to leave, this nevertheless ensured the country a national school system up to the university and academy levels. And so here too a national bourgeoisie arose as a bearer of national culture. In political life after 1868 the bourgeoisie gradually substituted the nobility.

However, the Croats did not feel they were a tribe of a unified Southern Slav people but rather a distinctive nation. The students of the 1830s had dreamt of Illyrian unity; but when the nobility seized leadership of the national movement for themselves, the battle cry was no longer the natural right of "Illyrians" to unity and freedom but rather the historic right of Croatia to have a constitutional state in which neither Serbs nor Slovenes had a part. The students influenced by the European Enlightenment may have regarded the distance between Catholic Croats and Orthodox Serbs to be no greater than that between Protestant and Catholic Germans; but when the Croat petty bourgeoisie and peasants entered the political arena led by the clergy, they brought with them their hatred of the Serb schismatics. Magyar dominion exploited this conflict and exacerbated it by supporting the Serbs "with no history" against the Croats who were demanding their historic right.

The idea of Yugoslav unity was still more alien to the Slovenes than to the mass of Croats. The Serbs had won their state in a revolutionary assault. In Croatia, national evolution could cling to the vestige of past state independence. The Slovenes had no state, no cities, and no bourgeoisie. To be sure, Austrian primary schools in the nineteenth century here too made a national literature possible by teaching the peasants and petty bourgeoisie to read. But literature—written not for the intelligentsia but for peasants—had to use the peasant vernacular if it was to find readers. It was on this that Illyrianism's attempt to win the Slovenes, too, to the common Serbo-Croatian literary language foundered, despite the close relationship between Slovenes and Croats; the Slovenes created their own literary language out of the Carniolan peasant vernacular. But the literature this small and poor people could produce had to be meager; and at first its political history also appeared meager. Only with gradual democratization could the Slovene petty bourgeoisie and peasants create the germ cells of national self-rule; after the granting of suffrage in 1882 to the "five-gulden men,"* the Slovene petty bourgeoisie conquered the town council of Laibach,† and the Slovene peasants one year later the Carniolan state parliament, which had up to then still been dominated by the big German landowners. Only through terribly arduous struggles could this small people wrest the minimal requisites for cultural life from the German-Austrian bourgeoisie, which, angry and insulted by the impertinence of Slovenes forcing it to grant some very few parallel classes in a German Gymnasium, overthrew a government in 1893.

But however great the impediments were against which all branches of the Southern Slav people had to push forward, the result of the whole nineteenth-century development was still the development everywhere—in Serbia as in Croatia, in Dalmatia and in Slovenia—of a national bourgeoisie that had assumed intellectual leadership of the Yugoslav peoples and through schools, the press, and organizations had also suffused the petty bourgeoisie and peasant masses with national consciousness. For this national consciousness the degrading status to which the Yugoslav people were still consigned at the beginning of the twentieth century had to be intolerable.

As late as the beginning of the twentieth century, the overwhelming majority of the Yugoslav people lived under foreign domination. In Old Serbia and Macedonia the Turks still ruled; there Bulgarians, Serbs, and Greeks fought against one another and against Turkish rule in wild guerrilla warfare. From 1878, the Habsburg Monarchy's military absolutism governed Bosnia. From 1883 Count Khuen-Hederváry held Croatia in chains "with horsewhip and oats." Only in Serbia and Montenegro did the Yugoslav people enjoy state independence. But what did this independence mean? The prince of the tiny country of Montenegro was a beneficiary of the Viennese and Saint Petersburg courts. In Serbia things were even worse. The family scandals of the degenerate Obrenović dynasty became the ill fate of the country. The detested family had imposed oriental despotism: parliamentary elections, votes in parliament, and juridical sentences occurred through direct orders from the princely court; prisoners were murdered in jail by royal command; as late as 1898, after the attempted assassination of Milan Obrenović, the lives of the oppositional party leaders were saved only through foreign appeals. And this regime, despotic to the core, was

---

* See Glossary.
† The Old-Austrian name for Ljubljana.

moreover servile to the outside world. Under Milan Obrenović, Serbia became a vassal state of Austria-Hungary; in exchange for the protection of its
shameless internal despotism, Milan and Alexander abjured any independence from their powerful neighbor. In the meanwhile, young people were
excitedly reading about the great history of the Italian Risorgimento. They
read that Italy too had once been fragmented and ruled by the Habsburgs.
And they dreamed that Serbia might be called upon to do for the Yugoslavs
what Piedmont had done for Italy. It was still a mere idea, almost preposter-
ous in view of the terrible reality. But the idea became a force.

In 1903 the Yugoslav Revolution began. The uprising in Macedonia,
the overthrow of the Obrenović dynasty in Serbia, and the overthrow of
Khuen-Héderváry in Croatia are the three events that marked the beginning of the revolutionary upheaval.

The bloody guerrilla warfare that had pitted the Bulgarian, Serb, and
the Greek Komitadji* in Macedonia against one another had finally forced
Turkey to confront the bands with an iron fist. The bands, which had up to
that point been battling one another, now united against the Turks. And as
soon as they turned against the hated feudal lords, they attracted the support of the peasants. By 1903 the war of the bands culminated in Macedonia's revolutionary uprising against Turkish domination. The great powers
now intervened. Russia, tied down in Manchuria, came to an agreement
with Austria-Hungary in October 1903 in Mürzsteg over a reform program
for Macedonia.[1] A European police force reestablished provisional peace in
the country. But the Balkan Question had been reopened.

In the same year in Serbia, Alexander Obrenović suspended the constitution and imposed a new one. The King's coup d'état was answered by the
military revolution. Alexander and Draga were murdered and Petar Karadjordjević was elected king. Despite its oriental forms it was an authentic
revolution: absolutism was broken, peasant radicalism and the petty bourgeoisie gained the upper hand, a democratic constitution was created, and
freedom of the press, of association, and of assembly were won. The new
regime sought to free the country of its dependency on the Habsburg Monarchy, but here it quickly came into conflict with Austria-Hungary. In 1906
the Habsburg Monarchy offered to renew its trade treaty with Serbia only
on condition that it forego exporting livestock to Austria and pledge that it
would get its ordnance and railway material only from Austria; when Serbia
rejected the diktat the Habsburg Monarchy closed its borders to Serbian agri-

---

* Rebel bands operating in the Balkans during the final years of the Ottoman Empire.

cultural products. The tariff war dealt Serb peasants a severe blow. And when Serbia sought a way out of the unbearable economic dependency through a tariff union with Bulgaria, Austria-Hungary menacingly objected. At this point the conflict between Serbia and Austro-Hungary quickly became exacerbated.

But 1903 also brought a change to the Yugoslavs in Austria-Hungary. The corrupt and ruthless Khuen-Hederváry regime in Croatia finally became intolerable. At the same time, however, the outbreak of the last great conflict between the Habsburg Monarchy and the Magyar landowning class raised hopes among the Yugoslav people. The struggle over the language of command of the Hungarian military forces had become the decisive confrontation over whether the armed forces were commanded by the Crown or Hungary's parliament of nobles. In his army edict of September 16, 1903, at Chłopy, Emperor Franz Joseph declared that he would never "relinquish the rights and powers reserved to the Supreme Commander. Joint and unitary as my army is, so must it remain." In the Hungarian parliament Stephan Tisza sought in vain to break the resistance of the Party of Independence to the King's military demands;[2] the new elections of 1905 gave a majority to the coalition of independence parties, the parliament rejected taxes and recruitment, and the counties did not collect taxes. At this point the Crown joined battle; in June 1905 the Fejérváry "bodyguard regime" was formed, and in February 1906 it had a Honvéd squadron* forcibly chase all deputies out of the parliament. The entire fabric of the Habsburg Monarchy was unravelling. Croats and Serbs were hoping to use the Empire's severe crisis for their own cause. On October 2, 1905, parliamentary deputies from Croatia, Dalmatia, and Istria met at Fiume† and agreed on the famous resolution authored by the Dalmatian politician Ante Trumbić, which established the framework of the new Yugoslav policy. "By blood ties and language Croats and Serbs," it proclaimed, "are one nation." It asserted that this nation, just as any other, "has the right to make independent decisions on its existence and destiny." On this basis, it stated, Croats and Serbs were offering the parties fighting for Hungary's independence an alliance against the "Viennese camarilla."

The Resolution of Fiume showed the profound transformation that had occurred in the thinking of South Slavs. The fact that Croats and

---

* Honvédség, the Royal Hungarian Landwehr, that is, the Hungarian armed forces of Austro-Hungary.
† Italian and Old-Austrian name of Rijeka in Croatia.

Serbs, whose mutual antagonisms Magyar rule had exploited for decades in order to dominate both, declared they were *one* nation, and that in the deep crisis of the Empire both no longer took the side of the Habsburgs against their Magyar oppressors as in 1848 but stood with them—all this showed for the first time that the South Slavs hoped for liberation now only from a severe convulsion of the Habsburg Empire. In fact, the alliance with the Magyar nobility that they then formed was by no means fruitless. To be sure, the Magyar nobility, frightened by the Crown's threat to impose general and equal suffrage, had already reestablished peace with it in May 1906. But the Hungarian Coalition, which now came to power under the Wekerle government, still had to make a concession to its Croatian and Serbian allies. For the first time, a Croatian Sabor was elected without government pressure. Hungary could no longer have Croatia governed by a submissive Sabor; if the conflict between Hungary and Croatia was still alive, it had to take the form of a conflict between the Ban and the Sabor and thus become a constitutional conflict. This in fact happened very soon. When in 1907 the Hungarian government wanted to resume the Magyarization policy applied to the Croatian railways, the Sabor took a strong stand against it. For the Ban, Baron Rauch, there was no choice but to push the Sabor aside and exercise naked absolutist rule.

In the meanwhile, the movement had already gained new momentum. After the Russo-Japanese War, England and Russia had become closer. The common conflict with Germany over its support of Turkey, and the common threat of the ferment in the Muslim world, which had already led in 1906 to a revolutionary outbreak in Persia, had brought the two powers closer together. In a blunder, Aehrenthal encouraged their convergence through a foray into the Balkans: The Austro-Hungarian concession for the construction of the Sanjak Railway (January 1908) not only elicited the protest of Italy and Serbia; it also provided Russia with the excuse for declaring the Mürzsteg Agreement null and void. The old conflict between Russia and Austria-Hungary was revived and so gave new hope to Serbia. In June 1908 at Reval,* Russia came to an understanding with England, and the Entente was established. Its first act was a new reform program for Macedonia. The national sentiment of the Turkish officers rose up against this program. On July 24, 1908 Abdul Hamid II had to capitulate to the Revolutionary Army. The Young Turk Revolution resonated strongly in Bosnia and Herzegovina.

---

* Tallinn before Estonian independence in 1918.

Austria-Hungary itself had once aroused expectations in Serbia for the acquisition of Bosnia and Herzegovina. In 1869 Andrássy and Kállay had promised Serbia the two still Turkish provinces in order to pry it away from Russian influence and to aggravate the conflict between Serbia and Croatia, which asserted a claim to these provinces. But these Serbian hopes were bitterly disappointed: The Berlin Congress that recognized Serbia's independence in 1878 at the same time empowered Austria-Hungary to occupy Bosnia. Already at that time popular passions in Serbia fiercely resisted the idea that once again a South Slav country should be surrendered to foreign domination. From then on, the Habsburg Monarchy governed the country with military absolutist methods. The commanding general acted like a viceroy in the country. The administration of the state was populated by foreign officials—Germans, Magyars, and Polish Jews. In the country itself the Monarchy relied on the Muslim nobility and maintained the Turkish feudal agricultural structure. This foreign domination was all the more unbearable since in Bosnia too, with economic development and the development of a school system, a national bourgeoisie began to evolve, which participated in the life of Belgrade and Agram.* Since absolutism was collapsing even in Turkey, it became untenable in Bosnia. And then Bosnia remembered that according to international law it was still a Turkish province and threatened to nominate Bosnian deputies to the Turkish parliament.

Thus, by 1908 the Monarchy was already in the tariff war with Serbia, involved in a serious constitutional conflict with Croatia, and facing dangerous turmoil in Bosnia; then it decided on an act that could demonstrate its power and intimidate the South Slavs. On October 5, 1908, the annexation of Bosnia was proclaimed. Now popular anger flared out of control. And Serbia was no longer alone this time. Russia, England, and France were leading its cause. The Yugoslavs began to see the Entente as their protectors against the Habsburgs.

In its struggle against the Magyar nobility, the Crown had in 1905 demanded general suffrage for the Hungarian parliament; in so doing it had fanned the hopes of Hungary's nations for their liberation from the rule of the Magyar nobility. Now the Crown bought the assent of the Magyar nobility to the annexation of Bosnia by abandoning the Hungarian nationalities to it. Andrássy's electoral reform received the preemptive ratification of the Crown in November 1908. In May 1912 Tisza put down the revolt of the Hungarian workers and forced through an electoral reform meant

---

* The Old-Austrian name for Zagreb.

to perpetuate the Hungarian nations' lack of rights. In so doing, all hope for the support of the Crown in the struggle against the Hungarian nobility was dashed for the Serbs of Vojvodina as it was for all of Hungary's nations. The effects of the annexation crisis were still stronger and more direct in Croatia. As Austria-Hungary began to concentrate its troops on the Serbian border, as it humiliated Serbia with the threat of war, it recognized how strong the Serbo-Croatian sense of unity had already become. The sympathies not only of the Serbs but also of a part of the Croats in the Monarchy were now with Serbia. Vienna and Budapest thought they could cope with this "high treason" through court rulings. But the Agram High Treason Trial led to a crushing defeat for the government; the proof that its records were forgeries fabricated by imperial diplomacy now added contempt to the Yugoslav people's hatred. The nation's capacity for resistance was reinforced; the Ban Tomasić sought in vain to create a majority in the Sabor through open terror. Since all of his efforts failed, Croatia's constitution was suspended on April 3, 1912, and the naked rule of force was established with Cuvaj as the "Royal Commissioner."

In fall 1912, the year in which Tisza's coup d'état in Hungary and Cuvaj's Commissariat in Croatia had destroyed all hope of a democratic evolution within the Habsburg Monarchy, Serbia, in alliance with Bulgaria and Greece, attacked Turkey, which had been weakened by the Italo-Turkish War. In valiant combat the Serbian army defeated Turkey and freed their countrymen in Old Serbia and Macedonia from the yoke of the Turkish feudal lords. These were no longer the barbaric Serbs of Obrenović on which Croats had proudly looked down. The heart of all South Slav peoples beat for the victors of Kumanovo. Even the Slovenes were carried away by the powerful wave of enthusiasm for the victorious Serbs. "There, near Chataldja," said Janez Evangelist Krek, a Catholic priest in the Austrian Chamber of Deputies, "they are also fighting for every last Slovenian peasant in threatened Carinthian villages." The thought of the national unity of Yugoslavs was now advancing victoriously. On November 20, 1912, ninety Slovene and Croat deputies of all South Slav crownlands resolved: "As Croats and Slovenes we are forming a national unit." But the Habsburg Monarchy once again, as it did throughout the whole Balkan War, confronted Serbia as an enemy; it once again mustered its troops threateningly on the Serbian border and laid itself open to scorn when it had its agents invent those lies about the castration of the Monarchy's consul, Oskar Prochaska, which was to provide the pretext for war. Thus, the Habsburgs pitted themselves in the severest opposition to the Yugoslavs' national sentiment, which had been tremendously inflamed by the war.

The Habsburgs now saw the entire Slav south of its Empire in revolt. It trembled in the face of the South Slav revolution. Fear whipped Austro-Hungary into war. The militarist faction in the Viennese Court, especially its head, Chief of the General Staff Franz Conrad von Hötzendorff, had long pushed for war. In a 1907 memorandum he had already posed the "incorporation of Serbia including the central region of Niš" as a goal; for "an independent Serbia is the constant epicenter of those aspirations and machinations that aim at the secession of all South Slav regions." During the annexation crisis he did everything in his power to push for striking out and annexing Serbia. It is true that Aehrenthal thought that for this purpose the regime had to wait for "a favorable European constellation," and Franz Joseph comforted Hötzendorff: "This war will in any case come on its own." However, people gradually became used to the idea. If Aehrenthal resisted, his successor Berchthold gave in. The assassination at Sarajevo provided the desired pretext. This time the decision was made that nothing was to impede going forward. The ultimatum was written so as to make war unavoidable.

The mechanism of alliances enlarged the clash between the Habsburg Monarchy and the Yugoslav people into a world war of unprecedented dimensions. But whatever war meant elsewhere in the world, on Yugoslav soil its meaning was clearly understood by every peasant: on the one side the Germans, the Magyars, and the Turks, the three nations that for centuries had subjugated the South Slav peasants and transformed them into their dependents, fragmenting the South Slav people; on the other side the Serb peasant who in a brilliant feat of arms had just liberated his countrymen in Old Serbia from the foreign domination of Turkish feudal lords and was now once again setting out to free them in the Habsburg Empire from foreign domination by German and Magyar landlords. Thus for the Yugoslav people the war was its national and social revolution.

During the days of the resounding collapse of the big offensive of the armies of Supreme Commander Potiorek and on the very day—December 7, 1914—that the Imperial Army was pushed back behind the Kolubara, the Serb government, in the Skupština* convoked in Niš, declared Serbia's war objective for the first time to be "the liberation and unification of all of our enslaved Serb, Croat, and Slovene brothers."

---

* Serb parliament.

This declaration had to elicit a strong response among the South Slavs within the Habsburg Monarchy. The Habsburg army had been deployed against the Serbs on South Slav soil, but it feared treason in every Serbian village. The Habsburgs had deployed South Slav reservists for war against Serbs; but every Serb in the Imperial Army was a treason suspect for the German and Magyar officers. As a result, the war machine operated with terrible violence; with few scruples its officers had Greek Orthodox priests in Bosnia, Slavonia, and Vojvodina hung from the nearest tree; the military courts pronounced death sentences every day; all politicians, intellectuals, clerics, and teachers suspected of Yugoslav patriotism were deported from their homeland to internment camps; the Monarchy waged war against its own citizens. Hatred grew among the mistreated ethnicity. In the Monarchy itself the brute force of war absolutism suppressed their voice. But those who emigrated could speak, and they did speak. Already by the beginning of the war, in America assemblies and congresses of émigrés from the Monarchy's southern regions passionately took up Serbia's cause against the Habsburg Monarchy. And this emigration found its leadership in a group of politicians from the south of the Monarchy who had been able to flee abroad at the beginning of the war. On May 1, 1915, the Yugoslav Committee (Jugoslavenski Odbor) was constituted in London and led by Ante Trumbić; it organized propaganda for the secession of the South Slav countries from the Monarchy and their unification with Serbia and Montenegro.

The Kingdom of Serbia and Yugoslav revolutionary émigrés had set the goal of the liberation and unification of South Slavs, but in this there were essential differences. The objective of the Serbian government was a Greater Serbia that was to incorporate the South Slav areas of the Habsburg Monarchy. The goal of the émigré revolutionaries was a Yugoslavia into which the Kingdoms of Serbia and Montenegro were to merge along with the other South Slav peoples of Austria-Hungary. The Serbian government imagined the future South Slav state under Serb hegemony. The Yugoslav émigré groups decidedly rejected Serb hegemony. "We are seven million, while you are only four," the South Slavs from the Monarchy pointed out to the Serbs from the Kingdom. The Yugoslav émigrés were pitted against the Greater Serbian orientation of Karadjordjević for several reasons: the self-consciousness of the old historic nation of Croats that felt itself to be culturally superior to a Serbian identity that had just risen in the last century out of a past without a history; the old tribal jealousies of Croats and Slovenes in the face of the

Serbs; the conflict between Croatian/Slovene Catholicism and Serbian Greek Orthodoxy; and the democratic, revolutionary, rationalist ideology of the intelligentsia in relation to the historical formation of the Serbian state.

The Greater Serbia idea imagined a future state of Serbs, Croats, and Slovenes as a unitary state under Serb leadership, while the Yugoslav idea posited a federation, a federal state of South Slav peoples with equal rights. The Greater Serbia orientation saw Belgrade as the capital of the South Slav state, while the Yugoslav conception saw Agram or Sarajevo as the capital. Greater Serbia supposed a monarchy under the Karadjordjević's, while Yugoslavia's supporters wanted the decision over its form of state to be taken by a constituent assembly to which the dynasties of Serbia and Montenegro as well as the South Slav peoples of Austria-Hungary would have to submit. Greater Serbia dreamed of the conquest and annexation by Serbia of the South Slav regions of the Monarchy; Yugoslavia saw the South Slav regions of Austria-Hungary, liberated from Habsburg domination, constituting an independent state, which would freely agree with Serbia and Montenegro on the conditions for unification. The Yugoslav concept also saw Bulgaria as a part of the Yugoslav people; it hoped that the future South Slav federation could assimilate the Bulgarians. By contrast, the Serbs saw the Bulgarians as hereditary and deadly enemies of their nation.

The revolutionary émigrés were oriented to the Adriatic; worried about the Slav countries of the Adriatic that were menaced by Italy, they attached little importance to the quarrel of the Serbs with the Bulgarians over Macedonia. On the other hand, Serbia, oriented as it was to the Aegean Sea, held on stubbornly to the possession of Macedonia and Old Serbia, the achievement of the two Balkan Wars that had been bought with rivers of blood, while the border disputes of Croats and Slovenes with Italy was a more distant concern.

The Yugoslav Committee regarded itself as the appointed representative of the South Slavs dominated by Austria-Hungary; it laid claim to the South Slav volunteer battalions composed of émigrés and prisoners of war who fought in the Entente armies. It demanded that a common regime be formed, during the war, from representatives of the Serbian government and the revolutionary émigrés, which would be the only entity with the right to lead and represent the whole nation. The Serbian government rejected this kind of revolutionary innovation and claimed the liberation and unification of the South Slav peoples as the historic task of the constitutional government and Skupština of the Kingdom of Serbia. In this way, the conflict between Greater Serbia and the Yugoslav ideal, between the Serbian government and the Yugoslav Committee, between Pašić and Trumbić, continued through the whole history of South Slav emigration during the war. It was comparable to the conflicts between Bismarck and the German National Association, or between Cavour and Mazzini.

Throughout 1915, the year of the great victories of the Central Powers, the goal of the revolutionary Yugoslav émigrés must have appeared to the masses of South Slav peoples in Austria-Hungary just as utopian as the idea of Greater Serbia; a war outcome in which the South Slav countries would break away from the Habsburg Monarchy seemed improbable to them. Although the thought that the war, which arose out of the struggle of the South Slav peoples for their liberation from foreign domination and for unification, would have to bring liberation and unification powerfully gripped the masses, it appeared unlikely that liberation and unification could be achieved against the Habsburgs, and so the idea suggested itself that it could be achieved with the Habsburgs. A third political conception confronted the Greater Serbia and Yugoslav outlooks: the idea of a unification of the South Slav countries of the Monarchy with Serbia and Montenegro to become a state under the sceptre of the Habsburgs, which would join Austria and Hungary as a third state of the Monarchy.

The idea of Trialism* was not new; at the court of Franz Ferdinand, since 1905, it was often considered in the deliberations of the militarist faction. It offered a justification for a military and annexationist Balkan policy as a means to transform the Yugoslav unification movement that threatened to blow up the Monarchy into an opportunity for its enlargement as well as an instrument of domestic policy. It hoped to use the transition from Dualism† to Trialism to buttress the unity of the Empire in setting narrower limits to Hungarian statehood. Many politicians in Agram and Laibach clung to the hope of these militarist faction plans. What we mainly need, they argued, is unification; whether unification occurs under Franz Joseph or Petar Karadjordjević is much less important. And unification under Franz Joseph appeared at the time not only to be more easily reachable than unification under Petar; it could even appear more tempting to Croat and Slovene particularism. Even if it did not bring full freedom, full independence, it would have to ensure the hegemony of Agram over Belgrade, of Croats over Serbs, of Catholics over Greek orthodoxy. Thus, the revolutionary Yugoslav ideal confronted on the one side Greater Serbia

---

* See Glossary.
† See Glossary.

and on the other a Greater Croatia concept that sought to solve the national problem in a Yugoslavia within the Habsburg Monarchy.

The events of the war in 1915 reinforced the Greater Croatia or Trialist tendency. On May 23, 1915, Italy declared war on the Habsburg Monarchy. The details of the Treaty of London, with which the Western powers purchased Italy's military assistance, might not have been common knowledge, but people were aware that the treaty had promised Italy Slav soil on the Adriatic. Italy's attack on the Monarchy appeared to the South Slavs as an aggression against South Slav territory. At the Isonzo,* the Imperial Army defended Slav soil against Italy's lust for conquest. The mood in the South Slav countries shifted toward the Monarchy. On June 14, 1915, the Croatian Sabor met. It issued no declarations against Serbia or Russia; instead, with boisterous shouts of "Long live the Croatian sea!" it called for the victory of the Imperial forces over Italy. "The animus towards Italy in our countries is immense and general. Our regiments are battling like lions at the Isonzo," wrote Dr. Trumbić on July 11, 1915.

If Italy's attack brought the South Slavs of the Monarchy closer to the Monarchy, the conquest of Serbia by Mackensen's armies in fall 1915 further strengthened the current hoping for the unification of South Slavs within the Monarchy. Now the whole Slav south was amenable to the Habsburgs. Now all Greater Serbian plans, all the wishes of the émigré revolutionaries, seemed completely futile, and instead the unification of all Yugoslav peoples under the Habsburg sceptre appeared to have moved into the realm of the possible.

With the conquest of Serbia, the impediments that stood in the way of a Greater Croatian solution to the Yugoslav problem became apparent. While Conrad von Hötzendorff now advocated the annexation of Serbia, Tisza unconditionally rejected it. He proposed annexing Belgrade and Mačva, giving Niš and Macedonia to the Bulgarians, but letting the remainder of Serbia exist as a powerless, poor peasant state. The Magyar ruling class did not want the annexation of Serbia; it understood that the enlargement of the Habsburgs' South Slav subjects would inevitably usher in Trialism and thus cut off Hungary from the sea, weakening Hungary's position of power within the Empire. Thus, even a complete victory of the Central Powers would have hardly been able to unite the whole Yugoslav people within the framework of the Monarchy.

However, the turn the war took in 1916 made such a complete victory of the Central Powers appear highly unlikely. And with this any hope of

---

* *Soča* in Slovenian.

the unification of the three Yugoslav peoples in a single Habsburg Yugoslavia disappeared; for if Croats and Slovenes, putting unity before freedom, were ready to agree to the annexation of Serbia by the Monarchy just in order to unify the whole nation within one state, the Serbs from the Kingdom had a completely different idea. They did not want to sacrifice their freedom to the hated Monarchy for the sake of unity; for them any South Slav who spoke in favor of Serbia's annexation by the Monarchy was a traitor. And behind Serbia stood the Entente, which assured Serbia that it could no more restore peace without Serbia's recovery than it could without Belgium's recovery.

Unification of the whole nation under one state thus seemed unattainable. For now, the South Slavs within the Monarchy had to set a more modest goal: the unification of the South Slavs living in Austria-Hungary into a single state within the Habsburg Monarchy. It was, however, clear that the Monarchy would not itself voluntarily opt for this solution. The land of the South Slavs cuts both German-Austria and Hungary off from the sea; it was obvious that the two ruling classes of the Empire, the German-Austrian bourgeoisie and the Magyar gentry, would put up the stiffest resistance to the handing over of Slovenia and Croatia to a South Slav state, a resistance that could only be broken by powerful external pressure. That the Entente would exert such pressure was the last hope that remained to the South Slavs. In its note of January 10, 1917 to President Wilson, the Entente cited the liberation of the Slavs of Austria-Hungary as one of its war objectives. It was evident that in the peace settlement the Entente planned to force a restructuring of Austria-Hungary in order to break the hegemony of the German bourgeoisie and the Magyar gentry in the Monarchy and through this to separate the Monarchy from the German Empire. Only such coercion exerted by the Entente could liberate the Slovenes from German and the Croats from Magyar rule and compel the unification of the South Slav regions of Austria, Hungary, and Bosnia into a state within the framework of the Habsburg Monarchy. Thus the South Slavs had to set all their hopes on the Entente. Both the Greater Serbian and the revolutionary Yugoslav orientation had stood from the beginning in the camp of the Entente; now also those Croatian and Slovenian parties who had still been seeking a solution within the Habsburg Monarchy could only base their hopes on protection by the Entente.

The outbreak of the Russian Revolution in March 1917 and the entrance of the United States into the war in April 1917 reinforced the South

Slav unity movement. The Russian Revolution cemented the conviction that major internal upheavals would come after the war. Wilson's propaganda for the self-determination of peoples resonated strongly in the Slav south. Since the Russian Revolution the Habsburgs had been trembling for their throne. They began secret peace negotiations with the Entente. The South Slavs believed that the moment was approaching in which Austria-Hungary would seek peace by offering internal restructuring.

In May 1917 the Austrian Parliament* met again for the first time since the beginning of the war. The interventions of the South Slav deputies left no doubt that their sympathy was on the side of the Entente and that they hoped for the Entente's victory. It was clear that they would no longer be content with a solution within the Dualist framework of the Monarchy, that the only thing that could now assuage the nation would be an independent Yugoslav state. However, it was also evident that they could envisage the formation of this state within the Habsburg Monarchy. The declaration of the Yugoslav Club, which Korošec read out in the Chamber of Deputies on May 30, 1917, demanded, "on the basis of the nationality principle and Croatian constitutional law, the unification of all regions of the Monarchy in which Slovenes, Croats, and Serbs live into an independent state based on democratic principles, free of domination by any nation, and under the sceptre of the Habsburg-Lorraine dynasty." This "May Declaration" was passionately seconded in Croatia's Sabor and in innumerable rallies of Slovene and Croat organizations. It appeared now as the actual program of South Slavs in the Monarchy.

Greater Serbianism and the revolutionary Yugoslavism of the émigrés were unsettled by the secret peace negotiations between the Monarchy and the Entente. They feared that a premature peace accord would leave Slovenia, Croatia, and Bosnia in the possession of the Monarchy. In order to reinforce the propaganda for the breakaway of South Slav countries from the Monarchy they tried to come to agreements with one another. In July 1917 the Serb government and the London Yugoslav Committee met on Corfu for negotiations. On July 20, Pašić and Trumbić signed the Corfu Declaration, a compromise between the Greater Serbian concept and revolutionary émigré Yugoslavism. It demanded the unification of all South Slav countries into a "Kingdom of the Serbs, Croats, and Slovenes." The kingdom was to be a "constitutional, democratic, and parliamentary monarchy with the Karadjordievič dynasty . . . at its head." Its constitu-

---

* Reichsrat—see Glossary.

tion, which was to ensure complete equality before the law to the three Yugoslav religious denominations, was to be established by a "Constituent Assembly," whose resolutions would however first require the sanction of the King.

And so the May Declaration stood alongside the Corfu Declaration, each contending for people's souls. The South Slav peoples under Habsburg rule now felt hopeful that they would not have to tolerate the incomplete solution of the May Declaration forever and could achieve complete unification and liberation of the whole nation in the sense of the Corfu Declaration. In this they were buoyed up by the Russian Revolution, which raised hopes that the war would everywhere be followed by revolutionary upheavals; Wilson's propaganda, which shored up the conviction that the war would give rise to a new world order that would ensure each people its unfettered right to self-determination; and signs of economic exhaustion, military corrosion, and revolutionary tensions in Austria-Hungary itself. The ideal of the revolutionary émigrés no longer appeared utopian to the South Slavs of the Monarchy, as it had in 1914 and 1915. In 1917 the proviso that an independent Yugoslav state had to live "under the sceptre of the Habsburg-Lorraine dynasty" gradually disappeared from the rallies of South Slav organizations for independence.

But revolutionary Yugoslavism still did not have the support of the Western powers, which still hoped they could move the Habsburg Monarchy to conclude a separate peace. To be sure, the negotiations that Emperor Karl conducted with France in the summer of 1917, through Prince Sixtus of Bourbon-Parma, had failed because of Italy's veto; and the negotiations that Czernin tried to undertake with France also proved fruitless. But at the end of 1917 and beginning of 1918 new networks were created; it was the time of Smuts's discussions with Mensdorff, of the Emperor's correspondence with Wilson. Hope for peace still determined the Entente's position on the South Slav problem. Wilson's Fourteen Points of January 8, 1918 demanded for Serbia only its restoration and access to the sea, for the South Slavs of the Monarchy only an "unmolested opportunity of autonomous development"; similarly Prime Minister Lloyd George, in a declaration in the British Parliament on January 9, 1918, demanded only autonomy for the nations of Austria-Hungary. Then, suddenly, Czernin cut these threads of peace. His speech of April 2, 1918, recklessly provoked French prime minister Clemenceau into disclosing the secret negotiations of 1917. With this, all hope was dashed for new negotiations.

The Entente gave up the thought of separate negotiations with Austria-Hungary. If they could no longer hope to break Austria-Hungary away from Germany, they decided to blow up the by now loosened structure of its state. Now the Entente's attitude toward the Habsburg Monarchy changed completely.

The London Yugoslav Committee reported the turnaround to the South Slavs. Italian airplanes dropped a proclamation by Trumbić that announced: "The idea that it is possible to reorganize Austria and separate it from Germany has been given up by all the Allies. All of the Allies are now convinced that Austria can no longer exist after the war. Now we can achieve our freedom, our unification." Complete liberation, complete unification appeared within reach. The idea of the breakaway of the South Slav regions of the Monarchy, the revolutionary conception of Yugoslav unity and freedom for which the émigrés had fought since 1914, now completely won over the South Slavs in the Monarchy.

The internal development of this idea strengthened its power of attraction. Since the Russian Revolution the republican idea had gained strength among the Yugoslav émigrés. The idea of a federative republic of Yugoslav peoples had to attract Croats and Slovenes more than the thought of a Karadjordjević monarchy in which they would have to fear Serb hegemony. And the republican idea now appeared by no means hopeless. In summer 1918 transcripts of a letter by Trumbić appeared which reassured readers that since America's entry into the war, a democratic tendency was prevalent among the Allies; Wilson's power, he wrote, guaranteed that decisions about both the form of the Yugoslav state and its borders would be based on the right of peoples to self-determination. The hopes raised by Wilson's propaganda warded off both fear of Serb hegemony and of Italy, which entertained a desire for conquest.

In summer 1918 the Entente recognized the Czechoslovak Legions as an allied combatant force and the Czechoslovak National Council as a de facto government. This meant that the Entente had in fact already decided the breakup of the Habsburg Monarchy. In so doing it strengthened the hope of Yugoslavs for full national independence; and this hope became much stronger when after July the tide of the war on the Western front turned in favor of the Entente. But the Monarchy, even now, was still unable to offer the South Slavs anything. Although it indeed discussed the South Slav problem, the Magyar gentry still wanted to offer the South Slavs nothing more than the unification of Dalmatia with Croatia, which was to remain under Hungarian overlordship, and the incorporation of Bosnia into the Kingdom of Hungary with its own ban and a separate constitution similar to Croatia's.

However, to the German-Austrian bourgeoisie it already seemed an almost insufferable sacrifice to relinquish Dalmatia and Bosnia to Hungary for the sake of this solution, and as for the Slovenes it believed it could deal with them through local autonomy within the historical borders. This was all that the Monarchy could hold out to the people whom the Entente had promised complete unification and freedom. The two ruling classes of the Monarchy remained obtuse to the very end. Still in September 1918, when the defeat of the Central Powers was already decided, Tisza, sent to Sarajevo as the Emperor's representative, thundered at the spokespersons of the Bosnian Croats and Serbs: "It is possible that we will go down, but before we do we will still be strong enough to smash you to pieces." And so the last loyalists of the Monarchy in the Slav south turned their backs on the Habsburgs. The process of revolutionizing the South Slavs was complete. The revolutionary idea of Yugoslav unity now dominated the whole nation.

Starting in the summer, Austria-Hungary's Yugoslavs saw the approaching military collapse of the Central Powers. In agreement with the London Yugoslav Committee, they drafted their plan of revolution. At first, the South Slav regions of the Monarchy were to be consolidated into an independent state, which was then to negotiate with the Serbs the conditions of the merger. By August 16, 1918, the Narodni Svet, composed of all Slovenian parties, constituted itself in Laibach; it publicly announced that its task was "to prepare, as a part of the general Yugoslav National Council in Agram that is to meet shortly, the acquisition of all rights of state sovereignty." The South Slavs prepared for the longed-for day of liberation.

CHAPTER 2

THE CZECHS AND THE EMPIRE

The Yugoslav Revolution drove the Habsburgs into the war. The war in turn triggered the Czech Revolution. Of the national-revolutionary movements of the Austrian nations that were unleashed by the war, the movement of the Czechs was the most powerful and had the most serious consequences; it decided the fate of the Habsburg Monarchy.

Among the driving forces of Habsburg foreign policy finally leading to war, the intensification of the national struggles between Czechs and Germans had long been one of the most serious. By the 1890s the national struggles within Austria, especially between Germans and Czechs, had become increasingly intense, taking an ever more dangerous form. From 1897, the Parliament was paralyzed by national obstruction,* its bureaucratic administration undermined by the national conflicts within the corps of civil servants; even the structure of the army was increasingly threatened by the national struggles. This process of disintegration pushed the Habsburgs toward a violent solution of the Austrian problem. At the court of Franz Ferdinand a plan for a military coup against the December Constitution†—which had in fact long since been made inoperative by the national struggles—had already been worked out. The actual aim of the militarist faction,‡ which had been pushing for war already by 1907, was not only to violently quash the Yugoslavs but to use the power of militarism reinforced by a victorious war to impose a constitutional change that would forcibly insert the recently rebelling nations into a restructured Habsburg Empire.

---

* Filibustering in the Austrian Parliament on the part of the various nationalities.
† Austria's first constitution, sanctioned on December 21, 1867.
‡ See Glossary, "militarist faction."

The national revolution was not only the result but also the cause of the war, and this revolution had essentially already begun in 1897, not 1918.

The social basis of this national revolution was the awakening of the petty bourgeoisie, the peasantry, and the working class to independent political life. The structure of the Austrian state remained unshaken only as long as public life was dominated by a small upper stratum of the peoples, by the feudal aristocracy and the big bourgeoisie. To the degree that the masses, with the democratization of public life, began to determine the life of the state themselves, the Austrian state was undermined by the national struggles. It is no coincidence that precisely in the parliament elected in 1897, the first to have at least partly resulted from elections with general suffrage, national obstruction broke out from which Austrian parliamentarism from then on was unable to free itself. This self-disintegration of Austrian parliamentarism through national obstruction was the real beginning of the national revolution.

From 1860 to 1890 Austria's political life was dominated by the antagonism between the centralist big bourgeoisie, on the one side, and the federalist feudal nobility, on the other. The former was represented by the German liberal parties. The federalist feudal nobility combined under its leadership the German clergy with the Old Czechs* and the South Slavs. This was not a national antagonism; there were Germans on both sides of the divide. The liberal bourgeoisie was German. But so was the feudal nobility's clerical following. However, both parties were "loyal Austrians." The point of contention was the shaping of the Austrian constitution, not the existence of the Austrian state. The German liberal bourgeoisie saw itself as the actual party of the state; its prime objective was the defense of the Austrian state's unity against the plans of federalists. In this period the attitude of the Old Czech bourgeoisie was no less "good Austrian"; following the feudal nobility it fought for the federalization of the Austrian state—for, as long as the German Empire was strong, the disintegration of the Austrian state would be tantamount to letting the lands of the old German Confederation from Bohemia to the Adriatic fall to the German Empire and thus transferring Czech lands to German rule. For fear of this, Czechs had already in 1848 sided with Austria against the national revolutions of the Germans, the Magyars, and the Italians; Palacký wrote that if Austria did not exist, it would have to be invented.

---

* The Old Czech faction of the Czech National Party (Národní Strana) from which the Young Czechs split.

Already in the 1880s opposition grew in the German and Czech camps* to, respectively, the big bourgeoisie and the feudal nobility. From 1878 to 1885, the feudal nobility had bought the allegiance of the Czechs through national concessions; the Czech school system was expanded, civil service posts were increasingly held by Czech officials, the use of the Czech language was expanded in administration and the courts, and many local councils were transferred from the hands of the German big bourgeoisie to the Czech petty bourgeoisie. German liberalism had hoped that the 1867 Austro-Hungarian Compromise would secure the power of the German bourgeoisie in Austria as it had secured the rule of the Magyar gentry in Hungary; in the 1880s the German bourgeoisie recognized that it was not able to assert its dominance over the majority Slav population. Under the impact of this disappointment, a German irredentism began to emerge among the German youth who dreamed of German-Austria being rescued by the Hohenzollern Empire. The enmity expressed by the German intelligentsia for the feudal-clerical regime turned into enmity for the Austrian state itself. The emerging German-National parties, in deliberate contrast to the German Liberals, counterposed the German national interest to the interest of the Austrian state. "In our struggle for the national rights of Germans, we would like to see no other concerns prevail than those derived from national interests themselves," declared the program of the German-National Movement after the 1885 elections. Its growth frightened the Court; in order not to rile German national consciousness, national concessions to the Czechs were reduced. The Old Czechs continued to support the feudal-clerical regime; but they could no longer demonstrate that they had won national concessions in exchange for this support. As a result, resistance grew among Czechs to Old Czech politics. Young Czech† opposition to the Old Czech loyalty to the feudal regime grew in parallel with the German-National Movement against the liberal big bourgeoisie. In the 1889 Bohemian regional elections, the Old Czechs were obliterated by the Young Czechs, and the Czech bourgeoisie was emancipated from feudal leadership. The "Iron Ring," which had brought the federalist parties together under feudal leadership, was now broken.

---

* That is, within the Austrian Empire.
† The Young Czech faction of the Czech National Party, and from 1874 the Young Czech Party (National Liberal Party).

But at the same time the working class* rose up. In 1890 it launched its struggle for suffrage,† the first result of which was the Electoral Reform of 1896. A new parliament, not comparable to the former ones, was convened in 1897. The liberals were crowded out by the German National and Christian Social parties, and the Old Czechs were supplanted by the Young Czechs. Despite this, the Badeni government tried once again to reestablish the old regime, the coalition of federalist parties, under feudal leadership. They purchased the support of the Young Czechs with their language regulation, just as Taaffe had bought the Old Czechs with the Stremayr language regulations in 1880. But Badeni was facing opponents who differed from Taaffe's. The German-National parties responded to the language regulations with vociferous obstruction, stirring up the masses and blocking any parliamentary work. When Badeni tried to forcibly quash the obstruction, the Social Democrats disrupted the parliament by joining the obstruction. When Thun substituted the absolutism of Paragraph 14‡ for the parliamentarism that had been destroyed, the working masses rose up. The Court capitulated. The Thun government, the last right-wing feudal-federalist government, was dismissed; the Clary government repealed the language regulations in 1899. The feudal Slav government system was now followed by a German bureaucratic one. The Czechs had suffered a serious defeat, but now they reached for the same weapon that the Germans had so successfully employed. German obstruction was superseded by Czech obstruction. The Austrian Parliament was never to be free of it again.

The period of national obstruction always filled broad popular strata with the passions of the national struggle, always made the nations into bitter enemies of one another, and caused relations between the nationalities to deteriorate ever more. If nationalism was first based in the intelligentsia and its petty bourgeois following, with the intensification of national struggles it gradually was able to subordinate the other classes as well to the leadership of the nationalistic bourgeoisie. First it was the peasantry that succumbed to it. The German and Slav clerical parliamentary representatives of peasants, until 1895 united in the Hohenwart Club to form a faction, were pulled apart and forced into "national citizenries" and thus subordinated to the leaderships of the national bourgeoisies.§ Then civil ser-

---

* That is, the German-speaking working class in all of the Austrian crownlands (Cisleithania).
† In Cisleithania.
‡ See Glossary.
§ That is, both the Czech and German-Austrian bourgeoisies.

vice personnel were drawn into the national struggle. Imperial nationalities ministries and the national people's councils fought over every office; the individual interest of each official in his own advancement was now coupled to a particular national interest in a power struggle between nations; and the officials began to subordinate themselves to the national people's councils. The Czech officials de facto re-introduced the Czech language for official domestic affairs, which had been abolished by the Clary regulations. The German judges overrode Czech linguistic rights introduced by the Stremayr regulations. Nationalism finally spread to the working class. As long as the Czech bourgeoisie supported the feudal Badeni and Thun governments, the Czech working class stood in fierce opposition to them; as soon as the Czech bourgeoisie, after 1899, fiercely opposed the German-bureaucratic governments, the Czech working class fell increasingly under the influence of Czech nationalism; Czech separatism exploded the Austrian International.[1] Thus, the fifteen-year battle of the Czech bourgeoisie against the German-bureaucratic governments from Clary to Stürgkh gradually developed the force that overcame all class and party antagonisms and united the entire nation against the Austrian government system.

Once again, this development was interrupted. Because of national obstruction, the Parliament based on the curia system had lost all capacity to be effective. The victories of the 1905 Russian Revolution lent new impetus to the Austrian proletariat's suffrage struggle. In 1905, the Emperor's conflict with Hungary's parliament of nobles had led to the installation of the Fejérváry-Kristóffy government, which frightened the rebellious Magyar gentry by threatening to introduce general suffrage; in order to intimidate the Hungarian parliament the Emperor granted general and equal suffrage in Austria. The democratic electoral reform unleashed powerful forces that were opposed to nationalism.* After the 1907 elections, Beck united the representatives of the German, Czech, and Polish bourgeoisie in a coalition government. A tremendous step forward seemed to have been accomplished. The bureaucratic authoritarian governments were replaced by a government based on a parliamentary majority. In place of feudal lords and bureaucrats, now the Prades and Pacáks, the Petscheks and Prášeks, the representatives of the German and Czech bourgeoisie and farmers, sat on the government front benches. In place of national obstruction, there was now the common government of the bourgeoisie and the peasantry of the three leading nations. Since the 1880s, the evolution of

---

* In Bohemia, Galicia, and German-Austria.

democracy had awakened and strengthened national forces, whose confluence had undermined the old authoritarian state; democracy's conquest of power now seemed to point to the uniting of these national forces to build a democratic state of the peoples together.

But the powers dethroned by the electoral reform immediately rallied against bourgeois democracy's seizure of power. The press of the big capitalists stirred up the national struggle. The feudal nobility intrigued. Militarism delivered the decisive blow. The militarist faction hated the Beck government, whose representation of militarism's claims against Hungary and against the Austrian Parliament it viewed as too weak. It prepared for the annexation of Bosnia and needed a "government with a strong hand" for this. On Franz Ferdinand's order Gessmann overthrew the Beck government. With Bienerth as Prime Minister the German-bureaucratic government system returned, but so did Czech obstruction. Imperialism had foiled the first and only attempt by democracy to solve, by its own means, the Austrian problem that its own development had created. Henceforth imperialism intended to solve this problem with its own means, by means of a belligerent foreign policy, and precisely because of this it transformed an internal Austrian problem into a broader European one.

A few weeks after the ousting of the Beck government, the annexation of Bosnia was proclaimed. The annexation crisis pitted the Habsburg Monarchy, under Germany's protection, against the Entente powers for the first time. The new world situation now began to determine the relationship of nationalities to the state.

The position of the German national bourgeoisie with respect to the state now quickly changed. The German-National parties had arisen in the 1880s in the struggle against liberalism's state policy, which identified German ethnic interest with Austria's state interest; from 1897 to 1899 in their struggles against Badeni and Thun, they had threateningly counterposed the Greater German* ideal to the Habsburg state. But now, under pressure of the new world situation, they returned to the Habsburg camp. In the west and the east, Germany was confronting powerful enemies. The danger of a war between Germany and the Entente powers was palpable. In the imminent war the Habsburg Monarchy had to fight on Germany's side. It now became clear to the German-National organizations what the historic destiny of the Habsburg Monarchy was: its task was to place the bayonets of forty million Slavs, Magyars, and Romanians under Ger-

* See Glossary, "Pan-German."

man command. Now the German national interest demanded that the Habsburg state be as strong and fully armed as possible. The German-Nationals* became—with fewer reservations—more black-yellow† than the liberals ever were. Their patriotic zeal vied with that of the Clerical Party. They stood by the side of the Habsburgs during the annexation crisis and the Balkan War. They enthusiastically approved the Conscription Law, arms credits, and the War Effort Law.

However, it was precisely in this that the position of the Czechs toward the Austrian state changed in the opposite direction. In Austria the Habsburgs had reestablished the German-bureaucratic regime to respond to the obstruction of the Czechs, the Slovenes, and the Ruthenians‡ with the absolutism of Paragraph 14. In Hungary the Habsburgs had made their peace with the Magyar noble class and had delivered the Slav nationalities to them once again. The Habsburgs threatened Serbia, and they armed for war against Russia. The more hostile the Habsburgs became toward the Slav powers, the more they were dependent on Germany's protection, and the more they appeared as vassals of the Hohenzollerns. To the Czechs too it appeared as the historic destiny of the Habsburg Monarchy to hold down the Slavs in Austria and Hungary in order to throw the weight of their ethnic power in the approaching great war, under German leadership and command, against the Slavs of Russia and the Balkans. In so doing, the relation of the Czechs to the Habsburg Monarchy had to change. Now their hostility to the German-bureaucratic regime turned into hostility to the state itself. It began with the annexation of Bosnia, was accelerated by the Habsburgs' anti-Slav policy during the Balkan War and culminated in the ultimatum issued to Serbia that unleashed the World War.

The Habsburg Conquest of 1620 not only destroyed the Bohemian state but also Czech culture. The rebellious Czech nobility was stamped out and the Czech bourgeoisie expelled from the country because of their Protestant faith. Whatever survived the assault of the bloody Habsburg Counter-Reformation succumbed to the turmoil of the Thirty Years' War. From 1620 to the first decades of the nineteenth century, the Czechs were serfs who confronted German landlords, a people without a bourgeoisie, without urban culture, without literature, without participation in the life

---

* See Glossary.

† The flag of the imperial k.u.k. entity (see Glossary) as a whole. The colors were synonymous with loyalty to the Emperor.

‡ See Glossary.

of the state, a nation without a history like the Slovenes. It was only with nineteenth-century capitalist development that a new bourgeoisie was born from the womb of the Czech peasantry, the Czech peasant freed from serfdom, and a self-conscious Czech proletariat appeared. In fierce struggles against the domination of the German bureaucracy, against the economic supremacy of the German bourgeoisie, against the superior power of attraction of German culture, the Czechs awoke to new national life in the course of a century. But in its beginnings, still in 1848, this movement seemed almost hopeless. At the time, the Sudeten lands were still a part of the German Confederation; within the confederation there were three to four million Czechs and forty million Germans. In the Czech territories themselves at the time a couple hundred intellectuals, supported by a weak petty bourgeois stratum, were the bearers of the national movement; the farmers still had no share in it; the bourgeoisie and bureaucracy, capital and industry, local councils, and schools were then German, everywhere, even in Bohemia. If it relied on its own strength alone, the young Czech movement appeared hopeless, and so it had to find strength in the thought that behind the small Czech people was the one hundred-million-large Slav race. Already by this point in the awakening of the Czech people the hope of the community of Slav peoples took root in its soul; since Kollár's "Slávy dcera," the first great poem of the re-emerging nation, Czech art had awakened and strengthened the Romantic enthusiasm of the following generations for the unity of the Slav race. Czech soldiers were bred in this tradition; they now had to be recruited to march against Serbs and Russians, against their "Slav brothers."

The Habsburg Monarchy had arisen when Ferdinand I united the Kingdoms of Bohemia and Hungary with the German Hereditary Lands. In 1620, 1749, and 1849, absolutism had annihilated Bohemia's state independence. When absolutism collapsed on the battlefields of Magenta and Solferino, the Czechs demanded, as did the Magyars, the reestablishment of their state independence. In 1865, as the Habsburgs prepared for war against Prussia, the Czechs believed they were close to achieving their goal; Belcredi suspended the centralist structure.* Prussia's victory had decided matters against the Czechs. The Compromise of 1867 was to subordinate them to the German-Austrian bourgeoisie, as it subordinated the Slavs in Hungary to the rule of the Magyar gentry. In 1869, as Beust prepared the war of revenge (on France's side) against Prussia, the Emperor turned once

---

* Reestablishing it, actually, on the basis of Dualism.

more to the Czechs; in 1871 the Hohenwart government wanted to reestablish the Bohemian state.[2] But after the Compromise of 1867, the power of
the Magyar nobility and, after the German victories in France, the Emper-
or's fear of German irredentism in Bohemia were too great for this plan to
succeed. Hohenwart fell, and the German-centralist structure triumphed.
In the long period of peace that followed, the Czechs had no more hopes
of reestablishing their state; in 1878 they gave up passive resistance to the
centralist structure and entered parliament, contenting themselves with a
"breadcrumbs policy," with gains within the centralist structure. However,
within the nation the hope was still strong that new European upheavals
would one day make it possible again to take up the struggle for the reestablishment of their state. After each of its major defeats, after 1867, after
1871, after 1899, and after 1908, the nation dreamed that "the unavoidable
world struggle of Germanism with Slavism will come," which would give
its state back to the nation. This is what Palacký had still said in 1871. After
the annexation crisis of 1908, after the German Reich Chancellor in 1913
had himself spoken of the threat of a struggle between Germanism and
Slavism, this thought came to life again. When in 1914 the Russian Army
rolled toward the German border, the hour of which the nation had so long
dreamed appeared to have arrived. And yet Czech soldiers were forced to
fight and die for the cause of Germanism against Slavism!

The mass sentiment that had run through the entire history of the nation
now had to rebel against the war. That the Habsburg Monarchy forced them
to fight and die for a cause that was not their own but rather that of their
enemy must have been felt by Czech soldiers as the most wretched servitude.
The soul of the nation had to rise up against the Habsburgs. "We must strive
for liberation from the Habsburg yoke," wrote Bohdan Pavlů, "in order to
escape from the horrible agony of having to fight on the side of our enemy."

However, it was not only feeling but also political calculation itself
that had to counterpose Czechs to Austria. The Czechs had not forgotten
that Königgrätz and Sedan had decided their defeat in the struggle for a
Bohemian constitutional state. If the Central Powers were victorious in
the World War, then Germany would become hegemonic in Europe; the
hegemony of the German Empire in Europe would necessarily strongly
reinforce the power of the Germans within the Habsburg Monarchy. If,
on the other hand, the Entente were victorious, then the reestablishment
of the Czech state would be a certainty. To be sure, very few Czechs at the
beginning of the war could consider the complete disintegration of the

Habsburg Empire possible or desirable. But if the Entente won, then it would obviously be in its interest to smash the rule of the German bourgeoisie and the Magyar nobility in the Monarchy and compel the Monarchy's reconstruction in a way that would ensure the leadership of the Slav majority population in order to permanently separate Austria from Germany. The Czech people could therefore only expect freedom and power from the defeat of the Central Powers.

Czech soldiers stood at the front. The machinery of militarism kept them under discipline. And on the battlefield they forgot all politics—those who shoot at us are our enemy. However, the Czech regiments could not be expected to deploy their full energy and passion, to really sacrifice themselves; this could only come from an enthusiastic struggle for one's own cause. If the enemy broke through their lines, if there was man-to-man combat, then they put up their hands; they were not willing to die for a cause that was foreign and hostile to them.

But the homeland was silent. It could not revolt openly. Counteracting all enthusiasm, all willingness to sacrifice for the war, however, were not only their feelings but also political calculation. "Do not do anything that could look like approval for the war," was Kramář's watchword; this was the only attitude that could ensure the nation of the Entente's protection when peace would be concluded.

In the meanwhile, the Russian armies had beaten Austria. The Russians were at the Dunajec River, in the Carpathians just at the gates of the Czech and Slovak areas of settlement. A manifesto from Russian Supreme Commander Nikolai Nikolaievich promised state independence to the Czechs. The Czech National Council in Russia offered the Bohemian crown to a Russian grand duke.[3] The nation listened attentively. The dream of a nation-state seemed now to enter the realm of possibility for the first time.

The political leaders remained silent. Wartime absolutism had sealed their mouths. But ordinary people were not able to contain their bursting hearts. Czech soldiers sang:

> *Fly, red neckerchief! Turn around!*
> *We are marching against the Russians and don't know why.*

And in the hinterland the Russian grand duke's manifesto was passed from hand to hand. And then the executioners began their work; in the first months of the war, in Moravia alone, there were 500 high-treason trials; death sentences were pronounced and executed.

The breakthrough at Gorlice put an end to Czech hopes. The Russian armies flooded back home. The Habsburg Monarchy triumphed, and the self-confidence of Austrian militarism was greatly strengthened. In its worst hours it had seen Czech regiments wavering, with an unreliable Czech hinterland. The leaders of the Czech bourgeoisie were arrested and condemned to death by military courts, not for their actions but for their views. Day after day the military courts pronounced their bloody sentences against Czech soldiers, workers, teachers, and women who had incautiously used some critical word, had saved a flyer, or had met with a Russian prisoner in too friendly a way. The Sokols* were disbanded. The police forced the newspapers to print patriotic articles. A war of confiscation began against Czech books of the prewar period and monuments of Czech history.

The German bourgeoisie† saw the national enemy put down by the iron fist of military force. Now believing its hour had come, it formulated its "interests." It demanded a coup d'état to impose German as the official language, the "special status" of Galicia, and a majority for the Germans in the Chamber of Deputies.

This was very serious. At Lutsk what remained of Austria-Hungary's independence collapsed. The whole Eastern Front was put under German command. "Mitteleuropa," the incorporation of Austria-Hungary in a confederation of states led by Germany, was being prepared. If Austria were to be absorbed into German "Mitteleuropa" then German hegemony had to be secured within Austria.

It was clear what a victory of the Central Powers would mean: the hegemony of German imperialism, which would forcibly suppress the Slav nations of the Monarchy through the German-Austrians and the Hungarians. And for this goal Czech soldiers were to bleed and die.

The era of persecution and plans for a coup d'état had two effects. It drove the leaders of the political parties into the arms of "opportunism." They made a show of Austrian patriotism in order to soften the pressure of military power and stave off the worst. The masses, however, did not understand this diplomacy of the nation's leaders. Defiance and hatred of the Empire and the Dynasty were growing among them. And this popular mood increasingly took hold of the soldiers at the front. Ever more frequently whole battalions went over to the enemy.

---

* Gymnastics organizations founded in the Czech lands of the Austrian Empire in 1862. The movement spread to other Slav nations.

† In both German-Austria and German-Bohemia.

Then in a single stroke all plans to tighten repression were frustrated by Russia's March Revolution. It was now clear that the war had to beget the revolution that would free the subject peoples. The United States entered the war. In the west Wilson and in the east revolution now both declared the right of self-determination of peoples to be the goal of the war. On the side of the Central Powers, blood justice, absolutism, and the "interests" of "Mitteleuropa"; on the other side, the promise of independent statehood for each nation. With all of their hearts and all their hopes the whole Czech people now expected their liberation to come from the defeat of the Central Powers.

The Russian Revolution had exploded Austrian wartime absolutism. In May 1917 Parliament was convened. Open discussion now became possible. The Czech deputies of all parties greeted the Parliament with a declaration on May 30, which demanded the establishment of a Czech state—to be sure, still in the framework of the Habsburg Monarchy. The opportunism of the national leaders allowed the Habsburgs to still hope for reconciliation with the Czech people. And they now clung to this hope. Since the Russian Revolution the Habsburgs feared for their throne. Emperor Karl sought peace with the Western powers. He negotiated with France through his brother-in-law Prince Sixtus of Bourbon-Parma. But as "Mitteleuropa" postulated German hegemony in Austria, in like manner an understanding with the Entente presupposed reconciliation with the Slav nations of the Monarchy. The Emperor wanted to open a path to reconciliation. In June he granted amnesty to the Czech "high traitors." But now the German-Nationals raged: "Did not German troops suffer severe losses as a result of the breakdown of Czech battalions? What are things coming to when treason goes unpunished?"

But if the Germans were bitter, the Czechs were also not satisfied. That the House of Parma* was creating a network of contacts between Vienna and Paris; that the Habsburgs were considering breaking away from Germany and turning toward the Entente; that such a turn would also upset the power relations within the Monarchy—the Czech masses had no sense of this. They were dominated by a hatred that grew from the bloody persecutions of the first two years of war. The great message of the Russian Revolution revolutionized them, and their hopes were fanned by the Western propaganda of the "right of small nations." The collapse of wartime absolutism was for them only a sign of their reviled enemy's weakness. The new era made it possible for them finally to openly profess what they had

---

* Empress Zita and her two brothers Sixtus and Franz Xaver of Bourbon-Parma.

to hide in their hearts under the pressure of absolutism. The masses rose up against the opportunistic leaderships of the Czech parties, and in fall 1917 the leadership of the Young Czechs, of the Czech National Social Party, and of the Social Democrats were overthrown and replaced with national-revolutionary leaderships.

The new tendency growing out of the mass mood of the revolutionized people was expressed in the Declaration of the General Regional Diet of all Czech deputies of January 6, 1918. In it the call was already heard for a completely independent Czech state; and the passage envisioning a Czech state living under the Habsburg Dynasty, which had been part of the May 30, 1917 Declaration, was struck out. With this, official Czech policy at home was situated on the terrain of the national revolution. The activism of the Czechs in the country was placed under the leadership of the revolutionary Czech émigrés. Since the beginning of the war there had been a strong movement among the Czech colonies abroad. Already in the first days of the war, the Czech colonies in Russia, France, England, Switzerland, and the United States had protested against it, demanded a "national state with a Slav king," and called for the formation of volunteer units to fight in the Entente armies against the Habsburgs. But this movement only took on greater significance when the homeland sent them the leader and the combatants—the leader in the person of Masaryk and the combatants represented by the masses of Czech prisoners of war who in the prison camps of Russia and Siberia, and of Serbia and Italy, had embraced the revolutionary propaganda of the Czech foreign colonies.

In December 1914 Professor Masaryk went abroad. For a lifetime he had fought against traditional Czech romanticism, against the prejudices of the nation—against the superstitious belief in the authenticity of the Dvůr Králové (Königinhof) Manuscript,* against the romantic historicism of the rights of the Bohemian Crown,† against anti-Semitic pogrom agitation, and against the naïve belief in a pan-Slavic spiritual community. And he continued to oppose traditional romanticism during his time abroad. To the ideal of reestablishing the crown of Saint Wenceslaus he counterposed the ideal of a democratic Czechoslovak republic, and against hope in Russian tsarism he set his hopes on Western democracy. Only in this way did he win over the workers, who made up the overwhelming majority of Czech émigrés, to the national movement. Only in this way

---

* A purportedly medieval manuscript forged in the nineteenth century containing epic poems boosting the notion of an early pan-Slavic consciousness.
† See Glossary.

could he sustain the movement after the Russian defeats in 1915 and draw new strength for it from the 1917 Russian Revolution. At the same time, his personality secured for the movement the sympathies of the western intelligentsia as well as connections to the governments of the Entente powers. After Masaryk went abroad in fall 1914, he first applied himself to organizing the Czech foreign colonies. He was able to consolidate them, create for them a unified executive organ in the form of the National Council constituted in May 1916 in Paris, whose leading figures were Masaryk, Beneš, and Štefanik. Within these colonies he pushed back the influences of the tsarophile tendency supported by the Russian government and raised the funds among the colonies themselves needed to carry out very effective propaganda for an independent Czechoslovak state. At the same time care was taken to keep the revolutionary Czech émigrés in close contact with the homeland. Already in fall 1914 in Prague, a secret association of revolutionary politicians was founded, which later formed the so-called Maffie* and maintained contact with the revolutionary émigrés. Through illegal channels they received information and instructions from Masaryk and sent him reports from the homeland. However, the émigré movement up to 1917 only had the character of a large propaganda operation. The Czech émigrés really came to power when they succeeded in creating an army in their service in one place in the world, which temporarily took on unique importance because of the war.

Already in fall 1914, the tsarist government had formed a Czech *druzhina*† out of Czechs located in Russia, which fought together with the Russian army. But the *druzhina* hardly counted more than a thousand men. Only after the Russian March Revolution had filled the Czech prisoners of war in Russian and Siberian camps with revolutionary fighting spirit, only when the tsarophile leadership of the Czech émigrés in Russia—whose reactionary ideology repelled the democratically oriented prisoners of war—was overturned along with the tsarist regime, only then did the military movement of Czechs in Russia expand. Now it was possible to form a Czech army of 42,000 men in the Ukraine within a few months. Its First Division fought in June 1917 near Zboriv against the Austrians. But when in fall 1917 the Imperial Russian Army began to dissolve, the Czech corps retained its structure, its discipline in the midst of this general disintegration. The Russian Army was dissolved by the social revolution; the idea of the national rev-

---

* See Glossary.
† Retinue.

olution gave the Czech corps a very strong underpinning. In winter 1917–18, in the weeks of Brest-Litovsk, the Czech corps was the only orderly, disciplined military force in the entire territory of Russia. When, after the separate peace with the Ukrainian Rada, the German and Austro-Hungarian troops broke through to the Ukraine, the Czech corps retreated, fighting, to the east. Shoulder to shoulder with the Bolshevik Red Guards it fought its rearguard action against the Germans near Bakhmach and Kiev. But when the Soviet government too concluded peace with the Central Powers, when it committed itself to tolerate no foreign armed formations on Russian soil, the representatives of the Paris National Council agreed with the Soviet government that the Czech soldiers would hand over their weapons to the Soviets and would be brought as "free citizens" in special trains through Siberia to Vladivostok; there they wanted to embark for France in order to continue to fight against the Central Powers on French soil.

But the plan could not be carried out. The poor condition of the Russian railways made the transportation of the Czech Legions impossible. For weeks, indeed for months, the Czech transports were stalled at different railway stations. In May the first three regiments reached Vladivostok. Four regiments still remained, divided among different transports, in western Siberia and Transbaikal in the vast area between Chelyabinsk and Chita. Three regiments, however, were still awaiting transport in European Russia, in the area of Penza.

During the months of waiting, however, increasing tensions developed between the Czech battalions, compelled to idly wait at railway stations for transports, and the local soviets governing in the nearby towns. The Russians looked on the Czech legionnaires with great mistrust. The fact that they had kept military order and discipline and remained under the command of their officers made them look like counterrevolutionaries. That they were continuing the war (even after the Russian people rose up for peace at any price) and wanted to carry on as an ally of French imperialism (which was hostile to the Soviet Republic) made them enemies of the proletarian revolution. On the other hand, the Czech legionnaires viewed the Russian Communists as traitors, because by concluding a peace agreement with the Central Powers they had wrested Slavic Russia from the Entente and in so doing had shaken hope for a defeat of the Central Powers, which was the only hope for the liberation of this small Slav nation and of a safe return for themselves. To this political antagonism were added national antagonisms. In Siberia, out of German, German-Austrian, and Magyar prisoners of war, the Bolsheviks had formed the "internationalist" battalions, which at the time constituted the Bolsheviks' strongest, and often their only, armed force in large parts of Siberia. In the antagonism between the "internationalists" and the Czech legionnaires, the national antagonisms of the homeland were revived in new guises. The Bolsheviks sought, with occasional success, to bring their agitation to the Czech battalions; the defensive struggle of the Czech officers against this agitation, which threatened to break down the national army, sharpened the antagonisms. The mutual mistrust of both parties grew. The Bolsheviks feared that the Czechs might ally with the Russian counterrevolution; in fact, at the Don some Czech divisions had already turned up associated with the White troops of General Alekseyev. The Czechs feared again that the Soviet government would deliver them to the Central Powers, to Austrian hangmen. The starker the antagonisms became, the more stubbornly did the Czechs refuse to hand over their weapons to the Soviets, as had been agreed. The antagonisms led to a crisis.

In April Japan had landed troops in Vladivostok. In Transbaikal the counterrevolutionary bands of Semyonov had taken possession of large areas, and the counterrevolutionary intervention of the Entente in the Far East had begun. Now the Soviet government decided to no longer permit the transport of the Czech legions to Vladivostok; it did not want to supply the counterrevolution with a powerful army. The Soviet government agreed with the representative of the Paris National Council in Moscow that the Czech regiments that were still in European Russia and in western Siberia should be brought to France not through Vladivostok but through Archangelsk. The regiments, which had covered part of the way to the east in months of unspeakable difficulties, were suddenly expected to turn back and take the route to the west. The legions rose up against this order. They felt strong. Russia had no army. It did not appear difficult to overrun the weak Red Guards, mostly composed in Siberia of German and Magyar prisoners of war. The idea grew in the Czech Legions to forcibly take possession of the Siberian Railway to force their transport to Vladivostok.

Already on May 14 the tensions led to a violent clash. At the railway station of Chelyabinsk the Czechs had slain a Magyar prisoner of war. When the Chelyabinsk soviet consequently had the Czech sentinel arrested, the Czechs pushed into the town; they threatened the soviet and disarmed a part of the Red Guards. Two days later in Chelyabinsk the delegates of the Legions held a congress. They resolved to refuse the journey to Archangelsk and to make their way, on their "own orders," to Vladivostok. Now the Soviet government decided on uncompromising intervention. On May 23 the military commissariat ordered that "all Czech transports be disarmed and disbanded and that parts of the Red Army or work detachments be formed from them." On May 25, Trotsky gave the order: "Every Czechoslovak who boards a train with weapon in hand is to be shot on sight. Every company in which even one armed Czechoslovak soldier is found is to be interned in a detention camp. All railway workers are to be informed that no railway car with Czechoslovaks is to move eastward."

On the same day that Trotsky issued this order, the Czechs cut loose in western Siberia. They took the railway stations, invaded the towns, overpowered and disarmed the weak red garrisons, and arrested the members of the soviets. Within a few days the whole Siberian Railway from Chelyabinsk to Baikal was in Czech hands.

At this point the regiments that remained in European Russia rose up as well. On May 29 they took Penza. From there they forced through their transport to the east. In Lipyag they beat red fighting forces that tried to block their path; Samara fell to them. Here, on the Volga, a new front formed. In the first period, Austrians were on both sides of the front that were waging the new war—on the one side Germans and Magyars under a red flag, on the other the Czechs. On June 6 connection between Samara and Chelyabinsk was established; from the Volga to Baikal the railway was now in the hands of the Legions.

In this entire expanse the Czechs had overthrown the soviets. Under the protection of Czech bayonets, the "democratic" governments of Samara and Omsk were formed, which took power in the name of the Russian Constituent Assembly disbanded by the Soviet government. It was the Right Socialist Revolutionaries and the Kadets who were inheriting the soviets. To these parties the Czechs associated a belief in democracy and hostility to the Treaty of Brest-Litovsk. With their armed protection, they aimed at reestablishing the great Slavic Russia, annulling the Treaty of Brest-Litovsk, and rebuilding the Eastern Front against the Central Powers. There was no longer any talk of Vladivostok. The aim now was to concentrate the Czech regiments in the new front on the Volga, maintaining it until Russian democracy established a new national army at their rear.

The May uprising of the Czech Legions was an event of historic importance. Its effect was counterrevolutionary against proletarian Russia, at the same time as it was revolutionary against feudal Austria-Hungary. The twofold character of every bourgeois revolution—which is revolutionary against the feudal regime but at the same time becomes counterrevolutionary against the proletariat—was particularly clear in the national revolution of the Czechs.

The Russian Revolution was seriously endangered by the uprising of the Czechs. The Volga area, the Urals, and all of Siberia were severed from the Soviet Republic. Russia lost its access to the Siberian breadbasket, the mines of the Urals, and the transport routes to the Caucasus and Turkestan. The Soviet Republic was thrown into the most severe food and raw material crisis. At the same time, the Soviet government had to establish a new army and wage a new war to fend off at the Volga the onslaught of the counterrevolution rallying under the protection of the Czech Legions. At first, it was petty bourgeois democracy to which the Czechs had given control of the areas wrested from the Soviet Republic. But democracy, only instituted by foreign troops, ended—to the extent that it tried to establish a new Russian army behind the Czech front—under the control of the counterrevolutionary Russian officer corps; and as soon as this corps, based on the newly formed army, was sufficiently strong it deposed the democratic governments and elevated the tsarist Admiral Kolchak to the position of dictator of the areas "liberated" by the Czechs. The destructive Civil War between the white and red dictatorship was the final result of the Czech uprising.

But as much as the effect of the Czech uprising on Russia was counterrevolutionary, its effect on Austria-Hungary was revolutionary. Because now, in a single stroke, the position of the Czech people in the world had completely changed. The Paris Czech National Council was no longer a mere propaganda society; it suddenly became a participating armed power with an army in a location that had become extremely important for the war.

The Treaty of Brest-Litovsk had committed the Soviet Republic to hand over to the Central Powers the millions of German, Austro-Hungarian, and Turkish prisoners of war who had been held in Siberia. This meant many new armies against the Entente! The Treaty of Brest-Litovsk enabled the Central Powers to have access (through Russia) to food and raw materials from Asia. This meant the breaking of the blockade. Cutting the Soviet Republic off from Siberia was a vital question for the Entente. The Czech Legions provided this service. Their uprising cordoned off Siberia from Russia; they thwarted the transport of prisoners of war and the supply of food and raw materials from Siberia to Germany; they secured access for the Entente to the Trans-Siberian Railway. Guinet accurately claimed that the Czech Legion and the Czech uprising meant nothing less than the "re-establishment of the Eastern Front against Germany." This front was maintained by no more than 50,000 men; but in the Russia of those years, in which there no longer was a tsarist army but the Red Army still did not exist, 50,000 men was a powerful force, and its Volga front completely cut off the Urals, Siberia, and Turkestan from European Russia; their bayonets controlled the entire Trans-Siberian Railway. And these 50,000 men executed the resolutions of the Paris National Council, which now became an ally of the Entente powers and could negotiate with them as an equal power.

The self-confidence of the Czech nation was powerfully reinforced by these events. For the first time in three hundred years there was an independent Czech army. For the first time since the defeat at White Mountain, the nation could intervene independently in world history. The idea of an independent Czech army now gathered increasing force. Volunteer Czech formations were already fighting on the French and Italian fronts; powerfully influenced by the events on the Volga, the Legion fighting on the Italian front grew in summer 1918 to 17,000 men with a strong influx from the prisoners-of-war camps. With increasing frequency Czech patrols in Italian uniforms broke through to Czech soldiers in Austrian trenches, calling on them to join them in fighting for the liberation of the Czech people. And when the Czech legionnaires were taken prisoners as defectors and marched to the gallows with heads held high, they were seen by Czech soldiers in imperial uniform as martyrs of the national idea. In the Czech territories themselves the national movement now took on an unequivocally revolutionary character. On July 13, the Národní Výbor* (National Committee) was formed in Prague. It began life with a declaration that left no doubt that it saw itself as the nucleus of the future revolutionary regime. In fact, it immediately began working out plans for the assumption of state power in the Czech territories. But the May uprising of the Czech army at the Volga and in Siberia had not only completed the revolutionizing of the consciousness of the Czech masses; it also completely overturned the relation of the Entente to the Czech Revolution.

As late as 1917 the destruction of Austria-Hungary was still not a war objective of the Entente. In the peace negotiations mediated by Prince Sixtus of Parma between the Viennese Court and the French government in spring 1917, in the peace offer conveyed in August 1917 by the General Staff

* See Glossary.

Colonel Count Armand to the Austrian diplomat invested with full powers by Czernin, Count Revertera, as well as in Wilson's Fourteen Points
of January 1918, there was no mention of the establishment of a sovereign Czech state. Only after all attempts to reach a peace had failed and
Czernin's speech of April 2, 1918 had made any further progress impossible
did the tendency prevail to smash Austria-Hungary and thus deprive Germany of its ally, which by now seemed impossible to detach from it. When
a few weeks later the May uprising of the Czech army in Russia suddenly
elevated the Czech National Council in Prague to the status of a belligerent power in its own right and strongly reinforced its authority in relation
to the Entente, Masaryk and Beneš could use this changed mood in order
to win the Entente's formal recognition for the Czech Revolution.

Already on June 4, under direct pressure of the May uprising, the
Entente governments communicated to the Soviet government that they
viewed the Czechoslovak troops as an allied belligerent power and would
view their disarming as a hostile act. On June 29, the French government
recognized the right of the Czech people to independence and the Paris
National Council as the supreme governing body of the Czech people; on
August 9, England and Japan recognized the Czech army as an allied fighting force. On August 2, the United States issued a similar declaration; in
it the Paris National Council was recognized as the de facto government.
Finally, on October 3, after the Czech Legion had distinguished itself on
the Italian front in its counterattack at Dosso Alto, Orlando stated that Italy too recognized the Paris National Council as the de facto government.
Thus, the independent action of the Czech army bore rich fruit: once the
Czechs at the Volga deployed their weapons in the service of the Entente,
which then recognized it as an allied military force, the establishment of
the Czechoslovak state and the destruction of the Austro-Hungarian Empire became a war objective of the Entente.

And this goal came within reach in August when the German Army
was severely beaten in France. As long as Germany was strong, Palacký's
dictum still held for the Czechs: "if Austria did not exist it would have to be
invented"; that is, the only goal could be a Czech state within the Habsburg
Empire. As soon as Germany was beaten, as soon as there no longer was the
danger that after the dissolution of the Habsburg Empire the Sudeten lands
could also fall to Germany, the Czech people no longer had an interest in
the existence of the Habsburg Empire. Now it had in mind something else
that Palacký had said: "We were here before Austria and we will be here af-

ter Austria." The Czech people no longer worried about the grotesque game, which had come into tragicomic contradiction with historical reality, of Austrian policy that—still in August when the German forces on the Western front had already collapsed, just before the catastrophe—proclaimed a "German course" in Austria in order to conciliate the German-Nationals, who were embittered against the Emperor ever since the disclosure of the 1917 Parma intrigues, by trying to impose German "concerns" through the division of the Bohemian Provincial Administration Commission into national sections. The Národní Výbor worked out plans for the takeover of state power in the Czech lands. The Czech people waited for the inevitable capitulation of the Habsburg Monarchy.

Three hundred years before, the Czech nobility had tried to save the national republic of the nobility from the aggression of Habsburg absolutism. It succumbed to the armies of the German Emperor. The nation paid for this defeat with two centuries of servitude and lack of history. But the development of capitalism and of democracy in the nineteenth century had roused the Czech masses. Their ascendancy occurred through increasingly severe conflict, and finally in open collision, with Habsburg imperialism. When the German Empire collapsed, the Czech masses could reestablish the national republic that the Czech nobility had squandered three centuries before.

CHAPTER 3

THE POLES AND
THE CENTRAL POWERS

When the war began, a large section of Galicia's Polish population cheered the Imperial armies marching against Russia, and thousands of Polish students, intellectuals, and workers volunteered in the Polish legions combating the Russians. If South Slavs and Czechs stood against the Habsburgs, here one of the Slav peoples of the Empire appeared to stand with the Habsburgs and draw hope from a Habsburg victory. But as the war drew to a close, all the desires and hopes of the Poles, just like the Yugoslavs and Czechs, were invested in the Entente; they too expected liberation from the fall of the Habsburgs. This great transformation among Galicia's Poles during the war is also an important chapter in the history of Austria's revolution.

In the stormy days of the Great French Revolution, the Polish aristocratic republic foundered. In the uprisings of 1794, 1830, 1846, and 1863, the Polish *szlachta** tried in vain to reconquer lost state independence. The terrible defeat of the 1863 January uprising broke the revolutionary energy of the Polish nobility. The fall of Napoleon III in 1870 robbed it of all hope that the Polish Question could be opened again. The task was no longer the reconquest of national statehood but the mere salvage of national existence; "organic work" instead of revolutionary romanticism was the slogan of the day. Already in 1846, the Austrian government had deployed Galicia's peasants against the rebelling nobility. In 1864 the Russian government had divided the noble es-

---

* Legally privileged noble class from the time of the Kingdom of Poland and Grand Duchy of Lithuania.

tates among the peasants in order to support them against the revolutionary szlachta. Similarly, Bismarck believed he could play the "loyal" Polish peasants against the rebellious szlachta. The nobility saw its class interests threatened when the governments protected the peasants against noblemen, and it therefore sought reconciliation with the governments of the three imperial powers. "Triple loyalty" was now the slogan that the Kraków *Stańczyks** gave the nobility of the three parts of Poland.

In Galicia, this policy was very fruitful. After the Austro-Hungarian Compromise of 1867, the Emperor and the German bourgeoisie made their peace with the Polish nobility. In the Austrian Parliament and its delegations, the szlachta became a trustworthy pillar of every Austrian government. But in exchange Galicia was totally at their mercy, and the Polish aristocratic republic reemerged. The administration and school system were Polish. And the Polish szlachta held unrestricted sway over Polish and Ruthenian peasants. Things were different in the Russian and Prussian parts of partitioned Poland. All the efforts of the szlachta there to win the favor of the rulers were of no avail. While the nobility in the Kingdom of Poland paid homage to the Tsar and the Koło Polskie† voted for military and naval bills, the Polish people were nevertheless denied a national school and all elements of national self-rule. Already in 1832 the Prussian government had introduced German as the language of administration in Poznań; in 1833 it suspended the district administrator (Landrat) elections there; in 1836 it had eliminated the *woyts*‡; it had named district commissioners to substitute these elected village heads; and the Poles responded to this demolition of all self-administration with their exit from the civil service. In 1873 Prussia introduced German as the language of instruction in schools; in 1886 the Prussian Settlement Commission began to buy up Polish land holdings and resettle German farmers on them. Thus, after the complete destruction of their self-government, Poles in Poznań and West Prussia stood under the domination of a foreign bureaucracy that sought to wrest the souls of their children from them through German schools and their land through resettlement policy. It was no different for the Poles in the Russian-ruled part after 1863 when all self-rule was destroyed; in 1869 all instruction was Russified, as was the judicial system in 1873. In Lithuania, Poles were prohibited from buying land, and in 1868 the public use of the Polish language was proscribed.

---

* See Glossary.

† The Polish Club in the German Reichstag.

‡ Rural district foremen, chief judges, and village headmen in Russian Poland.

But the harshness of this foreign domination did not impede economic and social development. In Poznań, whose peasants had much earlier become free landowners, where agriculture and schooling had reached a much higher level than in both other parts of the country, the struggle against the Prussian government's Germanizing school and resettlement policy awakened the Polish peasants. Since the 1880s, a dense network of peasant associations and cooperatives had developed under the leadership of the Catholic clergy. High-level politics was not the concern of the Poznań peasants, but in the persistent struggles on the level of everyday life they defended the nationality and land of the popular masses and frustrated all the plans of resettlement policy.

At the same time the leadership of the nation shifted from the nobility to the peasantry in Prussian Poland; in Russian Poland thanks to Russian protectionism since 1877, a significant industry developed through which the industrial bourgeoisie rose in fierce antagonism to the violent and corrupt Russian bureaucracy. But being dependent on the wider Russian market, closely tied to St. Petersburg's, Moscow's, and Riga's trade and industry, it was strongly influenced by Russian society.

If Galicia enjoyed more national and political freedom than the other two parts of Poland, it was, on the other hand, far below them on the economic and social level. It had neither the strong peasant organizations of the Prussian part nor the rising industrial bourgeoisie of the Russian part. Here, until 1914, power in the countryside and the leadership of the nation remained in the hands of the nobility. It is true that from the beginning of the 1890s a gradually growing opposition confronted the rule of the nobility. However, the vehicles of this opposition were neither the peasantry nor the industrial bourgeoisie but the petty bourgeois intelligentsia to which Galicia's Polish school system transmitted the revolutionary-patriotic traditions of the Polish émigrés from 1831 and 1863, the great traditions of Mickiewicz and Słowacki; neo-romantic literature was associated with this tradition, as were Wyspiański and Żeromski and the new historiographical school of Askenazy. And so this intelligentsia developed, dreaming of the revolutionary-patriotic struggle and the reestablishment of an independent Poland. In this struggle against the rule of the nobility, the intelligentsia could only base itself on the labor movement, which was young and underdeveloped; lacking a broad industrial base labor had to accept the leadership of the revolutionary-patriotic intelligentsia, filling itself with the latter's ideals.

Thus, by the time the Russo-Japanese War triggered the first Russian Revolution in 1905, the development of the three parts of Poland had already followed completely different paths. The Kingdom of Poland was pulled along by the powerful surge of the Russian Revolution. The workers rose, massive general strikes convulsed the country, and street fighting intimidated the owning classes. The frightened Polish bourgeoisie ran for cover under the protection of the Tsar's bayonets. The revolution was put down. But the fears it instilled continued. The Polish bourgeoisie now knew that every uprising against tsarism would bring the proletariat onto the scene and would have to threaten its own class rule. It now broke completely with the whole traditional ideology of national uprising, of national independence. Dmowski led National Democracy, the leading party of the Polish bourgeoisie, to reconciliation with Russia. The Russian Revolution had brought a constitution to Russia. On the floor of the Duma, representatives of the Polish bourgeoisie met the Russian liberals who in their struggle against the bureaucracy did not seem disinclined to concede autonomy to Poland within the Russian Empire. From then on National Democracy placed its hope on the rise of Russian liberalism with the goal of Polish autonomy within the Russian Empire.

Prussia's Poland policy fostered this rapprochement of the Polish bourgeoisie with Russia. In 1904 Prussia had promulgated an exceptional law against Polish land acquisition. In 1907 this was followed by an expropriation law that threatened Polish land tenure with forced expropriation. At the same time, the German law on associations forbade the use of the Polish language in assemblies. While Russian Poland had, with the 1905 Revolution, at least acquired freedom for private Polish elementary and middle schools, Prussia resorted to exceptional laws that proclaimed the forced displacement of Poles from their native soil. A wave of outrage swept through Polish territory. It was not Russia but Germany that now appeared as the nation's most dangerous enemy. The idea of a Slav community of interest against the Germans now gathered force in Poland as well; in 1908 Polish representatives appeared in the All-Slav Congress in Prague.

When the Polish bourgeoisie turned away from the idea of national independence, it thus met no resistance from the masses in Russian Poland. The peasantry there had taken no part in the tradition of the szlachta uprisings of 1831 and 1863; in every country village, crosses and stone monuments reminded the Polish peasant that it was only after the repression of the nobility's uprising in 1863 by the Russian Tsar that he received the lands of the Polish szlachta. The working class, which emerged out of this peasant milieu, was caught in the maelstrom of Russian class struggles. During the Revolution, a majority in the Polish Socialist Party (PPS) was won by the Left, which—just as the Social Democracy of the Kingdom of Poland and Lithuania, founded by Rosa Luxemburg, had earlier done— proclaimed the common revolutionary class struggle of the Russian and Polish proletariat and refused any separate national struggle of the Polish proletariat for national goals, aiming at achieving national autonomy for Poland through the revolution of the Russian proletariat. Thus, it was only with the 1905 Revolution that the Kingdom was spiritually annexed by Russia. Both the bourgeoisie and the proletariat allied with their class comrades in Russia, placing their hopes in the internal upheaval in Russia to achieve national autonomy within Russia.

There was, to be sure, a countertendency. Tsarism put down the revolution with great brutality. The Warsaw governor general Skałon signed a thousand death sentences. The prisons filled up. One transport after the other left for Siberia. The trade unions and the national school and Sokoł associations were dissolved. The times of Suvorov, Paskevich, and Mura-vyov returned. The old hatred of tsarism flared up. The idea of an armed uprising to liberate Poles from Russian domination came to life again. It was embodied in the patriotic "right" wing of the PPS, above all in its combat organization founded by Piłsudski. But the suppression of the revolution fragmented the partisan war of the combat organization against the tsarist lackeys into aimless banditry. Piłsudski and his people withdrew to Galicia, and here his watchword of national armed uprising against Russia resonated much more strongly among the revolutionary-patriotic intelligentsia and the working class led by it and united in Galicia's Polish Social Democratic Party (PPSD) than it did in Russian Poland.

The international situation was propitious for the idea of a national uprising against tsarism. Since the annexation of Bosnia, the conflict between Austria-Hungary and Russia had sharpened. Piłsudski hoped to take advantage of the impending war between Russia and the Central Powers to further Poland's liberation. The Austro-Hungarian general staff hoped that in the event of war they could use a Polish uprising against Russia for the Monarchy's war strategy. And so in 1910 Piłsudski could found his paramilitary Riflemen's Associations and drill them with weapons delivered by the k.u.k.* military authorities in plain sight of the Austrian authorities. In 1912, when the Balkan War further aggravated the Russian-Austrian

---

* See Glossary.

conflict, the unification of the independence parties took place; their immediate goal was an uprising against Russia and the organization of the Riflemen's Associations as cadres of the Polish legions, which were to be established in the event of war. The core of the unification was the right-wing PPS and the PPSD, along with a small party of intellectuals.

Opinions also began to differ in Galicia. On the one side, Prussia's Poland policy again stoked hatred of Germany and drove many into the ambit of the National Democrats, which had become Russophile since 1905. In 1912, the Prussian Settlement Commission began for the first time to make use of the Expropriation Law and expropriated four Polish manors. On the other side, Russia's Poland policy continually provided more wind in the sails of the independence parties. If Stolypin's coup of June 3, 1907 had weakened Polish representation in the Duma, if all efforts of the National Democrats to wrest advantages for Poland's cause on the floor of the Duma were unsuccessful, then Russia's separating of the Chełm Governorate from the administrative organizations of the Kingdom of Poland was felt by all Poles as a slap in the face. Thus caught between Prussian and Russian enmity, Galicia's intelligentsia argued whether in the impending war Poland would join the side of Russia or the Central Powers.

The parting of the ways took place in the conflict over how to deal with Galicia's Ruthenians. The Ruthenian peasants had been awakened. In the big agrarian strikes, they had risen up against the Polish estate owners. The Russian Revolution had a powerful effect on them. The first elections under universal suffrage showed how their self-confidence had grown. However, the young intelligentsia that led the peasants was divided into two parties, with the Ukrainians and Moscophiles contending for power. For the Ukrainian faction, the Little Russian peasantry was an independent nation; filled with hatred for Russia, which forbade the use of written Ukrainian and imposed the Russian written language on the Ukraine, and supported by the near-landless peasant masses, their orientation was democratic and revolutionary and filled with the spirit of the Russian Narodniki. By contrast, the Moscophiles saw the Little Russians as a tribe of the Great Russian nation; they loved the Slavic Russia of the Tsar and the Orthodox Church.

How unsustainable the domination of the Polish nobility in Eastern Galicia had become was shown by the energetic opposition of the Ukrainian delegates group in the Austrian Parliament since the introduction of universal suffrage (1907) and Siczynski's assassination of governor-general Potocki in 1908. Since the Habsburg Monarchy was preparing for war against Russia, it now tried to reconcile the Ukrainians with Austria, while attempting to violently suppress the Moscophiles. The appeasement of the Ukrainians would serve to democratize Galicia's aristocratic parliament, which governor-general Bobrzyński sought to accomplish. The Western Galician Stańczyks, always trying to secure the support of the Viennese Court for their class, did not want to come into conflict with a dictate of Austrian reason of state; by contrast, the Eastern Galician landowners, the "Podolians," directly threatened on their manors by the Ukrainian peasant movement, sided with the conservative Moscophiles. And the same fissure ran through all of Polish society in Galicia: the independence parties viewed the Ukrainians as their natural allies in the struggle against Russia; the National Democrats, threatened in Lemberg* by the rising Ukrainian tide, invoked "national patriotism" and "a policy of national power" in the struggle against the Ukrainians. Thus, the Stańczyks and the independence parties stood on one side, and the Podolians and National Democrats on the other—the distinction between the Austrian and the Russian orientation was already presaged.

The war broke out. On August 6, 1914, Piłsudski and two hundred Riflemen crossed the Russian border and occupied Kielce. This military gesture was greeted by the independence parties with great enthusiasm. They saw it as the beginning of the national liberation struggle for an independent Poland, and Piłsudski's riflemen as the successors to Dąbrowski's Legions, which had fought under the imperial eagles of Napoleon. A few days later in Kraków, the Naczelny Komitet Narodowy (NKN) was formed, conceived as the nucleus of the government of an independent Polish state. The Stańczyks and the independence parties determined its politics. An independent Polish state, composed of Russian Poland and Galicia, which would affiliate with the Habsburg dual monarchy as its third limb, was its immediate goal. But Russian Poland protested. In the Duma, Polish leaders took the side of the Entente. In Warsaw a national committee formed that denied the Kraków NKN's right to speak in the name of Poland and soon tried to recruit (with little success) a legion to fight on Russia's side against Piłsudski's Legions. Meanwhile, Russia's armies conquered the greater part of Galicia, and the Russian Supreme Commander, Grand Duke Nikolai Nikolaievich, issued a manifesto on August 14 promising unification to Poles of all three parts of the country in an autonomous Poland within the Russian Empire. Now in Galicia too the opposition dared to come out against the "Austrian orientation."

---

* Old-Austrian name of Lviv in present-day Ukraine.

The National Democrats and Podolians left the NKN and destroyed the Eastern Galician Legion. The conflict between the Austrian and Russian orientations within Galician Poland was now manifest.

The Austrian orientation was the struggle for a Polish state—to be sure a state without its nationally most seriously threatened Prussian portion. But at least it would be a state. If Polish statehood was to be reacquired in the first place, then it would be able to fight for the unification of all Poles in one nation-state.

The Russian orientation was the struggle for the unification of Poland—unification, to be sure, under tsarist rule. Unification above all, even if inside a prison! If twenty million Poles could first be united in a state, then they would be able to carve out an independent national existence.

The ideal of freedom, of state independence, thus entered into conflict with the idea of national unity. Polish society was torn between two camps.

In any case, the most active and energetic Galician Poles had declared themselves on the side of the Central Powers. They were peculiar allies. The Habsburgs and Hohenzollerns allied with the legions organized by revolutionary conspirators filled with the ideas of the democratic revolutions of the nineteenth century. Austria, which had gone to war to break the revolutionary principle of nationality in the South, championed the revolutionary principle of nationality in the North. And behind Austria Hakatist* Prussian Germany, which had to view the emergence of an independent Poland as a threat to its domination of Poznań and West Prussia.

In fact, the friction began immediately. It appeared when the k.u.k. Supreme Command demanded that the Legions swear loyalty to the Emperor. It continued in the running battles between the Army Supreme Command and Piłsudski. But it first took on significance when the 1915 Great Offensive subjugated Russian Poland to the Central Powers.

Now, above all, it was clear how different feelings were in Russian Poland from those in Galicia and how closely the Kingdom was to Russia ever since 1905. Warsaw gave Piłsudski's Legions a mute reception, without greeting them.

Only one act could shift the mood in the Russian section in favor of the Central Powers. But the Central Powers were incapable of it. The first to object to the Austro-Polish solution was Tisza; a third state within the

---

* Pejorative acronym for three founders of the German Eastern Marches Society—Hansemann, Kennemann, and Tidemann—which promoted the Germanization of Poles in Eastern Prussia.

Habsburg Monarchy with equal footing would have diminished Hungarian influence. As a result, the Viennese Court agreed that Russian Poland,
united with Galicia, would be an autonomous component of the Austrian
state. Thus, Austria was only offering autonomy, not statehood. Nikolai
Nikolaievich offered as much. But he also offered more—annexation of
the Prussian part on top of this.

It was not Austria but Germany that was to decide Poland's future.
And in Germany there was no unanimity. Prussia's power interests favored
a new division: annex a part of Russian Poland and either give back the
rest to Russia or make it into a small buffer state dependent on Germany.

While the Habsburgs and Hohenzollerns could not agree on Poland's
future, their outlook was identical on one point: they wanted Polish recruits
for their war. In the Kingdom, men were to be recruited for the Polish Legions. At this point a division appeared among the supporters of the Austrian
orientation. The Stańczyks promoted the recruitments. From fall 1915, the
PPS under Piłsudski's leadership opposed this, accepting recruitment for a
Polish army only if a government existed to command it. Everyone was now
united in the struggle against recruitments—the anti-Russian independence
parties with the Russophile National Democrats. Beseler's efforts to establish
a "Polish Wehrmacht" under German command were unsuccessful.

In summer 1916 Austria collapsed at Lutsk. The German Supreme
Army Command now controlled the entire Eastern Front. In summer 1916
Germany rejected the Austro-Polish solution. And in Germany Ludendorff
was in command. He needed Polish "human resources" and insisted on the
right to conscript recruits in Poland. Governor General Beseler believed
he could assemble fifteen divisions of Poles if the Central Powers promised Poland the reestablishment of its statehood. On November 5, 1916, the
Central Powers declared the Russian part an "independent state as a hereditary monarchy with a constitutional form of government," while Franz
Joseph promised Galicia an expansion of its autonomy within Austria.

The November 5 manifesto reserved the right to determine the borders
of the new Polish state; Prussia wanted to maintain the possibility of annexing a part of Russian Poland. The relationship of the new state to the
Central Powers was to be determined later; Berlin envisioned an economic
and military "affiliation" of Poland with the Empire. In Warsaw a Council
of State was established, but it was only an advisory body, with government
power remaining entirely in the hands of the German governor general.

Piłsudski stepped down from the command of his Legions and entered the Council of State in Warsaw. When his Legions entered Warsaw in 1915 alongside the Germans they had been received in silence. When in 1916, already in conflict with the Central Powers, he came alone to Warsaw he was greeted as a victor. He worked out plans in the Council of State for the establishment of a Polish army, but he adhered to his slogan: no army unless there is an independent Polish government to command it.

On March 15, 1917, the revolution was victorious in Russia. On March 30 the Russian revolutionary government issued a proclamation to Poland in which it recognized Poland's right to self-determination and promised it the support of revolutionary Russia in the establishment of a Polish state. The Western powers, until then bound to take into consideration their ally Russia, now declared the establishment of an independent Polish state necessarily comprising all three parts of the country to be one of their war objectives. When in May Brusilov's last offensive failed, all hesitation evaporated. It was now clear that Russia no longer posed a danger to Polish independence; only German plans for annexation could still endanger Poland. And only the Entente could still protect Poland from Germany. If German weapons had broken Russia's domination of Poland, it was only the Entente that could break the domination of the country by the two other partitioning powers. For Piłsudski, who in 1914 had mobilized the Legions for the Central Powers' battle against Russia, it was now appropriate to dissolve them and deploy the conspiratorial Polish Military Organization against Germany. When in summer 1917 the Legions were to swear an oath of loyalty to Kaiser Wilhelm while he was preparing a new division of Poland, Piłsudski's men refused the oath; they were interned in prison camps, with Piłsudski himself arrested by the German Command and held prisoner in Magdeburg. At the same time, however, on Russian soil, General Dowbor-Muśnicki united the Polish formations of the Russian Army to create a Polish corps that was to fight against the Central Powers for the liberation of Poland, while in France a Polish legion was formed in association with the French Army.

The Austrian orientation was dead. Already in May 1917, when Austria's Chamber of Deputies convened for the first time after a three-year hiatus, the new mood was evident in the resolutions of the Polish Club. The Polish Club now demanded "an independent united Poland with access to the sea" and attributed an "international character" to the Polish problem. The Austrian orientation was replaced by an Entente orientation.

Poland appeared lost to Austria. The Habsburg Monarchy believed it could now use Poland only as a negotiating chip. In February 1917, war weary and now after the Russian Revolution fearful of revolution, the Habsburgs offered the German Empire all of Poland including Galicia under condition that Germany declare itself ready to cede Alsace-Lorraine to France and thus make it possible to end the war; Austria-Hungary hoped it could compensate itself by incorporating a part of Romania. Germany rejected this. Michaelis answered in August 1917 that the surrender of Alsace-Lorraine was impossible for Germany and insisted that a peace settlement bring it the economic incorporation of Belgium and the mining regions of Longwy and Briey, as well as the military incorporation of Poland, Courland, and Lithuania.

A few weeks later the October Revolution broke out in Russia. The complete dismantlement of Russian military power seemed to revive the Austro-Polish solution. The German eastern armies had been relieved. Germany now hoped to achieve a breakthrough in the west, and German imperialism now believed it could found a great continental empire from the North Sea to the Persian Gulf, in which Courland, Livonia, Estonia, Lithuania and Poland, Austria and Hungary, Bulgaria, and Turkey would be incorporated within Germany militarily, economically, and politically. "Mitteleuropa," the close economic-military linking of the Danube Monarchy with the German Empire, was a component of this plan, with the incorporation of Poland in the Danube Monarchy as the price for the latter's integration into the German Empire.

But there were insuperable internal difficulties standing in the way of this plan. It was precisely the military incorporation of Austria-Hungary into Germany that Emperor Karl, long inwardly hostile to Germany, virtually forbade Czernin to negotiate. And the negotiations over a customs union were watered down to negotiations over a trade treaty. Austria-Hungary was not ready to pay the price for the Austro-Polish solution, all the less so that German imperialism tied the incorporation to unacceptable conditions. Czernin recounts: "The Germans demanded, apart from a quite enormous territorial pruning of Congress Poland, the suppression of Polish industry, co-ownership of Polish railways and state property, as well as the shifting of a part of the war debt onto the shoulders of the Poles. We could not affiliate to ourselves such a weakened, hardly viable Poland that would naturally have to be extremely unhappy."

Hungarian imperialism took advantage of the situation created by German imperialism. Poland along with Galicia was to be left to the German Empire in exchange for gaining Romania, brought under Hungary, so as to compensate Austria for the loss of Galicia and so that Hungary would relinquish its share of Bosnia and give it to Austria.

The Brest-Litovsk peace negotiations fell in the period of these fantasies of treating countries as chess pieces. In Brest-Litovsk Trotsky advocated Poland's right to self-determination against the Central Powers. However, alongside Trotsky there were the representatives of the Kiev Ukrainian Rada. The Central Powers wanted to use the Rada to play it against Soviet Russia, in order to sever Ukraine from Bolshevik Russia and take possession of Ukraine's huge grain reservoirs, which was to make continuation of the war possible.

But this Machiavellianism was caught in its own snare. The Rada's participation in the negotiations became a "Köpenickiade."* In Ukraine the Bolsheviks advanced victoriously. The Rada troops were pushed back to the Galician border. Behind the young people negotiating at Brest-Litovsk in the name of Ukraine, there was no longer a government, a military power, or state. In Austria, however, the food crisis had reached its high point; Czernin needed at any cost the "peace for bread" that the Ukrainian granary was to open up to starving Vienna. The Kiev delegates took advantage of the Danube Monarchy's difficulties. "The Ukrainians are not negotiating anymore; they are dictating!" Czernin wrote in his diary. And this at a time in which the Ukraine of the Rada no longer existed.

Czernin let himself be bluffed. And Prussia, always and everywhere concerned with weakening Poland, helped the Ukrainians. "The Ukrainian representatives could not be dissuaded from their demand for the Chełm territory," according to the protocol of the Austro-Hungarian peace delegation, "which we wanted to see decided through negotiations with Poland, but the Ukrainian representatives could not be brought around to this, and in this they evidently had the support of General Hoffmann. On the German military side, however, there was great receptivity to Ukrainian demands but thorough hostility to Polish demands." And so, on February 8, that tragicomic peace treaty came into being in which Austria-Hungary not only ceded Chełm Governate to messieurs Sevrjuk and Levicki but also committed, for their sake, to a restructuring of its own internal order—the separation of Eastern Galicia from Lesser Poland and the unification of Eastern Galicia with Bukovina to form a crownland.

A storm of outrage swept through Poland. Now it was clear what had become of the Austro-Polish solution: in the west annexations benefitting

---

* As in the real-life event depicted by Carl Zuckmayer's play *The Captain of Köpenick*. The term refers to an imposture in which an authority is impersonated.

Prussia; in the north annexations favoring Lithuania, which was to be "incorporated" into Germany, where a German prince was to be installed as Mindowe II*; in the east annexations to benefit Ukraine; the remainder was to be a pathetic vassal state of Germany. The Polish Club in the Viennese Parliament went over to the opposition, and for the Viennese government there was no longer any possibility of a parliamentary majority. At the front, the Polish Auxiliary Corps, the dismal vestige of Piłsudski's Legions, mutinied. A part of the mutineers under the command of General Haller succeeded in marching across the border, breaking through to the coast in hazardous marches and battles, from where they shipped to France; there Haller was put at the head of the Polish Legions that had fought against the Germans on the Western front. Another section of the mutineers was taken prisoner by Austro-Hungarian troops and went before the Austro-Hungarian military tribunal at Mármaroszigeth.† With Piłsudski captured in Magdeburg, his most loyal supporters among his legionnaires in part interned in the German Benjaminów and Szczpiora camps, in part tried by the military tribunal at Mármaroszigeth, but with Haller and his men fighting on French soil against the Central Powers this was the end of the attempt of a part of the Polish people to achieve freedom for Poland in league with Austria, through Austria.

The Habsburgs had lost the Poles. They hoped to win over the Ukrainians, but this too was self-delusion.

When the Russian armies advanced into Eastern Galicia, the Ruthenian peasants did not comprehend why they should see the Little Russian Cossacks, who spoke the same language and confessed the same religion as they did, as their enemies and the Royal Hungarian Hussars, who plundered their villages, as their protectors and liberators. The summary court martials by the k.u.k. army had brutally punished the Ruthenian peasants for their political incomprehension. From then on there was grumbling among the peasant masses.

Despite this, the petty-bourgeois Ukrainian intelligentsia placed their hopes in Austria and Germany. Their victory was to free the Ukraine from Moscow's domination. But their Austrian orientation had lost its rationale when, after the Russian March Revolution, a Rada—the government of an autonomous Ukraine—could be formed in Kiev. Nevertheless, the motivation returned when after the Russian October Revolution, Moscow undertook to quash the autonomous Ukraine. The Treaty of Brest-Litovsk,

---

* Mindaugas in Lithuanian.
† Sighetu Marmaţiei in Romanian.

in which the Central Powers recognized Ukraine as a sovereign state, was the greatest triumph of this Austrian orientation.

However, the picture then changed very quickly. German and Austro-Hungarian troops mobilized to snatch Ukraine from the Bolsheviks. They occupied the country. But they occupied it in order to rob the peasants of their stocks of grain, in order to give back to the Russian and Polish landowners the soil that the Ukrainian peasants had seized, and in order to carry out the hangman's bloody work against the rebelling peasants. It was not the petty bourgeois Rada but the Hetman Skoropaadskyi whom they put into power; it was not the patriotic-revolutionary Ukrainian intelligentsia but the old tsarist generals and governors who took control under the protection of German and Austrian bayonets. What the petty bourgeois intelligentsia hoped would be a work of national liberation became plunder, counterrevolution, and foreign domination.

And so the circle was closed. The Habsburgs had begun the war against the Yugoslavs, through the war it came into severe conflict with the Czechs, and in the course of the war it had lost the Poles and not won the Ukrainians. All Slav peoples now stood against the Habsburgs. They all hoped for the victory of the Entente. Austria-Hungary conducted the war not only against external enemies all around it but also against two-thirds of its own citizens. The fate of the Habsburg Monarchy was sealed.

CHAPTER 4

GERMAN-AUSTRIA
IN THE WAR

The conflict between our "German-ness" and our "Austrian-ness" runs through all of German-Austria's recent history.

The German-Austrian bourgeoisie arose in the century between 1750 and 1850. It emerged in the period in which the antagonism between Habsburg imperial power and the aspiring royal power of the Hohenzollerns dissolved the old Holy Roman Empire; it arose at a time when the German federal lands of Austria detached themselves from Germany and were absorbed into the bundle of lands making up the Habsburgs' hereditary lands, which gradually coalesced into a unified state on the basis of the unified Austrian economic and legal sphere. Although its language was German and a good deal of German culture, albeit idiosyncratic, developed from it, it nevertheless felt Austrian, not German; it was not the disintegrating Germany but the Austria rich in ethnicities that was its fatherland.

However, beginning with the July Revolution of 1830 a new species emerged. The young intelligentsia, which grew up in hatred of Metternich's absolutism, absorbed the ideas of aspiring European liberalism and fell under the spell of the period's German intellectual life. They no longer felt Austrian; they felt German. It was not the old, backward, un-German Austria that was their fatherland but the big Germany, which they intended to reunite through offensive struggles.

There has ever since been a struggle in the soul of the German-Austrian bourgeoisie between its German-ness and its Austrian-ness. It was evident in the turbulence of 1848 in the antagonism between "the black, red, and yellow" and "the black and yellow"*; it arose again at the beginning of the Constitutional Era† in the antagonism between German liberalism and the Austrian clericalism associated with the feudal nobility; in the last generation before the war it was expressed in the struggles between Schönerer and Lueger, between the German-Nationals and Christian Socials. The Old-Austrian tradition lives on in the Old-Viennese patriciate, in the Viennese petty bourgeoisie, and in the Alpine peasantry educated by the Catholic clergy. In the border areas, where the conflict with the Slav neighbors to the north and south dominates people's passions, the German tradition lives on in the intelligentsia, which fills the petty bourgeoisie and farmers with its ideas and feelings.

The Great European Crisis, which since 1908 has united the German Empire and Austria-Hungary against a world of enemies, overcame these differences of sentiment. German nationalism and Austrian patriotism now combined. Austrian patriotism saw its Empire endangered; from 1897 the struggle between Czechs and Germans had torn the state apart; from 1903 the turmoil in the Slav South grew dangerously, as it did from 1905 also in Galicia; Austrian patriots hoped that Franz Ferdinand, the successor to the throne, would wage war to overcome the external enemy and renew the Empire from within. German nationalism saw Germany threatened; since the 1908 Reval Accord, Germany confronted the frightening alliance of the Western powers with Russia; German nationalism pinned its hopes on war, which would crush the enemy before Russian population growth and railway construction expanded the danger. Already during the 1908–09 annexation crisis, already during the 1912 Balkan War, leading circles of Christian Socials and German-Nationals pushed for war. When war came in 1914 it was their war. For the one it was the war for Austria's assertion and renewal, for the other the war for Germany's power and greatness. But both cheered the war on, both supported the war absolutism of the first war years, both saw the struggle of the Slav peoples for their liberation as high treason to be put down with an iron fist. The conflict between the German-ness and Austrian-ness of the German-Austrian bourgeoisie seemed to have been overcome.

In the history of German-Austrian Social Democracy the conflict between German-ness and Austrian-ness appears in a completely different form.

The 1848 Revolution had, for the first time, confronted democracy with the Austrian problem. Italians, Hungarians, and Poles were fighting for their

---

* The colors of the German and Austrian flags, respectively.
† 1867–1918.

liberation from the shackles of the Habsburgs. The German people, however, pressed for their own unity and freedom. The national goal of the German Revolution of 1848 was a unified German Empire in place of the deplorable small-state provincialism within the German Confederation. But the Austrian state stood in the way of this goal. It united German federal lands—western Austria from Bohemia to the Adriatic—with Hungary, with Galicia, and with Lombardy and Venice. The German north wanted to incorporate Austria's federal lands, but not its Italian, Hungarian, and Polish provinces, into the German Empire. The unification of Germany thus presupposed the dissolution of the Habsburg Empire and the separation of Austria's federal German lands from Italy, Hungary, and Poland. This goal could not be attained through the dynasties but only against them. The Habsburgs did not want to bow to the Hohenzollerns, nor the Hohenzollerns to the Habsburgs; the revolution could only create the German Empire if it succeeded in overthrowing the dynasties in Vienna and Berlin, uniting all of Germany, including the German federal lands of Austria, in a German Republic, while leaving other Habsburg countries to a united Italy, an independent Hungary, and a free Poland. That was the national goal that the republicans championed in 1848 against the Habsburgs and against the Hohenzollerns.

This idea was revived after the War of 1859 and the Italian Revolution of 1860. The German bourgeoisie, frightened by the 1848 events, was no longer revolutionary. In northern Germany it placed all of its hopes in Prussia. German imperial rule with Prussian leadership was its goal; but this goal supposed the expulsion of Austria's federal lands from the Empire. The workers protested against this. They had remained revolutionary and hoped that a united Germany would be achieved not through the bayonets of German princes but by the fists of German workers. They counterposed the Pan-German* republican ideal of 1848 to the "smaller German" solution of the northern German bourgeoisie. In Germany, the divorce of proletarian from bourgeois democracy was completed in this struggle. "Grossdeutschland moins les dynasties" was Lasalle's formulation of emerging Social Democracy's national program. And when after 1866 the German-Austrian working class also began to move again, it too took up the Pan-German republican idea. The hope for a revolution that would overthrow the German dynasties, unite German-Austria with the rest of Germany in a German Republic, and give independent statehood back to the other nations of the Habsburg Monarchy was one of the leading ideas of emergent Social Democracy.

---

* See Glossary.

History at first worked against nascent Social Democracy. In 1866 Austria was expelled from the German Confederation; in 1871 the "smaller German" Empire was established. However, Social Democracy at first regarded this solution to the German question as only temporary. To his dying day, Engels maintained that "the complete dissolution of Austria is the first condition of Germany's unification." The thinking was that Austria still had a function as the bulwark against the expansionary tendencies of Russian tsarism but that it would lose this function as soon as the revolution traversed Europe again, whose "outermost points" would be St. Petersburg and Constantinople when it broke out again. The next phase of the European revolution would (so went the thinking) disband Austria, reunite its German areas with Germany, and give its other nations their freedom. The thought that the period of social revolution would have to entail the breakup of Austria into free nation-states and thus also the unification of German-Austria with the rest of Germany formed a part of the political tradition of Social Democracy from the beginning.

For the time being, however, Social Democracy had to wage its struggle on the terrain of the Austrian state. After 1890, when it became a large mass party, when after 1897 the national struggle of the bourgeoisie dominated all of Austria's official life, destroyed parliamentarism, and established the absolutism of Paragraph 14, when the unleashed passions of nationalism began to threaten the international unity of Austrian Social Democracy, it could no longer simply refer the diverse peoples to the coming revolution that would, along with the breakup of the Austrian state, also solve the national problem; now it had to oppose a common objective of the entire Austrian proletariat to the national objectives of the contending bourgeoisies.[1] Thus to the centralism of the German bourgeoisie, and the crownlands federalism of the feudal nobility and the Slavic bourgeoisie following in its wake, the Brünn* Party Congress of 1899 opposed a program of transforming Austria into a federal state of autonomous nations.

The serious crisis of the Empire in 1905, the conflict of the Habsburgs with the Magyar noble class, lent actuality to this program. Against the nationalism of the bickering bourgeoisies there stood, on the one side, the Crown whose Empire the national struggles threatened to destroy and, on the other, the proletariat whose ascent was impeded by the national struggle. In Austria, the pressure exerted by the Crown from above and by

---

* Old-Austrian name for Brno in the present-day Czech Republic.

the proletariat from below forced electoral reform on the limited parliament of privilege.* Through the electoral reform program of the Fejérváry-Kristoffy government in Hungary, the Crown deployed the proletariat and the nationalities against the Magyar nobility. It seemed plausible that the proletariat united with the Crown could smash the Dualist imperial constitution and force the nationalist bourgeoisies to establish a federal state of autonomous nations. The champion of this political idea was Karl Renner. In advocating the idea that the "supranational" power of the dynasty and the international power of the working class of all Austrian nations should together overthrow the nationalism of the warring bourgeoisies and rebuild Austria-Hungary into a federal state of free peoples, he revised the whole traditional position of Social Democracy on the Austrian problem.

It was in these years that Renner's *Grundlagen und Entwicklungsziele der österreichisch-ungarischen Monarchie* (Foundations and Development Goals of the Austro-Hungarian Monarchy) (1906) and my *Social Democracy and the Nationalities Question* were published.[2] While I saw any solution to the problem of Austrian nationalities within the Monarchy as only temporary, Renner celebrated the Austrian "imperial idea," the idea of a Swiss-style "confederation of Austrian nations," as a geographic and economic necessity. By that time he had already considered that the breakup of the Monarchy into small nation-states would only be the solution of reactionary nationalism. For him it was not the nation-state to which the future belonged but a "supranational state," in which autonomous nations were federated.

Renner's illusions seemed destroyed when the Emperor made peace again with the Magyar nobility and when the crisis of the Empire did not lead to the reconstruction of the Monarchy into a federal state of free peoples but ended with Tisza's coup d'état, with Cuvaj's commissariat, and Bienerth's absolutism.† The Nationalities Program of the 1899 Brünn Party Congress now took on another significance. Starting in 1908, the Monarchy was preparing for war against Serbia and from then on it believed that it could only bring the rebellious nations into line through military force. After 1908 Social Democracy struggled against the anti-Serb imperialism that was driving toward war. Our slogan in this struggle was: No war can solve the problem of the Austrian state; only its internal reconstruction into a federal state of autonomous nations can reconcile the nations to the state

---

* The curia parliament (see Glossary).
† See the Introduction to this volume.

and safeguard the peace threatened by the struggles of nations. Up to the very day of the declaration of war on Serbia, Social Democracy rejected any co-responsibility for it, counterposing its demand for "an Austria that is truly a federation of free peoples."

At the beginning of the war, Austria-Hungary stood alone against Russia. The German Army invaded Belgium and France; Austria-Hungary had to stave off the onslaught of the Russian armies. An Empire of fifty-two million inhabitants against one with 160 million; a half million men against one and a half million. At the end of the first big battle Galicia was lost and the Russians stood before Kraków and the Carpathian passes. One more thrust and the Russians could break through by way of Moravia to Vienna, which the Supreme Command already had girded with fortifications. One more thrust and Nikolai Nikolaievich could proclaim a Bohemian kingdom under the Romanov scepter on Czech soil. One more thrust and the Russian columns would roll through Hungary to the Balkans. Fear of the Tsar's huge armies reigned in German-Austria. The defeat of the Habsburg armies now meant the devastation of German-Austria by Russian troops; it meant the establishment of Slav vassal states of the Tsar right up to the gates of Vienna, of Nuremberg, of Dresden; it meant Russian despotism's subjugation of all of Eastern Europe from Petrograd to Tsargrad (Constantinople). Fear of tsarist victory gripped all classes of the German-Austrian people, including the German-Austrian working masses. They did not think of Serbia and Belgium, nor of the Habsburgs and Hohenzollerns. In the first months of the war, their desires accompanied the Imperial Army that defended the homeland through unparalleled bloody sacrifices against the frightfully superior power of the Russians.

In the first months of the war, German-Austrian Social Democracy was completely under the spell of this mass mood. It unhesitatingly aligned itself with the Central Powers and put its influence over the masses at the service of the war effort.

But against the Central Powers stood the Entente—whose propaganda contested the right to existence of the Habsburg Monarchy in the name of democracy, in the name of the right of peoples to self-determination, and in the name of the revolutionary principle of nationality. The resentment of its Slav peoples was directed against the Habsburg Monarchy, experiencing as unbearable serfdom and agony their obligation to fight for a cause that was foreign and inimical to them. Arguing against the Habsburg Monarchy was the fact that it had to wage war against the citizens of its own country and could only force its peoples to come together in the battle against the external enemy through war absolutism's violent means. This is how German-Austrian Social Democracy dealt with the problem of the Austrian state from the very first day of the war. Since 1897, Austria's undermining by the national struggles had deeply shaken the self-confidence of Austrian patriots. For them it was a happy surprise that the mobilization of summer 1914 was successful, that despite the grave defeats of September and October 1914 a powerful army could still be put together out of the sons of ten nations and stand up to the Russian onslaught in the Carpathians; that the nations in the hinterland bore the sacrifices of war silently and without rebellion, to be sure under the harsh constraints of war absolutism.

"The principle of the state has won over the nationality principle," Renner announced triumphantly; the state-building power of the nationality principle is exhausted, he claimed, and the reconstruction of national states on the ruins of the Monarchy has become a "reactionary utopia"; the superiority of the big "supranational state" over small national states, the necessity of a "large economic empire of small peoples," the interest of all nations of the Habsburg Empire in their "defense and economic community," had been decided by history itself. Were not Polish parties demanding the "Austro-Polish solution," the South Slav parties the "Greater Croatian solution"? The Habsburgs themselves would, Renner thought, have to accomplish the reconstruction of the Empire to become a federal state of autonomous nations in order to incorporate Poland and Serbia into its Empire. Thus by dint of the war, Austria would adapt its constitution to its nature and develop into a "democratic International." It was not the reestablishment of the old constitution destroyed by war absolutism that was the task; Renner hoped that an imposed war absolutism would be the instrument of internal reconstruction, of "Austria's renewal." Since he viewed the "supranational state" as a higher, more developed form of state than the national state, he advocated, quite in the sense of Habsburg imperialism, the "Austro-Polish solution" for the Polish and the "Greater Croatian solution" for the Yugoslav question; he sought German unity, in perfect conformity with the plans of Hohenzollern imperialism, in a "Central European economic and military union" in Naumann's sense. *Mitteleuropa,* an imperium federating the small nations under German leadership, would, so the idea went, represent a far higher-level social formation than the democratic states of the west. Those who remain stuck in the outdated "ideas of 1789," the "old liberals," may adore the democracy of the west; but socialists would have to see how the crisis of war forces the Central Powers to thoroughly absorb their economy into the state and thus to arrive at an economic constitution that is much closer to socialism and prepares the way to it. In the months in which the masses chiefly feared the Tsar's armies, in which Social Democracy, under the influence of this mass mood, unhesitatingly took the side of the Central Powers and deployed its influence among the masses for the war and victory of the Central Powers, it was Renner who supplied the ideology for this mood and the positions of the party.

But in the further course of the war, this Austrian-patriotic ideology had to come into increasingly sharp conflict with the mass mood. The blockade by the Entente had hit Austria much harder than Germany. Galicia was devastated by the Russian armies; Hungary cordoned itself off from Austria; and thus Austria experienced terrible food shortages, which the rationing measures of bureaucratic "war socialism" were only able to attenuate slightly. The frightful losses in the first months of the war necessitated ever more recruitments; militarism dragged children from their school desks, and old men went with their sons into the battlefields. Brutal force was applied to whip the hungering working masses of the war industry into working more; the factories were militarized and the workers placed under martial law, with military factory managers commanding in the workplaces. The Constitution was suspended, the Parliament shut down, the press muzzled, and the civilian population subjected to the blood justice of the military courts. The masses bore this enormous pressure silently as long as they were dominated by the fear of Russian invasion. But after the breakthrough at Gorlice, after the Russian armies were pushed far back, the fear of foreign invasion no longer held down resentment at the war's continuation. Mass exasperation grew.

The man who gave expression to this mass mood was Friedrich Adler. His central idea was: "We have a duty in this war to act as Social Democrats, to persevere in our Social Democratic convictions." The individual comrade, whether he is German or French, Austrian or Russian, may fulfill his soldier's duty on the battlefields; but the party must not "let itself be intellectually militarized"; it must not become a tool of the ruling classes' war effort; it must align its cause neither with the Central Powers nor with the Entente.

Renner believed that in a time of imperialist war the proletariat must be on the side of the imperialism of its own country in order not to be subjugated to foreign imperialism. Adler demanded that the proletariat remain in irreconcilable opposition to imperialism as a whole but above all must fight against the imperialism of its own state in order to end the war and for peace without annexations and reparations.

Renner viewed the defense and enlargement of the "supranational" state structure as a task of proletarian internationalism. Adler saw as a task of proletarian internationalism the reestablishment of the proletariat's international community of struggle against all national and "supranational" imperialisms.

Of war absolutism Renner demanded administrative reform and revision of the Constitution, which was to lay the groundwork for transforming Austria into a federal state of peoples. Renner celebrated the militarization, the "state management" of the economy through war absolutism as the beginning of socialization. Adler, on the other hand, called for a struggle against war absolutism: "In Austria and Russia there still is no question of the social revolution. Here the bourgeois revolution has still not won, here the settling of accounts with absolutism, the realization of democracy, is still to come. In opposing absolutism we do not first need the establishment of socialism, rather it is the old bourgeois revolution, the fulfillment of whose tasks has so far not occurred in Austria, that needs to be carried out."

In the face of the problem of the Austrian state, Adler adopted a "position of the strictest neutrality." He did not identify the cause of the proletariat with the cause of the national-revolutionary movements of the Slav nations. But he also declined to defend the existence of Austria against these movements, which would "compromise the cause of socialism through too close an entanglement with the destiny of a state." Above the turmoil of the struggles between states and nations, international social democracy had, in his view, to fulfill its special task of waging the struggle on its own front: the struggle against war despotism in the factories for the freedom of the workers, against war absolutism in the state for democracy, against war and for peace without annexations and reparations, against the passions and hatreds of war and for the international solidarity of the proletariat. It had to use its influence among the masses not to further the conduct of the war but to use the shortages and breakdowns caused by the war for revolutionizing the masses.

Friedrich Adler gathered around himself a small group of comrades who were organized in the Karl Marx Association and who defended their ideas in the columns of *Der Kampf* and in the party's imperial conferences against the overwhelming majority of the party.

But, at the beginning, insurmountable obstacles stood in the way of the activism of the Left organized by Adler. Above all it lacked the basis in parliamentarism enjoyed by its sister party in the German Empire, where conflicts in the party could be articulated; and censorship severely limited their room to carry out their struggle in the press. They thus had no access to the broader masses. Adler recognized increasingly clearly that, since absolutism had removed all possibility for the opposition of carrying out legal mass propaganda, it was only an extraordinary individual deed that could galvanize the masses and transform the latent energy of their muffled rancor into conscious political action. In fall 1916 any hope for imminent peace disappeared. The food crisis had become so unbearable that in September, despite severe martial law, a movement erupted in the militarized armaments industry, which forced the army administration to organize special food provisions for factories involved in the war effort. The exasperation with the absolutism of the Stürgkh government was felt by all classes. In the House of Lords, groups of the high nobility demanded the convening of Parliament; Stürgkh rejected this. The president of the Chamber of Deputies representing the German-National parliamentary group convened the chairmen of the parties; Stürgkh refused to take part in the chairmen's conference. University professors convened an assembly in which the presidents of the Chamber of Deputies were to speak; Stürgkh prohibited the assembly. There was no longer any possibility of legal opposition. That is when Fritz Adler decided to act. On October 24, 1916, he shot the Prime Minister.

Adler's act was a turning point in the history of the labor movement. To the masses who were living day to day in hopeless and passive desperation, he was a hero who sacrificed his life in order to avenge their suffering. The impact of the deed became greater as its immediate consequence became recognizable: Koerber, who followed Stürgkh as prime minister, relaxed the war absolutism; he more strongly opposed Tisza's dictatorship within the Empire; there was hope that Parliament would be convened. The Worker's Day mass rally of November 5, 1916* convened by the party and the trade unions could finally unveil the horror of the military despotism in the arms factories and so deliver a devastating report explaining what motivated Adler's deed.

This was followed a few weeks later by the March Revolution in Russia, which also revolutionized the thinking of the masses in German-Austria. The fear of Russian tsarism was now extinguished by enthusiasm for the

---

* A traditional annual mass rally.

Russian Revolution. It was against the Tsar that everyone had been struggling; but people did not want to wage war against the Revolution. And the struggle for peace was connected to the struggle for democracy; now also in the east the Central Powers were opposing democratic polities, as they already had in the west, and their war was nothing more than the war of semi-feudal military monarchies against democracy. The movement among the masses was expressed in ever more frequent strikes in the arms enterprises, which militarism, with all its violent means, could no longer prevent; the decree of March 18, 1917, which re-regulated working conditions in the arms industry and relaxed industrial war absolutism, was the first capitulation of absolutism to the mass movement.

On May 18 and 19, 1917, the trial of Friedrich Adler took place before the Extraordinary Court. The openly revolutionary language that Adler could use for the first time before the bench was passionately echoed by the masses. The picture of his personality revealed by the court proceedings affected and recruited people far beyond the working class; a picture in which critical, undogmatic thinking, nurtured by the spirit of modern relativism, was coupled with unconditional faithfulness to one's own principles leading to the ultimate level of self-sacrifice, faithfulness to one's own political-moral character, to moral duty, combining intellectual relativism and ethical absolutism in so rare a way. A few days later, on May 30, 1917, Parliament met after a three-year hiatus. It immediately took up the struggle against the terror of military power. The majority, composed of the Social Democrats and the representatives of the Slav nations, refused to approve the Paragraph 14 Emergency Decrees on the abrogation of jury trials and the subjection of civilians to military justice and thus wrested from militarism's reign of terror its most terrible weapon; through his revelation of judicial murder in the pages of the *Arbeiter-Zeitung*, Friedrich Austerlitz had effectively prepared this victory over martial law. With the reestablishment of the Constitution, the possibility of mass propaganda and mass action was won back, and the self-confidence of the masses, held down for two years through military terror, was powerfully reinforced.

In the course of all these events, under pressure of the changing mass mood, the attitude of the party had completely changed, albeit gradually. The Party Congress of October 19–21 in Vienna put the finishing touches on this development. The Declaration of the Left summarized once more the accusations against the party's attitude in the first years of the war. The resistance of the majority was by now merely a rearguard action. The Party

Congress was followed by huge mass demonstrations against the war and for the Russian Revolution. The image of the *Arbeiter-Zeitung* changed completely. In its pages, Austerlitz now led the battle for a democratic negotiated peace against Austro-Hungarian and above all German imperialism; in contrast to the days of Brest-Litovsk, the *Arbeiter-Zeitung* had moved away from the Reich-German majority socialists. By summer 1917 the Stockholm Conference had already stirred up hope among the masses that socialism would bring peace, but now the party, thanks to its decisive turn, became the spokesperson for the war-weary masses yearning for peace both at the front and in the hinterland; its influence grew far beyond its old cadre, and so it acquired the trust, the authority, and the power that enabled it to assume leadership of the imminent revolution.

A deep transformation had taken place since 1917 not only among Social Democrats but also in the ranks of the ruling classes. The old antagonism, overridden in the first years of the war, now flared up again—the antagonism between German-ness and Austrian-ness was rekindled.

It began at the front. The Prussian officers made the Austrian comrades feel that German divisions had to rescue their weaker ally after every Austrian defeat; Prussian arrogance irritated Austrian egos. Jealousies between the German Army High Command and the k.u.k. Army High Command, quarrels between the diplomats of the two empires over the Trentino, Poland, and Mitteleuropa aggravated the antagonism. The struggle for peace made it come into the open.

Friedrich Adler's deed, the outbreak of the Russian Revolution, and the May Declaration of the Czechs and South Slavs in the Parliament had scared the Viennese Court. It saw that after the Russian Revolution the movement to secede from the Empire was becoming stronger among Czechs, Poles, and South Slavs. The Viennese Court recognized that only a quickly concluded peace could still rescue the Empire. Throughout 1917 it made continuous attempts through secret negotiations to rapidly conclude peace with the Entente and to move its German allies to do the same.

But the Habsburgs were still not ready to make serious sacrifices to bring about peace. It is true that in April 1917 Czernin offered the German Empire the incorporation of Poland along with Galicia in order to induce it to cede Alsace-Lorraine to France; but it immediately undercut the offer by demanding the Polish royal crown for Archduke Karl Stephan. It is true that on May 1917 Emperor Karl declared his readiness to cede the Trentino to Italy; but the price he asked was the cession of Italy's colonies. It is true that in May 1917 Czernin repeated the offer to Germany to cede it Poland and Galicia; but this time the price he asked for it was the incorporation of Romania into the Monarchy. However, the worse the economic hardship became in the Monarchy, and the more threatening the revolutionary movement of its peoples, the greater was the Habsburgs' desire for peace, and the greater was the willingness of the Emperor to purchase peace even with major sacrifices in order to salvage his throne. But in Berlin he came up against a rigid attitude. The generals who determined the German Empire's policies still hoped for victory. Not only did they not want to hear anything of the cession of Alsace-Lorraine to France; they still spoke of the annexation of Liège, of control of the Flemish coast, of the incorporation of Russia's peripheral ethnicities. In Vienna there was growing exasperation with the German generals who were preventing the only thing that could save the Monarchy: a promptly negotiated peace. The Viennese Court began to weigh the possibility of separation from Germany and a separate peace with the Entente.

The Empress, who was from the Bourbon-Parma family and so brought up in German-hating French traditions, was pressing for a separate peace. And Magyar diplomats and Croatian generals were advising a separate peace. Bismarck's aphorism that no great nation "could ever be moved to sacrifice its existence on the altar of the sanctity of treaties" became the favorite quote at court. The Emperor vacillated. But in the end he did not risk a separate peace. Above all he feared the German generals. He was afraid that Germany would answer a separate peace with its armies invading the territory of the Monarchy. By March 1917 Prince Sixtus of Bourbon-Parma had assured the Emperor of the military assistance of the Entente against Germany in such a case. In November 1917 Czernin weighed the consequences of a separate peace: "The German generals will not be so stupid as to wait until the Entente breaks through to Germany through Austria but will ensure that Austria becomes a war theater. Through this we will not be ending the war; we would be merely switching enemies and in addition subject some hitherto spared provinces, such as Tyrol and Bohemia, to the fury of war, and only to be smashed to pieces ourselves in the end." After the Russian October Revolution, after the disbanding of the Russian Army had freed the great German Eastern Army, this danger was doubtless very serious.

And so all efforts to reach a peace failed. But they also had a very serious aftermath: In April 1918 Clemenceau revealed the secret of the peace negotiations led by Prince Sixtus. Just when the German Army on the Western front had commenced the second powerful offensive push, from which the German-Nationals hoped for a breakthrough to Paris and Calais and final victory—in this moment German-Austria learned that the Emperor had, through his brother-in-law who was serving in the enemy army, assured "the valiant French army" of his sympathies and behind Germany's back had empowered his brother-in-law to "communicate to Mr. Poincaré, the President of the French Republic, that with all means available to me and deploying all of my personal influence I will support France's just claim of the restitution of Alsace-Lorraine." Everyone in the Austrian bourgeoisie with German orientation was in angry revolt. They were unhappy with the Emperor for not daring, after the Russian Revolution, to impose their "interests." They were angry when, in the period of the peace efforts, he granted amnesty to the Czech "high traitors." Now that the Emperor's letter to the Bourbons was made public he appeared to them as nothing other than a traitor to the German allies who in the last four years had repeatedly saved the defeated Austrian Army by sacrificing their lives. Contempt for, and hatred and mistrust of the Emperor now prevailed in the German-National bourgeoisie.

The view of those with an Old-Austrian orientation was completely different. They too may have regarded the Emperor's methods as wrong. But they agreed with its aim. They agreed that only a quick peace, even if it had to be a separate one, could save the Empire, that Austria had to separate itself from Germany, throw itself into the arms of the Entente, and reconstitute itself as a federated state of autonomous nations, in order to avert complete collapse. Thus an idiosyncratic Austrian patriotism emerged, in which the human abhorrence of war and the pacifist belief in Wilson's message of peace combined with Old-Austrian patriotism, Old-Austrian hatred of Prussians, a concern for the existence of the Monarchy, and fear of the national and social revolution. Lammasch's personality lent importance to this tendency.[3]

On the one side, the German-Nationals who still hoped for a victory of the German forces and still wanted to hold out for a victorious peace that would increase Germany's power; on the other side, there was patriotic pacifism and Social Democracy, both of which called for peace and the internal restructuring of Austria into a federated state of free peoples. For a moment All-German-ness met the united opposition of pacifist Old-Austrianism and Social Democracy. When Lammasch bravely confronted Schönburg and Pattai in the House of Lords, the working masses cheered him on. But the alliance between patriotic pacifism and Social Democracy did not last long. It was dissolved by the internal development of Social Democracy.

In the years from 1914 to 1917, the Left had only partly accomplished its task within German-Austrian Social Democracy. At the moment it was only democratic pacifism that had prevailed in the party. Now the task was to lead the party from mere pacifism to the recognition of its revolutionary aims.

In fall 1917 it had become clear to us that if peace did not come soon, the war would end in revolution. And the outcome of this revolution could be predicted by everyone who had observed the internal development of the national movements of the Czechs, Poles, and South Slavs in 1917: if the revolution were to break the power apparatus that held the ten nations in submission, then the Czechs, Poles, and South Slavs would break away from Austria-Hungary, and Austria-Hungary would fall apart. The question was not whether the German-Austrian working class wanted the Empire to disintegrate; the question we had to answer was how the German-Austrian working class should act when the Czechs, Poles, and South Slavs broke up the Empire.

From 1899 we had been demanding the reformation of Austria into a federal state of free nations. In the course of the war it became clear that the Czechs, Poles, and South Slavs would no longer be satisfied with this solution of their national problem when the revolution broke out, at which point they would fight for their full national independence. Our problem was whether German-Austrian Social Democracy could oppose the national revolution of the Slav peoples. When the revolution came, should it try to force the nations demanding complete freedom to content themselves with autonomy within Austria?

The Brünn Nationalities Program was a revolutionary program when in 1899 we opposed it to the centralism of the German-Austrian bourgeoisie and the crownlands-federalism of the feudal nobility. It was revolutionary when from 1908 to 1914 we deployed it against militaristic imperialism. It could serve as a revolutionary rallying cry when in 1915 and 1916 the party aimed it against the war absolutism of Paragraph 14, against the "concerns" of the German-Austrian bourgeoisie. However, in 1917 it was already clear that once the revolution arrived, the watchword of the counterrevolution would be the reconstruction of the Monarchy into a federated state of autonomous nations; it would become the program that the dynasty, the German-Austrian bourgeoisie, and the Magyar gentry would counterpose to the nations fighting for their complete independence. Our question was whether in the coming revolution the German-Austrian working class should stand on the side of the dynasty, the German-Austrian bourgeoisie, and the Magyar gentry against the nations demanding their unconditional right to self-determination.

It was our view that if the hour of the revolution came, then only counterrevolutionary force could reinsert the nations into the association of the Austro-Hungarian state. But counterrevolutionary force cannot establish a democratic federated state of free peoples; it can only hold the suppressed peoples together through violence. If the revolution were to be victorious then Austria would not become a federated state of free peoples but would come apart. A victorious counterrevolution could not establish a federated state of free peoples but only a despotic tyranny that would hold down not only the oppressed nations but also the German-Austrian working masses. After considering the question we came to the conclusion that in the event of revolution, we would not defend the existence of Austria arm in arm with the counterrevolutionary powers, with the dynasty, with the German-Austrian bourgeoisie, and the Magyar gentry against the revolutionary nations. We would have to recognize the unconditional right of self-determination of the Slav nations and from this would have to conclude that recognizing their right of self-determination meant we would have to demand the same right of self-determination for the German-Austrian people. If the Slav nations were to realize their unity and freedom within new nation-states we would have to try to realize the unity and freedom of the German people through the annexation of German-Austria to Germany. If the national revolution of the Slav nations were to burst the Empire apart, we would have to use the revolutionary crisis for the cause of the social revolution; we would have to overturn the dynasty on our soil as well, establish the democratic republic, and on its basis begin the struggle for socialism.

If we wanted to intellectually prepare the party to fulfill its tasks in the approaching revolution, we would have to break the influence of Renner's doctrine of the necessity and superiority of the "supranational state," educate the masses for the unconditional recognition of the right of peoples to self-determination, overcome the 1899 Brünn Nationalities Program, and revert to the old tradition of republican democracy from 1848, so that the task of the Austrian Revolution would become the dissolution of the Austrian state itself and the establishment of free nation-states on its ruins.

Already before the war, in *Der Kampf,* I had taken the view that the approaching war would place the revolutionary nationality principle on the historical agenda. When I came home from a Russian prisoners-of-war camp in September, I began to propagate this thinking. Admittedly, if we wanted to speak to the masses publicly, we had to observe certain limits set by press censorship. We thus could not speak openly of the Revolution but had to paraphrase it as the "full victory of democracy," as the "calling of constituent national assemblies"; we could not openly proclaim the dissolution of Austria but could express it through the demand that only those matters should be left to be decided in common by the nations which they together freely determined to be common concerns. I therefore included in the Declaration, which the Left defended at the October Party Congress of 1917, the following sentence, which polemicized against Renner:

> Just as the social problem cannot be resolved into mere administrative work but only through the conquest of political power by the proletariat, so too the national problem cannot be solved by a couple of administrative laws but only through the *total victory of democracy.* Our slogan in the struggle for national autonomy cannot be district administration[4] but only the calling of constituent national assemblies in each of the nations, in which everyone *sovereignly* determines the constitution and administrative organization of their nation and *agrees on* dealing with concerns that are shared in common with the other nations.[5]

But this line of thinking was still so unfamiliar to the party in October 1917 that it was not at all understood by the Party Congress. The same Party Congress that shrank back from the concepts of the Left regarding the party's position on the war accepted a resolution of Renner's that demanded a democratic administrative reform as the basis of Austria's restructuring into a federated state of nationalities without even those representatives of the Left who were present at the Congress having been able to raise an objection to it. It was only the events of January 1918 that made the German-Austrian working class acquainted with the ideas of the right to self-determination of nations.

In Brest-Litovsk the representatives of the Central Powers negotiated peace with the delegation of the Soviet Republic. Against all the "incorporation" plans of German and Austrian imperialism Trotsky defended Poland's, Lithuania's, and Courland's right to self-determination. On January 12, General Hoffmann pounded his fist threateningly on the negotiating table; the protest assemblies that the party organized the next day in

Vienna showed the passionate agitation in the masses over the imperialist push of Germany's Supreme Command against the Soviet Republic. Bitterness over the dragging out of the peace negotiations was aggravated by a serious crisis of the nutrition services. When on January 14, 1918 the flour ration was cut in half, the workers in Wiener Neustadt went on strike. On the next day the strike spread to Ternitz, Wimpassing, Neunkirchen, Triesting Valley, and St. Pölten. The movement spread spontaneously from factory to factory, from locality to locality. The Party Directorate decided to unify them and give them a political goal. On January 16 the *Arbeiter-Zeitung* published a manifesto, which declared that the people did not want "to carry on the war against Russia so that the Emperor could be elected King of Poland and the King of Prussia could do economically and militarily as he liked with Courland and Lithuania." The manifesto closed with these words:

> Therefore we call on you workers to always to raise your voice loudly and emphatically and to struggle with us: for the quickest possible end to the war! for peace without open or concealed conquests! for peace on the foundation of a genuine right of the peoples to self-determination!

That the party leadership issued this manifesto and that the censors, following a directive imposed by Victor Adler and Seitz on Prime Minister Seidler, no longer dared to suppress it bespoke the deep transformation that had already been accomplished. Even without this manifesto, the Lower Austrian strike would probably also have drawn in Viennese factories; but the Manifesto united the whole movement. On January 16 the entire Viennese working class went on strike. On January 17 and 18, the Upper Austrian and Styrian industrial areas were caught up in the movement as well. On January 18, the Hungarian working class also joined the walkout. The enormous number of strikers, the fierce revolutionary passion of their mass rallies, the election of the first factory councils in the strike assemblies—all of this gave the movement a tremendously revolutionary character, stirring hope among the masses that they could directly transform the strike into the revolution, take power, and impose peace.

That was of course an illusion. The military commands were able to very quickly throw a significant number of troops into the strike areas, deploying only Romanian, Ruthenian, and Bosnian troops with which the striking workers could not communicate, and browbeaten young recruits who were firmly in the grip of their leaders. There was no doubt that these troops were strong and dependable enough to bloodily suppress any attempt by the masses to develop the strike into a revolutionary act of violence.

But even in the event Austrian militarism no longer had defense forces against a revolutionary uprising, what had become possible in October 1918 would not have been possible in January. For at that time, in the days of Brest-Litovsk, German imperialism was at the height of its power. After the October Revolution, the Russian Army had been completely dismantled. The giant army of Germany's eastern front had been freed up. In the following weeks German militarism could shift a million men from east to west. At the moment in which German imperialism had a bigger reserve army at its disposal than ever before or during the whole war, all the Austrian Revolution could have brought about was the invasion of Austria by the German Army. German armies would have occupied Austria, as only a short time later they had occupied incomparably larger areas in Russia and the Ukraine, and would have suppressed the Austrian Revolution as they did the revolution in Finland a short time later. And since the Revolution would at the same time have terminated the southern front, the Entente armies pushing forward from the south would have collided on Austrian territory with the German armies breaking through from the north; Austria would have become a war zone.

We knew how serious the danger of a German invasion was. We had information that it was only the fear of invasion that deterred the Viennese Court from a separate peace. We also knew that the Czech revolutionaries feared a German invasion. For us during the January strike, no symptom was more significant than the attitude of the Czech working class. It was only in Brünn, where the centralists* connected with the Viennese trade unions were in the leadership, that there was a strike. The whole greater Czech area in which Czech Social Democracy was the leading force remained quiet. The Czech Social Democrats had long been under the strong influence of the Czech revolutionary leaders who were preparing the Czech national revolution and who received their instructions from the National Council of Czech Émigrés. Obviously, the leaders of the Czech national revolution did not want Czech workers to participate in the strike. As allies of the Entente they could not want a strike, which could be seen as a demonstration for peace with Soviet Russia; the Entente had just broken with Soviet Russia because it

---

* The term "centralists" denotes those factions of the Social Democratic Party and trade unions in what was to become the Czechoslovak Republic, which during the process of the Empire's disintegration remained faithful to the central bodies in Vienna.

had decided to negotiate peace with the Central Powers. An escalation of the strike to become a revolution is something they had to want even less; their tactic during the entire war was dictated by the conviction that as long as German imperialism was not yet beaten, a Czech revolution could only lead to the occupation of Bohemia and Moravia by German troops.

All of this had to determine our decisions. We had wanted the strike as a great revolutionary demonstration. But the escalation of the strike into a revolution is something we could not want. Therefore, we had to see to it that the strike was ended before famine forced the strikers to capitulate and end it in such a way that the power and self-confidence of the masses was reinforced. Already on the first day of the Vienna strike, on January 16, the party directorate presented the government with a set of demands. The workers' council elected in the strike assemblies approved these demands in its first session on January 18. The government gave in. On January 19 the Prime Minister delivered to a delegation of the workers' council a declaration by Foreign Minister Czernin in which he solemnly pledged he would not let peace negotiations fail because of any territorial acquisitions at Russia's expense and would unconditionally recognize Poland's right to self-determination; in addition he promised reforms of the War Effort Law and the Nutrition Services as well as the democratization of the municipal electoral law. In the night of January 19–20, after passionate debates, the workers' council accepted the motion of the party directorate that they go back to work on Monday, January 21. This resolution met heavy resistance from the masses gripped by revolutionary passion. It was fought over in the giant turbulent assemblies. In most factories, work was only resumed on Tuesday, in many only on Wednesday or Thursday.

In the tumultuous assemblies before the end of the strike, the Left Radicals carried out fierce agitation. In summer 1917, at a conference in St. Ägyd in the Föhrenwald near Wiener Neustadt, this small group led by Franz Koritschoner had established links with the working class of the Wiener Neustadt industrial district. In January their agitation played a part in the spread of the Wiener Neustadt strike to the rest of the Lower Austrian industrial districts. They opposed the resolution to end the strike. Military squads in the areas of the strike, the negative attitude of the Czech workers, the million-strong army reserves of German imperialism—none of this troubled them; for them the ending of the strike was sheer "betrayal." They directed their attack not only against the party directorate but also against the Left because we supported the enactment of the resolutions issued by the workers' council. The paths taken by the Left and by the Left Radicals now diverged. While the Left gradually won over the party to its views, the Left Radicals positioned themselves against the party. In November 1918 they constituted themselves, together with a group of prisoners of war returning from Russia, as the Communist Party.

The January strike could not lead directly to the Revolution. But it was a revolutionary demonstration of great historical effectiveness that decidedly contributed to creating the preconditions of the October and November Revolution. At first the strike had intimidated the government. In the beginning, the thinking of the Court was to establish a military dictatorship that would put down the rebellious workers; General of the Cavalry Prince Schönburg was designated Prime Minister. But the Emperor no longer dared to provoke the workers. Shuddering at the prospect of another strike outbreak, militarism no longer risked fully deploying violent means against the working class. The influence of Social Democracy was strengthened, our freedom of movement expanded, and martial law in the factories significantly relaxed.

Still more serious was the effect of the strike on the army. The struggle of the working class for peace was strongly echoed by the war-weary starving soldiers. The ferment among the troops was expressed in a series of mutinies following the January strike. In Judenburg Slovenian troops mutinied, in Fünfkirchen Serb troops, in Rumburg Czech troops, and in Budapest Magyar troops. In the first days of February in Cattaro,* a strike of arsenal workers spread to the navy. Warship crews hoisted red flags, took officers as prisoners, and demanded a peace agreement on the basis of Wilson's Fourteen Points. Only the fleet division of Pola,† which the harbor-master called in to help, and supported by German submarines, could force the mutineers to capitulate. The mutinies were put down. But the degree to which the January strike had strengthened our power and intimidated the rulers was seen in the frequent success the Social Democratic deputies had in impeding the execution of the mutineers who had been condemned to death. Despite the repression, revolutionary ideas continued to spread ever more widely among the troops. These ideas were strengthened still more when after the peace agreement with the Soviet Republic tens of thousands of prisoners of war, who had experienced the revolution in Russia, came home and were reintegrated into the troops.

---

* Kotor, on the Adriatic coast of Montenegro, was a base of the Austrian Navy.
† Now Pula in Croatia, the main base of the Austro-Hungarian navy.

At the same time, however, the revolutionary idea itself also took on greater definition. The January strike had tied the demand for peace to the demand for the recognition of the right of peoples to self-determination. It was in and through the January strike that the conviction took hold of the German-Austrian workers that only the unconditional recognition of the right of nations to self-determination could put an end to the war. Now the German-Austrian working class began to understand the task with which the approaching national revolution of the Czechs, Yugoslavs, and Poles had to entrust it. This task now had to be more precisely defined.

On the same January 20 in which the tumultuous mass assemblies fought over ending the strike, a few representatives of the Left met with Czech centralists in the Railway Workers' Home in Vienna; a Polish and a Slovene Social Democrat also came. We were convinced that the moment of the Revolution had not yet come; we were therefore in agreement about ending the strike. But we were convinced that the moment of the Revolution was approaching; that is why we came together to agree on the concrete tasks of the proletariat in the national revolution. The result of these consultations was the Nationalities Program of the Left.

The analysis presented in the Nationalities Program was based on the assessment that the Slav nations of the Monarchy had reached a level of development in which they no longer could tolerate foreign domination and dismemberment. "They are demanding their full right to self-determination. They will achieve this as soon as the full victory of democracy overcomes the forces that subjugate the peoples."[6] What then—this is the question that the program tries to answer—will international social democracy have to do in the hour that is approaching? The program answers:

> As a democratic, international, and revolutionary party, German Social Democracy* cannot oppose this development. It must recognize the *right to self-determination of the Czech nation* and the right of the *Slovenes, Croats, and Serbs to be united in a South Slav commonwealth*. It has to support the demand for the *unification of the entire Polish people*, that is, also of the Polish people in Galicia and Silesia with the independent Poles.
>
> ...
>
> The Germans only make up a minority of Austria's population. The domination of the German bourgeoisie in Austria rests only on political and social privileges. It will therefore be shaken by the economic and cultural rise of the other nations. It will completely collapse through the

---

* That is, German-Austrian Social Democracy.

victory of democracy. Through this victory the Slav and Latin peoples of Austria-Hungary will attain their own statehood; it is precisely through this process, however, that *German-Austria as a specific community* is separating itself from the Austrian conglomerate of ethnicities. If this community is constituted then it will be able to arrange its own relations to the German Empire according to its needs and its wishes.

Democracy is necessary for the life of the proletariat. German Social Democracy thus cannot uphold the political and social privileges on which the national domination of the German bourgeoisie in Austria rests. However, it is precisely when the German working class dismantles these privileges, thus supporting the emancipatory stirrings of the non-German nations, that it will be preparing the *unity and freedom of the German nation, the unification of all Germans in one democratic German polity.*[7]

...

On the other hand, Czech, Polish, and South Slav social democracy have to oppose any attempt by the bourgeoisies of their nations to subjugate other nations to their own in the name of freedom. Czech Social Democracy must unconditionally oppose the demand of the Czech bourgeoisie for incorporation into the Czech state of the *German areas of Bohemia and Moravia* and the German and Polish areas of *Silesia*. Polish Social Democracy has to decisively reject the nationalist demand that the Ukrainian areas of *Eastern Galicia*, as well as the *Lithuanian and Belorussian* areas, be incorporated into the Polish state. South Slav Social Democracy has to unconditionally repulse every plan to enrich its people at the expense of the *Italians*, the *Albanians*, or the *Bulgarians.*[8]

Starting from these principles, the program demanded a completely sovereign Constituent National Assembly for each distinct linguistic territory, the settlement of border disputes through plebiscites, and no inter-state-laws other than those mutually and freely negotiated. The program drew all the conclusions implied by the recognition of the right of nations to self-determination in demanding for the first time the "unification of all Germans within a democratic German polity"—this is how we had to express the idea of the republic in the face of censorship—that is, the annexation of German-Austria to Germany. With this the program drew on the traditions of 1848 and of the 1860s—with a significant difference, it is true. In the year 1848 the Czechs and South Slavs were still underdeveloped peasant peoples; all bourgeois culture in Bohemia, Moravia, and Carniola*

---

* Carniola became a Habsburg crownland in the fourteenth century. It is now almost entirely located within Slovenia, with a small part in Italy.

was still German. At the time, their antagonism to the national revolution of the Germans, the Magyars, and the Italians made the Czechs and Slovenes pillars of the Habsburg counterrevolution. A Czech or Yugoslav national state was only conceivable then as a vassal state of tsarist Russia. This is why the democracy of 1848 by no means recognized the right of the Czechs and Slovenes to independent statehood. Its goal was the absorption of the historic German federal states of Austria, including the Czech and Slovene areas, into a German Republic, alongside which only the revolutionary historic nations—the Italians, Magyars, and Poles—were to found their independent nation-states.

In the seventy ensuing years the situation changed completely. Czechs and South Slavs developed their own bourgeois culture, they were now vehicles of the national revolution against the Habsburgs, and after the Russian Revolution they could no longer be tools of tsarism. The Nationalities Program of the Left could therefore only demand the annexation of Austria's German linguistic areas to Germany. It had to recognize the right of self-determination not only for the historic nations—the Italians, Poles, and Magyars—but also for those formerly without history: the Czechs, Yugoslavs, and Ukrainians.

The Nationalities Program of the Left was formulated in the days of Brest-Litovsk, in the days of the Russian Revolution's struggle with German imperialism. It was first conceived as a proclamation against German imperialism. At the time, after the dismantling of the Russian Army, German imperialism was more confident of victory than ever. It was the period of its most reckless plans. In Brest-Litovsk it wanted to annex Courland and Lithuania to Germany and divide Poland between Germany and Austria. A few days later, Germany's annexation plans extended even to Livonia and Estonia. In Finland German troops were to install a German prince; in the Ukraine they established the hetman as Germany's vassal. The Treaty of Bucharest was to make Romania dependent on the German economy. At the same time Ludendorff prepared a full-scale offensive in the west, which was to crush France and secure economic and military control of the Flemish coast for Germany. And so the idea of an immense empire took shape as the goal of the German war, which was to place the ten nations of Austria-Hungary under German command in a "Mitteleuropa" united as a military and economic community and in the west to place Belgium and the French mining regions of Longwy and Briey, in the East the Russian "peripheral peoples" from the Gulf of Finland to the Black Sea, in the Southeast Romania, the Balkans, and Turkey to the Persian Gulf, under German supremacy. To these plans for domination by German imperialism we opposed the principle of the right of peoples to self-determination, to the Greater German* idea of a "Mitteleuropa," through which the German bourgeoisie was to rule over twenty-five smaller nations, the old idea of the Pan-German republicans of 1848 that the German people will only achieve its unity and freedom when it recognizes the freedom and unity of other nations. The Pan-German concept of unity reemerged in the struggle against the Greater German plans for conquest. Later, Friedrich Adler was to formulate the distinction in this way: "Not Greater-German, that is, as far as the German sabre reaches, but Pan-German, that is, as far as the German language is heard." While German imperialism sacrificed the nation's wealth and blood for its fantastic project of extending its dominion over foreign peoples, we were planning ahead for the policy of the German future: the only path that the German people could take as soon as the inescapable occurred, that is, German imperialism's succumbing to the superior force of the peoples of the world, with all German dominion over foreign peoples collapsing.

The historical significance of the Nationalities Program of the Left was that it prepared the party for the tasks of the future when the leadership of the nation would have to fall to it. At first the Program provoked fierce resistance within the party; Renner in particular passionately opposed it. The Program led to a heated debate in the columns of *Der Kampf,* which flowed over into many party meetings and conferences. Through these debates the party gradually arrived at a clear concept of the coming revolution and of the tasks of the party in it. As party members came to recognize the defeat of the Central Powers and the internal dissolution of Austria in summer 1918, the concepts formulated by the Left in the Nationalities Program began to prevail. On October 3, the Club of the German Social Democratic Deputies adopted a resolution that appropriated the Program's principles. We will have more to say about this resolution, for the October Revolution actually began with it. During the preliminary discussions of the resolution, Renner, by now supported by only a few deputies, continued to oppose it. But a few days later he gave in to the decision that history had already made; he too recognized that from now on there was no path other than the one already prefigured by the Declaration of the Left in the October 1917 Party Congress, which was clearly outlined in the Nationalities Program of the Left during the January 1918 strike, and which the

---

* See Glossary, "Pan-German."

party gradually endorsed during summer 1918. Only then were the antagonisms in the party completely overcome. The party had acquired a unified
concept of its next tasks. In October and November 1918 it was unified in
taking up the path of the Nationalities Program of the Left.

The Left was the driving force of the great internal development that
the party had accomplished in the course of the war, which prepared it for
the tasks it had to complete during the Revolution. However, it is to the
credit of both orientations within the party, the right and the left, that
the antagonisms did not ossify into a split but were overcome through the
internal development of the party as a whole. Under the wise leadership
of Victor Adler, Seitz, and Austerlitz, the party majority, recognizing the
changed situation, gradually corrected its views, adapted its attitude to the
changing mood of the masses, and dissolved the antagonism that divided
left from right. The whole course of the Revolution was fundamentally
determined by the fact that the party entered the Revolution as a united
force.

PART II

THE
OVERTHROW

CHAPTER 5

THE FORMATION
OF THE NATIONAL STATES

Four years of war had corroded the k.u.k. army, the once so mighty instrument of domination that held the divergent nations of the Habsburgs under their sway. It still held its ground at the Piave.* It still occupied broad areas in Poland, the Ukraine, Serbia, Romania, Montenegro, and Albania. But each month its strength declined.

Its "human resources" had dried up. The Liaison Officer of the Army High Command reported at the end of September 1918 that "of 15 units of the Isonzo Army, seven of them dispose of less than a third, three of less than a half, and only five divisions of two-thirds of the required stocks of firearms." The artillery of some brigades no longer had enough crew to mount the complete artillery emplacement. In many formations, four, six, eight, indeed even ten horses had to be maintained by one man.

There was no longer the capacity to feed the troops. Meatless days became continually more frequent, and meatless days were days of famine. "In the morning and evening flavorless black coffee, for lunch an insubstantial dish of dehydrated vegetables without fat, accompanied in the best of cases by 60 grams of cheese or pumpkin"—according to official reports this was the food of the fighting troops at the Lower Piave by the end of September. "The men can no longer physically withstand a normal military training session lasting several hours," the commandants reported. "In a division, the average body weight of a man is 50 kilos," reported the command of the Sixth Army. "Months of improved nutrition would be needed

---

* The reference is to the Italian front in the war.

simply to make the army physically capable of mobile warfare again," the same command reported. "Any deserter in the hinterland, even if he has to hide in the forests, can feed himself better than the soldiers at the front," which is how officers and the men explained the increase in desertion to the Liaison Officer of the High Command.

What was true of food also applied to clothing. "On average each man has a set of underwear. But there are cases in which not even a full set is present, with undershirt or underdrawers missing. One has to have seen this underwear to form an idea of the misery that exists! One has a shirt without sleeves, the other has no back part, a third has only half under-drawers or shreds of footwraps. In a front regiment every third man lacks a coat," according to the General Staff Officer of the Army High Command assigned to the Isonzo Army. "The poorest Bosniak is ashamed of his rags in the face of the Venetian civil population; men from the poorest areas of Dalmatia say: 'Mi nismo junaci, nego prosjaci'" (we are not heroes but beggars), the same officer added.

With inadequate technical equipment the soldier saw himself abandoned to the enemy. Enemy artillery rained down on the infantry positions. One's own artillery had to remain silent because supplies for them had long since dried up. Directly in the face of enemy attack, many artillery pieces had to be withdrawn from their emplacements for lack of horses to which to harness them. In air combat the enemy was far superior; the infantryman saw himself unprotected and abandoned to enemy aircraft.

All this weighed heavily on people's souls. The lack of troops did not permit adequate relay and frequent enough leaves. The young boys who were dragged out of middle schools and appointed as commandants over old fathers of families possessed no moral authority. Every letter from home told of the desperation of the women and the hunger of children. And in the midst of all this despair the soldier saw the infuriating feasting and revelry among the higher staff, he heard of the profits of those gaining from the war at home, and he knew that in the chanceries of the hinterland hundreds of thousands of "indispensables" were exempt from service at the front.

Discipline began to collapse. Whole armies of deserters were hiding in the mountains and farms. Between the fronts there were armies of military-service dodgers doing business everywhere. In the forests of the south the "Green Cadres"* were gathering.

---

* The Green Cadres were deserters who were armed and organized militarily. They controlled certain areas and terrorized the population.

As late as June, there was an attempt to mount an offensive with this kind of army. With frightful human sacrifice the offensive achieved nothing; it only confirmed the ongoing disintegration. Now everyone knew it: the end was coming.

To be sure, Austro-Hungarian defeats were a familiar phenomenon since the beginning of the war. In hours of need German armies had always rescued their beaten allies. But now it was clear that even Germany could no longer come to the rescue. Ludendorff's large-scale offensive in the west had failed. On July 18, Marshal Foch had gone over to the counteroffensive. And what sooner or later had to happen did happen. The enemy had superior numbers. With access to the ocean, fertile plains, stores of raw materials, and the world's industries, the enemy had incomparably better fed soldiers and incomparably more complete technical equipment. Through dreadful struggles the German armies ceded the bloodily conquered soil step by step. By August 8, Germany's defeat could no longer be doubted. In anxious suspense everyone waited for the unimaginable, the inescapable that had to come.

And everyone knew that it had come when on September 15 General Franchet d'Espèrey's infantry broke through the Bulgarian front at Dobro Pole. The Bulgarian Army, long since physically, technically, and morally even more wasted than the Austro-Hungarian Army, completely disintegrated. The defeated troops stormed the Headquarters in Kyustendil and marched menacingly toward Sofia. On September 29, Bulgaria signed the Armistice.

On the same day Ludendorff requested that the Central Powers ask the Entente for an immediate ceasefire. The system of Prussian-German authoritarian government collapsed. In Berlin, under the direction of Prince Max of Baden and the participation of the Social Democrats, a parliamentary government was formed. In the night of October 3–4, Germany's request for a ceasefire and peace negotiations went to President Wilson; Austria-Hungary and Turkey added their voices to this request.

The Central Powers had accepted Wilson's Fourteen Points as the basis of peace negotiations. The tenth and fourteenth points had demanded the "possibility of autonomous development" for the peoples of Austria-Hungary. The Entente had solemnly promised liberation to the Czechs, the Poles, and the Yugoslavs. It was clear that without the liberation of the Slav peoples, peace could not be achieved. However, the Habsburgs still hoped to content the nations with autonomy within the Empire. On October

1, in the Chamber of Deputies, Prime Minister Hussarek identified the government's program as the federalization of Austria, the transformation of the Austrian state into a federated state of autonomous nations. In their dying hour, the Habsburgs tried to cling to what the Brünn Nationalities Program of the Austrian Social Democrats had demanded in 1899, what emerged as a possible goal in the imperial crisis of 1905, and what had become a utopia for ever after 1908 when the Habsburgs betrayed Hungarian democracy in the Bosnian Annexation Crisis. This is what the Habsburgs now grasped at in their dying hour. "Too late!" Czechs, Yugoslavs, and Poles answered Hussarek; nothing could satisfy them other than complete independence. The Habsburgs now helplessly faced the nations that saw their hour as having come.

And the German-Austrian bourgeoisie was just as helpless. They had just been outraged over the Czech "high traitors," had just cheered the renewed announcement by Prime Minister Seidler of a "German course," and had still hoped up to the last moment for the maintenance, indeed reinforcement, of German predominance within Austria.

The antagonisms between the German bourgeois parties and German-Austrian Social Democracy were never as harsh as they were in the last year of the war. But now that their entire policy had foundered, the bourgeois parties turned to the Social Democrats. "Among the Czechs, the bourgeois parties and social democrats have long been in the Český svaz,* among the Poles all parties were united in the Poland Club; could not such cooperation also be possible for us Germans?" On October 3, the Club of the German Social Democratic Deputies met in order to answer this request from the German bourgeois parties. Its answer:

> The representatives of the German working class in Austria *recognize the right of self-determination of the Slav and Romanian nations of Austria* and claim the same right for the German people in Austria. We recognize the right of the Slav nations to form their own nation-states; however, we unconditionally and permanently reject the subjugation of German areas within these national states. We demand that all German areas of Austria be united in a *German-Austrian state* that will decide its own relations to the other nations of Austria and to the German Empire, based on its own needs.[1]

Our answer was clear. As a condition for cooperation with the bour-

---

* See Glossary.

geois parties, we demanded a total break with previous German-Austrian policy and thus the recognition of the unconditional right of self-determination of the non-German nations. We called for a revolutionary act: it was not Greater-Austrian legislation that should determine our future and decide our relations to the other nations; we wanted to form our own German-Austrian state, which, irrespective of the previous Austrian legal situation, ought itself to decide whether it should unite with the national states that the other Austrian nations would create—in a federation of states—or join the German Empire.

On the same day in which the Club of the German Social Democratic Deputies adopted this resolution, the first parliamentary government was formed in Berlin, and in Sofia Ferdinand of Bulgaria abdicated; a few hours later the Central Powers sent their request to Wilson for a ceasefire agreement. Now for German-Austria there was no alternative to what the Social Democrats were proposing. Already on October 4 the German-National parties resolved to "accept the general principles of the resolution of the German* Social Democratic Party as the basis for further negotiations." The Christian Socials were still hesitating; only on October 9 did they too agree, but only with the proviso that Austria should be transformed into "a federation of free national communities," into which the still-to-be-created German-Austrian state would be incorporated.

Now the oral negotiations began between the German parties. The bourgeois parties at first still thought of forming a common party association within Austria's Chamber of Deputies on the example of the Český svaz and the Poland Club. We answered: Absolutely not! It is not the Austrian Chamber of Deputies, whose hour has struck, but the German-Austrian state, which has to be founded. All deputies of the German-Austrian electoral districts together should proclaim the founding of the German-Austrian state, constitute themselves as the Provisional National Assembly of this state, and install a government for it. It was a parliamentary revolution that we proposed. The bourgeois parties hesitated. But the events of the following days forced them to choose our road.

In the south, Franchet d'Espèrey's army quickly pressed forward. Yielding to superior forces, the weak German and Austro-Hungarian armed forces had to retreat step by step. Serb troops approached the borders of Bosnia and Croatia, and the South Slav countries prepared to receive them. On October 5 in Agram an assembly of deputies of all parties and all areas

---

* That is, German-Austrian.

of the Monarchy's South Slav lands was convened. On the next day they constituted the Narodno Vijeće.* In its proclamation to the nation, the Vijeće declared its task to be the "unification of all Slovenes, Croats, and Serbs in one national, free, and independent state," and on the following days it already began preparations to establish the emerging Yugoslav state.

On October 7 the Polish Regency Council in Warsaw proclaimed the formation of an independent Polish state consisting of all three parts of Poland. At the same time, the Regency Council dissolved the State Council and announced the establishment of a government. On October 9, the Poland Club in the Austrian Chamber of Deputies paid homage to the Regency Council. On October 15 the Polish Assembly of Deputies in Kraków issued a proclamation to the Polish people: "Independent, free, and united Poland is beginning to lead its own state life. We understand ourselves as citizens of the Polish state, to which alone we pledge loyalty and obedience." The Ukrainian deputies answered this rally with the announcement that they would call the Ukrainian National Council in Lemberg for October 19.

The Czech Národni Výbor organized large mass rallies against the export of food and coal from the Czech-speaking territories. Prague's Socialist Council resolved to tie these rallies to a demonstration for the republic. It was the first unambiguously republican rally: in all Czech areas work stopped and the demonstrating masses demanded an independent Czech republic. This rally, however, was more than a powerful demonstration. The masses had demonstrated against the export of food from the Sudeten lands to German-Austria and the front. And in fact this export began to slow down the very next day; Czech farmers ceased deliveries to the State Grain Supply Agency; Czech officials of the Prague branch of the War Grain Supply Agency no longer directed transports to Vienna; Czech rail workers held all food transports at the Lower and Upper Austrian borders. The Czechs had imposed a blockade on German-Austria and the front; it was palpable within a few days.

On October 14, the same day on which the general strike of Czech workers announced the revolution in the Czech territories, Dr. Beneš communicated to the Entente governments that "with the agreement of the political leaders of our areas" the first Czech government had been constituted in Paris; Masaryk, he said, had been named president, Beneš foreign minister, and Štefanik minister of war. By the next day France recognized this government. Two days later in Washington, on October 17, Masaryk

---

* National Council.

proclaimed that the Czechoslovak Republic had come into being.

In General Headquarters in Baden/Vienna it was known that the Italian Army Command was preparing a powerful offensive against the starving, ragged, and broken k.u.k. army in the Veneto. But Wilson still left the Habsburgs' request for a ceasefire unanswered. He exchanged notes with the German Empire on ceasefire conditions, but he did not dignify Austria-Hungary with a reply. A tremendous terror seized the Court: Did the Entente no longer want to grant the Monarchy any peace at all?

The Emperor tried to negotiate with the nations themselves. On October 12 in Baden he received thirty-two deputies from all nations. He was aiming at a "ministry of peoples." But the Czechs and South Slavs replied that they would have nothing more to do with an Austrian government. They had only two demands: transfer of all governmental power in their areas to their national councils and the evacuation of all troops of foreign nationality from their territories.

The Court saw that open insurgency was developing in Bohemia, in Croatia, and in Galicia. But did it still have the power to crush the revolt? Were the weak, starving Landsturm* formations in the hinterland still dependable against the popular masses? And if they were, everything would still depend on whether the Entente would concede a ceasefire before the beginning of the menacing Italian offensive. Could one hope for the Entente's mercy if one were bloodily crushing the peoples whom the Entente had recognized as their allies? Considering this, the Habsburgs gave up any resistance.

The German bourgeois parties, too, now saw that the German-Austrian people should not cling to the foundering Empire but should take its destiny into its own hands. They finally agreed to our demand that the German-Austrian deputies constitute themselves as the Provisional National Assembly of the German-Austrian state and claim full legislative and executive power in it. There was nothing more for the Emperor to do than maintain the appearance of power through expressly allowing what had already been decided without his permission and was already being carried out. And so he resolved to publish the Manifesto of October 16. In its words, "Austria should become a federated state in which every ethnicity forms its own body politic on its area of settlement. This is in no way meant to forestall the unification of the Polish areas of Austria with the independent Polish state." The peoples should "contribute" to this reconstruction

---

* A reserve and local defense force, divided, from 1867, into a k.k. (Cisleithania) and a royal Hungarian Landsturm (Honvéd).

"through national councils made up of the Austrian Parliament deputies of each nation, who should represent the interests of the peoples in relation to each other as well as to My government." As far as the Manifesto called for the formation of national councils, it was only legalizing a process that was already underway. At the same time, however, the Manifesto showed once again how impossible it was to reconcile the rebelling nations with the Monarchy. The Hungarian government had succeeded in having included in the Manifesto the provision that Austria's reconstruction must "not in any way touch the integrity of the territories of the Holy Hungarian Crown"; this allowed the South Slavs national unification only within the imperial framework, and the Czechs would be refused incorporation of Slovakia. And the Manifesto wanted to carry out the whole reconstruction "in a legal manner"—as if the peoples would still be prepared to have the degree of their independence specified by the Crown and the two houses of the Austrian Imperial Parliament! All Slav peoples scornfully rejected this Manifesto. Nothing less than full independence!—this was the answer of the Národni Výbor, which met on October 19 in Prague, and of the Narodno Vijeće in Agram on the same day.

Then, finally, German-Austria too defined itself within a framework of the national revolution. On October 21, the Austrian Parliament deputies of all German electoral districts met in the conference hall of the Lower Austrian Diet. Dr. Waldner, the chairman of the Association of German-National Parties, opened the assembly. "History," he said, "made us Germans into the founders of the old state of Austria, and through the centuries we have given the best of ourselves in terms of culture and economy to this state with steadfast loyalty and selfless devotion. *We now leave this state without being thanked,* in order to concentrate our ethnic force on us alone and—full of hope—to build from its inexhaustible source a new body politic that will serve our people alone."[2] The assembly unanimously passed the following resolution:

> The German people in Austria have resolved *to determine their future state order themselves,* to form an *independent German-Austrian state,* and to decide its relations to *other nations* through *free agreements* with them.
>
> The German-Austrian state claims territorial jurisdiction over the *whole German area of settlement,* especially including the Sudeten lands. Any annexation of territories inhabited by German farmers, workers, and bourgeois by other nations will be resisted by the German-Austrian state. The German people will seek to secure its access to the Adriatic

through agreements reached with the other nations.

The German people in Austria will elect a *Constituent National Assembly*. The Constituent National Assembly elected on the basis of general and equal suffrage will establish the *constitution* of the German-Austrian state.

Until the convening of the Constituent National Assembly the Imperial Assembly deputies of the German electoral districts have the duty of representing the German people in Austria. The totality of German deputies of the Austrian Imperial Assembly therefore constitutes the *Provisional National Assembly* for German-Austria.

Until the Constituent National Assembly convenes, the Provisional National Assembly claims the right to represent the German people in peace negotiations, to negotiate with other nations concerning the *transfer of administrative power to the new national states* and the reconstruction of relations between the nations, and to establish a *legislative and executive authority*. The Provisional National Assembly will determine the *electoral rules* on whose basis the Constituent National Assembly will be elected, and it will prepare the organization of the domestic administration[3] of the German-Austrian state. The Provisional National Assembly will give special attention to the grave economic distress of the German people in Austria; it will above all seek to cope with the dangers arising from the slowdown in *food supply* and for this purpose will carry out the necessary negotiations.[4]

Accordingly, the assembly of deputies resolved to constitute itself as the Provisional National Assembly and to elect an Executive Committee as the germ of the still-to-be-created German-Austrian government.

Victor Adler spoke for the Social Democrats. He began with greetings to the neighboring peoples. "In this hour we offer our fraternal greetings to our Slav and Latin comrades. We congratulate them that their people are finally near realizing the right to self-determination for which they so tenaciously and selflessly strove. We recognize this right to self-determination without reservations and without restrictions. We also demand it without reservations and without restrictions for our own German people."[5] German-Austria should "unite with its neighboring people in a free league of nations if the peoples want this. However, if the other peoples reject such a community or only agree to it under certain conditions that do not correspond to the economic and national needs of the German people, then the German-Austrian state, which on its own would not be an entity capable of economic development, will be forced to affiliate as a special federal state to the German Empire." In any case, German-Austria ought to constitute itself as a democratic republic and promptly begin to form a German-Austrian government, "without being hindered by the limitations of the previous, completely collapsed constitution," which would have to take over the administration of German-Austria as soon as possible. The first tasks were thus clear: the formation of a government, the real assumption of governmental power, and annexation to Germany. But the bourgeois parties did not go that far. Schraffl declared in the name of the Christian Socials and Steinwender in the name of the German-Nationals that they would hold on to the idea of a constitutional monarchy. Only the events of the next weeks tore down these barriers as well.

On October 18, Wilson had finally answered Austria-Hungary's request for a ceasefire—on the same day that Masaryk had handed the Czech Declaration of Independence to the State Department in Washington. Wilson's answer, which was first made known in Vienna on October 21, the day of the constitution of the Provisional National Assembly, robbed the Habsburgs of their last hope. It read:

> Since that sentence was written and uttered to the Congress of the United States the Government of the United States has recognized that a state of belligerency exists between the Czecho-Slovaks and the German and Austro-Hungarian Empires and that the Czecho-Slovak National Council is a de facto belligerent government clothed with proper authority to direct the military and political affairs of the Czecho-Slovaks. It has also recognized in the fullest manner the justice of the nationalistic aspirations of the Jugo-Slavs for freedom.
>
> The President is, therefore, no longer at liberty to accept the mere "autonomy" of these peoples as a basis of peace, but is obliged to insist that they, and not he, shall be the judges of what action on the part of the Austro-Hungarian Government will satisfy their aspirations and their conception of their rights and destiny as members of the family of nations.[6]

The president declared: No peace without full satisfaction for the Czechs and Yugoslavs. The Czechs and Yugoslavs had, however, long since declared that nothing other than full independence could satisfy them. Complete independence of the Czechs and Yugoslavs had become the condition of an armistice.

However, the Habsburgs could wait no longer for the armistice. The beginning of the great Italian offensive on the Italian front was imminent. On October 24 it actually began. It was clear that the starving, ragged, poorly equipped army would not be able to stand up to the attack. It was all the clearer that there were increasing signs of dissolution within the army itself. Since October 20 there were daily reports of mutinies of Magyar and Slav troops in the Balkan theater of war. Since October 24, the Magyar troops in Tyrol and the Veneto had been demanding their evacuation to Hungary where they wanted to defend their threatened homeland. On October 23, Croatian troops in Fiume had hoisted the national flag, disarmed the Hungarian Honvéds and municipal police, and taken control of the city. At any price, the Habsburgs had to try to end the battle at the Italian front, which would have to lead to the complete smashing of the army, and reach an immediate ceasefire to save at least a part of the army. Only if they succeeded in this could the Habsburgs hope to still assert their rule at least in German-Austria and in Hungary.

In the meanwhile, the exchange of notes between Wilson and the German government continued. On October 24, the day the Italian offensive began, a new note of Wilson's to the German government was made known. In it he declared: "If it [the United States] must deal with the military masters and the monarchical autocrats of Germany now, or if it is likely to have to deal with them later in regard to the international obligations of the German Empire, it must demand, not peace negotiations, but surrender."[7] This raised the question of the monarchical state form for Germany and made clear that Austria-Hungary could not obtain an immediate ceasefire if it were on Germany's side. By offering a separate peace, the Habsburgs had hoped to obtain an immediate ceasefire, to separate their fate from the Hohenzollerns, whose overthrow Wilson demanded, and to rescue the monarchist state form in the territory that might remain to the Habsburg Monarchy. On October 26, the same day on which Ludendorff was removed from office, Emperor Karl telegraphed Kaiser Wilhelm:

> Internal order and the *monarchist principle* are in grave danger if we do not put an immediate end to the hostilities. Even the deepest fraternal feelings have to take second place to the consideration that I must rescue the existence of these states whose fates Divine Providence has entrusted to me. Therefore I must inform you that I have made the irreversible decision to seek a *separate peace* and an immediate ceasefire within 24 hours.

The Magyar oligarchy had pushed for a separate peace, which it believed to be the only way to save Hungary. Their representative Count Julius Andrássy had already been named Foreign Minister on October 24. At the same time, the Emperor had charged Lammasch with the reconstruction of the Austrian government; since the Court had decided on a separate peace and on capitulation to the Czechs and the Yugoslavs, it sought refuge in patriotic pacifism, which had long since believed that the only way to save the Empire was by breaking with Germany, reaching an understanding with the Entente, and reconciling with the Empire's nations. On October 26, the day of the telegram to Kaiser Wilhelm, the Lammasch government was formed, whose most important members were Josef Redlich and Ignaz Seipel.* Since according to Wilson's answer the transfer of de facto governmental authority to the Czechs and the Yugoslavs had to be recognized as the condition for armistice, the Lammasch government was charged with the task of "carrying out in continual agreement with the national governments the transfer of central administration to the administration of the national states." In the night of October 27–28, Andrássy's answer was sent to Wilson, and at the same time General of the Infantry Weber was given the order to transmit the request to the Italian Headquarters for an immediate ceasefire.

Andrássy's answer to Wilson was the death certificate of the Monarchy. The Austro-Hungarian government declared that it "agreed with the conception contained in the last note of the President on the rights of the peoples of Austria-Hungary, especially those of the Czechoslovaks and Yugoslavs." With this the independence of Czechoslovakia and Yugoslavia was really recognized, and the Habsburgs gave up any resistance to their separation from the Monarchy. At the same time, Austria-Hungary declared its readiness, "without waiting for the results of other negotiations, to enter into negotiations over a peace between Austria-Hungary and the adversary states and over an immediate armistice." In so doing the Habsburgs had agreed to a separate peace, they had broken with the German Empire, and through this the relation of the German-Austrian bourgeoisie to the Habsburgs was turned completely upside down, and the Revolution was spurred on in German-Austria as well.

On October 28, Andrássy's note was made known in Prague. The masses poured cheering into the streets. Houses were decorated with the national flags. People spoke, sang, and danced in the streets. Austrian national emblems were torn down from buildings. Soldiers decorated their caps with the national cockade. In the meanwhile, representatives of the Národni Výbor went into the War Grain Supply Agency, then into the Governor's Office and the building of the Provincial Administration Commission to assume

---

* See the Introduction to this volume.

authority in the name of the Národni Výbor. They encountered no resistance. Everywhere the officials immediately pledged loyalty to the Národni Výbor. At 3 p.m. the military command called out a Hungarian battalion onto the Old Town Square; but at the Národni Výbor's energetic insistence the battalion was withdrawn. At the same time, the most important squares of the city were occupied by the armed companies of Czech Sokols*; they received weapons from the crews of some military depots and formations. In the evening hours thousands of Czech officers along with the Czech squads present in Prague placed themselves in the service of the Národni Výbor; military sections were formed out of them, which reinforced the Sokols. At 8 p.m. the representatives of the Národni Výbor negotiated with the commanding General Kestřanek, while armed Sokols penetrated into the building of the military command. The general recognized that the Czech officers and soldiers who had gone over to the service of the Národni Výbor were under the command of the Sokols, and he pledged to do nothing against those now in power but retained command of the German and Hungarian body of troops in Prague until their evacuation.

On the next day the Národni Výbor proclaimed that the Czechoslovak state had come into being and that government power in the whole Czech linguistic area was in its hands. The Bohemian governor, who was just then returning from Vienna to Prague, was arrested on arrival. On the same day, the k.k. state police placed itself under the Národni Výbor. However, military power was still not entirely in its hands. On the same day conflicts arose between the new Czech and the still existing k.u.k. military command. On October 30, Czech troops penetrated into the military command, the Hungarian troops handed over weapons and ammunition without resistance, and General Kestřanek stepped down from his position of command and transferred it to the Národni Výbor. At this point all power had been transferred to the new national government.

The events in Croatia were more dramatic and emotional. The mutiny of Croatian troops in Fiume on October 23 had ushered in the movement. Mass demonstrations in the area of Ogulin followed for whose suppression the military authorities were no longer capable of recruiting assistance. On October 28, the Croatian crew of the naval fleet, passively supported by the crews of other nations, began to mutiny; on every ship crew committees were formed, which took over command by the following day. The Sabor convened on October 29 in Zagreb. It resolved:

---

* See Glossary.

> All national-legal relations and connections between the Kingdom of
> Croatia, Slavonia and Dalmatia, on the one hand, and the Kingdom of
> Hungary and the Empire of Austria, on the other, are discharged.
>   The Croato-Hungarian Compromise (Article I) is declared null and
> void. . . . Dalmatia, Croatia, Slavonia with Rijeka are proclaimed an
> independent state with respect to Hungary and Austria and become the
> joint people's sovereign state of Slovenes, Croats and Serbs.[8]

The Sabor recognized the Narodno Vijeće as the supreme ruling
power. On the basis of this resolution of the constitutional regional parliament, the Narodno Vijeće took over the government. Ban Mihalović and
the commanding General Šnjarić subordinated themselves to the national
government. On the following day the mutinying sailors in Pola forced
the formal surrender of the whole k.u.k. naval fleet to the South Slav state.

At the same time the republican movement gained strength in German-
Austria as well. It emanated from the working class. It was awakened by the
republican demonstration of the Czech workers on October 14 and took its
slogan from the declaration that Victor Adler had made at the constitution of
the Provisional National Assembly on October 21, in which he called for the
republic. As soon as the Prague events of October 28 became known in Vienna, the movement pushed for consummation. On October 29 the workers
of many Viennese factories sent delegations to Parliament, which demanded
that the party immediately organize a mass demonstration for the republic.

But since Andrássy's request for a separate peace, the republican
movement had suddenly taken hold of the German-National bourgeoisie as well. Already since Clemenceau's unveiling of the Emperor's peace
intrigues with Sixtus of Bourbon-Parma, the German-Nationals were full
of mistrust and contempt for him. Now that the Habsburgs, in Germany's greatest hour of need, had broken with Germany, they broke with
the Habsburgs. They had supported the Habsburgs' bloody tyranny as
long as it ensured German command over the human resources of the Slav
and Latin peoples. Now that the Habsburgs separated themselves from
Germany and threw themselves on the mercy of the Entente in hopes of
rescuing the rest of their Empire, the rule of the Habsburgs could only
mean the opposite: the incorporation of German-Austria into an empire
subservient to the Entente and dominated by Hungary. However divergent their motivations were, German-Nationals and Social Democrats now
agreed that German-Austria must create, without worrying about the imperial government and the rights of the Emperor, a provisional constitution

and establish a national government to take over the government in the German-Austrian region. To this end the Provisional National Assembly was called for October 30; but the Social Democrats called on the working class to stop work at 3 p.m. that day and come to the seat of the state parliament where the National Assembly was to convene.

The Emperor saw that the fate of the dynasty was in danger of reaching a point of no return. He hit on the desperate idea of appealing to the loyalty of the soldiers to the dynasty. On October 29 the High Command telegraphed to the troops:

> The national councils are making efforts towards the propagation of the republican state form in the areas to be created. In this, however, the army in the field is not being consulted, although it comprises all men from 18 to 50 years of age and actually represents the peoples.
>
> By telegraph, declarations of troops and formations of all nationalities desirable to speak out for the Monarchy and the Dynasty without being compelled by officers. Relay immediately to the Army High Command, which should immediately forward them.
>
> Very urgent consultation of those of German nationality, since on the 30th at noon a decisive session of the German National Council is to take place in Vienna.[9]

This question from the Emperor no longer reached the front troops. At the base some commandants let the troops and officers vote on the issue of monarchy vs. republic. In so doing they only hastened the process of dissolution in the army.

Enormous masses of people heeded our call on October 30. The rally in front of the old building of the Lower Austrian Diets dispersed into an endless number of mass assemblies. The republic and the release of Friedrich Adler from jail were the demands of the day. Among the demonstrators were great numbers of soldiers. In the evening hours disorganized masses of soldiers and young people moved through the city. They tore the imperial eagles from buildings. The soldiers tore out the rosettes with the imperial insignia from their caps; they forced the officers they encountered to do the same.

Meanwhile, the Provisional National Assembly met in the Landhaus. It resolved what the masses on the street were passionately demanding. To be sure, it still avoided formally proclaiming the republic; the bourgeois parties still held on to the idea that a Constituent National Assembly had to first decide on the form of state. But in fact the Provisional National

Assembly already decided on a republican constitution that day. The resolution on the "fundamental institutions of state power" stated: "Legislative power is exercised by the Provisional National Assembly itself."[10] Governmental and executive power is transferred by the National Assembly to a Staatsrat* it elects[11]; the Staatsrat names the state secretaries who are to lead the individual government offices.[12] The Staatsrat was elected and charged with immediately taking over the actual government of the German-Austrian area. There was thus no more room in this provisional constitution for imperial power; on October 30, exactly seventy years after the day that Windischgrätz besieged Vienna and placed the revolutionary capital at the Emperor's feet, German-Austria became a republic.

On the following day, the Revolution swept through all of Austria. On October 31 in Laibach, the Narodni Svet took over state power and established a government. In Trieste a welfare committee took power. In Kraków, in the name of the Reczpospolita† a liquidation commission empowered by the Polish deputies took over all civil and military power. The Ukrainian National Council took possession of Lemberg with the support of some Ruthenian troops. On November 1, General Sarkotić surrendered government power in Bosnia to the Narodno Vijeće. Nowhere did the Habsburgs put up any resistance to the movement. And yet the Habsburgs believed, as did their generals and diplomats, that their cause was not at all lost. For in the south, retreating in a terrifying struggle with the enemy, the Imperial Army still lived despite all. If only a part of the beaten army could be saved from general disintegration and be maintained in the hands of its commandants, then one might still hope to suppress the Revolution, at least in German-Austria and in Hungary. That was the hope of the Imperial generals. "What is playing out in the hinterland is only intoxication, which will be over tomorrow," Field Marshal Boroević still comforted the Army High Command on October 30. Admittedly, under one condition: "If only the army, for which only the hinterland still has respect, does not disappear." In fact, it was not in the inexpensive victories of the Revolution in the hinterland but there in the south, where even as late as October 30, Italian attacks on Monte Asolone and Pertica had collapsed and bravely fighting rear guards still covered the retreat of the Sixth and Isonzo Armies, that the fate of the Empire had to be decided.

---

* Council of State.
† See Glossary.

CHAPTER 6

THE DISSOLUTION
OF THE EMPIRE

Hungary had entered the war under completely different conditions than Austria had. In Austria, all nations had long since produced a national bourgeoisie that led the masses in the national struggle. Already by 1897 the national struggle had shaken the foundation of the Austrian state. During the war, national antagonisms appeared increasingly stark, and the national revolution in October 1918 seemed the natural conclusion of Austria's internal development. The ruling class itself, the German-Austrian bourgeoisie, finally gave up its resistance to the revolutionary nationality principle and aligned itself with it. The situation was completely different in Hungary. There Magyar landlords and Magyar bourgeois continued to rule illiterate Slav and Romanian peasants. There the Slovaks, Walachians, and Ruthenians remained peasant peoples with no history. Hungary was still a national state, ruled by the Magyar ruling class alone. There the claims of the Czechs to Slovakia, of the Romanians to Transylvania, and the Yugo-slavs to the Banat did not look like internal national development but rather like the lust of foreign conquerors for annexation, and all of Magyar society defended the "integrity" of historical Hungary against them.

German-Austria had long ago emancipated itself from the leadership of the landlord class. The bourgeoisie, the peasantry, and the working class had long had a presence in parliament and outside it as organized powers in relation to one another. In Hungary, on the other hand, parliament was based on census suffrage and still dominated by the nobility, which per-mitted only a thin layer of the large financial and trade bourgeoisie to share

135

its power. The petty bourgeoisie, the working class, and the peasantry still stood "outside the sanctuary of the constitution."

The war had greatly reinforced the power of the Magyar ruling noble class. In comparison to disintegrating Austria, Hungary was superior, ruled as it was by the iron hand of its oligarchy. In a sense, Stephan Tisza was the actual ruler of the Monarchy. At the same time, however, the war also developed the forces of Magyar democracy.

In 1905 the King of Hungary* threatened the recalcitrant parliament of nobles with universal suffrage. The nobility prostrated itself before the King in order to escape democracy. The Independence Party then split in 1909, while the majority, led by Ferenc Kossuth, renounced the tradition of Lajos Kossuth and abandoned the struggle for national independence in order to purchase the King's relinquishment of democratic electoral reform. But a minority, led by Justh, thought differently. The experience of 1905 had taught them that the Hungarian Parliament was unable to achieve national independence as long as democracy could at any moment become an instrument of the Habsburgs against national parliamentarism. True to the ideals of 1848, they wanted to knock this weapon from the hands of the dynasty, against whom they hoped to transform democracy into an instrument of national parliamentarism. The wing of the Independence Party led by Justh now itself inscribed universal suffrage onto its banners. If the majority of the parliament of nobles wanted to approve the King's military requests in order to circumvent democratic electoral reform, Justh opposed this capitulation with the slogan: approve no military requests before democratic electoral reform is carried out. This slogan allowed the forces of the new Hungary, which had emerged from industrial development, to gather around him. They attacked the old Hungary embodied in the parliament of nobles; they included the bourgeois radicalism associated with the Budapest Sociological Society and the journal *Huszadik Század*, which represented the young bourgeois intelligentsia filled with the thinking of the Western democracies, as well as the social democratic working class.[1] Tisza had violently put down the proletarian resistance of Justh's party and the workers' street revolts of May 1912; but the democratic coalition that had arisen in these struggles lived on.

Count Mihály Károlyi stepped into Justh's shoes. He was the last representative of the Kossuth tradition; his name and goal linked modern democracy to the historical Hungary. His goal was the dismantling of the

---

* Franz Josef, Emperor of Austria and King of Hungary.

Compromise of 1867 and thus the establishment of national independence. He wanted to mobilize the Magyar peasant masses through democratic electoral and agrarian reform in the struggle for Hungary's independence, which had been betrayed by the gentry. Ever since the annexation of Bosnia, the foreign policy of the ruling oligarchy had become continuously more subaltern to German imperialism; following the tradition of kuruc* and Kossuth, Károlyi counterposed a Western to a German orientation. Before the war he had sought connections to Western democracy and Russian liberalism. During the war he advocated democratic pacifism, which was inimical to German imperialism. The party that bore his name was still small, but bourgeois radicalism provided it with a staff of eloquent and effective intellectuals, and Social Democracy connected it to the organized working masses experienced in struggle. These were the democratic forces that confronted the oligarchy in the October days.

The collapse of Bulgaria put Hungary in the greatest danger. In Serbia the army of General Franchet d'Espèrey was approaching the Hungarian border. The occupation of Bulgaria by Entente troops reestablished Romania's connection with the Allies' army at the Salonika Front; now Romania rose up against the ignominious peace that Czernin had dictated in Bucharest at the behest of the Hungarian oligarchy. Austria fell apart; the Czechs and Yugoslavs raised claims to Hungarian soil. And in Hungary itself the previously mute and downtrodden peoples now finally dared to make their demands heard. On October 18, the deputy Alexander Vajda read a declaration in the Hungarian parliament in which he contested the right of the Hungarian government to conduct negotiations in the name of the Romanians of Transylvania. On October 19, in the parliament, the deputy Ferdiš Juriga demanded the right of Slovaks to self-determination. On October 23, the Magyar troops in Fiume were disarmed by a Croatian regiment.

Just a few weeks before, the Magyars had still felt very secure: Austria might fall apart, but Hungary would live. Now they suddenly saw their thousand-year Empire threatened by a terrible catastrophe. In wild panic and with passionate patriotism, the thinking was now: What do we care about Trent and Trieste? Hungarian troops belong at home to defend our soil against Romanians and Serbs. Austria and Germany are lost. Let us separate from them. Let us throw ourselves into the arms of the Entente to rescue Hungary.

---

* See Glossary.

It was in this spirit that Magyar democracy rose up. On October 16, the deputies of the Károlyi Party demonstrated in parliament in favor of the Entente, maintaining that the connection with Austria and the alliance with Germany had put Hungary in jeopardy and that only joining the Entente could save the integrity of the fatherland—"Cancel all constitutional ties to Austria! Break with Germany! Separate peace with the Entente!" Above all, they declared that Hungarian troops ought no longer to fight for a foreign cause against the Entente, that it was madness for Hungarian troops to defend Austrian vested interests in Tyrol while Hungary's borders with Romania and Serbia went unprotected. The call therefore was for the immediate withdrawal of Hungarian troops from the Italian front in order to defend Hungary's own threatened borders.

Public opinion turned toward democracy. It was not the class that had led Hungary into the war and led it in that war that could save Hungary's integrity; people thought that Károlyi, who had already established friendly relations with Western democracy before the war, and the democracy that had opposed the imperialist war would be treated more mercifully by the Entente. The oligarchy had oppressed the nationalities, but the radicals and Social Democrats, who had long advocated political equality and national autonomy for the nationalities, would be able to win the Slovaks, Romanians, and Serbs for Hungary. Public opinion demanded the transfer of power to democracy.

But power was still in the hands of the oligarchy. However, it too now believed that Hungary and its oligarchic rule could only be saved by breaking with Austria and Germany. On October 16, the day on which Emperor Karl signed the Manifesto on the reconstruction of Austria into a federal state, Prime Minister Wekerle declared in the Hungarian parliament that with the federalization of Austria the conditions for the Compromise of 1867 would be destroyed; between Hungary and Austria there could from now on be no other relation but that of mere personal union.* On October 22, Wekerle declared in parliament that the government too was considering bringing the Hungarian regiments home. On October 24, the oligarchy pushed through the appointment of Andrássy as Foreign Minister who was to offer the Entente a separate peace. There was essentially no

---

* "Personal union" refers to the connection between the two states, a unity based only on the fact that the Austrian Emperor was also the King of Hungary; the laws, political structures, and other features of the two states, with the exception of the Imperial Army High Command, remained distinct.

difference any longer between the policy of the oligarchy and the policy of democracy; but the oligarchy did not want power to leave its hands.

The King, to be sure, did negotiate with Károlyi. But the oligarchy was still strong enough to impede entrusting him with the formation of a government. Count János Hadik, not Károlyi, was named Prime Minister on October 29. The National Council, which had been formed by the three democratic parties and counterposed itself to the parliament of nobles, now considered whether it should seize power in a revolutionary lightning attack. It postponed the deed. But some mutinous companies, which on October 30 had resisted the order to decamp from Budapest and had put themselves at the disposal of the National Council, acted on their own initiative. In the name of the National Council, they seized the headquarters and administrative institutions on the night of October 30–31. The Court still sought to save itself by legalizing ex post facto what had already been accomplished by the right of revolution: on October 31 the King named Count Károlyi as Prime Minister, and the new government swore allegiance to Archduke Josef as the representative of the King. But the working class rose up against this: "No government of the King anymore! Károlyi is Prime Minister by the right of revolution!" The King was to immediately relieve the government of its oath. And so on October 31, Hungary was a de facto republic.

The loss of Hungary had decided the fate of the Habsburgs. Before the movement that was occurring throughout Hungary had achieved victory in Budapest, it had already taken hold of the troops at the front and unleashed the national revolution in the most crucial location—the army. It was not any secret "emissaries" of Károlyi or proclamations of the National Council that had triggered the revolution in the army. The historical events themselves that had plunged the thousand-year Empire of the Magyars into catastrophe filled the Magyar officers and soldiers at the front with the same passion as the Magyar popular masses in the hinterland, with the passion of a burning patriotism born of panic, from which the Hungarian Revolution arose at the Brenta and the Piave as well as the Danube.

On October 24, the Italian Offensive began in the area of Monte Grappa, between the Brenta and the Piave. The enemy had decisive superiority: 780 Austro-Hungarian battalions confronted 841 enemy battalions. And this superiority was to be resisted by the starving, ragged Imperial and Royal army, this army with divisions in which the average body weight of a man was fifty kilos, with regiments in which no one still had a full set of underwear, with batteries that no longer had horses or ammunition for its guns. But it was not only in numbers and materiel that the enemy was far superior—its spirit was above all superior. Here an army that no longer believed in the possibility of victory and whose battalions patched together out of ten nations no longer had a common fatherland to defend; there an army that after four years of futile struggle now finally saw the possibility of wresting victory and peace in one major blow. "It was with a sense of grave concern," Lieutenant-Colonel Glaise-Horstenau recounted, "that the military leaders on the Austrian side awaited the first reports from the battlefield. Only a divine miracle could save the situation."

Nevertheless, the strong suggestive power, through which the military machinery in times of combat is able to keep the officers and men in its grip, continued to be effective. Once again Germans and Czechs, Poles and Ukrainians, Magyars and Slovaks courageously fighting side by side sacrificed life and limb for a fatherland that no longer existed. The reports from the Italian Army High Command provide a vivid picture of the last feat of arms of the k.u.k. army. Of the situation on October 24, they reported: "Monte Asolone, which was taken on the first try, had to be evacuated under pressure of heavy enemy counterattacks. The Pesaro Brigade took Monte Pertica, the 23rd Storm Battalion and other divisions the 1,484-meter heights of the Prassolan, but, melted down due to enemy fire, these too had to stop at the positions achieved." Of the situation on October 25: "The enemy, after recovering from the surprise, carried out counterattacks from all sides against the storm troops who pushed through the breach and managed to get back through the enemy forces to the starting point, bringing prisoners with them." It was the Fourth Infantry Troop Division, two-thirds of whom were Czechs, that pushed back the Italians in the Asalone phase; it was soldiers from Egerland, along with Székelys, Slovaks, and Romanians, Magyars, and Czechs, whose "fierce resistance" was noted by the Italian army report. Not without justification the Austro-Hungarian army report of October 26 boasted: "The achievements of our troops in no way take second place to the greatest feats of arms of earlier battles."

In the hinterland the Empire was already in complete dissolution. Here at the front it seemed to still be alive in the unity of the army embracing all the nations. The situation of the summer of 1848 seemed to have returned:

> *In your camp is Austria,*
> *We others are individual ruins.* *

---

* From the poem "Feldmarschall Radetzky" by Grillparzer.

And yet this was mere illusion. The popular army of 1918 could not remain unaffected by the national revolution as Radetzky's small professional army was in 1848. The army of 1918—beaten in hundreds of battles, starving, decaying, beleaguered by frighteningly superior forces—could not save the Monarchy as the triumphant army of 1848 could through a quick and easy victory. While the combat troops on Monte Grappa fended off the onslaught of the enemy for the last time, in the immediate vicinity threatening signs appeared that the Revolution had penetrated the army itself.

Already by October 24, the day the Italian Offensive began, the armies reported menacing phenomena. The Sixth Army reported that the march battalions of two Hungarian regiments demanded to be brought back to Hungary to defend their endangered homeland. The Belluno Group Command reported that the 42nd Croatian Division was in such a state that the Command could hardly still dare to deploy it. The Army Group Boroević Command reported mutinies of Bosnian troops. Even so, all this could be seen as just individual cases without greater significance; the bulk of the army still seemed solid. Only on the following day, October 25, did the national revolution actually begin in the army. The movement sprang from the 38th Honvéd Infantry Division, recruited from Transylvania, and the Upper Hungarian 27th Infantry Division. The Transylvanians had just fought courageously at Monte Sisemol. And even now they remained orderly and within military discipline. But they refused to fight any longer; they demanded to be sent home. From newspapers, letters, and the accounts of returning furloughed soldiers, they knew that Romania was rising up again, that the borders of Transylvania were threatened, that the border population was in flight; they did not want to defend foreign Tyrol but their own homeland.

Archduke Joseph, who was with the Division on October 26, reported to the Army High Command:

> In the troop review I held, the standby 22nd Honvéd Infantry Division was particularly disciplined. Not a single one of them spoke. The Battalion Commandant told me that it was the same on 25 October, with the exception of one man who told him that they would not go into battle position. When he demanded that this man be arrested the whole battalion cried out in unison, "We won't put up with that," followed by a return to total discipline. I gathered the regiment around me, addressed them according to my sovereign instructions and was enthusiastically acclaimed. But when the "at ease!" order was given and I spoke with several of them individually, infantrymen of several companies declared,

without being asked, that they would not go into battle position. They promised to be brave, disciplined, and faithful to the end, but in Transylvania, on their border, so as not to have to experience again what occurred in 1916 when parents or women and children were murdered by the Romanians before they arrived. Thus their evacuation to Transylvania was their most urgent plea.

It proved impossible to bring the two divisions back to obedience in the midst of battle. Their demand had to be met. On October 26 the evacuation of the two divisions was ordered. The example was set. Now the movement quickly spread among the Hungarian units. "It cannot be denied," reported the Sixth Army Command, "that among the Hungarian troops, both the officers and men, the thought has been awakened that the fatherland is being threatened by an enemy invasion and that the Hungarian troops need to be called back to the immediate protection of the homeland." On October 26, the 40th Honvéd Infantry Division, and on October 27 the Seventh Infantry Division and other Magyar divisions were caught up in the movement. And now the movement spread to the Slav units as well. The mood of the Slav soldiers had long been no different from that of the Slav masses in the hinterland. Despite the hatred they harbored for the Empire, they had continued to fight for it. Fear still kept them obedient. Now that the Hungarians—with the German-Austrians the stablest core of the army—set the example of insubordination, the Czech and South Slav battalions also took courage. Where Magyar units refused orders, the mutiny spread to the adjacent Slav divisions. They too refused the orders to advance. They too began to desert their posts. Already on October 27, the Army Group Boroević Command reported mutinies of Czech, Slovene, Polish, and Ukrainian battalions.

However, the movement became truly widespread when defeat began to break up the iron mechanism of discipline, which still impeded the revolutionary movement among the troops.

On October 26, English troops managed to cross the Piave. On October 28, the day of the upheaval in Prague, the Austro-Hungarian front on the east bank of the Piave was breached. On October 29, the Czech troops who had been deployed for the counterattack refused orders. On the same day the Army High Command ordered the evacuation of the Veneto. The army now flooded back along the whole Venetian front. The disintegrating impact of the defeat and retreat on discipline was now total. The insubordination of the Hungarian and Slav troops spread throughout the whole army. Magyars and Slavs no longer wanted to fight for the hated Austria. But the German-Austrians still stood firm. They were continuing to defend their threatened homeland: If the army disintegrated in great disorder before the advancing enemy, then the Alpine valleys to the back of them would be threatened with frightful devastation. But as everything to the right and left of the German battalions* disintegrated, in the end they too could no longer resist.

In a report from the Tyrol Army Group Command to the Army High Command on October 27, a German formation was for the first time designated as no longer trustworthy. It was not a regiment subverted by a Bolshevik returnee, nor one made up of Social Democratic workers. It was the most loyal of the loyal who first began to waver. It was the Tyrolean rifle companies, the old Tyrolean farmers, who, now that South Tyrol appeared threatened, became anxious about their wives, children, and property and wanted to get back to their villages.

On October 28, some German formations did in fact mutiny: the Alpine, overwhelmingly farmer formations of the Edelweiss Division, some Tyrolean Kaiserjäger and Kaiserschütze Battalions, the Upper Austrian Regiment No. 14, and the Salzburg Regiment No. 59. When the two Hungarian divisions, from which the whole movement had originated, were relieved and evacuated, the Command sent these German formations in their place. At this point the Alpine farmers became furious: "We are not here to fight in place of the Hungarians."

Still, these were only occasional incidents. The mass of German-Austrian soldiers could still be trusted. When after the defeats of October 28 and 29 the Slav and Magyar troops refused orders almost throughout the entire front, the German units were everywhere thrown against the advancing enemy. It was a useless sacrifice: since to the right and left of them the non-German units no longer wanted to fight, the German-Austrians were threatened everywhere with encirclement and annihilation. And so they too began to revolt; thus the rebellion now also embraced the German battalions.

All bonds of discipline loosened. It was a spectacle such as the history of warfare had never known. The enemy advanced fiercely with frighteningly superior force. In some places—especially in the area of the so-called Isonzo Army, which was positioned around the tailwater of the Piave—the

---

* That is, German-Austrian battalions.

troops that were still in the hands of their leaders offered the enemy stubborn resistance in fierce rearguard action. But in other places the rearguard was already swept away by the rebellion; they ran away without a fight. Where the Commands ordered counterblows against the advancing enemy, they could not tell what forces were still available: while some battalions were still preparing for the counterattack, others no longer paid attention to orders. The rear echelons were in total disarray; the troops, unconcerned with orders and abandoning military equipment, marched unauthorized toward their homeland. The revolution in the hinterland completed the disbandment. On October 31, the Slovene Narodni Svet had taken control of the means of transportation and communication of the most important supply line; it declared its neutrality, ordered the disarming of all foreign troops on its territory, and cut off the most important telegraph and telephone lines to the front.

Defeat and revolution thus combined to form an indissoluble unity. Certainly, the Revolution had hastened and compounded the defeat—if the army's material means of power were already inferior to those of the enemy, now the Revolution robbed the army even of its sources of moral strength; the Slavs and Magyars no longer fought for the Empire that was no longer their fatherland. But it was only defeat that completely unleashed the revolution in the army. Only after the October 28 defeat did the Revolution gain greater ground. The 11th Army, stationed between the Stilfser Pass and the Pasubio, was not attacked by the Italians and had not known defeat; it was entirely untouched by the Revolution and had been completely orderly until November 3. The course of events also very clearly showed the character of the Revolution, which had shattered the army and, with it, the Empire. It was still not a social revolution but a national one. It was not the regiments of the industrial workers of Vienna and Lower Austria, of German-Bohemia and Styria, that were the base of this movement but the Magyar and Slav peasant regiments.

On October 29, the Monarchy asked for a ceasefire. Italy's Army Command, however, dragged out the ceasefire negotiations under continually new pretexts. After the ingloriously conducted war, it did not want to lose the opportunity of the glory of a total victory, which could now be gotten so cheaply. Only on November 1 were the ceasefire conditions delivered to General Weber.

On the day before, the Revolution had triumphed in Hungary. The Magyar democracy had protested that Hungarian troops still had to fight against Italy. Its first act was the attempt to end this combat. On November 1, the Károlyi government's minister of war, Lieutenant-Colonel of the General Staff Béla Linder, issued the order to the army commands to have the Hungarian troops lay down their weapons and march back unarmed to their homeland. Linder's message was relayed by the Baden High Command's wireless station without the High Command giving instructions as to whether his order should be carried out. Field Marshal Boroević telegraphed the High Command: "I am compelled to report that the ambiguous behavior of the High Command and its lack of clear will is highly dangerous to the proper conduct of the troops. I take no responsibility for this army command, since it threatens not only to destroy the existence of the army but also its honor."

But in German-Austria as well, many pushed for unconditional surrender. There was a tremendous climate of fear in Tyrol. People dreaded plunder, devastation, and arson if the army, without discipline and supplies, were to stream back through the country. On October 26, the Austrian Parliament and Regional Diet deputies of German Tyrol constituted themselves as a provincial assembly and elected a Tyrolean National Council from among this assembly, which on November 1 proclaimed that it was taking over "total civilian and military control of German Tyrol." The National Council demanded the "sealing off" of North Tyrol from the retreating army. To this end it first asked for the deployment of Imperial German, and then even Entente, troops. Better that the whole army should be taken prisoners than all of Tyrol be devastated.

The ruling class in Vienna had no less fear of the returning army. Since October 30 Vienna had daily witnessed turbulent gatherings of soldiers. The Court and the High Command, the generals and the diplomats, the nobility and the bourgeoisie all quaked at the expected vengeance of the returning troops. They too now thought it best to let the army be taken prisoner.

And even individual commands at the front thought no differently. On November 2, the Tyrol Army Group Command telegraphed the Chief of the General Staff that if an immediate ceasefire could not be achieved, the only salvation would be the entire army's laying down of arms.

The High Command was under this kind of influence when it finally received the Entente's ceasefire conditions. At first, it was completely at a loss. The Entente demanded the full right to march through Austrian territory; Tyrol was to become the area where it would concentrate its troops against southern Germany. The Emperor knew what effect his defection from Germany had had in German-Austria. He feared a wild outburst of rage in German-Austria if he were to agree to this demand of the Entente as well. While anarchy at the front grew with every passing hour, the whole of November 2 was spent in inconclusive discussions.

The Emperor tried to pass the decision-making on to the German-Austrian Staatsrat, which it declined to accept. In its view, German-Austria had no army, and a ceasefire could only be signed by the power that had waged the war and still commanded the army.* It would be its final task, but it would be no one else's task.

In the night of November 2–3, the Emperor finally gave the order to accept the ceasefire conditions. At the same time he ordered the troops to immediately cease combat. When the Army High Command relayed this order, it had to know that many hours would pass before the order to sign the ceasefire treaty could reach General Weber in Villa Giusti, more hours until the treaty could really be signed, and yet more hours before the front line of Italian troops could get news of the ceasefire. If despite this the High Command were to order the Austrian troops to immediately cease combat, it could expect that the enemy, even in the best of cases, would only lay down arms many hours after its own troops had. It had to know that the order would deliver a large part of its own army into enemy captivity.

In reality the situation was even worse—for the High Command had issued the ceasefire order without even seeing the definitive text of the ceasefire agreement. This text contained the provision that hostilities were to cease only twenty-four hours after the signing of the ceasefire agreement.

Through this unilateral ceasefire order, the High Command and the Emperor themselves destroyed what still remained of the army. The Austro-Hungarian troops, in accordance with the imperial order, ceased combat operations in the morning hours of November 3. The Italians, following the letter of the ceasefire agreement, continued hostilities until 3 p.m. on November 4. Italian tank, cavalry, and bicycle divisions broke through the lines of the Austro-Hungarian troops who were no longer defending themselves, pushed forward as far as possible, and took as prisoners all those who were to the south and west of the line they had reached up to November 4 at 3 p.m. Hundreds of thousands of Austrian soldiers were taken prisoners, including those who, as in the case of the 11th Army and much of the Isonzo Army, had maintained complete military discipline up to the very end. Whoever could still evade captivity pushed chaotically backward

---

* That is, the Emperor and his High Command.

in panicked fear. This accumulation of soldiers who pressed on to the rail-roads, plundered depots, commandeered railroad trains, forcing them to travel home, was no longer an army. On November 3 the Imperial Army had ceased to exist; the Emperor himself had dealt it the final mortal blow.

The iron mechanism that had held together ten diverging nations, maintaining them under Habsburg rule, was destroyed. And with this the Empire was dissolved and Habsburg rule at an end.

CHAPTER 7

THE GERMAN-AUSTRIAN REPUBLIC

In just four days (October 28–31), the Habsburg Monarchy had disintegrated. In just four days the army had collapsed at the front and the new national governments in the hinterland had taken control. It was a national and a democratic revolution; in German-Austria, as well as among the Czechs, in Galicia, and the South Slav area, national popular governments composed of representatives of bourgeois, peasant, and worker parties took power, replacing the dynasty and its "supra-regional" bureaucracy, generals, and diplomats. But at the same time the collapse of the old powers unleashed working masses who had until then been held down by militarist force. The turbulent daily soldier demonstrations that had begun in Vienna with the huge mass rally on October 30 signalled that the national-democratic revolution was also propelling the social revolution, that the transition of government power from the dynasty to the peoples was also introducing the class struggle within the people and a shift of power relations among the classes of the nation. The development of this threefold revolutionary process of the democratic, national, and social revolution is the history of the emerging German-Austrian state from October 30 to November 12.

On October 30, the Provisional National Assembly mandated the Staatsrat to take control of the government in German-Austria and install a German-Austrian government. German-Austria, along with all the other emerging national states at that time, was confronted with the problem of forming a government. Unlike the normal forming of governments, this

148

did not mean the transfer of existing state power from one power group to another but rather the creation of new states, of not yet existing state authorities. The governments that were formed at first had no material instruments of power—neither an administrative apparatus nor a military force; it was only through their moral authority that they could prevail, subordinating the administrative machinery of the disintegrating Monarchy to create a national defense force. If the moral authority of the new governments was to be adequate to this task, if it was to prevail in the big cities as well as the villages, in the industrial areas as well as among farmers, in administrative bodies as well as barracks, then the new governments had to be composed of persons of trust from all social classes. This is why all the new national states had to be made up of representatives of all large political parties within the nations being constituted. That "bourgeois, farmers, and workers" together had to form the new government was the watchword of the day.

The German-Austrian state too had essentially emerged from a *contrat social*, a state-founding contract between the classes represented by the political parties. All the German-Austrian deputies had constituted themselves as a Provisional National Assembly and proclaimed the German-Austrian state on the basis of agreements between the parties. And only this entirety could now take over government power. The Staatsrat elected by the Provisional National Assembly according to proportional representation (that is, composed of representatives of all parties) formed the actual government. It was only as its appointees that the state secretaries took over the direction of the individual state offices from the Staatsrat; it was not to them but to the Staatsrat itself that the provisional constitution of October 30 assigned the power to issue regulations. Just as the Staatsrat itself was composed of all parties represented in the Provisional National Assembly, so all state secretaries it appointed were also chosen from all parties. It was thus the first time that Social Democrats directed state offices. But in keeping with the national character of the revolution, they could at first only lay claim to a modest share in the government. Victor Adler became State Secretary of the Exterior; only a Social Democrat could introduce the new foreign policy of German-Austria, which was to be based on the right of peoples to self-determination. Ferdinand Hanusch was appointed State Secretary for Social Administration; at a time when the war industry was being dismantled, the working class had the strongest interest in getting this state office under its control. We left the direction of all other state offices at first to the bourgeois parties. Karl Renner was appointed Chief of the Chancellery of the Staatsrat. To the Christian Democratic State Secretary of the Interior we added the Social Democrat Otto Glöckel as Under-State Secretary and Julius Deutsch[1] as Under-State Secretary to the German-National State Secretary of the Armed Forces. It was only the events of the following days, which propelled the national revolution to become a social one, that increased our weight in the government. Only these events made the Chief of the Chancellery of the Staatsrat into the State Chancellor. Only these events made the bourgeois state secretaries of the two most important state offices—the Office of the Interior, which controlled domestic administration, the police, and the gendarmerie, and the Office of the Army, which had to direct the demobilization and establish a new army—recede far behind the Social Democratic under-secretaries. It was a power shift that was taking place through the events themselves, in which the process of the Revolution was being expressed.

Emerging from the war, the social revolution did not come out of the factory as much as it did from the barracks. When great numbers of soldiers and officers took part in the mass rally of October 30; when on this day red cockades began to appear on the soldier's caps and black-red-yellow cockades on the officers' caps;* when on the evening of October 30 masses of soldiers in the streets tore the rosettes with the imperial initials from the caps of officers, it was clear that military discipline in Vienna's barracks had completely collapsed. The tremendous omnipotence that the war's military organization had lent the officer corps all of a sudden turned into complete impotence; the four-year-long suppression of the soldiers' human dignity now came home to roost in the men's wildly burning hatred for the officers. Where silent obedience had previously prevailed, now an elementary, instinctive, and anarchistic ferment set in. Masses of soldiers, led by returnees from Russia, gathered next to the Rossau Barracks and were intoxicated by fiery speeches. They attempted to form a "Red Guard," they went armed through the city, "expropriating" automobiles and "confiscating" food rations. The officers themselves were taken up by the movement. Reserve officers from the ranks of the intelligentsia participated, carried away by the revolutionary romanticism of Bolshevism, in the formation of the Red Guard, while German-National officers entered the Parliament building as "soldiers' councils." However, the overwhelming majority of

---

* The red indicating the socialist inclinations of the soldiers and the black-red-yellow the orientation to the unity of the German nation on the part of the officers.

the soldiers felt the irresistible desire to go back to their homes, to their wives and children. The Slav soldiers hurried back home in an unorganized fashion as soon as they learned of the formation of national states in their homeland; their example immediately made the movement to desert spread to the German soldiers as well. Nobody fulfilled their duty any longer, the cadres thinned out, the guards ran away, the most important depots and magazines were unguarded. War feralization, famine, and criminality took advantage of this self-dissolution of the garrisons. Plunder began. Foreign prisoners of war were no longer guarded in detention camps. For a couple of hours a Vienna that the self-dissolution of the garrison had rendered defenseless trembled at the advance of Italian prisoners of war from the camp at Sigmundsherberg; after the desertion of the Austrian guards they had seized an arsenal and were marching toward Vienna. The danger in the railways was no less great. Every train brought starving undisciplined and armed returnees from the front; every day saw shootings in the railway stations; every day there was the danger of plunder of the cities by Slav and Magyar returnees who were heading for their homeland through German-Austrian territory. Only the establishment of a newly armed force could prevent complete anarchy.

The Staatsrat first tried to put into commission the remains of the garrisons of the old army. They pledged oaths of loyalty to the provisional constitution. And since restoring the authority of officers at first seemed hopeless, the Staatsrat asked the men themselves to elect soldiers' councils from among their number, which were to establish order and discipline in the barracks. But these initial attempts were unsuccessful. The soldiers swore the oaths but still dispersed and went back to their wives and children. To keep the reservists in the armed forces was impossible. There was only one solution: recruit paid volunteers and create a new army with them. On November 3, the day of the ceasefire, the Staatsrat accordingly decreed the recruiting of the Volkswehr.* And this is where the Social Democrats' initiative came in.

An idea immediately suggested itself: the reserve units of the old army could be deployed as cadres of the Volkswehr that was to be established. But it was a dangerous idea. These troops gathered together professional officers of the old army, the last repositories of the Old Austrian spirit loyal to the Monarchy. If the Volkswehr were not to become its tool, then its establishment would have to occur completely independently of the for-

* Popular defense force or militia.

mations of the k.u.k. army. This is what Julius Deutsch at first pushed through in the State Office of the Armed Forces. From now on there was no more attempt to hopelessly resist the immediate demobilization of the men who had either remained with the replacement formations in the hinterland or were returning from the front with their detachments. The immediate discharge of all men and reserve officers was now directly decreed; the officers who were still with the replacement cadres of the old army became harmless since they no longer had access to troops. Instead the Volkswehr battalions were established in complete independence from these replacement cadres.

The farmers' sons hurried back to their villages to finally eat their fill after the hungry years of their wartime service, and nothing tempted the sons of the bourgeoisie into the Volkswehr. But it was otherwise with the industrial working class. The war industry had shut down. Tens of thousands returning from the front found no work. The comparatively high soldier's pay of six kronen tempted the unemployed into the defense force. Consequently, the Volkswehr battalions consisted almost exclusively of industrial workers. However, it was mostly politically unschooled people run ragged by the war and susceptible to the attractions of any political adventurism and the temptations of the revolutionary romanticism of those days who came together at first into the new battalions; and not a few criminal elements had reported for soldiers duty. To bring this mass under solid leadership, protect them from likely misuse of their political naïveté, and edge out the lumpenproletarian elements among them—this was the task of the Social Democrats.

Even during the war, the links between the comrades in the barracks and the Social Democratic party organizations were never completely cut. The comrades who had been called into military service socialized in the workers' centers,* bringing their grievances to the party secretariats. In summer 1918 Julius Deutsch had consolidated and organized this loose connection to Vienna's barracks. In each troop unit, he designated some comrades as representatives who would remain in personal contact with him. During the war this system of representatives only served to inform us of everything going on in the barracks. Now, however, we could use these representatives to gain influence over the formation of the Volkswehr. It was above all they who, passing into the battalions being formed,

---

* The Arbeiterheime were the local party branches where people met and where cultural services were provided.

had to bring as many trustworthy comrades as possible from the cadres of the old army into the battalions of the Volkswehr, organize the election of soldiers' councils in the new battalions, and attract the leadership of the new battalions. At the same time, the party organizations began agitating for the Volkswehr; they took pains to induce old, trustworthy comrades to enter it and explain what their task would be within it. In this way cadres of organized Social Democrats formed within the new battalions, who put the Volkswehr under its leadership and thus under the leadership of the party, filled it with its ideology, fended off and channelled the onrush of political adventurism in fierce, tenacious struggles, and tried to gradually push the criminal elements out of the Volkswehr.

From the beginning, the Volkswehr was not a party troop. In the period of its emergence it was a ragtag bunch of poor, uneducated people brutalized by the war who had been lured into the barracks by soldier's pay. If left to their own devices, these people would have become mercenary bands using their weapons only to plunder the country and become the prey of the political adventurism and naïveté of the times, which believed that only a couple of hundred armed men and two machine guns in Ternitz or Traisen would be enough to overthrow Europe's social order. If the new troops were not to become a serious danger, they had to be placed under firm, conscious leadership. There were only two ways to do this. One was to restore the power of the officers. But this could hardly work in a period in which the authority of the officer corps had completely collapsed and hatred for them, stemming from the experience of war, was the popular passion of the day; and if it did succeed the revolution would have placed itself in the most serious danger, handing over armed power in the emerging republic to the counterrevolutionary, monarchist-oriented officer corps. Thus, only the other way was open. In these days of the collapse of all traditional authority, the Social Democrats' authority was greater than ever. They alone could discipline the mass of armed proletarians who gathered in the barracks, tie them to their leadership, fill them with their ideology, and thus save them from the temptation, after four years of war, to misuse their weapons.

The establishment of the Volkswehr saved the country from the imminent danger of anarchy. The Volkswehr took over custody of the depots and magazines. In bloody battles on November 14 and 15, Volkswehr battalions repelled the attacks of Czech and Magyar troops being transported back home through German-Austrian territory. The Volkswehr incorpo-

rated the Red Guard and forced it to submit to its command and rules.*
But it was Social Democratic-led troops, marching with red flags to the
strains of the German Workers' Marseillaise, who now had to watch over
the security of the country.[2] Through this the establishment of the Volkswehr became a revolutionary act, the first act of the proletarian revolution
into which the national revolution then began to turn.

In the classic historic revolutions, decisions had to be made on the barricades. Through victory on the barricades, the revolution disarmed the
forces of the old regime, and its own armed force arose from these battles.
What occurred simultaneously in barricade battles took place in two acts
within the German-Austrian Revolution. The disarming of the old regime
was completed through the self-dissolution of the Imperial Army. The
armed force of the new regime arose in the Volkswehr. The transfer of armed
power from the hands of the old to those of the new regime, which in other
revolutions could only occur in bloody civil war, could be accomplished
here after the self-dissolution of the old army without a bloody battle, as a
mere organizational act through the establishment of the Volkswehr. That
this act could do without the romance of battle on the barricades should
not obscure the fact that its historical effect was the same as what in other
revolutions could only be won on the barricades. The republican Volkswehr
took the place of the Imperial Army, and the Volkswehr was a proletarian
army filled with a socialist spirit. The actual control of the armed force not
only shifted from the Emperor to the people; it also shifted within the people from the owning classes to the proletariat.

This revolution in the barracks immediately unleashed the revolution
in the factories. During the war the industrial entrepreneurs had ruled
over the workers with the direct protection of the military—military factory managers commanded in the factories and military guards kept the
workers under strict discipline. Now with the collapse of military power,
the whole authority of the entrepreneurs and their organs also collapsed.
Workers' self-confidence and awareness of their power underwent massive
growth. The impending ferment in the workers' districts intimidated the
bourgeois parties and subordinated them to the will of the Social Democrats. And so the Revolution continued to take its course.

On October 30, German-Austria had in fact given itself a republican
constitution; but in Vienna the Emperor was still not giving up his throne.

---

* The Red Guard was the most radical unit of the Volkswehr and was under the influence
of the Communist Party. See Glossary.

The state secretaries appointed by the Staatsrat had taken over the branches of the k.k. ministries that had to administer German-Austrian territory. But alongside them, those departments continued to exist, as "ministries to be liquidated," which administered the apparatuses and assets of the old Empire, which the German-Austrian government had not dared to take over because they were still regarded as the common possession of all the Empire's successor states. Thus, these "ministries-to-be-liquidated" provisionally remained under the administration of the Lammasch government. In all central offices the Austrian ministers appointed by the Emperor still sat alongside the German-Austrian state secretaries appointed by the Staatsrat. This dualism of republican and monarchist administration on the same soil was untenable. It became unbearable when imperial rule finally also collapsed in the German Empire.

When Germany became a republic on November 9, the republican movement of the working masses pressed for the elimination of the last vestiges of the monarchical order. On the next day, in German-Austria, the Social Democratic representatives in the Staatsrat declared to the bourgeois parties that violent upheaval was unavoidable if a republic was not immediately proclaimed in German-Austria as well. The bourgeois parties, intimidated by the movement in the factories and barracks, no longer dared put up any resistance. The Christian Social Party, which had still stood by the Monarchy on November 9 and 10, resolved on November 11 to give up its resistance, since a resolution the Tyrolean National Council had just passed in favor of the republic, and reports from Upper Austria and Carinthia, showed that a powerful republican wave was evident even among the peasantry. The Staatsrat decided by majority vote to call the Provisional National Assembly for November 12 and to present it with a draft law on the proclamation of the republic. Even the Emperor, advised by Lammasch, now gave up all resistance. On November 11, the last Habsburg now formally renounced governance. In the words of the Emperor's proclamation: "Filled with an unalterable love for my peoples I will not, with my person, be a hindrance to their free development. I acknowledge in advance the decision that German-Austria will make on its future form of state. The people has, by its deputies, taken over the Government. I relinquish every participation in the administration of the State. Likewise I have released the members of my Austrian Government from their offices."

Already in October, the idea of the republic had been linked to the annexation of German-Austria to Germany. The idea of annexation was first expressed in our Nationalities Program of the Left. As soon as the revolutionary situation appeared for which the Program was conceived, we began to propagate it. Already on October 13, I had initiated a series of articles in the *Arbeiter-Zeitung*, which put the idea of annexation on the agenda. It quickly gained momentum.

With the collapse of its rule over other nations, the German-National bourgeoisie saw its historical mission ended for whose sake it had up to then willingly tolerated the separation from the German motherland; if separation from the German Empire and its own rule over the other peoples of the Habsburg Empire no longer served the German nation's power position, then it hoped that annexation to the German Empire would protect it from falling under foreign domination where it had until then exercised foreign rule. The only alternatives open to Germans in Bohemia, Silesia, and Northern Moravia, geographically separated by Czech territory from the German Alpine areas, was foreign domination by the Czechs or annexation to the German Empire. The six million Germans of the Alpine areas, closely tied for centuries to the three million Germans of the Sudeten lands, could only sustain this relationship in the framework of the German Empire. How helpless German-Austria stood in the face of the new national states had already been seen in the first beginnings of the Revolution: Famine had immediately occurred in German-Austria when the Czechs ceased supplying food and coal. The first step of the emerging German-Austrian state had to be requesting the Berlin government's help with grain supply. The German-Austrian economy, based on the larger Austro-Hungarian economic area, necessarily had to get into dire straits due to the breakup of this area. Alone it became defenseless prey to the hostility of the new national states; only the support of the big economically powerful Empire could reinforce its economic position of power vis-à-vis the neighboring states and facilitate the needed reordering of the German-Austrian economy. By October, under the powerful influence of these considerations, interests, and feelings, broad sectors of both the bourgeoisie and the intelligentsia had already derived comfort from the hope of annexation as a remedy for the collapse of their old edifice of dominion.

On the other hand, the mass of workers were still cool toward the idea of annexation, although Social Democrats were its first heralds; they had hated German imperialism during the war too much to now feel enthusiasm for annexation to that same Germany. Only when imperial rule was overthrown in the German Empire on November 9 were the masses won over to the idea. Only when imperial rule was overthrown in the German Empire and a socialist government, based on workers' and soldiers' councils, had seized power, when the German Revolution in a single powerful stroke seemed to far overtake our own, did the working masses begin to understand that the big, highly industrialized Empire offered much more advantageous conditions for the struggle for socialism than those of the small German-Austria, which was hopelessly dependent on neighboring agrarian countries, although it itself was half agrarian.

But just as the victory of the Republic within the Empire* had conquered the masses in Austria for annexation, so too in German-Austria itself the ideas of republic and annexation mutually reinforced one another. The republican movement derived much strength from the demand for annexation. For it was obvious that a Habsburg Austria could not be absorbed into the Empire, that is, that German-Austria had to break with the Habsburgs to be eligible for annexation. Thus, the concept of annexation attracted allies within the bourgeoisie to the proletariat's demand for a republic. But the idea of annexation itself derived much strength from the republican movement. The conflict between the Habsburgs and the Hohenzollerns had separated German-Austria from Germany; if Habsburg and Hohenzollern rule collapsed, then at the same time the unification of a people within a common state seemed to be the natural consequence of the fall of the dynasties that had torn it apart. Thus, the movement, in marrying the idea of the republic to that of German unity, took up again the tradition of democracy from 1848.

The ceasefire had just been concluded on the basis of Wilson's Fourteen Points, which promised all peoples the right to self-determination. If German-Austria wanted to assert annexation with no other weapon than the appeal to this right, which was promised to it as well, then annexation could not be the dream or the program of single parties; the German-Austrian people had to show that, in the same moment as it had gained its freedom and taken its fate into its own hands, it was at once united in setting itself this goal. Therefore, the Social Democratic representatives in the Staatsrat moved that annexation should be proclaimed simultaneously with the republic. This motion was accepted on November 11 by majority vote.

On the following day, the Provisional National Assembly met for its third session. That day's resolution summarized the results of the great

---

* That is, the German Empire.

upheaval. It completed the democratic revolution; it declared German-Austria as a democratic republic, transferred all rights of the Emperor to the Staatsrat, nullified all prerogatives of the Habsburg family, abolished all bodies based on political privileges (the delegations, the House of Lords, the regional parliaments, and local councils elected through census suffrage), and decreed the election of a Constituent National Assembly and the new election of provincial and local councils on the basis of the universal and equal suffrage of all citizens without regard to gender based on proportional representation. The Republic, the demolition of the plutocratic electoral privileges in the provinces and localities, women's suffrage, and proportional representation were the achievements of the democratic revolution. At the same time, the act drew the final logical conclusion from the national revolution: "German-Austria," Article 2 declared, "is a component of the German Republic." And this resolution of the democratic and national revolution was at once the first act of the social revolution, of the power shift that had occurred between the classes. For it was the will of the working class that had forced the Republic on the owning classes. On October 21, in the first session of the Provisional National Assembly, the two major bourgeois parties had still declared themselves for the constitutional monarchy; on November 12, in the third session of the Provisional National Assembly, both of them, trembling at the impending uprising of the proletariat, had voted for the Republic. Here too what Marx portrayed as having happened in Paris on February 25, 1848 occurred: the proletariat commanded the bourgeoisie to proclaim the republic.

On November 12, the working masses left off work. While the Provisional National Assembly met in the hall of the House of Lords, Viennese workers gathered in front of the Parliament building. But here too the powerful social ferment among the masses was evident in this giant demonstration. When the red-white-red flag (which the Republic gave itself in place of the black-yellow Habsburg flag) was to be hoisted for the first time on the flagpole of the Parliament building, revolutionary workers tore the white strips out of the flag. A short while afterward, a throng of communist soldiers fell upon the Parliament gate and began an aimless and senseless shootout, which cost two lives and scattered the assembled mass. As senseless as it was, the jarring note with which the rally ended was nevertheless a symptom and symbol of the agitation, of the ferment, of the elementary movement in the masses, which pushed beyond the achieved political freedom and equality.

In April 1919 the Republic declared November 12, the day of the completion of the democratic-national revolution, as the national holiday. The bourgeoisie, however, has never recognized it as a legal holiday; from its vantage point it always represented the day of its capitulation to the proletariat. The working class, on the other hand, celebrates it every year as the day of its victory. It expresses a deep historical context: the goal of the bourgeoisie had been the maintenance and solidification of its rule over the other nations, and when its national policy collapsed, the proletariat took over leadership of the nation. The German-Austrian state was founded under the spiritual leadership of Social Democracy; under pressure of the working masses it had broken away from the Habsburg Empire, abjuring any attempt at reunification with the young liberated nations, and set itself the goal of unification with Germany. The national revolution became the business of the proletariat and the proletarian revolution the bearer of the national revolution.

On November 12 we achieved what the Left had already outlined on January 18 as the first necessary stage of the approaching Austrian Revolution, which the whole party then, overcoming the opposition between left and right under the powerful influence of the world-historical turn, set as its principal goal in the first October days. And we achieved this goal in the course of six weeks without street battles and civil war, without the use of violence and bloodshed. Certainly, like any revolution this too was an act of violence. But the violence that enabled the revolution did not operate in the streets of Vienna. It was on the battlefields in the Balkans and the Veneto that it had smashed the iron mechanism that stood in the way of the Revolution. Therefore in the hinterland we could complete the Revolution without violence. In these decisive weeks from October 3 to November 12, we completed it by only doing each day what had already matured, always demanding only what was already feasible without heavy casualties; in this way, proceeding step by step, we finally achieved all that we had set ourselves as a goal. For the last time Victor Adler led the party's action. Each day his incomparable sense of reality grasped what had already just become possible and necessary. His sense of responsibility could not tolerate us trying to take today, at the cost of heavy casualties, what tomorrow would have to fall into our lap as ripe fruit. His respect, his human understanding for the defeated opponent, made it easier for the losers to retreat. He died on November 11 in sight of the accomplished deed. He died when the education, the organization, and the power of the Austrian working class, which was the result of his life's work, celebrated its greatest triumph; as the victory of the party, which he had unified in his youth, which in later life he had led to power, whose unity he had saved in his last years, transcending its inner contradictions, when in the revolutionary experience of his last years the national dream of his youth was combined with the social project of his middle years. He left the working class the great heritage of a revolutionary victory, which was not gotten with hand grenades and machine guns but as a moral and intellectual feat, as the work of tactical skill and organizational effort, which allowed the further development of the revolutionary process as a cultural transformation and the self-determination of the masses.

The revolutionary process continued. It involved continuously broader social strata; geographically it achieved ever greater extension. Spreading from Vienna, it had already long since gripped the provinces and unleashed a movement there as well, which in its beginnings sprouted from the same revolutionary germ as the Viennese movement but which in its further course inevitably had to come into contradiction with revolutionary Vienna.

When after October 14 the closing of the Czech border terribly exacerbated the food shortage in German-Austria, the industrial entrepreneurs' organization and the industrial workers' organization in Styria entered into negotiations over the securing of food supplies for workers in industry. Since the nutrition services of the k.k. governor's office had completely failed in this, the two organizations determined to take nutrition services into their own hands. Together with representatives of the political parties they formed the Welfare Committee in Graz, which already by October 25 had taken hold of the entire administrative apparatus of the k.k. governor's office, transferring its management to the industry representative Dr. Wutte as the Economics Commissioner and to the Social Democrat Dr. Eisler as Vice-Commissioner;[3] the imperial governor stepped down.

Just as the food shortage in Styria had done, so now in Tyrol the fear of a countryside devastated by the troops flooding back from the front led the parties to take hold of the provincial government. On October 26, the Austrian-Parliament and Provincial-Parliament deputies of Tyrol elected a "National" Council, which took over the provincial government on November 1. Vorarlberg, up to then co-administered by the Tyrol governor's office, immediately followed suit; it separated itself from the Tyrol, and the autonomous provincial committee took over the affairs of the k.k. governor's office.

On October 28, the Czechs had taken over the Bohemian and Moravian governor's office. However, the actual power of the Czech state that had emerged on this day extended only to the Czech language area. The German areas of the Sudeten lands, which had unanimously rejected subjection to the Czech state authority and professed their identification with the German-Austrian state, broke their ties to the k.k. Bohemian and Moravian governor's office. For these areas therefore a completely new administrative organization had to be created. On October 29, the Austrian Parliament deputies of German-Bohemia established themselves as a German-Bohemian provincial assembly and elected from among their numbers a German-Bohemian provincial government, which established its seat in Reichenberg.* On the next day, the Austrian Parliament deputies of the contiguous German districts of Silesia, Northern Moravia, and Eastern Bohemia met, resolved to unify these areas within a new country to which they gave the name "Sudetenland," and elected a new provincial government for this country. The new provincial governments of the two areas,† geographically separated as they were from the rest of German-Austria, had, with enormous difficulty, to establish a completely new administrative organization and new railroad, postal, financial, and judiciary authorities in order to detach the administration of these spheres from the Czech authorities in Prague and Brünn and provisionally assure the continuity of administration, communications, and food supply. In the German territories bordering on Lower and Upper Austria, that is, in Southern Moravia and Southern Bohemia, an analogous organization had to be accomplished, though here under somewhat more favorable conditions; in the first days of November these areas were constituted as Znaimer Kreis‡ and Böhmerwaldgau,§ which established autonomous county governments. As short-lived as all these entities were, they not only enabled the administration of these areas in the transitional period up to their forcible subjection to the Czechoslovak Republic and secured their food supply but through their actions also announced to the whole world the claim of their inhabitants to self-determination, their protest against their annexation by Czechoslovakia.

In all these revolutionary entities in Styria and in Tyrol, in German-Bohemia as well as in the Sudetenland, however, a new type of provin-

---

* *Liberec* in Czech.
† That is, Sudetenland and German-Bohemia.
‡ See Glossary.
§ Bohemian Forest Region.

cial government emerged. The k.k. governors were replaced by provincial governments elected by the representatives of the people of the area and proportionately made up of its political parties. The dualism of princely and autonomous administration—specific to Old Austrian administrative organization and deriving from the estate-based body politic—was overcome, with the popularly elected provincial government taking over the functions of the imperial governor. In all countries now the movement pressed toward this goal: the substitution of the k.k. governor by autonomous provincial government appeared to be the necessary consequence of the collapse of imperial rule. The Staatsrat was powerless to oppose this movement. The Provisional National Assembly could only approve what had already been accomplished through the revolution in the provinces. Thus the Basic Law of November 12 was completed by the law on the takeover of state power in the provinces, which the Provisional National Assembly passed on November 14. The law put provisional provincial assemblies in the place of the provincial parliaments that had been elected by privileged suffrage; the new entities were built in such a way that representatives of the working class now joined the parliamentary deputies of the bourgeoisie and the peasantry. These provincial assemblies had to elect the provincial governments that took over the official duties previously assigned to the governors. The new governments were elected with proportional suffrage so that the working class, up to now completely shut out of the provincial parliaments, everywhere had direct participation in provincial government. However, in the process the relation of provinces to the central state was completely upturned. The governor, who had been appointed and dismissed on the Emperor's orders, had been an organ of the central government. The new chief provincial officer* elected by the provincial assembly, who could only be recalled by it, was completely independent of the central government; the resolutions of the provincial assembly determined the administration of his office. With this the provinces in fact became independent republics and the state a loose federation of countries. The constitutional struggle between the state and the provinces and the development of German-Austria into a federal state was already predetermined here.

It was the democratic revolution in the Alpine lands and the national revolution in the Sudeten provinces that had compelled the substitution of authoritarian government with self-administration in the provinces. But

* Landeshauptmann

these results of the democratic and national revolution also necessarily acquired immediate social significance. The central state was under the powerful pressure of the proletariat in Vienna and the industrial areas. The provincial governments of the agrarian Alpine provinces necessarily had to come under the decisive influence of the peasantry and the small-town bourgeoisie. From the very start, the class antagonism was part of the antagonism between the state and the provinces.

The beginnings of this development were already evident in the stormy days of the Revolution. The first province[4] that adopted a hostile stance toward the state was Tyrol. Under the influence of the panic that had arisen in Tyrol in the days of the dissolution of the old army, the Tyrolean "National" Council had at first asked the German Empire to block the Brenner Pass with Imperial German troops to protect North Tyrol from devastation by troops flooding back home. But when the Germans really crossed the Tyrolean border, the Tyrolean National Council feared that Tyrol could become a theater of war between the Germans and the Entente. Now the Tyrolean National Council protested against the German invasion it had called for and sought help from the Entente. It sent an official delegation to Switzerland, which was to take up immediate negotiations with the Entente. The Staatsrat had to protest against these attempts at an independent foreign policy on the part of Tyrol. The conflict quickly deepened. The Tyrolean National Council, fearing for the fate of German South Tyrol, believed that by severing Tyrol from German-Austria it could attract the clemency of the victor. This hope lay behind the Tyrolean independence movement. But the antagonism between the particular regional interest and the general national interest was intertwined with the class antagonism. In the war the Tyrolean peasantry had learned to hate militarism. The republican idea quickly won them over. On November 11 the Tyrolean National Council proclaimed the Republic. But it very soon took exception to the proletarian character the Republic was beginning to acquire in Vienna. Peasant, petty-bourgeois Tyrol opposed "Red" Vienna. Consequently, the Tyrolean provincial assembly issued an official declaration of independence on November 21. The connection of Tyrol to the other German-Austrian provinces had, it asserted, rested on the Pragmatic Sanction* of 1713, on the union of the ruling dynasty. With the end of the Habsburgs right to govern it, it considered this bond to be broken and Tyrol free to decide its own future; its merely interim national affiliation with

---

* See Glossary.

German-Austria could not negate its regained right to self-determination. The Tyrolean example affected the other Alpine countries. Everywhere the peasant-bourgeois majority defended the independence of its regions from proletarian Vienna.

However, while the Alpine provinces began to rise up against the state unity of German-Austria, to the north German-Bohemia and the Sudetenland, the Böhmerwaldgau, and the Znaimer Kreis waged the fiercest battle for affiliation to German-Austria against the young Czech Republic, which laid claim to all these German areas. In German-Austria the national policy of the bourgeoisie had collapsed, and leadership of the nation had passed into the hands of the proletariat; it was no longer the dominion over other nations but the assertion of the right to self-determination of one's own nation that was now the content of national policy. In Czechoslovakia, on the other hand, on October 28 the national policy of the bourgeoisie had achieved its greatest victory; the triumphant national idea had subordinated the popular masses to its leadership, and, itself just having been freed from foreign domination, it was already grasping at the domination of foreign peoples. The young Czech imperialism caused endless difficulties for the establishment of a German-Austrian administration in German-Bohemia and in the Sudetenland, and for the maintenance of communications and food supply. In the border areas there were daily conflicts and frequent skirmishes between the German-Austrian Volkswehr and Czech troops. The German-Bohemian provincial government tried to reach an agreement with the Czech provincial government to assure peaceful cooperation between both administrations until the Peace Congress decided the fate of German-Bohemia. But the Czech minister Rašín answered the German-Bohemian Vice-Chief Provincial Officer Seliger on November 4: "We do not negotiate with rebels." The Czech bourgeoisie, which had recently been persecuted for high treason against Austria because it had fought for its people's right to self-determination, now regarded the German-Bohemians fighting for their right to self-determination as high traitors. And so the young Republic was menaced by a fierce conflict with Czechoslovakia. And at the same time the Slovene troops of General Majstr were already threatening German cities in Lower Styria and the German areas of Carinthia.

If the national revolution in Vienna and in the industrial zones of German-Austria had developed into the proletarian revolution, the barriers to the expansion of the proletarian revolution were already discernible. It was evident in the resistance of the peasantry and the bourgeoisie of the Alpine provinces, which opposed the further development of the Revolution beyond the framework of bourgeois democracy, as well as in the threat from the bourgeoisie of liberated neighboring peoples, which, reaching beyond their borders, sought to subject German-Bohemia and the Sudetenland—German-Austria's greatest industrial areas, the location of the German-Austrian proletariat's greatest strength—to its rule. The Republic, which had first arisen precisely from the will of the German-Austrian proletariat, was already threatened by the country particularism of the Alpine peasantry within and the imperialism of the Czech and Yugoslav bourgeoisie from without. On November 12 the Republic had only been proclaimed; but it took years of work and struggle to create and secure it.

CHAPTER 8

NATIONAL AND
SOCIAL REVOLUTION

We have presented the course of events from the national struggles, which dragged the Habsburg Monarchy into the war, in the light of the national movements of the war period through to the dissolution of the Monarchy. At this point we should pause and cast another glance at the events to which the Habsburg Empire was subjected after 400 years of existence, in an attempt to extract its essential content from the confusing plethora of phenomena.

The antagonisms between the world powers had expanded the war, which had broken out in 1914 from the clash between the Habsburg Monarchy and the Yugoslav people's desire for unity and freedom, into a world war. The war itself had changed character during its course. Originally nothing more than a battle between two imperialist power groups, it had become a struggle between two political systems ever since the collapse of Russian tsarism in March 1917 and the United States's entrance into the war.

On the one side stood England, France, Italy, and the United States—countries with parliamentary governments, with the bourgeoisie using democratic forms of rule. On the other side was the German Empire, governed by the Junkers through forms of the military-bureaucratic authoritarian state, which only admitted into co-rule with it the upper stratum of the bourgeoisie, finance capital, and heavy industry; and there was Austria-Hungary, dominated by the dynasty, the generals, the bureaucracy, and the episcopate and where Magyar magnates, Bohemian feudal powers, Polish szlachta, and the German-Austrian bourgeoisie indirectly co-ruled.

There the rule of the bourgeoisie, here the supremacy of the dynasties, the generals, the nobility—this was the actual social contrast. There democracy, here the authoritarian state—this was the conflict of the ruling ideologies.

The Western powers had to unleash all of their popular force in order to win. Their victory depended on the will and strength of the masses, of the masses in the fields and in the war industries. They used the power of democratic ideologies, of the great traditions of the bourgeois revolution to ignite the will to victory among their masses. They could represent their war as the war of the democracies against militarism, absolutism, and feudalism, as soon as tsarism was no longer fighting at their side. Since that moment, Woodrow Wilson's impactful words gave their war its powerful democratic ideology.

The victory of the bourgeoisie over the dynasties, the nobility, and the military caste, the victory of democracy over the authoritarian state is the content of all bourgeois revolutions. This victory, won on the barricades of all such revolutions, was again won on French battlefields in 1918. The victory of the Western powers over the Central Powers was the victory of bourgeois democracy over the oligarchic military monarchies. It was the biggest, bloodiest bourgeois revolution in world history.

The Austrian Revolution took place in the context of this general bourgeois revolution during the war. It too was a bourgeois revolution. In its origin and character it was the revolution of the Yugoslav, the Czech, and the Polish bourgeoisie.

At the beginning of the nineteenth century, the Czechs and Yugoslavs were still peasant peoples dominated by foreign ruling classes. In the course of that century, a national bourgeois revolution had developed in their womb. With the development of public primary schools and the press, with the democratization of public life, this national bourgeoisie had gradually filled the petty bourgeoisie, the peasantry, and the workers with its national ideology and led it into the struggle against the national relations of domination arising from the epoch of feudalism and absolutism, into the struggle against the supremacy of the German bourgeoisie and the Magyar gentry, and into the struggle for national statehood. By 1903 and 1908 this struggle became menacingly vehement.

Among the Polish people too a bourgeoisie had developed in the course of the nineteenth century, which had gradually taken over leadership of the nation from the nobility. Since the toughening of Prussia's Polish policy, it had come into continually sharper conflict with the German world. After the 1905 Russian Revolution, the Polish people's desire for unity again became stronger.

The intensification of the national antagonisms shook the Empire. Through the war the Monarchy tried externally to overcome its permanent internal crisis. This is why it threw itself into it. But in so doing it made its very existence dependent on the outcome of the war.

The tremendous sacrifice of blood and property that the war demanded hit the Slav peoples doubly hard; to them it seemed a sacrifice for a state that was foreign to them, for a cause hostile to them. Thus, the longer the war lasted, the more it strengthened the national revolutionary movement in the Slav countries against Austria. The goal this movement first set itself was national statehood in a federation of peoples under the Habsburg scepter. But two world-historical events, which the war generated, finally made it possible for them to set the goal of completely sovereign national states and thus the total destruction of the Habsburg Monarchy.

The first of these events was the Russian Revolution. As long as Russian tsarism remained unbroken, the existence of the Austro-Hungarian Monarchy was a European necessity. If the Monarchy were to disintegrate, then the Slav states that would have to emerge from them would inevitably become vassal states of Russia; its disintegration would have established tsarist rule over Europe. "The only factor that has served as a justification for the existence of Austria as a political entity since the middle of the eighteenth century," Marx wrote in 1860, "has been its resistance to the advance of Russia in Eastern Europe, a resistance conducted in a helpless, inconsistent and cowardly, but obstinate manner."[1] This "helpless, inconsistent and cowardly, but obstinate" resistance was offered by the Imperial Army for the last time in the great winter battle of 1914–15 in the Carpathians. Tsarism's offensive capability was broken at the Dukla Basin near Mezőlaborcz and at the Uzsok Pass. The Russian forces were worn down; in the 1915 spring campaign they were broken. The way was free for the Russian Revolution.

The Russian Revolution revolutionized all peoples of the Habsburg Monarchy. It heartened the Yugoslav movement. It united the Poles, who had previously been wavering between an Austrian and a Russian orientation, against the Central Powers. It gave the Czechs the opportunity to gain recognition by the Western powers as a belligerent power through its independent presence at the Volga and in Siberia. With this it decided the downfall of the Habsburg Monarchy.

In 1888 Friedrich Engels wrote that the "breaking-up of Austria" would have been calamitous "before the imminent triumph of the revolution in Russia (after which it would become superfluous because the now redundant Austria would disintegrate of itself)."[2] This falling apart on its own is something we experienced in October and November 1918 in the formation of national states in the hinterland and in the self-dissolution of the Imperial Army in the Venetian Plain.

The victory of the Russian Revolution spurred on the national revolution of the Czechs, Poles, and Yugoslavs toward the struggle for full state independence, for the complete dissolution of the Habsburg Monarchy. The defeat of the German Empire ensured victory for this revolution. As long as the German Empire stood tall, Austria could not fall apart; German power guaranteed Austria's existence because through the German-Austrians and Magyars, Germany kept the Slav and Latin peoples of the Monarchy under its sway. As long as the German Empire stood, even the Slav peoples could not want the Monarchy to collapse; Czechs and Slovenes had to fear that the German Empire would penetrate up to the Adriatic and incorporate the old German lands* if Austria disintegrated. Only when tremendous superiority broke the strength of the German Army on the Western front could the revolution of the Czechs, South Slavs, and Poles achieve complete victory. Thus, the national revolution of the three Slavic peoples presupposed the victory of the Western powers. Crushing the Habsburg Monarchy was not at all the objective of the Western powers in the first three and a half years of the war. Only after the negotiations with Austria-Hungary over a separate peace in 1917 proved fruitless, only after the dictated peace of the Central Powers at Brest-Litovsk and Bucharest, and after Czernin's attack on Clemenceau on April 2, 1918, had made the resumption of negotiations impossible, only after the Czech Legions "restored the Eastern Front" at a point of vital importance for the Western powers—only then could the revolutionary émigrés win the Western powers over to the goal of the complete dismantling of the Danube Monarchy. Only then did the goal of the bourgeois revolution of the Czechs, Poles, and South Slavs become an objective of the incomparably larger general bourgeois revolution, which the war of the Western powers against the Central Powers had become.

The German-Austrians and the Magyars were not the vehicles of this revolution; they were its victims. When the victory of the Western powers tore the other nations loose from the Habsburg Monarchy, the Germans

---

* The German lands of the German Confederation.

and Magyars lagged behind. The state, in which they had until then occupied the leading position, dissolved itself. The bases of their economic life
were destroyed. Large sections of both peoples were in danger of subjection
to foreign rule. Only then did the revolution spread to German-Austria
and Hungary. The revolution of the German-Austrians and Magyars began only when the complete victory of the Czech, Polish, and Yugoslav
revolutions was imminent and unpreventable. Emerging from the national
revolutions all around them, the revolution of the German-Austrians and
Magyars at first also set national goals. Since the previous forms of their
state life were destroyed by the bourgeois revolution occurring all around
them, both nations at first harkened back to the ideas of their bourgeois
revolution, the Revolution of 1848. The Magyars sought to salvage themselves from the collapse of the Habsburg Monarchy by proclaiming their
independence. The German-Austrians, despairing at the prospect of carrying on an improbable national independent economic life as a mere vestige
of the old great Austria, proclaimed unification with Germany.

But even if the revolutions of the German-Austrians and the Magyars
began as national revolutions, they acquired a completely different social
content than the national revolutions of the Czechs, the Poles, and the
Yugoslavs.

In Czechoslovakia, in Yugoslavia, and in Poland, the bourgeoisie and
proletariat had fought together for national liberation. The jointly achieved
victory for the moment completely subordinated the proletariat to the
bourgeoisie's national idea. In the triumph of national victory during the
months of the revolution, the proletariat found complete satisfaction in
the establishment, development, and reinforcement of the national polity.
It did not push beyond the limits of a bourgeois, national revolution. The
situation was completely different in German-Austria and Hungary. In the
war, the German-Austrian bourgeoisie and the Magyar ruling class had not
fought for national liberation but for the preservation of their domination
of other nations. Here the national revolution that blew up the Habsburg
Monarchy was not the final victory but the final defeat of the national idea
of the bourgeoisie. Here, with the defeat of the Habsburgs and Hohenzollerns, the bourgeoisie was defeated. Its authority had collapsed. With
the disbanding of the Imperial Army, its means of domination were destroyed, and the masses rose up against it. In Vienna and Budapest armed
power fell into the hands of the proletariat. Here the revolution pushed
beyond the national framework to the social, the proletarian revolution.

The immense old Empire and its enormous economic area was not smashed by the social revolution of the German-Austrian and Magyar proletariat but by the national revolution of the Czech, Polish, and Yugoslav bourgeoisies. As long as the Empire was viable, the German-Austrian proletariat did not struggle against its existence but for its restructuring into a federated state of free peoples—the only solution to the problem of the Austro-Hungarian Empire, if indeed there was any solution, that could have permitted its survival. Only when the Slav nations seceded from the Empire, only when the collapse of the Empire had become inevitable and imminent did the proletariat in German-Austria and Hungary rise up. It was not through the proletarian revolution that the Empire was dissolved; rather, it was through the dissolution of the Empire that the proletarian revolution was awakened and unleashed. However, the national and social problems continued to be closely intertwined precisely because the proletarian revolution in German-Austria and Hungary was triggered and unleashed by the victory of the national revolution of the Slav peoples, which demolished the Empire.

German-Austria is not an organically evolved entity. It is only the vestige of the old Empire, which was left after the other nations broke away from it. It remained as a loose cluster of divergent countries whose shared political identity and economic bases of existence were destroyed by the disintegration of the old Empire and the old economic area. In the Empire the German-Austrians had been the politically dominant and economically leading people: Vienna was not only the location of the Empire's bureaucracy but also the center of the banking system and trade in the old Empire; the Germans* had not only supplied the old Empire with its officers and officials but also its managers of industry and its merchants. The dissolution of the old Empire thus was bound to dispossess a large part of the German-Austrian people of their function and with it of the economic bases of their lives. German-Austria had been the industrial region of the enormous, overwhelmingly agrarian economic area of the Habsburg Monarchy; its industry had depended on the sources of raw materials and the markets, on the feeding of its industrial workers, on the agriculture and livestock farming provided by the other countries of the Monarchy. The breakup of the old Empire thus had to convulse German-Austrian industry and dramatically affect the food supply of the industrial masses. At the time of the Revolution, no one believed that this vestige of the old

* That is, German-Austrians.

Monarchy, torn away from its economic body through a violent operation, would be in a condition to lead a viable life independently. At the eleventh hour, the Old-Austrian idea* had tried to salvage the interrelationship of the nations of the Danube Monarchy in a new form; this was the effort made by the Lammasch government. It had to fail after the revolution in Russia and Germany's defeat had raised the stakes of the Slav nations' liberation struggle to become a struggle for full, unrestricted sovereignty. Consequently, German-Austria sought the new form of its state life in the return to the mother nation, in its annexation to Germany. But in so doing it necessarily came into conflict with French imperialism, whose triumph occurred at this very moment. Independence, a Danubian federation, or annexation? This was the question. In what international law context and what kind of constitutional relationship could German-Austria, after the old forms of its existence had been destroyed by the national revolution of the Slav peoples, find new bases for an economic and state life? This was the national problem of the German-Austrian Revolution.

This national problem, however, was closely interconnected with the social problem of the Revolution. After the complete collapse of the political and economic system of domination of the German-Austrian bourgeoisie, the leadership of the German-Austrian people had to fall into the hands of the proletariat. The national revolution had to become a proletarian revolution. But all around us, just as our proletarian revolution began, a bourgeois revolution was overthrowing the dynasties and aristocracies, only to install the bourgeoisie in power. The victory of the Entente was a bourgeois revolution; it broke the supremacy of the Hohenzollerns and the Prussian Junkers in Europe; in its place it put the unrestricted rule of the Western European bourgeoisie over all of Western and Central Europe. The victory of the Czechs, the Poles, and the Yugoslavs was a bourgeois revolution; it broke the power of the Habsburgs, of the German-Austrian bourgeoisie, and of the Magyar gentry; in its place it put the rule of the Czech, Polish, and Yugoslav bourgeoisie organized in the new nation-states whose triumphant national ideal kept the proletariat in its camp. But in the same moment as the Western European bourgeoisie subjugated all of Central Europe and, under its wing, the Slav bourgeoisies established their domination on the territory of the old Habsburg Monarchy, the authority of the bourgeoisie in German-Austria collapsed; at the hour of the greatest international victory of the bourgeoisie, in German-Austria and Hungary

---

* Altösterreichertum.

the proletariat rose up. There the proletarian revolution inevitably came into conflict with the bourgeois revolution all around it. A proletarian revolution in German-Austria and in Hungary in the bosom of the bourgeois revolution occurring all around it—this was the problem. Could the German-Austrian proletariat seize and exercise power when German-Austria itself was completely abandoned to the military and economic power of the victorious Western bourgeoisies and surrounded by the emergent Slav nation-states legitimized by the Western bourgeoisies and thus subservient to them? That was the social problem of the German-Austrian Revolution.

The development of this national and social problem, the struggle to resolve it, is the history of the German-Austrian Revolution, to which we now turn.

PART III

THE HEGEMONY OF THE WORKING CLASS

CHAPTER 9

REVOLUTIONARY AND COUNTERREVOLUTIONARY FORCES

The Habsburgs and Hohenzollerns succumbed to the armies of the Western powers on the battlefield and to the Revolution in the hinterlands. When defeat and revolution swept the dynasties away, the two victors were left to face each other directly: on the one side the imperialism of the Western powers, on the other the Central European Revolution.

As in all bourgeois revolutions, the bourgeoisie, as soon as it has smashed feudalism and absolutism, turns against the proletariat that has risen up in its wake; just as the bourgeoisie, still revolutionary in the face of the old powers, becomes counterrevolutionary against the proletariat the day after its victory, so the triumphant bourgeoisie of the Western powers turned, the day after their victory over the Central European dynasties, against the Central European Revolution unleashed by this victory. Western bourgeois democracy, revolutionary only as long as it confronted the Central Europe of the Habsburgs and Hohenzollerns, became counterrevolutionary as soon as it faced the proletarian revolution.

While still at war with the Habsburgs and Hohenzollerns, the Western powers immediately made war on Bolshevism their most important task. Preventing the proletarian revolution from expanding beyond Russia's borders, not letting the Central European Revolution go beyond the framework of a bourgeois revolution, not letting it push forward beyond the establishment of bourgeois democracies—this became their chief aim the moment military victory brought Central Europe under their sway.

The Armistice of Villa Giusti maintained the Entente's blockade of Austria. After the Armistice, the German-Austrian government had immediately turned to Wilson requesting that he allow the import of foreign food supplies to the starving country. On November 24, Wilson's answer reached us. It promised the supply of provisions but only under one condition: that "peace and order" be maintained. Wilson's October 18 note had unleashed the national revolution. His November 24 note demanded the termination of the social revolution. The Western powers now stepped forward as the guardians of bourgeois order against the proletarian revolution in German-Austria. The self-liquidation of the Imperial Army had unchained the German-Austrian proletariat. The army whose bayonets had held down German-Austria's proletariat and upheld bourgeois order no longer existed. The only remaining organized armed power in the country was no longer in the hands of the bourgeoisie but of the proletariat. The proletariat felt omnipotent against the bourgeoisie. But, at the same time, the self-dissolution of the Imperial Army had left German-Austria completely defenseless against the powers that had become Central Europe's masters through their victories on the battlefields. While the German-Austrian proletariat felt omnipotent in the face of the domestic bourgeoisie, it stood powerless before the bourgeoisie of the Western powers, which now came forward as the protector of bourgeois order in German-Austria.

The greater Austro-Hungarian economic area had been dissolved, and this in a time of the most frightful deprivation. After four years of war and blockade, there was a severe shortage in all the new nation-states of food, clothing, shoes, linens, coal, and raw materials. Each state did everything it its power to obtain what it could. Already in the first days of their existence, they insulated themselves from each other and forbade any export. However, German-Austria was blockaded not only by the Entente but also by the new states. Czech territory sealed us off from German-Bohemia and the Sudetenland; Inner Austria—Vienna and the Alpine provinces—had to fend for itself.

Inner Austria had no coal. Our monthly coal requirement was 1,150,000 tons. But our domestic mines could only supply 155,000 tons of mostly low-quality coal. We had always gotten our coal from the Ostrau-Karwin district,* Upper Silesia, and northwest Bohemia; now the Czech government cut off all supplies. There was dire coal deprivation. Tremendous efforts were

---

* Old-Austrian names of Ostrava and Karviná in the present-day Czech Republic.

necessary to meet even a small part of our coal needs; on December 4, 1918, I reported to the Provisional National Assembly that we had to conduct five diplomatic negotiations with the Czech government to have a single coal train pass through Czech territory. In the end the only thing that guaranteed our coal supply was an inter-Allied Commission that took over the regulation of Silesian coal and coal transport. And this too could not assure us sufficient supplies. Our rail transport had to be severely restricted, with passenger rail travel completely suspended for weeks on end and freight traffic limited to food transports. In Vienna, streetcar service had to be repeatedly interrupted for a total of fourteen days a year because the power plant lacked coal. In smaller localities the gas works also had to be closed down. Factories had constantly to suspend production because power plants could no longer supply them with electrical energy and because coal could not be procured to heat the steam boilers. In Upper Styria all but one blast furnace and three of the region's fourteen Siemens-Martin furnaces were shut off. Household coal could no longer be distributed. The freezing population went into the woods, cut down trees without consideration of property rights, and carried the wood back home. But even this very scanty coal supply could only be maintained with the help of the inter-Allied Commission; if it had refused us all help, then rail traffic and industrial production would have had to be completely stopped. Thus, the coal shortage threw us into the most onerous dependency on the victorious powers.

The state of our food supply was equally dire. The area of Inner Austria had always been fed by Hungarian grain, Bohemian and Galician potatoes, Hungarian cattle, and Bohemian sugar; after four years of war, it was less able than ever to feed itself. Our livestock had been destroyed by the war; the cattle-rich Alpine areas had been the communications and requisition area of the Southern Army. As a result of the lack of manure and labor power, our agricultural production had been much set back. The land area under cultivation had shrunk, fallow land expanded from 65,000 to 295,000 hectares, and between 1913 and 1918 the average yield per hectare fell: for wheat, from 14.7 to 8.7 centners;* for rye, from 14.8 to 8.6; for potatoes, from 93.6 to 50.3; and for hay and second-growth hay, from 37.6 to 22.5. That is, compared to the 1913 figures, the 1918 harvest yielded only 48 percent in wheat, 45 percent in rye, and 39 percent in potatoes. Our domestic production could, in the best of cases, with the lowest rations and the most successful imaginable application, cover a fourth of our flour require-

* A centner equals 50 kilograms.

ments, a fifth of our potato, a third of our meat, a twentieth of our cooking fat, and a fourteenth of our sugar requirements. In the first weeks after the collapse of the Monarchy we lived on the military food-supply stocks and from supplies sent to us by Germany despite its own shortages; and we were still only able to cover our needs for a few weeks.

Our efforts finally succeeded in getting aid from the victors. Herbert Hoover, the American Food Controller, organized a steady food supply to German-Austria. These provisions too were very meager. The rations remained far below the physiological subsistence level. Malnourishment lowered the intensity of labor and kept mortality levels way above peacetime levels. Of 186,000 Viennese school children whose nutritional condition was observed by physicians, 96,000 were classified as very undernourished, 19,000 as somewhat undernourished, and only 6,732 as not undernourished. And even the scanty provisions they relied on rested almost completely on Hoover's supplies. But there were no reserves; what came in today had to be eaten tomorrow. Had Hoover suspended his food trains for only a few days, we would have had no more bread, no more cooking flour. Thus, we were very much in Hoover's hands. And along with economic hardship our military powerlessness delivered us entirely into the hands of the Entente. The Armistice Convention gave the Allied Powers the right to occupy our cities and rail lines. Tyrol and a part of Carinthia were occupied by Italian troops. An inter-Allied Armistice Commission headed by the Italian general Roberto Segre resided in Vienna. German-Austria's bourgeoisie, trembling at the advance of the proletariat, pleaded with General Segre to occupy Vienna with Italian troops; fear of the working class had blotted out their hatred of the "arch enemy." In the first months after the Armistice, hardly a week went by in which General Segre did not issue us an ultimatum; either with the suspension of coal and food supplies, or threatening an Italian troop invasion, he extorted the handing over of military equipment, railroad material, paintings, or monetary payments as atonement for an insult to an Italian courier in a Styrian railway station or to a Czech legionnaire in Italian uniform in a Tyrolean railway station. We were thus continually threatened with occupation by foreign troops; we knew that this would have meant the defeat of the proletariat by foreign bayonets.

The situation became even more dangerous when we came into conflict with Czechoslovakia and Yugoslavia. In the north, as soon as the Czech Legions that had fought together with the Italian army were brought to

Bohemia and launched attacks on the Sudetenland and German-Bohemia, and in the south when the battles between the Carinthian militias and Slovene troops began, the danger of a military confrontation with our neighboring countries became very serious. The Armistice had severely restricted the number of soldiers we were allowed to have under our flag. If the Czechs were to march on Vienna, we would have no time to organize a general draft call—Vienna is a day's march from the Czech border. Moreover, we knew that we ought not to overestimate the combat capacity of our Volkswehr. Although the authority of the imperial officer corps had been broken, we had still not been able to train a republican, not to mention proletarian, officer corps. If it were the wish of the Entente to let the Czechs attack Vienna, our capital, then the decisive position of power of the German-Austrian working class would be seriously jeopardized.

Entente imperialism opposed the proletarian revolution in German-Austria. And the Entente could shut off our coal and food supplies and consign us to a famine catastrophe: it could have our country occupied by its troops or abandon us to the attack of the neighboring countries. The power of the victors thus imposed firm restraints on the proletarian revolution in German-Austria. This objective situation of the proletarian revolution contrasted sharply with the subjective illusions that the Revolution had called forth among broad strata of the proletariat.

The war had fundamentally altered the structure and frame of mind of the proletariat. It had torn the workers out of the factory and workshop. They had experienced untold suffering in the trenches, which filled their souls with hatred for the draft dodgers and war profiteers in the hinterland who made money from misery, while they looked death in the eye hour after hour, and against the generals and officers who feasted lavishly while they starved. In the trenches they read newspapers that promised grateful welfare from the Fatherland to the heroes who defended it. In the trenches they heard the accounts of those who had returned home, who had experienced, as prisoners of war in Russia, the first phase of the Bolshevik Revolution, the phase of the Civil War, the bloody terror against officers, capitalists, and peasants, and the phase of expropriations, requisitions, and nationalization. Their years in the trenches made them unaccustomed to productive labor and used to forced requisitions, robbery, and theft, and filled them with a belief in violence. Now came the Revolution and homecoming. But back home hunger, cold, and unemployment awaited them. The four long years of pent-up hatred and resentment had to find an outlet.

Now they demanded revenge against all those who had mistreated them for four years. Now they called for a revolution that would expel the Emperor and overthrow all the mighty, the rich, those who were responsible. Now they wanted to see it, this promised thanks of the Fatherland to its heroes. And since the only answer they got was deprivation and misery, they now believed that a couple thousand resolute men with guns and cartridges had to be in a position to put an end, in one blow, to the heinous social order that had brought them war, want, and misery.

For four long years in the war industry factories, it had been the military factory managers who had given commands. Labor discipline there had been founded on military force, but with the collapse of military power this discipline disintegrated. Industry was in a chaotic state. Military order suddenly vanished; conversion to peacetime production faced the obstacle of lack of coal and raw materials, the collapse of labor discipline, the disinclination to work of a working class that had been depleted by hunger, exhausted by overwork in wartime, and shaken to its core by the experience of revolution. The factories turned into discussion halls. Industry could not absorb the masses returning from the front and streaming back from the production sites of the munitions industry. The mass of unemployed swelled from month to month, reaching its highest level in May 1919: 186,030 unemployed were registered, 131,500 in Vienna alone.

In the Volkswehr barracks there was wild ferment. The Volkswehr felt it was the bearer of the Revolution, the vanguard of the proletariat. Within the soldiers' councils, Social Democrats and Communists fought out their harshest battles. The militiamen were filled with the hope that they would decide the victory of the proletariat as soon as they had weapons in hand. And among the wildly excited returnees, the desperate unemployed, one could find militiamen filled with the romance of the Revolution as well as war invalids who sought personal revenge against the social order responsible for their fate; there were also pathologically incensed women whose husbands had languished for years in war captivity, intellectuals and literati of all kinds who suddenly coming upon socialism were filled with the utopian radicalism of the neophyte, and Bolshevik agitators who had been sent home from Russia. Every newspaper had news of Spartacus's struggles in Germany. Every speech proclaimed the glories of the Great Russian Revolution, which in a single stroke had abolished all exploitation forever. The masses who had just witnessed the fall of the once so mighty Empire had no sense of the strength of Entente capitalism; they believed that in a flash the Revolution would now also take hold in the victorious countries. "Dictatorship of the proletariat!" "All power to the soviets!" Here at home these cries echoed in the streets as well.

The workers councils had already emerged during the January strike in German-Austria. The young institution was quickly spread by the Revolution. In them the reinforced consciousness of power, the now awakened desire of the unleashed masses to act, sought and found its first sphere of action. Economic deprivation gave this thirst for action the direction, and the organization of the wartime economy gave it rich possibilities, for having an impact. The workers' councils took over the activity of the now intimidated district authorities. Together with the soldiers' councils and the incipient farmers' councils they established municipal, district, and agricultural commissions. They controlled the procurement of the harvests and livestock and the requisition and assignment of dwellings. They organized the capture of black marketers. They sought to terrorize profiteers. They impeded the export of food from their area to other districts and provinces. As a rule they cooperated with the legal authorities; formally the authorities availed themselves of the workers' councils and their control organs; in reality the authorities submitted to the dictates of the councils. At times, however, the councils proceeded independently without the authorities or against them. It happened that they independently ordered requisitions and, with the support of the Volkswehr, saw to it that people who had violated the wartime economic regulations were subpoenaed and threatened by the terror of the proletariat.

In the initial months the whole movement was elementary and unorganized; there was still no connection between the workers' councils of individual districts. It achieved its greatest extension in Upper Austria; there the workers' councils became chiefly an organ for sealing off the region, for the defense of its comparatively rich cereals and livestock production against the Viennese black-marketeering that beset the area.

It was in this activity of the workers' councils that their original ideology grew. The idea was that since the councils had extended their administrative operations, which they claimed for themselves as the right of revolution, they would—to the extent that the practical need of the proletariat required and its power allowed—gradually in part subordinate, deactivate, or demolish the authorities, and would finally wrest all power for themselves. Therefore, the councils cannot be "anchored in the Constitution"; any legal delimitation of their rights would, so the argument

went, only fix the momentary power relations between the council organization and the official administrative apparatus and thus erect obstacles
to the further revolutionary expansion of council power in relation to the
official apparatus. This ideology of the council movement gained influence far beyond the ranks of the industrial working class; in the spring
of 1919 public servants, private employees, and intellectuals took massive
part in the council elections. The Social Democratic literature of the time
too was under the influence of this movement. Alexander Täubler, who
had experienced the development of the soviets in the first phase of the
Russian Revolution, formulated the theory of the autonomous expansion
of the revolutionary administrative activity of the councils. In a similar
way, Max Adler celebrated the councils as the organ of the "revolution in
permanence."

It was not only the urban and industrial proletariat that was revolutionized by the war. A powerful movement also swept through the agricultural masses, for farmers too had returned from the trenches full of hatred
for war and militarism, for the bureaucracy and plutocracy. They cheered
on the new freedom, the Republic, the overthrow of militarism. They were
happy that farmer representatives now governed in the regional parliaments where k.k. governors had previously ruled. Just like the worker, the
farmer also expected from the political revolution a revolution in the relations of property. Since the 1870s feudal lords and capitalists had carried
out peasant clearance, gathering together farmlands to create large hunting
reserves; the lord's stags now grazed where the farmers' cattle had once
pastured. The time had come, the farmers felt, to give back the stolen farm-
land to the progeny of *Jakob der Letzte*.* In wartime the profiteers had used
their new wealth to buy up large estates; now, it was thought, the moment
had come to distribute to the farmers the property acquired from the blood
of the people. The forest and pasturage easements, which in 1853 after the
victory of the counterrevolution were regulated according to the needs of
the feudal lords, now had to be abrogated; now the farmers' communal
woods were extended at the expense of the lords' woods. Hunting rights,
which under pressure of the Viennese Court had only been managed according to the needs of the lords of the hunt, now had to be accommodated to the needs of the farmers. The movement that swept through the
peasantry at that time was truly democratic. But peasant and proletarian

---

* *Jakob der Letzte* (Jacob the Last) is a novel by Peter Rosegger, which depicts the pushing
out of farmers from the Alpine regions.

democracy are not identical. In the minds of the farmers the new freedom that they, like the workers, wanted to use immediately acquired a content directly opposed to the needs of the proletariat.

The monstrous military requisitioning apparatus of the wartime economy had borne down on the peasantry with terrible violence. It had destroyed the most valuable possession of Alpine farmers: their livestock. The stronger the passive resistance of the Empire's Slavs to the state's requisitioning service, the more the German Alpine regions had to provide for the army's needs. The quantity of hay that the individual areas had to provide was stipulated according to the size of the cultivated area; the meadows in the highlands, mown once a year, thus had to deliver just as much as the meadows in the lowlands, mown three times a year. In one harvest year, hay was requisitioned three times in succession; a farmer was never sure how much hay would remain to him or how much livestock he would be able to keep through the winter. The requisitioned hay often remained lying on the meadows; finally, in late autumn, the military administration released it to the farmers after it had been lying on the moist ground and had rotted. The farmers had no hay; but their animals were reserved for state requisitioning and they could not slaughter them or sell them at their own discretion. In the spring months of the last war years, farmers fed their animals with fir twigs. Then the requisition bodies came and randomly dragged the animals out of the stalls. First class dairy cows were taken away as slaughter cattle. The farmers saw that they were at the mercy of corrupt procurement commissioners and their whims. And they saw that the military administration unnecessarily let the cattle that it had taken from them go to ruin. For days on end whole trains with full cattle cars stood in railway stations without the animals being fed or watered. Hatred for this requisition system had revolutionized the farmers. Being compelled to dissipate the products of their labor far below the free market price seemed to them to be a new *robot** that the new revolution had to quash. The freedom that farmers expected from the Revolution that had exterminated militarism was above all freedom from the war economy.

But the Revolution had to disappoint that expectation; at a time of tremendous food scarcity, it could not do without a centralized requisitioning and rationing system. Blockaded as we were by all neighboring states, the supply of our cities and industrial zones, above all Vienna, could not have been ensured without state control of the economy. Farmers saw that

---

* The Slavic term for *corvée*.

the Revolution refused them what they thought of as "freedom." They saw that instead of the military requisition commands, it was now the workers' councils that enforced procurement, prosecuted illegal traffic, and fought against violations of government price controls. Farmers sometimes saw that, like the former k.k. troops, Volkswehr units were stationed in their village until they delivered the required grain, cattle, and wood. In the proletariat, farmers saw their enemy who denied them free disposal of the products of their labor. Farmers now began to hate the proletariat in the way they had formerly hated militarism.

Other phenomena further intensified the peasantry's hatred for the proletariat. The Revolution had also aroused agricultural workers. They began to organize. They presented wage demands and occasionally won them through strikes. Occasionally farmers were compelled to conclude formal collective contracts with their farm hands and maidservants, which stipulated exactly what wages the "senior servant" and the "junior servant" were to receive. Farmers saw that the proletariat's movement began to encroach on their own home and threaten their own authority.

The anti-proletarian mood of the peasantry was fostered by the town bourgeoisie of the Alpine regions and by the clergy. The town tradesmen were the natural allies of the farmer against the centralized economic control system. In the mass of farmers the town bourgeoisie saw their base of support against the proletariat. The clergy encouraged and organized the farmers' movement as the most powerful counterforce opposing the proletarian revolution. Newspapers and sermons told the farmers that their grain, livestock, and wood were being requisitioned so that hundreds of thousands of unemployed in Vienna could live in leisure, fed by the state; that the war economy that had oppressed the farmers was being maintained by an alliance of Jewish war profiteers in the central offices with Jewish labor leaders in the government; that the Revolution wanted to socialize their property and destroy their churches.

The farmers resisted. They sabotaged the requisitions. At times they confronted the requisitioning organs with violent resistance; farmers' councils were established, and they conducted a fierce struggle within the district and agricultural commissions against the workers' councils. If the workers' councils tried to terrorize the district commissioners, the farmers' councils did the same; workers' and farmers' councils were now struggling for power over the administrative apparatus. And the farmers were aware of their strength. They had enough food in their cupboards, and they could shut off supply to the city. It was not the farmers but the workers who would starve in the event of a civil war. And they had no lack of weapons. When the army dissolved, the retreating soldiers sold their weapons to the farmers in the Tyrol, in Carinthia, and Styria, or left them behind as booty for the farmers; large stocks of weapons were in the hands of the peasantry. In Carinthia and Styria, to deal with incursions by the Yugoslavs, farmers had formed militarily organized homeland defense units. Originally organized against the external enemy, they soon appeared as armed class organizations of the peasantry against the native working class.

The antagonism of the peasantry to the working class was closely connected with the antagonism of the provinces to Vienna. Before the collapse of the Empire, the provisioning of Vienna depended mainly on supplies from the Sudeten lands, Galicia, and Hungary; cut off now from these regions, Vienna had to demand much more food, firewood, and raw materials from Inner Austrian provinces than it formerly had. And this precisely at a time in which production was at a standstill due to the lack of coal and raw materials; at a time when Vienna was unable to give anything in return to the provinces to whose agricultural products it laid claim. Vienna then necessarily appeared to the provinces as a parasite feeding on their body without working. The provinces, which themselves lacked most necessary items, put up a defense against Vienna's claims.

The working class itself broke the first ground.[1] The local workers' councils impeded the export of food from the individual provinces; their control organs undertook the surveillance of the rail lines. The peasantry supported this cordon policy of the workers' councils. In its eyes the hated war economy, which the Republic retained, appeared to be a requisitioning apparatus aimed at plundering the provinces to Vienna's benefit. Above all, for them the separation from Vienna meant liberation from the war economy. If the peasantry could not immediately smash the war economy, it at least wanted to reduce delivery to the level required by the feeding of the cities of their own provinces; they fed the cities of their own regions but did not want to feed Vienna. As fierce as the struggles between the workers' and peasants' councils around delivery were, they agreed that what was to be delivered should not be exported beyond the borders of the provinces. The struggle between the working class and the peasantry around the continuation of the war economy first led to the provincial fragmentation of the war economy. The provinces cordoned themselves off against one another and against Vienna. The dissolution of the large Austro-Hungarian economic area into national economic areas was followed by the dissolution of the German-Austrian economic area into the midget economic areas of the provinces.

The new autonomous provincial governments that had arisen from the Revolution were the centers of this economic particularism. Since the central state government had to defend itself against the economic separation of the provinces, it came into sharp conflict with them. They refused to obey its instructions and threatened secession from Vienna. The bourgeoisie encouraged the insurrection of the provinces against the state. In the provinces with little industry, it found in the large peasant-bourgeois majority a solid bulwark against the state government dominated by the Viennese proletariat. If the spontaneous action of the workers' councils had themselves cemented the economic particularism of the provinces, it was now precisely provincial particularism behind which the bourgeoisie, leaning on the peasantry, entrenched itself against the power of the proletarian revolution concentrated in Vienna.

German-Austria is divided into two regions of nearly equal population: On the one side, there is the large industrial district comprising Vienna and a quarter of the Vienna Woods and Upper Styria; on the other side, the large agricultural area made up of all the other provinces. In the great industrial district all real power was in the hands of the proletariat. In the large agricultural areas, sprinkled with very few populous towns and industrial districts, the proletariat was certainly not powerless, but the peasantry constituted the strongest force and could not be crushed. It was impossible to govern the large industrial district against the working class and just as impossible to govern the large agricultural areas against the peasantry. The country's economic structure thus produced a state of equilibrium between the class forces that could only have been resolved by the violence of a bloody civil war. And it was for such a civil war that broad masses of the proletariat pressed. The proletarians in Vienna, in Wiener Neustadt, and in Donawitz only saw their enormously powerful position in the industrial district. They did not see the unshakable power of the peasantry in the agricultural areas. Still less did they see the menacing power of Entente imperialism beyond the country's borders. And so they believed it was possible to establish the dictatorship of the proletariat.

But the attempt to set up a council dictatorship would simply have meant the self-destruction of the Revolution. In the large industrial district, the proletariat could have established its dictatorship without insurmountable resistance. But in the large agricultural part of the country, the attempt would have failed. There the peasantry was strong enough to hold down the proletariat. The provinces would have responded to the proclamation of dictatorship by seceding from Vienna, by their secession from the state. They would have blockaded our transport routes and supplies. They would have put down the proletariat that would rise up against them in the provinces. The struggle against the counterrevolution of the agricultural provinces would have made a bloody civil war inevitable. But civil war would have brought the Entente onto the scene, which would not have tolerated the ensuing interruption of transportation in the country, representing their transport routes from the Adriatic to Czechoslovakia and Poland. The Entente was determined not to permit the development of the Revolution beyond the limits of democracy.[2] If the "law and order" it demanded were to be disturbed, it would have stopped the food and coal trains and immediately thrown the entire industrial district into a famine catastrophe; it would have given the Czechs and Yugoslavs permission to march toward us; it would have let the most important railway hubs and cities be occupied by Italian troops and thus put an end to the Revolution. The dictatorship of the proletariat would have ended with the dictatorship of foreign occupying troops.

Broad masses of the proletariat did not see this danger. But it was Social Democracy's duty to see it. And so Social Democracy was confronted with a twofold task: On the one hand, to take advantage of the huge revolutionary ferment in the proletariat and the profound shock to the whole capitalist social order in order to capture for the proletariat the strongest and most lasting possible positions of power in the state and the municipalities, in the factories, the barracks, and the schools; and, on the other hand, to prevent this revolutionary ferment from developing into open civil war and open collision with the supremacy of Entente imperialism, thereby ushering in famine, invasion, and counterrevolution.

If the power struggle of the classes was not to be conducted with weapons, then it had to be conducted and decided through the forms of democracy. Consequently, our first task was to organize the election of the Constituent National Assembly. Elections were held on February 16, 1919. They could, in fact, only be held in Inner Austria; the German areas of the Sudetenland were already occupied by the Czechs. The Social Democrats received 1,211,814 votes, the Christian Socials 1,068,382, and the German-National parties 545,938. Of the 159 seats, 69 went to the Social

Democrats, 63 to the Christian Socials, and 24 to the German-National parties, which from then on called themselves the Pan-Germans. The German-Nationals, still the strongest party in the Provisional National Assembly, became the weakest in the Constituent National Assembly. The Social Democrats, in the Provisional National Assembly still the weakest of the three large parties, became the strongest in the Constituent National Assembly. True, we did not have an absolute majority in the newly elected parliament. We could have acquired it if highly industrialized German-Bohemia would have been able to vote with us; but the Czech occupation of German-Bohemia made it possible for the bourgeoisie and peasantry to capture a majority in the German-Austrian National Assembly. However, if we did not have a majority, we were still the strongest party, and leadership of the new parliament fell to us.

The elections were first of all a referendum on monarchy versus republic. Their result was unequivocal. In its first act, the newly elected National Assembly solemnly repeated the resolutions of November 12: the proclamation of German-Austria as a democratic republic and annexation to Germany. On November 11, Karl Habsburg had promised to submit to the decision of the German-Austrian people on their constitution. The people had now made their decision. Renner told Habsburg that he could remain in German-Austria only if he kept his promise to relinquish his and his family's claim to the throne. Karl refused the required abdication and on March 23 travelled to Switzerland under English protection. The National Assembly responded to this decision of Habsburg with the April 2, 1919 law that expelled all Habsburgs from the country and confiscated their family property to benefit war invalids.

On November 12, 1918, the National Assembly went about erecting the Republic. In November the Provisional National Assembly had itself taken power; its executive organ, the Staatsrat, composed of all parties, was the actual government, the state secretaries were merely its agents. The November 12 Basic Law,[3] which had provided for the governing Staatsrat to result from proportional elections in the Parliament, had been accommodated to the needs of the period of state construction, which required the cooperation of all parties, the collaboration of "bourgeois, peasants, and workers." But it was no longer appropriate for a time in which class antagonisms—on the foundation of the already constituted state—developed further and the Parliament had to divide into governing majority and opposition. Therefore the Staatsrat was abolished through the March 14 Law on the Governance of the State.[4] Some of its powers were transferred to the President of the National Assembly who thus at the same time took over the function of a President of the Republic; Karl Seitz was elected as the first President. The actual government power, however, passed to the state government, which was now directly elected by the Parliament. With this the period of cooperation between all parties ended. From now on the task was to form a majority within the Parliament, which would elect and support the government.

During this time the government continually faced passionate demonstrations by returnees, the unemployed, and war invalids. It faced the Volkswehr, which was filled with the spirit of proletarian revolution. It daily faced serious and dangerous conflicts in the factories and the railways. And the government had no coercive instruments at its disposal: armed force was no instrument to use against the proletarian masses filled with revolutionary passions. Only through daily appeals to the intelligence, the knowledge, and the sense of responsibility of starving, freezing masses stirred up by war and revolution could the government prevent the revolutionary movement from turning into a civil war that would destroy the Revolution. No bourgeois government could have managed this task. It would have been defenseless in the face of the mistrust and hatred of the proletarian masses. After eight days they would have been overthrown by street riots and arrested by their own soldiers. Only Social Democrats could accomplish this task of unparalleled difficulty. They were the only force trusted by the proletarian masses. Only they could convince the masses that the appalling misery of this first winter after the war was not the fault of the government but the inevitable effect of a world-historical upheaval, which could not be broken through violent overthrow but could only be overcome gradually. Only the Social Democrats could peacefully end wildly excited demonstrations by negotiations and appeals, only the Social Democrats could communicate with the unemployed, lead the Volkswehr, and keep the working masses from temptation by revolutionary adventures, which would have been fatal for the Revolution. This function—which at that time was the government's most important function—could only be fulfilled by the Social Democrats. The profound shock to the bourgeois social order was most strikingly expressed in the fact that a bourgeois government without Social Democrats had simply become impossible.

But as impossible as a bourgeois government was, so too was a purely Social Democratic government. Just as a purely bourgeois government would have been impossible for the great industrial district of Vienna, Wiener Neustadt, and Upper Styria, so would a purely Social Democratic government be unsustainable for the agricultural areas of the provinces. A purely Social Democratic government would have lost any influence on the provincial governments; it could not have prevented the secession of the provinces; it would have been powerless in the face of the open rebellion of the peasantry. Without a majority in the Parliament, it would have had to resort to dictatorial measures and necessarily unleash a civil war in which the Revolution would have been destroyed. No government was possible without or against the workers' representatives. No government was possible without or against the peasants' representatives. A common government of workers and peasants was the only possible solution. Workers and peasants had to communicate within the government; they had to try and govern together if they were not soon to end up facing one another in open civil war.

In the countryside, the Christian Socials were the mass party of the farmers. The farmer representatives, who made up the overwhelming majority of the Christian Social deputies, were under the pressure of the powerful movement that swept through the peasantry. The two-sided character of this movement determined the politics of the Christian Social peasant representatives. They could have called on the peasantry to wage civil war against a dictatorship of the proletariat; but on the basis of a radical, republican, anti-militarist, and anti-plutocratic democracy they wished to cooperate with the proletariat. A completely different mood dominated the Christian Social deputies of the urban (above all the Viennese) bourgeoisie. To the bourgeoisie the Revolution meant nothing other than the collapse of its domination over its districts and in its factories, its subjugation under the powerful force of the working class. Therefore its mood was openly counterrevolutionary, and it was completely under the influence of Monarchist circles: the high clergy, the clerical nobility, and the counterrevolutionary officers. While the Christian Social peasant representatives, in common with the Social Democrats, demanded prosecution of the war crimes of the generals and officers, the urban Christian Socials emerged as the guardians and defenders of the officers. In the consultation over the laws regarding the expulsion of the Habsburgs, the confiscation of their property, and the abolition of aristocratic titles, rural and urban Christian Socials openly opposed one another. The church's power apparatus could prevent a split of the Christian Social Party, which for a while seemed possible; but the fissure through it still ran deep enough that we, leaving its urban wing aside, could communicate with its peasant wing. The cooperation of workers and peasants found its parliamentary expression in the coalition of the Social Democrats with the Christian Social Party dominated by its peasant majority.

However, the forces were by no means equal within this coalition. The powerful revolutionary movement in the proletarian masses put the peasantry on the defensive; in the proletarian–peasant coalition, the party of the proletariat was by far the strongest partner. This relation of forces within the coalition was reflected in the composition of the coalition government elected on March 15, 1919. All state offices that had to perform the principal governance functions fell to the Social Democrats: Renner took over the Chancellorship and the Ministry of the Interior, Deutsch the Armed Forces, and I became Foreign Secretary. Beyond these we secured for ourselves the ministries where the social revolution first needed to be active: Hanusch took over the Ministry for Social Welfare, Glöckel the Ministry of Education, and I the direction of the newly founded Socialization Commission. Among the Christian Socials the Vorarlberg farmer Fink became Vice Chancellor in the government, the Lower Austrian peasant leader Stöckler took over the Ministry of Agriculture, Zerdik Commerce, and Miklas Culture. This division of ministries expressed the dominant position that fell to Social Democracy. With the formation of the first coalition government, the working class did not govern alone but it had conquered hegemony in the Republic.

CHAPTER 10

BETWEEN IMPERIALISM
AND BOLSHEVISM

The World War had arisen from the national struggles in the Habsburg Monarchy, and it threatened to become a war between its nations. During the war, Habsburg soldiers had already confronted one another with weapons in hand. In the Urals and in Siberia they had fought against each other: the Germans* and Magyars under a red flag and the Czechs and Yugoslavs under a white flag. When in October 1918 the shackles that had tied the ten nations to one another under Habsburg rule were broken, the greatest of all dangers was that the liberated nations would contend for pieces of the Habsburg Monarchy through a bloody war among themselves.

The old hatred of the Slav nations for Vienna, the seat and center of foreign domination, was now turned against the young Republic. The German-Austrian proletariat innocently inherited the legacy of hatred from the neighboring peoples, a burden that passed to the German-Austrian people from the guilt of the German-Austrian bourgeoisie. Not only in the fall of 1918 but throughout the whole first half of 1919, we were continually threatened with military entanglements with the Czechs and South Slavs. Each such conflict would have meant economic death for the young Republic, military collapse, and the loss of our independence. Economic death because war would have blocked our coal and food provisions; military collapse because our war-weary people, who had become timid as a result of defeat and suffering, would confront neighboring peoples in a the

---

* That is, Germans and German-Austrians.

rush of their historic triumphs and in a belligerent mood; it would have set our weak Volkswehren against the Czech Legions now welded together in the Italian theater of war, and against the Serb Army, which was experienced in combat; and loss of our independence because war would have led to the occupation of our country by foreign armies. Keeping the peace with the neighboring peoples was our most important task, because only peace guaranteed us our small bread rations. Only peace would let us assert our young freedom.

The old Empire had disintegrated. But its administrative apparatus outlived it. In Vienna there were central authorities and institutions that still had to wind up business involving the economic, legal, and military interests of all successor states. If we were to avoid conflict with the successor states, we had to create an apparatus that could enable the smoothest possible conclusion of these still common operations. This was achieved through great effort and sacrifice. To begin with, it was possible to bring together all the successor states' envoys to Vienna in an ambassadors' conference that met weekly in the Foreign Ministry, assuming management of the conclusion of still common matters. It appointed an International Liquidation Commission and international councils of plenipotentiaries for the specific "ministries to be liquidated." It was a laborious and costly mechanism. And it was a great sacrifice for us that until the Treaty of Saint-Germain,* we had to tolerate on our soil—alongside our government ministries—still other "liquidating ministries" that were under the control of the successor states. But it was only this mechanism that enabled the old common administration to be wound down without dangerous conflicts with the successor states and gradually to transfer its operations to the administration of the national states.

Incomparably more serious conflicts emerged from the disputes over the borders of the new states. We claimed all areas with a German majority population. We demanded that these areas remain under our administration until the Peace Treaty decided their state affiliation. We demanded that this decision on all disputed areas occur through free referendums under neutral control. The Czechs and Yugoslavs rejected our demands. Before the conclusion of the peace treaty, they tried forcibly to gain possession of the areas claimed.

First, the Czechs proceeded to attack German-Bohemia and the Sudetenland. These two areas were geographically completely separated from

---

* The treaty between the Entente powers and German-Austria.

us. We could not send them weapons. We could not organize their food supply. It was not with German-Austrian support but only with the help of the German Reich that German-Bohemia and the Sudetenland could have defended themselves. But the German Reich, itself in dire straits, did not dare to intervene with weapons and food consignments outside the Reich's borders. Thus, German-Bohemia and the Sudetenland had to fend for themselves. The Czechs began by blocking their food supply. Sealed off from the agricultural area of Central Bohemia and Moravia, they suffered severe hardship. Famine crippled the masses' capacity to resist. And when, as in Aussig,* famine led to looting, the German bourgeoisie itself called for Czech occupation. And so Czech troops occupied German-Bohemia and the Sudetenland in the period from November 28 to December 16 without encountering resistance. On December 11, the German-Bohemian regional government fled to Dresden; the Sudeten regional government resigned on December 19. But if German-Bohemia and the Sudetenland could not defy Czech occupation arms in hand, they put up a strong moral resistance to Czech foreign domination. This resistance reached its high point in March 1919. Czechoslovakia overprinted its kronen; this was abhorrent to the German areas and seen as the economic annexation that followed military occupation. At the same moment in Vienna the Constituent National Assembly met on March 4; German-Bohemia and the Sudetenland protested that Czech occupation had denied them participation in the election of the National Assembly. On March 4, work stopped in the occupied areas; by means of a general strike and large mass rallies, the workers of German-Bohemia and the Sudetenland demonstrated for affiliation to German-Austria. Czech troops scattered the demonstrating masses; twenty-five Germans in Kaaden and sixteen in Sternberg paid for the rally with their lives.†

After the occupation of German-Bohemia and the Sudetenland, the Czechs advanced on the Böhmerwaldgau and the Znaimer Kreis districts, which bordered on Upper and Lower Austria, and here we had to face the question of whether we should carry out armed resistance. The Czechs pointed to the Armistice Convention, which gave the Entente powers the right to occupy all points in Austria designated as strategically important;

---

* Now Ústí nad Labem in the Czech Republic.
† Kaaden is the Old-Austrian name of Kadaň in Northern Bohemia (now in the Czech Republic); Sternberg is the Old-Austrian name of Šternberk in the Olomouc region of Moravia (now in the Czech Republic).

on this basis they determined that as an Entente power, they should occupy both districts. And they indeed got the support of the Entente for this course of action. When they came upon Viennese Volkswehr companies near Znaim and Nikolsburg,* French officers went ahead of the Czech troops as a sign that Czech occupation was occurring in the name of the Entente on the basis of the Amistice of Villa Giusti. If this already complicated any resistance, then our economic dependency on Czech coal deliveries made it truly impossible. Our Volkswehr formations therefore received orders to retreat in the event that Czech troops pushed forward under the leadership of Entente officers. In this way the Czechs were able to occupy the German border districts of Southern Bohemia and Southern Moravia.

Despite our retreat, the occupation of the German areas of the Sudetenland drew us into a series of acute conflicts with Czechoslovakia. Twice, at the beginning of December and the beginning of March, these conflicts escalated dangerously; there were moments in which we had reason to fear the outbreak of war. Thanks to the trusting personal relations between Tusar, the Czech ambassador to Vienna, and myself based on longtime party connections, and thanks to the support of the English and American representatives in Vienna, we were able to avert this danger.

The struggle around the southern borders developed in complete contrast to the situation in the north. In the north we faced the power of the Czechoslovak state, which had very rapidly consolidated itself, was militarily superior to us from the start, and on whom we were economically dependent from the outset. In the south the formation of the state was far more difficult. The Yugoslav state founded on October 29, 1918 at first comprised only the Southern Slav areas of Austro-Hungary; its founders first wanted to negotiate the union with Serbia as one power to another. But from the day of its founding, the Yugoslav state was in dire straits. Immediately after the collapse of the Austro-Hungarian army, Italian troops penetrated deep into the Southern Slav area. Italy did not recognize the handing over of the Austro-Hungarian fleet to Yugoslavia and demanded its handover to Italy on grounds of the Armistice Convention. The mobilization ordered on November 2 by the Narodno Vijeće failed; the war-weary farmers did not enlist. The central government of the Narodno Vijeće could not prevail against the regional governments—the governments of the Ban in Agram, the Narodni Svet in Laibach, and the Narodno Vijeće in Sarajevo. The Narodno Vijeće thus had no choice but to throw itself into the arms of Ser-

---

* The Old-Austrian name of Mikulov in Southern Moravia in the present-day Czech Republic.

bia. On November 24, it decided on union of the Yugoslav state with Serbia, which was proclaimed on December 1 in Belgrade. But many months passed before the central government in Belgrade really subordinated the local administration of the individual South Slav countries and could integrate their independent troops with the army of the Kingdom. In the first months after the Revolution, we were faced in the south not yet with the state power of Belgrade but still with the Slovene provincial government in Ljubljana, whose independent actions were regarded all the more warily and all the more weakly supported by the Belgrade regime the more the power of the South Slav Kingdom was tied down by its serious conflict with Italy. Slovenia was an incomparably weaker opponent than Czechoslovakia, and we were much less economically dependent on it. Thus in the south we could put up much greater resistance than in the north. However, here too the capacity for resistance was severely limited: to the extent that the new state configuration was consolidated in the south in the course of 1919, we had to assume that in the case of a serious crisis it would be not merely the weak forces of Slovenia that would confront us but also the far stronger forces of Greater Serbia.

In the days of the overthrow of the Monarchy, the Slovene general Majstr occupied not only the Slovene area of Lower Styria but also the German border towns of Marburg and Radkersburg.* At the same time he sent weak fighting forces into Carinthia. But here he very quickly met with resistance.

The Carinthian Wends,† separated from Carniola by the wall of the Karawanks and lacking their own urban center, had very little part in the national movement of the Slovenes. Among this small peasant people the sense of Carinthia as home was stronger than a Slovene national sense. The zigzags of the linguistic border in Carinthia make a neat distinction between the two nations impossible; the Wend farmers could not pass to Slovenia without German town settlements passing to foreign Slovene rule. Carinthian patriotism rebelled against such a mutilation of the country.

---

* Marburg is the Old-Austrian name for Maribor in present-day Slovenia. Radkersburg is Bad Radkersburg in present-day Austria; its Slovenian name is Radgona.

† *Wend, Wendenland, windisch:* Terms originally referring to Sorbs and Sorb lands but that became customary in the Austrian Empire to refer to Slavs and Slav lands, and almost exclusively to Slovenes and Slovene areas. *Windische Mark* indicates *slovenska krajina* (Windic March or Slovene March), which more or less corresponds to Dolenjska or Lower Carniola in present-day Slovenia.

When the Slovenes crossed the Drava and occupied Völkermarkt,* when it became clear that they were advancing on Klagenfurt, the Carinthians prepared for battle. On November 28, 1918, the regional soldiers' council declared that the Volkswehr was ready to join battle against the Slovene encroachments. On December 5, the regional assembly passed the resolution: "Entente troops are to be allowed to pass through unimpeded; South Slav troops are to be resisted." When on December 14 a South Slav half-battalion occupied Grafenstein fifteen kilometers east of Klagenfurt, the Volkswehr attacked the half battalion and took it prisoner. A few days later the population of the Lavant Valley rose up and captured a large part of the weak Slovene troops. At this point the regional commander Colonel Ludwig Hülgerth decided on a more extensive attack, which began on January 5. The Volkswehr, reinforced by volunteer formations, advanced in four groups: the Gailtal Group captured the Slovene occupation troops in Arnoldstein and advanced on Fürnitz; the Villach Volkswehr Battalion advanced just beyond the Faakersee; the Velen Group took the bridge at Rosegg and joined the Villach Volkswehr in Rosenbach; and the Klagenfurt Volkswehr battalions and volunteer formations were able to take the Hollenburg bridge and Ferlach. With this, the South Slav occupation was restricted to the southeast part of the country and the bridgehead of Völkermarkt. This state of affairs was provisionally fixed by the Armistice concluded on January 13, 1919.

In the meanwhile we succeeded in winning over the American "Inquiry" study group headed by Professor Coolidge, which was stationed in Vienna, to the idea of our participating in the armistice negotiations. The negotiations determined that the demarcation line should be decided by US Lieutenant Colonel Sherman Miles as arbitrator. To this end Miles toured Carinthia. His trip was very largely responsible for ensuring that the Peace Conference was well informed on Carinthia; however, his arbitration ruling, clearly favorable to German-Austria, was never published because of South Slav objection in Paris. There was a danger of hostilities breaking out again. Both sides prepared. In April the South Slavs resolved to attack Klagenfurt.

On April 29, the Yugoslavs attacked along the whole front. From the Völkermarkt bridgehead they were able to reach the vicinity of Klagenfurt. The danger appeared very great. We sent the Carinthians Viennese Volkswehr guns and artillery ammunition as help. But by then the Carinthians

---

* A town in Carinthia, Austria. Its Slovene name is Velikovec.

had already managed to bring the enemy attack to a halt. As soon as the reinforcements arrived, Colonel Hülgerth proceeded to counterattack. On May 2, the bridgehead of Völkermarkt was attacked and taken. On May 4, the Carinthians attacked the left flank of the Yugoslav front: St. Margareten in the Rosental and the Abtei plateau were taken and the strongly fortified exit of the Karawank Tunnel at Rosenbach was stormed. These defeats broke the resistance of the Yugoslav troops. They began to vacate the Drava line and retreated without resistance. In the meanwhile, General Segre, the head of the Entente's Armistice Commission, intervened. He protested our crossing of the Drava line and demanded that a new demarcation line be drawn in the armistice negotiations with his mediation. We thought it best to accept his proposal. After our victory we could, under the influence of Italian mediation (little disposed as it was to the Yugoslavs) arrive at a demarcation line favorable to us. But if we were to reject Segre's mediation, if we continued to pursue the defeated opponent, we would have to take into account that soon it would be no longer the weak Yugoslav forces that had thus far fought in Carinthia—these consisted of approximately forty companies, among them at the most three Serbian ones with only fifty-six guns—that we would face but the strong regular Serb armed forces. We therefore requested that the Carinthian provincial government cease the advance of their troops. But the Carinthians would not hear of anyone impeding them from taking advantage of their victory. While the Viennese Volkswehr, in accordance with the order of the State Secretary for the Armed Forces, remained at the Drava line, the Carinthians, despite all our warnings, pushed the enemy (which was retreating without a fight) up to the border of the province.

What we had warned the Carinthians of now occurred. The fourth Serb Army Command pulled together nine infantry regiments with strong artillery for the counterattack, which was carried out on May 28. The Carinthian troops could not bear up under Serb superiority. On the evening of the first day of battle, they had to withdraw to the Drava. On June 2 the enemy was able to dismantle our left flank in the Lavant Valley. With this defeat, Völkermarkt fell into the hands of the enemy on June 4. Therefore, Klagenfurt had to be evacuated on the following day; on June 6 it was occupied by the Yugoslavs. In the next days Italian troops occupied the Tarvisio–St. Veit railway. This put an end to the Carinthian defense struggle.

The battle had cost Carinthia 200 dead and 800 wounded. After two nice victories, it had still ended with the defeat of our forces. Nevertheless

it was not ineffective. It strongly influenced the course of the peace negotiations in Paris, in this way strongly contributing to saving Carinthia
from impending foreign Slav domination. But the struggles there gave the ·
government of the Republic a very difficult task. On the one side, we had
to support Carinthia as far as possible; on the other, we had to prevent
this local struggle from drawing us into a general armed conflict with the
Yugoslav Kingdom—for an advance of regular Serb forces on Graz would
have led to the collapse of German-Austria. Thus, we had to localize the
conflict in Carinthia and prevent its extension to Styria, maintain diplomatic relations with the Yugoslav Kingdom during the Carinthian struggles, and through arduous negotiations demonstrate that we were always
ready for a peaceful resolution of the conflict. In this way we were able to
prevent a break with Yugoslavia and thus maintain peace in the south.
But the heavy sacrifices we had to make in the north and in the south to
avert the danger of war with the Slav neighboring states was not enough to
save the peace; the most serious danger of war arose not from the dispute
over our borders to the north and to the south but from the effects of the
Hungarian Revolution on our internal relations—effects that threatened
to draw us into the war between Hungary and its neighbors.

In Hungary as well as in German-Austria, the October Revolution had
established the hegemony of the working class. Far more than the proletariat in German-Austria, however, the proletariat in Hungary pressed to turn
its hegemony into undivided rule, into its dictatorship. German-Austria
could not survive without the food and coal supplies from the Entente;
Hungary had food and coal in its own country. The Hungarian proletariat thus had much less to fear from a conflict with the Entente than did
the German-Austrian proletariat. In German-Austria the proletariat confronted an active and strong peasantry that had been schooled and organized by decades of political development; in Hungary the peasantry was
still unschooled and impassive; the plains docilely deferred to the political
decisions taken in the capital. The German-Austrian proletariat understood
that it had to share power with the farmers; the Hungarian proletariat believed it could easily subjugate the farmers to its dictatorship. In Austria,
the national revolution was the result of decades of national struggles; the
German-Austrian Revolution recognized the right to self-determination of
the neighboring peoples. The Hungarian Revolution, by contrast, viewed
the occupation of Slovakia by the Czechs, Transylvania by the Romanians,
of the Bačka and the Banat by the Yugoslavs as the annexations of foreign

conquerors; against them it defended the "integrity" of historic Hungary. The struggle for "integrity" was linked to the struggle for the dictatorship of the proletariat. In October, Hungary had hoped to save its integrity by overthrowing the ruling classes that had been the supporters of the alliance with Germany and union with Austria and by putting into power an Entente-friendly democracy. But when the Entente promised Hungarian territory to the Czechs, the Rumanians, and the Yugoslavs, its faith in democracy was deeply shattered; Hungary now threw itself into the arms of communist dictatorship in order, in alliance with Soviet Russia, to defend its integrity against the Entente. On March 20, 1919, the French lieutenant colonel Vyx handed the Károlyi government a note pushing the demarcation line deep into Hungarian territory, the Károlyi government abdicated, and Social Democracy, no longer strong enough to fend off the communist onslaught, capitulated to communist leadership. On March 21, the Hungarian Soviet Republic was established.

Having arisen from disputes over borders, the Soviet Republic was immediately drawn into the war against Romania and Czechoslovakia. Romanians and Czechs pushed toward the new demarcation line drawn by the Entente. The Romanians attacked at Debrecen, Grosswardein,* and Arad. The Czechs occupied Salgótarján, Miskolcz, and Sátoraljaújhely. Hungary was at war over its borders. It needed ordnance and munitions factories and thought that Austria could provide what it needed to carry on the war. The Hungarian Soviet government therefore tried to force the establishment of a soviet republic on German-Austria which, allied with the Hungarian Soviet Republic, would provide it with arms. "The entire equipment of the Austro-Hungarian army, all of its munitions," Ernst Bettelheim wrote,

> were piled up in Austria; tens of thousands of machine guns, thousands of canons of various calibers; large weapons and munitions factories from which Hungary's retreating red troops could have been supplied. In Austria there was the Austro-Hungarian Bank with its complete printing facilities. The scourge of white money† which produced a counter-revolutionary effect would have been eliminated in one stroke. Austria is an industrialized state, and with the aid of industrial articles produced in Austria, the Hungarian peasant would have been inseparably linked to the proletarian dictatorship.[1]

---

* The Old-Austrian name for Oradea in present-day Romania.
† Money circulated by the counterrevolutionaries.

But this importance of German-Austria for Hungary's war capacity was not only recognized by Hungary; Hungary's enemies saw it too. It was clear from the start that the proclamation of a soviet republic in Vienna would mean German-Austria's alliance with Hungary; an alliance with Hungary would mean war with Czechoslovakia, the termination of coal and food supplies, and the advance of the Czech Legions on Vienna.

The Hungarian Soviet government turned to us right after the March Revolution. We did not withhold our support to the proletarian revolution in Hungary. While all other states blockaded the Hungarian Soviet Republic, we authorized its embassy and trade mission and enabled Hungary to have access to a great quantity of Austrian manufactured goods. We could not officially send military equipment to Hungary without breaching our obligation to remain neutral in the Czech-Hungarian War; but, unhindered by us, the Social Democratic workers of the Wiener Neustadt district could smuggle significant amounts of military equipment over the Hungarian border. Shortly after Hungary's March Revolution, when the Entente lifted the blockade of German-Austria (which was still maintained by the Armistice Convention) only under condition that the imported goods not be transferred to Hungary, we had to comply with this condition; however, we still had the possibility of giving Hungary various kinds of economic aid. Nevertheless, all aid we gave Hungary's proletariat was limited because we could not afford to be involved in an armed conflict with our other neighbors. We could support Hungary's Soviet Republic, but we had to prevent the proclamation of a Soviet Republic in German-Austria. Béla Kun had at first expected that German-Austrian Social Democracy would imitate the Hungarian example, unite with the Communists, and establish a soviet dictatorship in German-Austria. As soon as he became aware that we had no intention of doing so, he initiated a campaign against us. Hungary's embassy in Vienna became a center of agitation. Great sums of money flowed from Hungary to the Communist Party of German-Austria, which served not only to reinforce its propaganda but was also used to bribe individual worker and soldier representatives. Communist propaganda sought to convince the workers that Hungary had large food supplies that sufficed to abundantly satisfy German-Austria's needs and that the army of the Russian Soviet Republic had already penetrated to Galicia and would soon cross the Carpathians to unite with the Hungarian Red Army. The terrible privation in German-Austria and the mass unemployment, which reached its highest level in May, provided fertile soil for the

Communist propaganda. It gained strength, when on April 7 a soviet republic was also proclaimed in Munich and when in May the Hungarian Red Army achieved significant victories over Czech troops in Slovakia.

The defense against communism was carried out at the level of the workers' councils. During the first weeks after the October Revolution, the councils operated independently of one another in the different localities and concentrated their activity on controlling food deliveries. It was only during the spring of 1919 that the local workers' councils were consolidated into a single organization that became the locus of the decisive political struggles within the proletariat, the instrument for the proletariat's most important political decisions. The impetus for this came from the Upper Austrian workers' councils. In Upper Austria—the only region of German-Austria that had grain surpluses—the economic activity of the workers' councils was the most extensive, and so they had gained considerable influence there. The Linz workers' council was the first to encourage the coordination of all local workers' councils. On February 19 in Linz it held a conference of all workers' councils, which asked the Social Democratic Party leadership to call a general Reich[2] conference of all workers' councils in German-Austria. This conference (held on March 1) issued unified statutes for the workers' councils, which regulated the election of local workers' councils and their coordination in Bezirk, Kreis and Land* workers' councils and in a Reich workers' council.[3] In the following weeks the workers' councils were reelected in accordance with these statutes. If these new elections—in which not only the mass of workers and employees but also a very large part of public officials participated—enhanced the authority of the workers' councils, then their federation ensured they would have a unitary political leadership. This leadership fell to Friedrich Adler, whose revolutionary conduct during the war had guaranteed him the unqualified trust of the revolutionary working class. Under his direction an exceedingly difficult struggle was carried out against communist adventurism within the workers' councils; under his direction the workers' councils came to recognize that within existing conditions the attempt to establish a soviet dictatorship in German-Austria would mean nothing other than suicide for the German-Austrian Revolution. The revolutionary authority of the workers' councils conveyed this recognition to the working masses. A soviet dictatorship became impracticable because the councils themselves rejected dictatorship.

---

* See Glossary, "Gemeinde, Bezirk, Kreis, Land."

More difficult still than in the workers' councils was the battle in the soldiers' councils. Communist propaganda had a powerful influence on the Volkswehr battalions. Josef Frey, who headed the Executive Committee of the Soldiers' Councils, was untrustworthy. Julius Deutsch's trusted colleagues—principally Braunthal, Leo Deutsch, Hofmann, Köhler, Schuhbauer,[4] and Weiss—waged a difficult struggle against the communist temptations that bore down on the Volkswehr. Here too the revolutionary authority of the workers' councils decided the struggle. The soldiers' councils resolved that the Volkswehr be seen as the armed force of the working class and therefore subordinated to the political direction of the workers' councils. Since the workers' councils rejected council dictatorship, this resolution, which grew out of council ideology, meant the rejection of soviet dictatorship by the armed forces.

Our action on the foundation of the workers' and soldiers' councils kept the masses away from the Communists. The Communists now tried to trigger violent clashes of the declassed elements under its influence among the unemployed, the returnees, and invalids with the state authority in order to incite the masses against the government of the Republic. On April 18, Holy Thursday, a few days after the establishment of the Communist dictatorship in Munich, the Communists induced a couple of hundred starving, unwitting, desperate unemployed and war invalids to attack the Parliament building. The demonstrators tried to set fire to the building; and when the police confronted them, they used their firearms against the police. A firefight began. The Volkswehr was called out. Despite Communist agitation they fulfilled their duty. They relieved the police, occupied the burning building, and chased away the demonstrators. The incident had exacted a heavy toll—six security guards and ten Volkswehr members died, and a few security guards and thirty demonstrators were wounded in the fray.

But at the same time, the day had shed light on the appalling misery that existed in Vienna: the demonstrators had pounced on the fallen horses of the security guards in order to tear pieces of flesh from the still warm bodies of the dead animals and carry them home as welcome spoils, as delicacies such as they had not known for a long time.

The day's most important lesson, however, was the attitude of the Volkswehr. It demonstrated the ineffectiveness of Communist agitation in the Volkswehr barracks. But Communist agitation of the Volkswehr now was even intensified, and the Entente furnished a convenient pretext for it so. The inter-Allied Armistice Commission demanded the abolition of the

Volkswehr, since with it the number of our soldiers would exceed the upper limit stipulated in the Armistice Convention. In this period of high unemployment, soldiers feared discharge from the Volkswehr; the Communists sought to take advantage of their arousal to win them to a putsch attempt. In the second half of May, Ernst Bettelheim came to Vienna as an emissary of the Hungarian Soviet government. He acted here as representative of the Communist International in whose name he overthrew the leadership of the Communist Party and put in its place a Directorium that was to organize the putsch.[5] Since the inter-Allied Armistice Commission demanded that the discharge of the members of the Volkswehr (which was to be dismantled) be completed by June 15, Bettelheim scheduled the putsch for this day. Communist flyers called on the Volkswehr members to take part, armed, in the street demonstration called for June 15. The Communist Revolutionary Soldiers Committee issued instructions to the Initiative Committees in the Battalions for the street battle and for the occupation of public buildings. At the same time, the communist Directorium asked Béla Kun to have the Hungarian Transdanubian Corps occupy the German-Austrian border until June 14 and on the following day move some detachments across the border.

We knew of these preparations and struck back. On June 12, I communicated to the Entente's Military Mission that we were not in a position to carry out the required dismantling of the Volkswehr. The Entente, fearing the spread of Bolshevism to Vienna, acquiesced in this rejection of their demands; and thus the Volkswehr members were freed from the danger of discharge, which was driving them toward the Communists. On June 13, the newly elected Viennese Kreis Workers' Council met for its first session. After an address by Friedrich Adler, it resolved that it had the sole right to decide on and carry out actions taken by the Viennese working class; the putsch attempt by the Communists was declared to be a rebellion against the revolutionary authority of the workers' council. On June 14 Julius Deutsch was able to get the soldiers' councils of the Communist Volkswehr Battalion No. 41—which had arisen from the Red Guard of the days of the uprising—to promise that the Battalion would maintain discipline and comply with the directive to not leave the barrack on this day without an order; in addition, Deutsch placed a trustworthy Volkswehr detachment under the command of Captain Marek near the barrack of the Communist No. 41, so that they could if necessary counter it by force of arms.

Impressed by our countermeasures, the Communists themselves were indecisive on June 14; a part of the Communist leaders opposed the putsch.

Yet still on June 14, as Bettelheim recounts, Béla Kun telegraphed the Viennese Directorium: "I have everything ready. Forward courageously and wisely! The thing's success is a matter of life and death." Since all signs indicated that the putsch plan had not been given up, Eldersch, who headed the Home Ministry while Renner led the peace delegation in Saint-Germain, had the key Communist organizers arrested.

On June 15, a crowd of several thousand Communists made its way to the police prison in order to free the leaders. In Hörlgasse they were met by a detachment of the City Guard,* a formation made up of Social Democratic workers. When the demonstrators tried to break through the ranks of the City Guard, it made use of its firearms. Twenty dead and eighty wounded lay on the pavement. The demonstrators streamed back; some Volkswehr battalions that had occupied the Ringstrasse maintained order with exemplary calm and prevented further clashes. In the meantime, the Communists tried to bring the Communist Volkswehr Battalion No. 41 into play. The soldiers' councils confronted them—with revolver in hand they defended the barrack gate and impeded the Communist Volkswehr members from leaving the barrack. In this way, the danger of an armed clash on the streets was averted. Now Eldersch could set free the imprisoned Communist leaders, and calm came back to the barrack. The putsch attempt had been thwarted.[6]

At first the Communists believed they could repeat the attempt. The second Reich conference of the workers' councils on June 30 turned into a major confrontation with the Communists. In the meantime, the strength of Hungarian Communism had begun to flag. In deference to an ultimatum of Clemenceau, Béla Kun had withdrawn the Red Army in Slovakia to the demarcation line. In Inner Hungary, growing economic hardships appeared, as did growing worker dissatisfaction and growing resistance from the farmers. On the Theiss,† Romania prepared an attack. The unmistakable collapse of the Hungarian Revolution also weakened its outposts in German-Austria. The June 15 experiences sharpened the antagonisms within the Communist Party. It could no longer dare a second attempt. When on August 1 the Hungarian soviet dictatorship collapsed and the bloody counterrevolution followed, the German-Austrian proletariat had a vivid demonstration of the fate from which Social Democracy had saved them. A short while later, Deutsch was able to disarm and dis-

* Stadtschutzwache.
† The Tisza River.

solve Volkswehr Battalion No. 41 without encountering resistance; and with this the putschists' only remaining dangerous position of power was taken from them.

The defensive battle against Bolshevism in German-Austria was not a class struggle between the bourgeoisie and the proletariat but a struggle within the working class. The bourgeoisie looked on without influence or comprehension. Later they tried to interpret the events to make the Vienna Police and Police President Schober responsible for having saved Vienna from Bolshevism. It is a foolish legend. Even on Holy Thursday and on June 15, it was not the police but the Volkswehr that restored order; and yet only a small minority of the proletariat was involved. If the workers' and soldiers' councils had decided in favor of a council dictatorship, they would have had at their disposal the whole working class, all armed formations made up of workers that had been founded since the October Revolution, the Volkswehr, the Municipal Police, and the railway police; the bourgeoisie could not have resisted them in Vienna, nor in the industrial districts of Lower Austria and Styria; the police would have been completely powerless. It was only in the struggle within the workers' and soldiers' councils that the onslaught of Bolshevism was repelled. And this struggle within the working class was not decided by weapons but in the struggle of intellects. Friedrich Adler's purposeful leadership in the workers' councils and that of Julius Deutsch and his circle of friends in the soldiers' councils decided the struggle. But this victory over Bolshevism meant nothing less than the self-assertion of the German-Austrian Revolution. If Bolshevism had been victorious for even a day, then the inevitable consequences would have been famine, war, and the occupation of the country by foreign troops.

The entire history of the German-Austrian Revolution from October 1918 to July 1919 is the history of its struggle for peace. We had to manage our border conflict with Czech and Yugoslav nationalism so as to avoid war with our two neighboring peoples. We had to stave off the onslaught of Hungarian Bolshevism so as to not be drawn into a war with our neighbors. The imperative of maintaining peace had inflicted heavy sacrifices on the national and social revolution. But only so long as the Revolution restricted itself to what was possible without war with the neighboring peoples could it protect itself from war and certain ruin, from counterrevolution under the cover of foreign bayonets.

However, preventing the outbreak of a new war was no less important than liquidating the Great War. The period of our conflicts with Slav nationalism and Magyar Bolshevism coincided with our peace negotiations with Entente imperialism. The maintenance of peace with the neighboring nations salvaged our existence as a state; it was only thanks to this that we could negotiate with the Entente as an independent state. The sacrifices with which we had to buy peace with our neighbors and the devastating misery in which we lived as an independent state in these first years after the Armistice showed us that German-Austria could live independently only with appalling privation, in oppressive dependency on foreign countries, and powerlessly in the face of neighboring peoples. This experience had to determine our objective in dealing with Entente imperialism; our most important goal had to be the defense of our right to union with Germany.

When on November 12 the Provisional National Assembly declared German-Austria to be a part of the German Republic, we were hoping we could actually accomplish union with the German Reich* without waiting for the peace negotiations and thus present the Peace Conference with a fait accompli. But it quickly became evident how much resistance this met. France objected emphatically and strenuously. In the German Reich there was fear that the price for incorporating German-Austria would be the ceding of large areas in the western and eastern parts of the Reich. France demanded the Rhine border. Poland demanded Danzig,† West Prussia, and Upper Silesia. That the lost war would end with a significant increase in the German Reich's population was improbable; Germany therefore feared that it would have to pay for union with German-Austria with the loss of the areas claimed by France and Poland. For this reason it hesitated to advance along the Danube at the moment the decision on the Rhine and the Vistula was still pending. In German-Austria, however, similar anxieties also stood in the way of our negotiations. Here there was concern not only that the completion of union would unfavorably influence the Peace Conference's decision on the fate of German South Tyrol, Carinthia, Lower Styria, Znaimer Kreis, and the Bohemian Forest; much greater still was the danger that as soon as we actually tried to enact annexation, France could instigate the Czechs and Yugoslavs to occupy German-Austrian territory and involve us in a war with our neighbors. It therefore seemed too dangerous to accomplish union at one stroke. We had to proceed by steps.

Thus in the first weeks after the Armistice, the government and public opinion in the Reich looked upon annexation with greater trepidation

---

* Germany's official name from 1871 to 1945 was "Deutsches Reich."
† Now Gdańsk.

and unease than was the case in German-Austria. We sent Ludo Hartmann as our envoy to Berlin, where he succeeded in promoting understanding and enthusiasm for annexation. When the German Constituent
National Assembly met in Weimar, the Committee of States, which replaced the old Bundesrat, consulted Hartmann. For the first time since
1866, when Bismarck abolished the Frankfurt Bundesrat, a representative
of German-Austria took part in the council of German states. The draft
of the Reich Constitution presented by Preuss to the Weimar Constituent
Assembly left open for German-Austria the possibility of entry into the
Reich. But all of this was only a demonstrative act. If we wanted to take
a serious step toward really accomplishing union, then it had to be at the
economic level.

    An opportunity to do so appeared when Yugoslavia and Czechoslo-
vakia overprinted the krone bills that circulated in their state territories,
an act that broke down the monetary community that still covered all
successor states of the Habsburg Monarchy. It was to be expected that
the value of our krone would quickly drop as soon as its circulation area
was restricted to German-Austria. The obvious move was not to create an
independent German-Austrian currency but to answer the overprinting in
Yugoslavia and Czechoslovakia with transition to the mark, that is, with
German-Austria's entry into the German monetary community. We proposed that Germany's Reichsbank grant a German-Austrian central bank a
loan in paper marks. This loan would enable the German-Austrian central
bank to honor the obligation to exchange every German-Austrian krone
note on demand of its owner against a mark at a fixed rate. In this way a
core mark currency could first be created in German-Austria that would
have brought the krone into a stable exchange rate with the mark and thus
signify our real entry into the German monetary community. At the beginning of March 1919, I went to Weimar and Berlin to negotiate this plan
with the German government.

    But the German government could not agree to our proposal. The resis-
tance came from the Reichsbank. We and the Reich were facing the peace
negotiations. No one could foresee what the Peace Treaty would say about
the krone bills circulating in the successor states and abroad or what it would
stipulate about the Austro-Hungarian Bank;* no one could predict the
shape of state finances either here or there after the peace treaties or to what
degree both states would be forced to draw on credit from the central banks

---

* See Glossary, "Bank, Austro-Hungarian and Austrian National."

to cover the deficit in the public budget. Under such conditions, adopting our proposal appeared to the Reichsbank to be a burden with intangible and unpredictable difficulties. The decision was postponed. This meant that union before the decisions of the Peace Conference was unfeasible.

This imprinted another character on the Berlin negotiations. With Count Brockdorff-Rantzau, Germany's Reich Foreign Minister, I concluded a treaty regulating how incorporation of German-Austria into the Reich should occur in the event the peace treaties did not prevent it. This treaty was highly favorable to German-Austria. Its provisions could have greatly strengthened the movement for union in German-Austria if it could have been immediately published, but this was not done for fear it would have an adverse impact on the peace negotiations. The German government had conceded to us that in the event of its incorporation into the Reich, German-Austria would be treated in terms of finance as if it had already belonged to the Reich since 1914. This would have meant that a great part of our war debt would be taken over by the Reich. It seemed imprudent to publish this treaty provision specifically because it could have led the Entente to impose the whole war debt burden of old-Austria on the German-Austrian Republic. The German government had conceded to us that German-Austria, even after its incorporation into the German customs area, could for several years still levy internal tariffs on German industrial products in order to protect its own industry, while German-Austrian products could be imported duty-free into the old German territory. With publication of the provision, the Entente would have included trade-policy provisions in the Peace Treaty that would have made it impossible to actually implement the agreement. And so it could not be used to influence the movement for annexation.

The decision on annexation had to fall to the Peace Conference and the peace treaties. Our chief task was thus to influence the Peace Conference such that it would put no obstacles in the way of annexation.

In the last years of the war, the Austrian problem was the subject of lively debate in the Allied countries. The conservative parties were mostly in favor of not destroying the Habsburg Monarchy while insisting on its internal restructuring; under Slav leadership the Monarchy could become a link in the iron chain with which the Entente wanted to encircle Germany. The democratic tendencies, on the other hand, worked for recognition of the right of self-determination for the Czechs, Poles, and Yugoslavs; they concluded that the part of old-Austria that remained after the founding of the independent national states of the Slav peoples would inevitably fall to Germany. Thus, the idea that the dissolution of the Habsburg Monarchy would necessarily mean the annexation of German-Austria to Germany was by no means foreign to public opinion in the Entente countries, having often been expressed there already in 1917 and 1918. Our campaign for annexation could thus plausibly count on the support of strong tendencies in the victor countries.

On September 21, 1918, and thus before the collapse of the Central Powers, US Secretary of State Robert Lansing drafted a memorandum on problems of peace for internal government use.[7] It provided for the dissolution of the Habsburg Monarchy, the founding of independent nation-states by the Czechs, Yugoslavs, and Poles, and contained the following proposal concerning the remainder of Austria: "Reduction of Austria to the ancient boundaries and title of the Archduchy of Austria. Incorporation of Archduchy in the Imperial German Confederation."[8]

We naturally did not know of this memorandum at the time; Lansing first published it in 1921.* But in this matter we could appeal to the United States not only on the basis that Wilson's programmatic declarations, which underlay the Armistice, also promised us the right to self-determination; we also knew that influential statesmen in the United States had recognized the annexation of German-Austria to Germany as in itself the necessary consequence of the dissolution of the Habsburg Monarchy even before German-Austria evoked the right to self-determination proclaimed by the US president in setting annexation as its goal.

Nor did we expect resistance from Italy to the goal of annexation. Italy viewed the dissolution of the Habsburg Monarchy as the actual achievement of its victory. It feared nothing so much as its reconstitution under the heading of a "Danube Confederation." A small, weak German-Austria could be forced into such a federation; it could become a bridge between Czechoslovakia and Yugoslavia and connect the Yugoslav Army to Czech industry; if German-Austria fell to the German Empire, then all plans for a Danube Federation would collapse; a bulwark would be inserted between the Czechs and the Yugoslavs. At the same time Italy would become a direct neighbor of Germany. The more Italy's differences with Yugoslavia and France grew in the course of the Paris Peace Conference, the more the tendency grew in Italy to regard our annexation to the Reich as in Italy's interest.

---

* The original edition incorrectly gives the date as 1920.

In England opinion was much less inclined toward annexation. The thought that Germany's defeat should end with an increase in the Reich's population was disagreeable to English policy. The vague plans for a federation of successor states had the most adherents in England. Nevertheless, it did not seem impossible that in the end England too would reject France's demand to insert a prohibition of union in the Peace Treaty. At the Peace Conference in March and April, the antagonism between England and France was at its height. The Hungarian March Revolution had made a strong impression on Lloyd George; he feared that Germany too, menaced by an unacceptable peace, would throw itself into the arms of Bolshevism. On March 25, 1919, he handed the Paris Conference a memorandum[9]—subsequently published by Nitti—that warned of the danger of "spartacism from the Urals to the Rhine." ". . . the news which came from Hungary yesterday," Lloyd George wrote, "shows only too clearly that this danger is no fantasy. And what are the reasons alleged for this decision? They are mainly the belief that large numbers of Magyars are to be handed over to the control of others." On these grounds Lloyd George protested against transferring more Germans than absolutely necessary to Polish and Czech rule. Could we not then hope that England would at least advocate the union of German-Bohemia with Germany? "If we are wise," Lloyd George wrote, "we shall offer to Germany a peace, which, while just, will be preferable for all sensible men to the alternative of Bolshevism." At the time, the Entente feared foremost the spread of Bolshevism from Hungary to German-Austria; was it unthinkable that Lloyd George was trying to bring about a peace that would grant us affiliation to Germany, so that we would prefer this peace to national-Bolshevik rebellion against the Entente? "Our terms may be severe," he wrote, "and even ruthless but at the same time they can be so just that the country on which they are imposed will feel in its heart that it has no right to complain." Was it inconceivable that England, even if it could not fend off the demands of French and Polish imperialism, would at least try to offer Germany compensation in the South? That it would allow union in order to convince the German people that peace despite all its severity nevertheless provided justice by letting the principle of the right of peoples to self-determination work not only against Germany but for Germany?

For the above reasons we did not consider it impossible to induce the United States, Italy, and Great Britain to reject insertion of a clause into the Peace Treaty prohibiting annexation. That we had not misjudged the politics of the Great Powers was later proven by the publication of Lansing's and Lloyd George's memoranda and above all by Tardieu's history of the peace negotiations. Tardieu, Clemenceau's closest collaborator at the Peace Conference, wrote: "France advocated for Austria remaining separate from Germany. Great Britain and the United States vacillated and discussed this question for a full three months."

For three months! What could we do to influence the powers in these three months in which German-Austria's fate was being decided? We had no entry to the conference of the victorious powers meeting in Paris. We only had one weapon: propaganda. We had to convince the statesmen of the Entente powers that German-Austria left to its own resources was not viable, that a federation of successor states would be impossible to achieve in the face of Czechoslovak and Yugoslav resistance, and that annexation to Germany was therefore the only possible solution, the only one that could prevent the complete economic collapse of German-Austria with serious social repercussions and the danger of war in Central Europe.

Through memoranda, papers, newspaper articles, and speeches, we tried to bring these ideas home to the statesmen of the Entente powers. At the same time, our propaganda had to be directed to our own population. If our appeal to the Entente was not to fall on deaf ears, we had to show them that our struggle for annexation was supported by the whole German-Austrian people, determined by their united will, that annexation was an economic necessity whose satisfaction could not be denied by sheer mechanical force, and that it was being fought for by a moral force that in the long run no other force could bring to heel—this was what we had to convince the Entente powers of. But our attempt was defeated by the rebellion of the bourgeoisie. As we tried to convince the victorious powers of the necessity of annexation and of the unified support for it among the German-Austrian people, the German-Austrian bourgeoisie stabbed us in the back.

The profound social convulsions that Germany experienced in the winter of 1918–19 frightened our bourgeoisie. It feared that Germany would fall into the hands of Bolshevism and did not want to become incorporated into "Spartacist Germany." And the general fear the bourgeoisie had of social revolution combined with the specific interests of big business. The large banks were particularly anxious to maintain their holdings in the successor states. They believed that Vienna would continue to be the financial center of these states if German-Austria remained alone; the Entente, they believed, would liquidate its branches and holdings in the national states if German-Austria was absorbed into Germany. Similar concerns were voiced by the major industrialists. Their enterprises had plants here in German-Austria as well as in the successor states. A Danube Federation could reunite their holdings within one economic area. For their German-Austrian plants, annexation to Germany meant the threat posed by the superior Reich-German competition; for their plants in the successor states it meant the danger of liquidation to meet German reparation obligations.

The capitalists' economic class interests were allied to the political class interests of the dethroned aristocracy, the high clergy, and of the officer corps divested of its privileges and careers. These classes still hoped for a restoration of the Monarchy. Union would have buried their hope for a return of the Habsburgs; German-Austria had to stay outside Germany if the Habsburgs were to return home.

The economic opposition of the capitalist class and the political opposition of the Monarchists revived the Old-Austrian traditions of Vieneseness. The traditional gulf between Austrian and German sensibilities came to life again. The Old-Viennese patricians and Vienna's petty bourgeoisie did not want to believe that the old great Austria had disappeared forever, hoping it could be resurrected, whether in a new form or under the name of a "Danube Federation." Their old aversion to the Prussian, northern German character gained strength. They began to agitate against our policy of annexation to Germany. Meanwhile, the provinces had their own foreign policy. On March 12, in the Constituent National Assembly, Tyrol's Christian Social deputies protested against the reaffirmation of the resolution on annexation; they believed that German South Tyrol could more easily be saved from incorporation by Italy if Tyrol did not fall to Germany. Similar sentiments prevailed at the time of Carinthia's struggle against the Yugoslav invasion; there was a complete repudiation of the nationality principle, which threatened to tear the country apart:

> *Not to the Ljubljana'ers and not to the Viennese,*
> *not to the Serbs and not to the Berliners,*
> *Carinthia to the Carinthians!*

In Vorarlberg the majority of the state parliament declared that the province should on no account fall to Germany. Already by the beginning of March, the provincial assembly opened negotiations with Switzerland; on May 11, in a plebiscite, the province voted 47,208 to 11,248 for union with Switzerland and against annexation to Germany.

Thus, the traditional Austrianism of the Old-Viennese patriciate and the Old-Viennese petty bourgeoisie, on the one side, and the particularism of the provinces, on the other, were allied with the bourgeoisie's general fear of Spartacism, with the specific economic interests of big financial and industrial capital, and with the hopes for political restoration of the Monarchist aristocracy, the Monarchist high clergy, and the Monarchist officer corps. All these forces together fought against our annexation policy.

This opposition was used by French imperialism for its own ends. Operating from Switzerland, French press agencies established a news service in Vienna. The French envoy Allizé knew how to get the liberal and Christian Social press to work to his advantage. French propaganda worked calculatedly to create the impression that German-Austria would retain the contested German border areas in Tyrol, Carinthia, and Lower Styria, in Southern Bohemia, and Southern Moravia and, from the economic point of view, receive much more advantageous peace terms than the Reich, if it would only renounce the project of annexation. The annexation opponents' front now became stronger and more united. The whole of Vienna's big liberal press and a large part of the Christian Social press in Vienna and the provinces were in its service.

Our propaganda, which was directed at winning the United States, Italy, and Great Britain for the cause of annexation, was thwarted by this domestic opposition. We showered the statesmen of the victorious powers with memoranda demonstrating that German-Austria's economic collapse was inevitable if we were not permitted annexation to Germany. France's statesmen could answer us that it was precisely the leading figures of Austria's national economy, the big bankers and industrialists, that daily assured the Entente diplomats in Vienna that German-Austria did not need annexation, that with a few favorable peace terms it could live quite well alone. We tried to convince the Entente's statesmen that all German-Austrian people wanted annexation. France's diplomats could easily refute this by calling as witnesses against us nearly all of the bourgeois press of Vienna and referring to the mood of a great part of the Alpine provinces. In the Paris negotiations, France could now say that only the Socialists and the Greater-Germans wished for annexation, that the middle class and peasantry wanted an independent Austria and considered it completely viable. The bourgeoisie's rebellion against our leadership thus became the strongest weapon of French imperialism in those three months of discussion in which the decision regarding annexation was finally made on the basis of Tardieu's testimony.

We intended to hold a plebiscite on annexation to convince the victors of the unity and firmness of the Austrian people's desire for it. Before the Paris Peace Conference's decision, in the period in which the three Great Powers still "vacillated and debated," this kind of popular demonstration would not have been ineffectual. But now we could not chance it since the fierce counterpropaganda of the annexation opponents could have influenced significant minorities, in some provinces perhaps even the majority of eligible voters, to vote against annexation.

On May 7, the draft of the peace treaty that the Entente intended to dictate to the German Reich was handed to the German peace delegation. Its terribly harsh peace terms immediately became a weapon in the hands of our domestic annexation opponents. They could now say that if annexation were to be implemented, German-Austria would have to co-pay the onerous war reparations that the victors imposed on the German Reich. If we would renounce annexation, then the Entente would, as Allizé so often promised, "build bridges" to us. At the same time the draft of the Treaty of Versailles dashed all the hopes of the proponents of annexation. Article 80 of the draft obliged the German Reich to "respect strictly the independence of Austria," agreeing "that this independence shall be inalienable, except with the consent of the Council of the League of Nations." The inclusion of this provision in the draft treaty appeared to prove that the time of vacillation and debate within the Entente was over. As Keynes recounted, the discussion ended with one of those characteristic compromises between Clemenceau and Wilson, between France's power politics and the democratic ideology represented by the US president, in which, as always, imperialism triumphed in actuality and democracy in phraseology. There was no simple prohibition of the principle of annexation because this would have violated the right of peoples to self-determination; but the exercise of this right was tied to the agreement of the League of Nations and thus made impossible in practice. "And who knows," Keynes asked, "but that the President forgot that another part of the Treaty provides that for this purpose the Council of the League must be *unanimous*."[10]

Under the impact of this decision, our delegation headed by Renner travelled to Saint-Germain for the peace negotiations. On June 2 it was handed the first draft of the Peace Treaty. It was a terrible document. The Entente promised German-Bohemia, the Sudetenland, the Böhmerwaldgau, Znaimer Kreis, and the Lower Austrian border districts to the

Czechs, German South Tyrol to the Italians, and most of Carinthia with its capital Klagenfurt and the German cities of Lower Styria to the Yugoslavs. The draft's economic terms were just as harsh. They were simply copied from the German Peace Treaty; the property of German-Austrian citizens in the successor states was to be confiscated just like the property of Reich Germans in England; and the debts of German-Austrian citizens owed to citizens of the successor states were to be valorized in the same way as our debts to France or Italy. In the context of the close economic relationship of Vienna to the successor states, this would have quickly meant Vienna's ruin.

In Vienna these terrible conditions produced a sentiment in favor of capitulation. The cry now was to expressly renounce annexation in any form in order to buy milder peace terms. I had to oppose this mood of capitulation. For in the June 2 draft there was no mention of annexation; a provision analogous to that of Article 80 of the draft of the German Peace Treaty was not included. This led us to conclude that the period of "vacillation and debate" within the Entente was still not over; and this gave room for hope that the victor might yet accede to the objections of the German peace delegation to Article 80 and delete it, or at least temper it, for example by allowing a majority decision in the Council of the League, as had been done in the decision on the Saar coal districts. Thus I strongly opposed the idea of buying ameliorations of the peace terms by renouncing annexation. In my June 7 speech to the National Assembly, in which I responded to the draft peace treaty, I said:

> The draft treaty dispels the sad illusions of those who seek salvation in separation from the German Reich; in its territorial and economic conditions much harsher still than the draft presented to the German Reich, it proves that it is not the degree of hatred that determines the content of the Peace Treaty but the assessment of what remains of the defeated country's strength. Therefore among our people the conviction is now stronger than ever that it can only have a tolerable future in the framework of a Greater German Republic.

France's diplomats could see that a mood of capitulation prevailed in the bourgeois parties and press. Since I opposed capitulation, they launched a personal campaign against me, carried out not just in the Parisian but also in the Viennese press. Significantly, this was also the period of the struggle around the socialization laws. I was not only Foreign Secretary but also president of the Socialization Commission. The bourgeois press fought the

Foreign Secretary in order to strike a blow at the president of the Socialization Commission. Thus they increasingly put themselves at the service of the campaign organized by the French Mission. At the same time, our conflict with French diplomacy was aggravated by other circumstances. Since Hungary's March Revolution, France was anxious to unite all of Hungary's neighbors into a coalition against its Council Republic. It mobilized Romania, Czechoslovakia, and Yugoslavia against Hungary and tried to force us into this coalition. It was our duty to resist this imposition. Even if the Hungarian Revolution followed a path we considered dangerous and disastrous from the very beginning, it was still a proletarian revolution against which we would not ally with capitalist powers. With all our might we had to prevent the Hungarian Revolution from forcing the German-Austrian proletariat to follow in its path, but our struggle against Hungarian Communism was still only a struggle within the proletariat; against the capitalist powers red Hungary had a rightful claim to our support. The German-Austrian proletariat would never have tolerated any other policy; if we had done imperialism's business against Soviet Hungary, the German-Austrian proletariat would have rebelled, and precisely because of a policy hostile to Communism it would have fallen into the arms of Communism. At the same time such a policy would have inevitably involved us in the most serious conflict with the Council Republic, which was far superior to us militarily. Any antagonism of German-Austria toward Council Hungary would have ended with an uprising of the German-Austrian working class and invasion by the Hungarian Red Army. German-Austria could not allow itself to join the hostile corral encircling Red Hungary.

Since Hungary's March Revolution, we had provided various kinds of aid. This alone led to friction with the Western powers. But the conflict really worsened when in May the Hungarian Red Army beat Czech troops in Slovakia and reconquered large parts of its territory. Czechoslovakia was in a most difficult situation. It could not militarily equip the new formations it sent into battle against the Red Army. France demanded that we help the Czechs with weapons and ammunition from our stocks. We refused. Then France issued an ultimatum: if shipment of ammunition did not begin by June 6, coal deliveries from Czechoslovakia would be discontinued. The threat did not frighten us, because particularly at that time the Entente's fear of Bolshevism spreading to German-Austria was too great for it to dare trigger economic catastrophe in Vienna. The military equipment was not delivered. And when shortly afterward we had to deliver certain equipment that the Entente demanded according to the Armistice Convention, we did not send it to the Czechs and the French but to the Italians in Innsbruck; in this way we could be certain that if it ever reached Czechoslovakia it would come too late to have any impact on the conflict. French diplomacy and the French military mission were extremely agitated by this resistance of ours. The press campaign against me became more heated still. If up to then the Parisian press had attacked me as a "Pan-German," it now called me a Bolshevik. Just when Béla Kun's emissaries in Vienna tried to organize a putsch against us, when his embassy became the center of the fiercest agitation against us, when he continually provoked conflicts with our Budapest embassy in order to deliver agitation material against us to his Vienna embassy, in the month of June when Hungarian Communism deployed all means to overthrow us, we came into severe conflict with France because we refused to let ourselves be used by the capitalist powers against the proletarian revolution in Hungary.

In Vienna, France and Italy jealously vied with one another for influence. In our conflict with France we sought support from Italy. Italy was not as hostile to our annexation policy as France. Italy also had nothing to object to in our Hungarian policy; because of its conflict with Yugoslavia, Italy had always treated the Magyars as future allies against Yugoslavia, and in the Hungarian Soviet period Italy was far less hostile to Hungary than the Western powers were. We had succeeded in interesting Italy in our border dispute with Yugoslavia. Italy supported our claims to Carinthia, Marburg, and Radkersburg. Only Italy's claims to German South Tyrol stood between us. We had to try and override this dispute in order to secure the protection of at least one of the Great Powers in the Peace Conference.

In the Treaty of London of April 26, 1915, Great Britain and France had pledged South Tyrol up to the Brenner Pass to the Kingdom of Italy if Italy would enter the war against the Central Powers. But the United States never joined in this treaty. And Italy itself flouted the treaty by demanding Fiume, which according to the Treaty of London had to be ceded to Yugoslavia. The battle for Fiume made it appear possible that the Treaty of London might be revised. Tardieu confirms that in April, France and England offered Italy a revision of the Treaty; if it came to that we could hope that the decision on South Tyrol too could be changed. In this period we were at pains to win over American statesmen for salvaging German South Tyrol. But President Wilson was completely taken up by the problems in the Adriatic. He denied the Italians not only Fiume but also the areas of Dalmatia and Istria that had been guaranteed to it in the Treaty of London. Since Wilson came into sharp conflict with Italy over these Slav areas, he wanted to avoid further enlarging the conflict to include the German areas in South Tyrol. "The American government," Tardieu recounted, "accepted the clauses of the Treaty of London on the Alps but rejected those concerning a part of Istria, of Dalmatia, and the islands of the Adriatic Sea." However, England and France declared that they were bound by the Treaty and that, as agreed, South Tyrol must remain with Italy and Fiume with the Yugoslavs. Still, we never lost hope. When Orlando left Paris on April 24, and the open break surfaced between Italy and the Western powers, we still hoped that the further development of the conflict would yet lead to a revision of the Treaty of London, and so in this period too we sought to influence the decision on Tyrol through our propaganda in the West. Only when the Italians returned to Paris on May 5 was it obvious that Tyrol could no longer hope to be salvaged by the Western powers. If German South Tyrol could be saved at all, it could only be through direct negotiations with Italy.

This is what we attempted in May. Italy advanced strategic arguments for annexing German South Tyrol. We therefore proposed to the Italian government that German South Tyrol remain with German-Austria but be militarily neutralized. We said we were even prepared to go beyond mere neutralization and concede far-reaching military rights to Italy up to the Brenner Pass, if the area between Salurner Klause* and Brenner only remained to us in other respects. As a prize for relinquishing their claim to German South Tyrol, we offered Italy concessions. We knew that Italian capitalists hoped to acquire shares in many enterprises located in the Adriatic and in Yugoslavia and to participate in German-Austrian enterprises. We said we were ready to fulfill all these wishes as soon as Italy showed willingness to negotiate German South Tyrol. The Italian government made us wait a long time for an answer. Only in July did it inform us that it had to decline our offer. At the Paris Conference Italy had been defeated in its struggle over the Adriatic and the Levant; it could not then agree to relinquish still another part of the spoils of war Paris had promised it. With this our attempt to come to an understanding with Italy collapsed.

As a result, our predicament was considerable. We were in serious conflict with France, and we could not reach an understanding with It-

---

* Italian: *Chiusa di Salomo* or *Stretta di Salomo*.

aly. At the same time, a large section of the co-governing Christian Social Party, and all of public opinion represented by the capitalist press, rebelled against our policy of affiliation to Germany. And yet it was precisely in this period of conflict that our foreign policy obtained its greatest success. On July 20, the second draft of the Peace Treaty was presented, and it represented significant progress over the first draft of June 2.

The first draft had promised the greater part of Carinthia with its capital to Yugoslavia. The second draft revised this and stipulated, as we had demanded from the start, that the Carinthian people were themselves to decide their state affiliation in a free plebiscite. With this the larger part of Carinthia was saved for German-Austria. On July 31, 1919, at the behest of the Supreme Council in Paris, Klagenfurt was vacated by the Yugoslavs. On October 10, 1920, the Carinthian people freely decided in favor of the Austrian Republic. This major success was the result, on the one side, of the stalwart defensive struggles of the Carinthian people and, on the other, Italy's support at the Peace Conference, which we succeeded in obtaining at least on this matter.

With the salvage of Carinthia, the second draft had also brought the liberation of Burgenland. Already during the war, in memoranda of the Czech and Yugoslav émigré organizations, and probably for the first time in a memorandum from Masaryk to Sir Edward Grey in April 1915, the demand surfaced to connect the future Czech and Yugoslav nation-states through a "corridor." To this end the Hungarian counties overwhelmingly inhabited by Germans—Ödenburg,* Wieselburg, and Eisenstadt—were to be divided between the Czechoslovak and the Yugoslav state. This demand was also brought to the Paris Peace Conference by the Czechs and supported by France. We had to ward off this danger of a Slav barrier between German-Austria and Hungary; we had to oppose it with the demand that the people of Western Hungary's German counties had themselves to decide the state to which they wanted to belong. When the revolutionary nationality principle tore down the historic state borders in October 1918, we demanded that this principle apply not only in the north and the south to the benefit of the Czechs, the South Slavs, and the Italians but also in the east where a neighboring German people lived under Magyar domination. We rejected any annexation of this area but at the Peace Conference presented the demand that the people of German-West Hungary themselves decide in a free referendum whether they wished to remain in Hungary or fall to German-Austria.

---

* Present-day Sopron in Hungary.

When Great Britain and the United States rejected the Czech demand for a Czech-Yugoslav "corridor" in Western Hungary, the Czechs recommended a division of Western Hungary between German-Austria and Hungary. They wanted this in order first to make German-Austria an enemy of Hungary and so prevent an alliance of both states against Czechoslovakia. Moreover, it was in its interest that the two railway lines connecting Slovakia with Croatia were not in the hands of only one state. The victorious allies rejected our demand for a plebiscite in Western Hungary and in the July 20 draft divided the country by giving the greater part of it to us and the smaller part to Hungary. At a time in which extensive German areas were under foreign domination in the west, east, and south, here we succeeded in liberating a German population from foreign domination. The Entente had made this decision in the weeks in which the German-Austrian working class had warded off the assault of Bolshevism mobilized from Hungary. It wanted to fortify our position against Bolshevism by holding out to us a compensation for our major losses to the north and south with a gain to the east at the cost of Bolshevik Hungary.

Finally, the second Peace Treaty draft brought us substantial improvement over the economic provisions of the first draft. While the June 2 draft regulated our economic relations with the successor states according to the same principles as our relations with the Entente powers, this principle was abandoned in the July 20 draft. This was most importantly seen in the removal of the dangerous provision on the liquidation of the property of German-Austrian citizens in the successor states. The provisions on the distribution of the public debt also accommodated our demands to a certain extent. These very important successes were the fruit of our struggle for annexation to Germany. In resisting our contention that German-Austria could not be viable on its own, French imperialism repeatedly promised it would make German-Austria viable through more favorable economic provisions in the Peace Treaty. It had to fulfill at least a part of its promises, at least by striking out those clauses in the first draft that would have brought about the immediate economic collapse of Vienna and completely annihilated the viability of German-Austria.

But as significant as the progress was that we made with the July 20 draft, it was evident that we had to continue our efforts for further improvements in the peace treaty. We had come into conflict with France for two reasons: first, because of our adherence to annexation to Germany, and second, because of our refusal to let ourselves be drawn into the unanimous coalition against the Hungarian Soviet Republic. But by now history had done away with both causes of conflict. On the one hand, the Entente had dismissed the objections of the Reich-German peace delegation against Article 80 of the German Peace Treaty; the Reich had to resign itself to this, and it signed the June 28 Peace Treaty. With this the provision that German-Austria could be taken into the German Reich only after a unanimous vote of the League's Council had become part of international law. On the other hand, we knew that the Hungarian soviet government had been severely undermined; there could be no doubt that its collapse was imminent. Under such conditions neither the German nor the Hungarian question could justify persevering in the conflict with France. And rapprochement with France seemed not only possible but necessary. Our attempt to get Italy to support us against France had foundered on Italy's insistence on annexing German-South Tyrol. And France's hostility to us could become much more dangerous once Bolshevism fell in Hungary than it was when fear of the spread of Bolshevism to German-Austria had set limits to what France might do against us. We thus now had to try to get France to take a softer approach toward us.

After the second draft of the Peace Treaty had been handed to our delegation, I met Renner in Feldkirch; there we agreed on the shift in tactics. Naturally, I could not be the one to transact this rapprochement with France; my personal conflict with French diplomacy had been far too sharp. I resigned, and on July 26 the National Assembly entrusted Renner with the direction of the Foreign Ministry. His skillful conduct in Saint-Germain had significantly bolstered his standing in German-Austria and also earned him sympathy in France. Renner clearly summarized the tactical shift of these days when he publicly declared that German-Austria now wanted to adopt a "Western orientation."

The success of this shift was seen when the third and final text of the Peace Treaty was presented on September 2. The third draft clearly brought us less far-reaching improvements than the second had; rapprochement with France produced less for us than conflict with France had. But this did not negate the need for the shift of tactics in July; it only proved that after the signing of the Treaty of Versailles and the collapse of the Hungarian Soviet dictatorship, less could be achieved than previously. At any rate, the third draft restored Radkersburg to us and gave us a by no means inconsiderable improvement in many economic provisions of the Treaty. Then again it was only now in the third draft that the Entente inserted Article 188, which obliged us to regard our "independence" as "inalienable" as long as the Council of the League did not allow us annexation to Germany. This limit to our right of self-determination had still not been in the July 20 draft, although the Entente had previously imposed the obligation on the German Reich not to take us in without the consent of the League's Council. Only after my resignation, after the new "Western orientation" of our policy, was this provision also added to the Austrian Peace Treaty.

Thus, we were defeated in our struggle for annexation to Germany. And yet this struggle was by no means useless. At the moment of old-Austria's collapse, it gave the new Republic a new national ideal and the bleeding German-Austrian people a soul, an aim in life, the will to live. This national ideal had immensely strengthened the young Republic. Habsburg restoration would have made annexation impossible; the national ideal won over large sections of the bourgeoisie to republican ideas. This ideal reconciled the German-Austrian bourgeoisie with the disintegration of its old Empire and won it to the principle of the right of self-determination of peoples; the right to self-determination now meant more to it than the mere collapse of its domination of other peoples; it also meant its claim to unify its own people. It was thus only this national ideal that enabled all of the young Republic's foreign policy to be based on the unrestricted recognition of the right to self-determination of the neighboring peoples and through this to save it from all the excesses of the struggle for "integrity," which had plunged the Hungarian Revolution into such catastrophic adventures. But it was above all our struggle for annexation that was our mightiest weapon against Entente imperialism. The fear that our thesis might be true that German-Austria would on its own be unable to live forced the Entente to grant us economic aid and milder peace terms. Nevertheless, as fruitful as the struggle for annexation was despite the final defeat, the defeat was still fateful. Forcibly torn out of the large economic area whose center was formed by German-Austria, with insufficient capacity to complete the accommodation to the new conditions of life with its own means, the young Republic had to lead an independent life since its incorporation into the much more economically strong Reich was prohibited—a life that could only be one of destitution, a life of oppressive dependency on foreign countries. The final result of this "independence" to which Saint-Germain had condemned us is the international financial control to which Geneva has subjected us.

The Peace Treaty of Saint-Germain was the result, on the one hand, of the bourgeois-national revolution of the Slav nations and, on the other, of

Entente imperialism's victory. As a result of the national revolution, it had freed Czechs, Yugoslavs, and Poles from foreign domination and, on the ruins of the power relations inherited from feudalism and absolutism to which they had been subjected, created space for bourgeois democracy on their soil. But as a result of the victory of Entente imperialism, it distorted and violated all the results of the national revolution. Instead of a Czecho-slovak national state, it created a nationalities state in which millions of Germans, Magyars, Poles, and Carpathian Russians were subjected to the domination of the Czech bourgeoisie. Thus, the treaty did not remove na-tional foreign domination but just made the lord into a servant and the servant into a lord. The fatal decision that determined the composition of the Czechoslovak Republic had not only arisen from the power interests of French imperialism, which needed Czechoslovakia as an obedient vassal against Germany, but also from counterrevolutionary motives. At the end of March, one of France's notes written by Tardieu to the Peace Confer-ence, which attempted to demonstrate the need to subordinate German-Bohemia to the Czech state, read: "If Poles and Czechs have until now resisted Bolshevism it has been out of national sentiment. If this sentiment is violated they will fall prey to Bolshevism; the barrier that separates Rus-sian from German Bolshevism will be destroyed." It was the Entente bour-geoisie's fear of the social revolution's expansion that caused the national borders of the Czech state to be extended far beyond the national borders of the Czech people. And since counterrevolutionary aims determined its borders, counterrevolutionary elements also altered the nature of the state architecture born in the revolution. Since the state had millions of citizens whom it could only subordinate and rule by force, it had to become—and in this it was the true heir to old-Austria—a militarist state whose force, directed against the dominated nationalities, annexation also was directed against the working class of the ruling nationality. What had so long ap-plied to the Germans was now true of the Czechs: they could not be free as long as they denied freedom to the neighboring peoples. What applied to Czechoslovakia also applied to Poland, which, enlarged far beyond the national borders of the Polish people, enriched both at Russia's and Ger-many's expense and thus making enemies of both these large neighboring peoples, had necessarily to become the tool of French imperialism against the German Republic and against the Russian Revolution. And it also applied to Yugoslavia where Serbian militarism had—instead of the free federation of the South Slav peoples—installed its system of domination violating the historically distinct ethnicities and against which the Croats and Slovenes rebelled almost as passionately as they had against foreign domination by Austria and Hungary.

German-Austria, however, became the victim of this violation of the national revolution by imperialism. The Peace Treaty robbed the Republic even of its name. In the October days, the time of the triumph of the right of peoples to self-determination, we had called it German-Austria; the name was meant to convey our wish not to claim the Habsburgs' heritage nor control of the foreign nations enslaved by the Habsburgs but instead to unite only the German areas of the Habsburg Monarchy into a free community. The Peace Treaty forced us to give the Republic the old name of Austria; it forced this hated name on us because it insisted on penance from the working-class-led German-Austrian Republic for the crimes that the ruling classes of the Habsburg Monarchy had committed against the peoples. The Peace Treaty robbed our Republic of areas inhabited by more than three million Germans; a third of the German-Austrian people fell under foreign rule. But to the remaining area, the Peace Treaty denied not only the right to self-determination, the right to annexation; it also imposed economic hardships on it that had to make our involuntary independence doubly hard to bear. It is true that the Entente was never able to enforce the Peace Treaty's reparation obligations. But the general right of lien in support of these obligations annihilated our state credit. And the Peace Treaty's provisions regarding the value adjustment of the prewar debt, for the liquidation of the Austro-Hungarian Bank, the sequestering of Austrian property abroad, for the restriction of our freedom of movement in customs and trade policy, and for our authority over rail-ticket and freight prices wrecked our currency and depressed our economy.

This assault on the Revolution by imperialism determined its further course in German-Austria. The victory of the Entente armies in October had unleashed the peoples of the Habsburg Monarchy and in so doing made possible the hegemony of the working class in German-Austria. In the first months after the Entente victories, this hegemony had not only been founded on the relation of class forces in the country itself but was at the same time a necessity for foreign policy. It was not the bourgeois parties, which had to the very end clung to the Habsburg Monarchy's system of rule, but only Social Democracy, which had championed the right of peoples to self-determination against this system of rule, that could lead German-Austria, after the fall of the Habsburgs, along the paths of its new foreign policy founded on this right. Nor could the bourgeois parties—which at the beginning of the war had hailed the ultimatum to Serbia and during the war had screamed for the bloody suppression of the Czech "high traitors"—gradually, after the victories of the Serbs and Czechs, disarm the hatred of the liberated neighboring peoples toward Vienna, win their confidence in the young Republic, and establish friendly neighborly relations with them. Again, it was not the bourgeois parties, which had looked on in helpless fear at the domestic struggle within the working class, but only Social Democracy that could fend off the onslaught of Hungarian Bolshevism.

The urgent need to keep peace with the neighboring peoples in the first months after the October Revolution therefore required the leadership of Social Democracy. But this leadership was undermined in the course of 1919 by the peace negotiations with the Western powers. When French imperialism wanted to force German-Austria into the iron ring around the Hungarian Council Republic, Social Democracy was the stubborn obstacle to this design and the reactionary elements of the bourgeoisie its obedient tool. When French imperialism wanted to break German-Austria's desire for annexation to Germany, it was opposed by Social Democracy while the Christian Social and liberal bourgeoisie did imperialism's work. The whole influence of French imperialism in Vienna now began to operate in favor of bourgeois reaction and against Social Democracy. When Entente imperialism overthrew the Hungarian Soviet Republic with the weapons of its Romanian vassals, when it established the counterrevolution in Hungary under the protection of its Budapest missions, the German-Austrian bourgeoisie was freed of its fear of the social revolution, and its self-confidence and power of resistance grew rapidly. When, in the peace negotiations, French imperialism prevailed over the democratic ideals that the Entente had used as a weapon during the war, when Entente imperialism forced a brutal peace on Germany and German-Austria, many intellectuals, officials, and petty bourgeois in German-Austria turned away from Social Democracy. In autumn 1918, at the time of Entente democracy's greatest triumph, these strata had been attracted by democratic ideas and Wilson's principles and swelled the ranks of Social Democracy as the only advocate of democracy in German-Austria. Now, when Wilson proved to be ambiguous and impotent, when Entente democracy turned out to be a mask for Entente imperialism, their faith in democracy was shattered and they quickly reverted to their old reactionary world of ideas. When, finally, the economic threat contained in the draft treaties depressed the krone from week to week, when this devaluation of our currency raised the cost of living in German-Austria, which impoverished officials, intellectuals, and those living on small pensions while affording opportunities for endless profiteering, the discontent of the masses unschooled in economics turned not against Entente imperialism, which had caused the devaluation, but against the government led by the Social Democrats, which was unable to prevent the inescapable consequences of the currency depreciation. In this way Entente imperialism undermined the hegemony of the working class in German-Austria. If the victory of the Entente armies in autumn 1918 unleashed the Revolution, the victory of Entente imperialism over Entente democracy in the 1919 Paris Conference set fixed limits on the further development of the national and social revolution in Central Europe, thus breaking the power of the Revolution and paving the way for the bourgeois reaction.

On October 17, 1919, the Constituent National Assembly had to ratify the Peace Treaty of Saint-Germain. On the same day the first coalition government resigned and the second was appointed. The second coalition government was of a wholly different character from the first. The day on which the Treaty of Saint-Germain had to be ratified was the day when the proletariat's hegemony in German-Austria came to an end.

CHAPTER 11

THE REVOLUTION
IN THE FACTORIES

The Revolution had seriously shaken the capitalist production regime. All of production had been organized to meet the requirements of war. When the war ended, the machines suddenly came to a halt. The energy for all industry was supplied by the coal beds of Silesia, Moravia, and Bohemia; when coal deliveries from Czechoslovakia ceased, the furnace fires went out. The work discipline of the war industry had been based on military obedience; when the Revolution threw out the military factory managers, all workplace discipline broke down. For four years the war regime had forced undernourished labor power to perform endless overwork; with the regime broken, the exhausted, overtired nerves and muscles refused service, and the four-year-long disproportion between nourishment and expenditure of labor, between supplied and expended energy, was followed by the disinclination to work and a decline in labor intensity as the inevitable reaction.

The condition of dissolution in which the whole of capitalist production had fallen shook people's faith in capitalism. During 1918 in Russia all of industry was nationalized and the agrarian transformation completed. In November 1918 in the German Reich, the Socialization Committee began its work, and in the tumultuous winter of 1918–19 the German government continued to officially announce that socialization was "on the march." In spring 1919 the Hungarian Soviet Republic socialized all of industry. The German-Austrian working class, in an elemental and tempestuous movement, also demanded the right of self-determination in its workplaces. In

229

single cases—as for example on April 7, 1919 in the Donawitz Works of the Alpine Montangesellschaft—the workers deposed the managers and elected a committee to continue running the factory.

Capitalist society's belief in itself was undermined. Under state command the war economy had organized capitalist production into compulsory cartels. Was it not now incumbent on the working class to claim this inheritance from the military regime and transform this large organizational structure into a socialist one? The finances of the defeated states had fallen into a state of decay, which no longer seemed possible to overcome. Was it not inevitable that the state take to itself a great part of the accumulated private assets in order to put its budget in order? Even the bourgeois world saw the advent of a "new economic order." University professors of economics, among the German-Austrians especially Schumpeter, Grünberg, Lederer, Amonn,[1] Schwiedland, as well as scholars from the bourgeois camp like Goldscheid and Neurath, wrote treatises on socialization as the task of the day. In Vienna, as in Berlin and Leipzig, they placed themselves at the service of the Socialization Commissions, developing socialization projects, often scolding Social Democracy for dragging its feet in this great task. Within a few months an entire literature of socialization arose. It was the ideological reflection of the profound economic shock the capitalist social order had suffered from war and revolution. Although very little of the manifold competing projects was realized, the economic shock reflected in this literature still created practical needs crying out for solutions, which in the end did indeed essentially reshape the capitalist production regime and add wholly new elements, germ cells of a socialist organization of the future.

In the days of the October Revolution, Ferdinand Hanusch took over direction of the Ministry for Social Administration. In close collaboration with the Trade-Union Commission, he transformed the Ministry into an executive organ of the trade unions. With great prudence but also much energy, he set out to satisfy the practical needs of the day.

At the beginning, demobilization was the main task. The collapsed industries could not absorb those returning from the front nor the working masses expelled from the closed war industry factories. The ranks of the unemployed swelled. The first necessity was to facilitate their return to the workplace. By November 4, 1918, the Staatsrat promulgated two executive orders, one of which regulated the organization of employment bureaus and the other which created District Industrial Commissions, organs with equal representation of entrepreneurs and workers for overseeing the employment bureaus. In these District Industrial Commissions, Hanusch created local centers of social administration whose effective reach soon could be extended far beyond their original scope. The executive order on state unemployment support came only two days later, on November 6. While previously the state had left unemployment relief to the trade unions and the poor-relief system, it now guaranteed every unemployed worker support from state funds at the same level as sickness benefits as well as family income supplements to those supporting families. This not only kept the unemployed from physical and moral decay but also damped the pressure of the unemployed on the wages of those still working. But it very soon became clear that in times of a profound breakdown in capitalist production, organizing employment bureaus and unemployment relief was not enough; there needed to be more far-reaching intervention.

Many entrepreneurs, discouraged by the disintegration of the usual conditions of production and by the rebellion of the working class, made no effort to shift their factories to peacetime production or to look for raw materials for their factories and markets for their goods; they preferred to take their capital out of production, invest it in foreign currencies, and deposit it in foreign banks. This sabotage by the entrepreneurs had to be countered; they had to be forced to exercise their entrepreneurial function. They were prevented from laying off their workers and forced to pay them. That meant forcing them to seek productive employment for these workers. Already on November 18, the Staatsrat decreed that those employees returning from the war who were covered by the Commercial Clerks Law had to be rehired in the offices they occupied before the war. But in May 1919, at a time when unemployment had reached its highest level and the menace from Hungarian Bolshevism had most weakened the bourgeois parties' power of resistance, Hanusch carried out a much more radical intervention into the rights of private enterprise. On May 14, he decreed that each business owner who on April 26 had employed at least fifteen workers or employees had to employ a fifth more workers and employees in his workplace and could not reduce this level without permission of the District Industrial Commission. In fact, with this instrument a part of the unemployed could be brought back into the workplaces. The District Industrial Commissions, it is true, could not have refused permission for reducing workforces where it seemed impossible to employ the larger workforce productively. But since the reduction of the workforces continued to require the permission of the Industrial Commissions, the laying off of workers was removed from the arbitrariness of the entrepreneurs; unemployment, even if at the price of short-time work, was contained; a limit was set to the sabotage by entrepreneurs; and the exercise of entrepreneurial function was placed under joint control. How well this intervention into the self-governance of entrepreneurs has stood the test is shown by the fact that Hanusch's decree, originally intended as an emergency measure, is still in effect today.

Our social legislation faced a second task, which arose from the physical condition in which the working class had emerged from the war. The constitution of the workers had been appallingly weakened by four years of malnourishment. The blockade that the newly founded national states imposed on us had immediately aggravated our food crisis still further. The amount of work performed by workers had to be adjusted to their diminished capacity caused by undernourishment. Compliance with the old demand of the working class for an eight-hour day had become a physiological necessity. There were urgent economic reasons for the eight-hour day: A long workday in which machines ran and factories were lit and heated was a waste of coal if the debilitated bodies of the workers could not intensively use the long working time; the goal thus had to be a shorter but more intensively used workday.

There were also important social-policy reasons for an eight-hour day: In the continuously operating factories, the transition from two twelve-hour to three eight-hour shifts required a 50 percent increase in the workforce and thus enabled the absorption of part of the unemployed into the factories. The entrepreneurs' resistance to the eight-hour day was very weak in the first months after the Revolution. Already during the war the continuously operating plants had foreseen that the working class would no longer sustain a twelve-hour day—eighteen hours with the weekly shift change; certain large steel plants had already been preparing for a transition to the eight-hour day. But factories not in continuous operation had obviously absolutely no interest in resisting the eight-hour day.

The head factory inspector Tauss wrote in his report for 1919:

> The dismal situation of industrial and commercial production after the end of the war, which has become increasingly critical due to the worsening shortage of fuel and raw materials, has forced almost all enterprises to institute far-reaching restrictions of production. In most of these, the workers could therefore only be employed at sharply reduced working times or only on some days of the week. This explains why, at a time of such stagnation of productive employment, the introduction

of the eight-hour workday, in other words a forty-eight hour workweek, became generally possible without significant disturbance to industry.

And the Viennese factory inspector Ehrenhofer says on this point: "the legal introduction of the eight-hour day could hardly have come at a more opportune time than in those weeks of rapidly sinking employment and industrial activity."

Then again we also had to be aware that in the long run, regulation of working times had to be adjusted to the level of competition between German-Austrian industry and the most important foreign competitors. Therefore Hanusch proceeded very cautiously in introducing the eight-hour day. The law of December 19, 1918[2] fixed the eight-hour maximum workday only for factory enterprises; and this law was to expire with the signing of the peace. It was only the experience of succeeding months that made it possible for us to go further. On the one hand, we saw that during the first months after the Revolution, the eight-hour day became a fact in almost all enterprises, that is, also in those not subject to the law; on the other hand, in the course of that year the eight-hour day was enacted not only in all countries undergoing revolutions but also in the neutral and victor countries, partly through laws and partly through trade union action. Thus, we could from now on go far beyond the first eight-hour-day law. The law of December 17, 1919[3] established the law on the eight-hour day generally and permanently, and it was no longer limited to factory-type enterprises.

The eight-hour-day law was rounded out by the Holiday Act of July 30, 1919,[4] which guaranteed every worker a fully paid annual vacation. The vacation length was one or two weeks depending on how long the worker had been employed at the enterprise, while in 1919 apprentices and young workers were guaranteed a four-week vacation—which they could in part spend at state-run holiday homes—so that youth who had grown up during the war could be provided some measure of protection from the danger of tuberculosis, which confronted them in a particularly severe way. The introduction of worker vacations did not cause a serious loss of labor output because in many collective contracts industrial workers forwent time off for most Catholic holidays, exchanging them for the right to a vacation. For restoring public health devastated by war and malnourishment, a continuous one- or two-week vacation per year did much more than individual days off scattered throughout the year.

After the eight-hour day, the Holiday Act arguably contributed most to the astoundingly rapid improvement in health conditions in the first three years after the war. The cultural significance of these two laws, however, is just as great as their hygienic impact. The shortening of the workday gave workers for the first time the leisure for rich cultural, social, and economic activity (about which we will say more later). The establishment of worker holidays enabled the undreamt of development of worker tourism, which opened up to workers finer recreational pleasures, more conducive to their physical and mental development than any they had previously known.

It was not only in these laws that the newly achieved power of the working class was seen. The working class had to use its hegemonic position in the Republic, which it owed to the Revolution, to adapt the entire system of our social-policy legislation to the new relations of power. And so the whole first year of the Republic was filled with fruitful social legislation. Workers' rights were reshaped through the abolition of the time book and the threat of punishment for breach of contract by workers. And labor protection laws were expanded by the prohibition of night work for women and youth, by the regulation of child labor and home work, and through special legislation for bakers, miners, and clerks.

But however important this social legislation was, the urgent needs of the period could not be satisfied by a mere extension of the legislation inherited from a previous historic period. The working class demanded more. It pushed for the overturn of the entire production regime. "Socialization" was the catchword of the day. But what workers meant by this slogan was not what bureaucrats meant. To the bureaucrats trained in the school of the war economy, socialization was the state organization and regulation of the economy. The workers' idea of it was completely different. They no longer wanted to be the living tools of the entrepreneurs. Where they co-worked they wanted to co-rule; in the industries in which they co-produced they wanted to co-manage. If we were to take even a first step toward socialization in the interest of the workers, a preliminary requisite was the constitution of the working class of each enterprise as a whole, as a community, and providing it its own organs which would subject the enterprise to its control, to its co-determination. The working class pressed for this everywhere. After the October Revolution in Russia, Bolshevism had immediately created factory councils as organs of "worker control in the factories." In Germany, workers' committees had already appeared in the war industry. In England the "Whitley Committee" within the Reconstruction Committee[5] had designed a large-scale project to organize industry, whose basis was to consist of the Works Committees. When, in

German-Austria after the February elections, the Socialization Commission was established and I was elected its president, the first task I presented to the Commission was the working out of a draft law on the factory councils. After painstaking preparatory work in which the trade unions (under the leadership of Hueber, Domes, and Wiedenhofer) took an active part, the draft Factory Council Act was presented to the National Assembly on April 24 and adopted on May 15, 1919.[6]

Apart from Soviet Russia, German-Austria was the first state whose legislation created factory councils; in this we were followed in 1920 by the German Reich and in 1921 by Czechoslovakia. In German-Austria we took advantage of the high tide of Central European revolution—the month in which soviet dictatorships ruled in Budapest and Munich—to force the Factory Council Act on the entrepreneurs. This is why in some respects our Factory Council Act intervenes more deeply in the capitalist production regime than the later laws adopted in Germany and Czechoslovakia at a time when the revolutionary wave was receding. Most importantly, our law does not fix a limit on the powers of the factory councils through a complete enumeration of these powers. It invests the factory councils with the unlimited right to look after the "economic, social, and cultural interests" of the workers and employees. It lists the individual tasks of the factory council only by way of example and does not limit the councils to these branches of activity. Thus it is only the power of the working class and the capability of its factory councils that determine how it is able to take advantage of the new institution.

In reality, the factory councils evolved in very different ways in the various enterprises. In industry and commerce, where an old and stable trade union organization already existed, the experienced representatives of the trade unions took over the functions of the factory councils. They soon understood how to use the law, which made the recognition of the representatives, having previously depended on the will of the entrepreneur, into an obligation for the entrepreneur, protected the representatives from any steps taken against them due to their activity, and extended their sphere of activity far beyond immediate trade union tasks. The law, however, imposed the establishment of factory councils not only in industry and trade but in every kind of enterprise. Factory councils were elected in hospitals, in theaters, in taverns, in trading companies, in the timber industry, and in quarries, penetrating enterprises where no trade union organization (or only a very underdeveloped one) had previously existed. Here they became a fulcrum of the development and extension of the trade unions; on the other hand, these enterprises at first lacked a staff of trained representatives who would have known how to make good use of the new institution. Consequently, there were at first many abuses and mistakes, which could only gradually be overcome by the self-education of the masses in practice.

The factory councils were decisively shaped by the rapid currency devaluation that continually required adjusting wages to the falling value of money. The rapid shifts in wages occupied the attention of the factory councils and made it difficult for them to become familiarized with other areas of activity. In this respect, the period was very unpropitious for the development and training of the factory councils. On the other hand, it was precisely this serious economic collapse that set the factory councils special tasks whose fulfillment soon appreciably increased their importance for the enterprise and their authority over both the entrepreneur and the workers and employees.

The main task was to restore labor discipline. The old autocratic factory discipline had been destroyed; if production was to get underway again, a new, democratic labor discipline had to be put in its place, and so the factory councils became organs to reestablish discipline. If the workers no longer passively obeyed the orders of the managers, then they themselves had to see to it that each worker fit in with the organization of the whole and the needs of the production process.

The factory inspectors reported that some individual plant managers had factory councils elected even before the law came into force because they could restore the relaxed labor discipline only with the help of the councils. The Viennese factory inspector Osswald wrote in his report for 1919 that many factory councils had "done fine work in that they directed their attention to the improvement of labor discipline." Another Vienna factory inspector, Hauck, wrote in his report for 1920: "In many of the largest enterprises the factory councils maintain strict discipline among the workers and in this regard assist the management. In many factories the factory councils have established fines for slackened discipline or for violations of the industrial safety provisions. The issuing of fines, the management of this revenue, and its use are in the competence of the factory council."

It goes without saying that labor discipline could only gradually be restored. It returned to the degree that the working class overcame the state of exhaustion and fatigue in which it emerged from the war and the state of passionate excitement into which it had been plunged by the Revolution;

and it was restored when better coal, raw material, and food deliveries once again made possible regular, uninterrupted work, and better nourishment. But if the restoration of discipline had only been gradual and only possible with the gradual restoration of its physiological, psychological, and technological prerequisites, this possibility could only be utilized in the large and middle-sized factories with and through the factory councils. Precisely these functions made the factory councils into indispensable organs of production itself and assured them a strong position of power in the production sites. As the entrepreneurs recognized that discipline could only be restored through the factory councils, they had to grant them more influence in the workplaces. In this way the anarchy into which the Revolution had thrown the factories was gradually overcome. But the result of this improvement is a new industrial statute within which the power of the workers in the factory has been greatly strengthened, with the workers as a whole co-managing the factory through the factory council they elect. The strengthened power of the whole workforce guarantees each worker his personal freedom, dignity, and welfare within the enterprise.

The hardships of the period in which the factory councils emerged confronted them with other challenges as well. They organized, often together with the workers' consumer cooperatives, the supply of food, heating fuel, and fabric for clothing. But they soon also began to look after the provision of coal and raw materials to the factories. The factory councils of manufacturing plants travelled to the coal-mining districts and induced the miners to work overtime and on Sundays in order to supply coal to the factories and schools in the industrial districts. The miners' councils then made sure that the coal they produced by working overtime was actually used for the specified purposes. In many instances, the factory councils travelled to Vienna to approach comrades working in state bureaus in order to secure better allocations of food to their districts and more coal for their production sites, or import or export licenses. Certainly, in such activities inexperienced factory councils often allowed themselves to be misused by the enterprises. But even in cases of misuse this kind of activity proved very important, for, on the one hand, it made the factory councils indispensable to the employers and thus strengthened their position and, on the other hand, it schooled them in the economic and technical management of factories, thus training them and enabling them gradually to extend their activity beyond the sphere of trade-union tasks to include the management of the plants themselves.

It is true that when the food and coal shortages were gradually overcome and centralized economic management gradually abolished, this area of the factory councils' activity declined in importance. But ever new areas of activity opened up to them. In large enterprises the factory councils developed into extensive administrative organisms with their own offices and frequently a quite complicated division of labor emerged within them. In his 1919 report, the Vienna factory inspector Ehrenhofer recounted that the factory councils of large enterprises were beginning to divide into subcommittees, each of which exercised specific functions.

The factory statute of the enterprises of common economic interest* provides that each factory council must elect one consultant each for operational-technical, labor-protection, wage and wage-agreement, and fiscal questions and establish special subcommittees for organization and balance sheets, for welfare services, and for apprenticeships. Even this subdivision does not fully reflect the councils' range of activity. For example, many factory councils have also established factory libraries and organized courses of instruction. The factory council of one enterprise of common economic interest, the Österreichische Werke, has even assumed control of a technical school for engineering, which trains workers to be foremen.

It goes without saying that the factory councils can only gradually acquire the experience and knowledge they need to successfully fulfill their many functions. Factory inspector reports furnish examples of how the councils gradually learned to perform their tasks. In the reports for 1919, there are repeated complaints that the councils showed little understanding of factory hygiene and accident prevention. On the other hand, Vienna factory inspector Naske wrote in 1920:

> The valuable collaboration of the factory councils in the work of inspections deserves special recognition; it is not only that the presence of the factory councils during inspections appears to increase the owners' sense of responsibility and effectively produces a feeling of obligation toward their workers, but at the same time the labor representatives present assume the responsibility of guaranteeing that the measures recommended by the factory inspector are really carried out without the need to put official pressure on the factory owner. The factory councils also constitute a valuable support for the factory inspector because they are well acquainted with local conditions and in a position to point out dangers that might easily escape the attention of the inspector. It also often hap-

---

* See Glossary.

pens that factory councils send written requests to the inspection office for remediation of grievances.

In a 1920 report the Wiener Neustadt factory inspector Astolfi wrote a similar assessment, while inspectors from areas with a more backward working class, for example the Vorarlberg inspector Eberl, reported that the factory councils could not evaluate issues of technical industrial safety.

The development of the factory councils depends to a very large extent on the development of the relations between workers and employees.* Differences of education, ways of life, political outlook, and the fact that the employees relate to the workers as superiors exercising entrepreneurial functions—all of these factors make difficult the close cooperation between the workers' and employees' councils that is essential to assure the employees' councils the strong support of the workers and to place the greater technical and commercial knowledge of the employees at the service of the workers' councils. These difficulties too can only be overcome gradually through the self-education of the factory councils in the course of their activity.

The factory councils are thus still in an early developmental phase. The Revolution could do no more than create them, but their development can occur only through practice. Only in gradual development, in gradual self-education in the activity of the factory councils, can the working class produce a staff of trained representatives able to take full advantage of the new institution. This self-education of the working class in and through the practice of factory councils creates the prerequisites of a socialist mode of production. The example of Russia, where the democratic organization of industry attempted immediately after the October Revolution had so quickly yielded to a bureaucratic state capitalism, shows that only bureaucratic state socialism, which merely substitutes the despotism of the entrepreneur with the despotism of the bureaucrat, is possible as long as the working class has not yet acquired the capacity for self-government in its work process. Democratic socialism—the socialism that the working class intends and wants, which realizes the workers' right to self-determination in the labor process—is only possible if the working class is capable of governing production without destroying it. As a great school of proletarian self-government in the production process, the factory councils are a preliminary stage of the socialist mode of production. Consequently, their

---

* *Angestellte*—white-collar workers.

origin and development means much more for the development of a socialist social order than any sort of violent expropriation if its result is to be
more than bureaucratically administered state and municipal enterprises.

The war economy had put capitalist enterprises under bureaucratic
governance and made these compulsory capitalist-bureaucratic trusts into
a requisitioning machine for the needs of the army. It militarized the individual capitalist enterprises, putting the coercive power of the military
bureaucracy at the service of capitalist domination and capitalist domination at the service of the coercive military organization. Both capitalist
enterprises and the state bureaucracy were allied against the working class.
The revolt of the working class was directed against both forces. If the
first consequence of the revolt against the domination of capitalist enterprises was the creation of factory councils, then the first result of the revolt against the state bureaucracy was the analogous creation of office staff
councils, which were first instituted in the public transportation agencies
and acquired strong influence on the administration of these agencies. But
neither of these institutions satisfied the masses of workers, who pressed
for the socialization of industry, which was to free industry from the domination of the capitalist entrepreneur without subjecting workers to the
domination of the state bureaucracy. A factory statute had to be found that
was neither capitalist nor bureaucratic. This was one of the first problems I
attempted to solve in a series of newspaper articles, which first appeared in
the *Arbeiter-Zeitung* and were subsequently published as a booklet with the
title *Der Weg zum Sozialismus* (The Road to Socialism).

The plan of organization that I sketched in these articles was inspired on
the one hand by English Guild Socialism, whose fundamental ideas I had
become acquainted with before the war from G. D. H. Cole's *The World of
Labour* (London, 1913), and on the other hand by the early organizational
experiments of Russian Bolshevism, which were formulated at the All-Russia Congress of Representatives of Financial Departments of Soviets in May
1918.[7] Both sought to base the administration of socialized industry on the
cooperation of the state, as the representative of the whole community, and
the trade union, as the representative of the special interests of workers and
employees active in the socialized branch of industry. My plan of organization added the organization of consumers as a third partner with the same
rights. I proposed that each socialized branch of industry be governed by
a special administrative body, which would be composed of workers and
employees working in each branch of industry, of representatives of the con-

sumers for whom the products are intended, and of state representatives as the arbitrators among the conflicting interests of the producers and consumers. At that time similar proposals were made wherever the working class initiated a struggle for socialization. Examples are the plan for a "German Coal Community" drawn up by Germany's Socialization Commission; Justice Sankey's recommendations for the British coal mines; the Plumb Plan[8] for the organization of railways in the United States of America; the proposal of the Confédération Générale du Travail for the socialization of the French railways; and later the proposals made by Sidney and Beatrice Webb in their *Constitution for the Socialist Commonwealth* (London, 1920).[9] While these proposals were never put into practice elsewhere, we in German-Austria were able to start realizing them, although only modestly at first.

When I became chair of the Socialization Commission, the first task I gave myself was the creation of a legal form for the new type of enterprise I had proposed. I submitted to the National Assembly a bill for the establishment of the enterprises of common economic interest at the same time as the bill establishing the factory councils. The bill was carefully revised by the Assembly's Socialization Committee and passed by the Assembly on July 29, 1919.[10] As soon as the legal preconditions had been created, we set about to test the new form of enterprise.

The dismantling of the war economy created new needs whose satisfaction required the new form of enterprise. The Republic had inherited many large firms, which had been the property of the army administration and operated under military control to meet the needs of the army. After the Armistice these firms were taken over by the civil administration—the Directorate General for State Industry.*

But their bureaucratic managers did not know how to adapt the war industries to peacetime production. A great deal of the valuable raw material that had accumulated in the factories was abandoned to profiteers. The managers refrained from laying off the workers so as not to swell the ranks of the unemployed, but they made no attempt to employ them productively. Thus, these enterprises became a heavy burden for the state. It was not advisable to lease or sell the enterprises to private capital. At a time in which entrepreneurial spirit had been paralyzed, firms were weighed down with enormous deficits, and the rapid currency devaluation made every appraisal of valuable plants impossible and quickly devalued the state-approved purchase prices; the selling off of the factories would have

---

* Generaldirektion der staatlichen Industriewerke.

meant dissipating valuable state property. But it was equally impossible to leave the firms in the hands of the technically and commercially incompetent bureaucrats. Thus, the wretched condition into which the state's war industries had fallen demanded a new form of organization that kept the factories as public property but gave them a commercially flexible management freed from the bureaucratic straitjacket. And the workers in the war-industry plants had to have an important share in their management. After the political upheaval the workers in these industries, concerned about their jobs, had defended the factories against the plundering of profiteers colluding with the bureaucracy. The workers had saved the plants and their raw material stocks for the state. Since the factories' bureaucratic management was incompetent to manage them and restore order, the workers assumed ever more control over them. It was therefore obvious that the factories could only be brought back into orderly production with the active participation of the factory councils, and so the direct involvement of factory councils in management was unavoidable. Thus, practical necessity tended to impose the new common-economic-interest form of enterprise.

Our first attempts were on a small scale. The first "enterprise of common economic interest" we established was the Vereinigte Leder- und Schufabriken.* They were founded by the state together with the Austrian Cooperative Wholesale Society† as the representative of proletarian consumers and the Agricultural Trading Center‡ as the representative of peasant consumers. The state brought its shoe factory in Brunn am Gebirge into the enterprise, while the two consumer organizations provided the working capital and took over the marketing of the products. The Enterprise Assembly,§ in which ultimate responsibility rests and which appoints the Executive Board, is composed of representatives of the state, of the two consumer organizations, and of representatives of the factory council and trade union of the workers who operate the factory. This first foundation was a resounding success. Within a short time, it was possible to start up production and intensify the work. The first annual balance sheet showed a substantial net profit. The second institution, the Austrian Central Medicine Dispensary,¶ launched immediately afterward was equally successful.

---

* United Leather and Shoe Factories.
† Grosseinkaufsgesellschaft österreichischer Konsumvereine.
‡ Landwirtschaftliche Warenverkehrsstelle.
§ Anstaltsversammlung.
¶ Die österreichische Heilmittelstelle.

It was founded by the state together with the Vienna Hospital Funds* and Health Insurance Fund,† which took over the management of the former Army Dispensary Authority.‡ They organized the provision of pharmaceuticals and therapeutic appliances to the sanatoria and convalescent homes and, through the introduction of prepackaged medicines, reformed public healthcare. The success of these first two enterprises of common economic interest encouraged the founding of others.

After I resigned from the chairmanship of the Socialization Commission during the formation of the second coalition government in October 1919, the work was continued with great tenacity by Ellenbogen as its president and Chief Government Building Supervisor Ried as its office head. Thus, a whole system of enterprises of general economic interest gradually emerged.

Several wartime industries were transferred bodily to this type of enterprise; for example, the large industrial plants of the Vienna Arsenal were transferred to the Österreichische Werke and the plant in Puntigam to the Steirische Fahrzeugwerke.§ In other cases, the wartime industrial areas were transferred to institutions of common economic interest, which however then transferred the individual factories to mixed-economy enterprises founded and managed together with private capital. Alongside them there arose enterprises of common economic interest not based on former wartime factories but serving newly arisen needs, for example, the Common-economy Settlement and Building-Material Agency¶ and Holzmarkt.** Finally, enterprises were formed whose legal form was not that of companies of general economic interest but rather joint-stock companies, though composed in the same way as the enterprises of common economic interest or similar to them. An example is the Wäsche- und Bekleidungs-A.-G.†† managed by the state together with the Wholesale Cooperative Society and the Agricultural Trading Center, as well as the Wiener Holz- und Kohlengesellschaft‡‡ managed by the Municipality of Vienna together with the Wholesale Cooperative Society.

Thus, the Revolution created a new type of enterprise. Before then

---

* Wiener Krankenanstaltenfonds.

† Krankenkassen.

‡ Militärmedikamentendirektion.

§ Styrian Automobile Works.

¶ Gemeinwirtschaftliche Siedlungs- und Baustoffanstalt.

** Lumber Market.

†† Linens and Clothing Corporation.

‡‡ Vienna Lumber and Coal Company.

we had been familiar with bureaucratically managed state and municipal enterprises on the one hand and cooperative enterprises on the other. Now a new combination appeared. The enterprise of common economic interest was as a rule managed by the state, or a municipality, together with the consumer cooperative institutions. The state furnished the plant; the co-operative societies provided commercially trained managers and organized the marketing of the products. But added to this cooperation of the state with consumer cooperative organizations was the crucial presence of the factory councils and trade unions of the workers employed in the enter-prises of common economic interest. Often they are represented not only in the company assembly but frequently directly in the company's man-aging board; thus, they have much more direct influence on management than they have in state and municipal enterprises or in the factories of cooperative societies. The idea of direct control of industry by the workers and employees active in it has been realized here to an extent that goes far beyond the Factory Council Act. The division of power between the three partners of the enterprises of common economic interest differs according to what the enterprise does. In enterprises working directly to satisfy the needs of public entities—for example the Central Medical Dispensary or the Wiener Holz- und Kohlengesellschaft—the influence of the public en-tities, of the state or municipality, is preponderant. In the enterprises work-ing directly to satisfy the needs of the cooperatives—for example in the Vereinigte Leder- und Schufabriken and in the Housing and Building-Ma-terial Agency*—cooperatives have the most influence. In the enterprises working for the free market and competing freely with capitalist enter-prises—such as the Österreichische Werke—the main influence is that of the trade unions and factory councils. But in all cases, the enterprises of common economic interest have been the means of replacing the absolute rule of bureaucracy over public enterprises by co-management on the part of proletarian organizations: through cooperatives on the one hand and factory councils and trade unions on the other hand.

To be sure, not only proletarian organizations were involved; in all en-terprises we find the Produce Exchange Office,† which is partly controlled by the agricultural cooperatives along with the Wholesale Buying Society of the Consumer Associations.‡ This was an economic application of the

---

* Siedlungs- und Baustoffanstalt.
† Warenverkehrsstelle.
‡ Grosseinkaufsgesellschaft der Konsumvereine.

idea of cooperation between workers and farmers, which underlay the first coalition government, and by this means an attempt was made to interest the peasants in the "socialized" enterprises and so win their support for the ideas of socialization.

The newly founded enterprises of common economic interest had and have great difficulties to overcome everywhere. The industries that they have taken over were exclusively adapted to military requirements. Only with great difficulty and at great expense can they be restructured for peacetime production. For example, the Österreichische Werke took over a large cannon factory, which now has to be adapted to the most varied new purposes. Gradually, this factory was transformed into a machine-tool factory, a sports gun factory, a production site for agricultural implements, an automobile factory, and a cabinet-making factory. But the enterprises lacked capital with which to carry out a rapid transformation, as they came into existence at a time of rapid currency depreciation. In this situation every industrial enterprise is obliged constantly to increase its working capital. The capitalist joint-stock companies do so by occasionally issuing new stock and by making greater use of bank credit. Neither method was feasible for the enterprises of common economic interest. They could of course not issue stock; by law they were granted the right to issue bonds at fixed interest rates. But the issuing of fixed-interest-rate bonds is impossible at a time of rapid money depreciation. Clause 8 of the Law,* however, conferred on the Minister of Finance the right to force the banks to invest a portion of their foreign currency determined by the Minister and their reserve fund in the bonds issued by the enterprises of common economic interest. But the government never decided to make use of this right. Nor could the enterprises of common economic interest receive sufficient bank credit in other forms. The banks extend credit to enterprises they control and in which they participate; they denied credit to enterprises not subjected to their control the more the continuously hostile agitation of the capitalist press tried to undermine confidence in these enterprises. Consequently, the enterprises of common economic interest were repeatedly obliged to request state subsidies to provide their working capital. Since they needed to enlarge their working capital, they remained dependent on these subsidies even though their balance sheets at the end of the first year showed net profits that were not inconsiderable. But the state, in dire financial straits itself, only insufficiently satisfied the enterprises' need for money. In con-

* The July 29, 1919 Law on Enterprises of Common Economic Interest (StGBl. 389/1919).

sequence, their development, especially the necessary investments for conversion to peacetime production, was retarded. The enterprises were forced to transfer a part of their businesses, which they could not keep afloat due to money shortages, to mixed-economy enterprises that they created together with private capitalists. In this way a great many associations and intermediate forms between enterprises of common economic interest and capitalist enterprises were generated. These financial difficulties will probably be overcome if the currency depreciation is halted. But only experience will be able to show how the still insufficiently consolidated enterprises will weather the market-outlet crisis, which has followed the stabilization of the currency.

Although the initial difficulties faced by the common economy have by no means been overcome, the new form of enterprise has doubtless already proven its superiority to the bureaucratic form. The war-industry enterprises immediately took on a completely different appearance when they were removed from the bureaucratic Directorate General of State Industries and transferred to the enterprises of general economic interest. The management became commercially flexible, production got underway again, and labor intensity and discipline rapidly improved with the active involvement of the factory councils and trade unions; the deficits, which had become very large under bureaucratic management, were very quickly reduced. If the enterprises can be supplied with sufficient working and investment capital, there is no doubt that they can become viable and productive.

The Law on Enterprises of Common Economic Interest also attempted to give them the opportunity to extend their influence beyond their own areas of operation and penetrate into capitalist enterprises. Clause 37 of the Law empowers the government, in the case of the creation of joint-stock companies or of capital increases in already existing ones, to demand a share amounting at most to one half of the company's capital under conditions no less favorable than those under which the new shares were allotted to the founders of the new company or the holders of the old shares. At a time when the currency depreciation compelled all joint-stock companies to continuously increase their working capital, this provision could be used to induce the state, or the enterprises of common economic interest created by the state, to acquire shares in capitalist enterprises; it also helped prevent private capital from reaping "founders profits" from receiving new shares on preferential terms—allowing the polity to do so as well. It is true that in the beginning the state was prevented by its financial straits from effectively using Clause 37. Later, however, the Vienna municipality did use it to acquire shares in many industrial enterprises, and in some cases the enterprises of common economic interest too could acquire preference shares in joint-stock companies. Thus, the Vereinigte Leder- und Schufabriken acquired shares in a large leather factory and a capitalist shoe factory.

When the economic power of the enterprises of common economic interest is improved and the political power of the working class systematically applies Clause 37, this provision can become an instrument for subjecting capitalist enterprises themselves to the gradually tightening control of the enterprises of common interest.

The common-interest economy has today penetrated many industries—in the metal and machine industry through the Österreichische Werke and Steyrische Automobilwerke, in the chemical industry through the Central Medicine Dispensary and the Blumau mixed-economy enterprises, in the timber industry through the Wiener Holzwerke* (founded together with the Settlement and Building Material Agency, which manages the cabinet-making production in the Arsenal); we see it in the textile industry with the Wäsche- und Bekleidungs-A.-G. (which has put into operation the weaving mills of the former military enterprises in Brunn am Gebirge and in Fischamend), and in the construction industry with the Housing and Building Material Agency. Thus, within all these industries the nuclei of a common-interest economy have been implanted that, when they are able to grow sufficiently, can gradually conquer spaces at the cost of capitalist industry and penetrate the latter. Above all, however, the enterprises of common economic interest offer the possibility of gradually working out the methods of a socialized administration of these branches of industry and gradually educating state officials, cooperative members, and trade unionists in these methods. This is indeed the most important function this sector fulfills in the transition to a socialist social order. As long as they do not have the capacities to administer the expropriated means of production, the workers cannot expropriate the capitalists without devastating production. To develop their capacities to work out the best methods for the administration of the public enterprises, and to educate to this end a trained staff of representatives, is the task of the social economy, which develops in the womb of capitalist society.

In the turbulent period in which the law regulating the enterprises of common economic interest arose, there was little patience for such a

---

* Vienna Lumber Works.

protracted development of the elements of the socialist future. In the winter and spring months of 1919, that is, the period of the great struggles in Germany around council dictatorship and socialization and the time of the council dictatorship in Hungary, the masses in German-Austria also demanded the socialization of private industry, and we too could not foresee whether victories of the socialization movement in our neighbor states could also make possible, and necessary, the socialization of individual branches of industry in our country. Projects for the socialization of individual branches of industry were drawn up by the Socialization Commission under the direction of Professor Emil Lederer of Heidelberg. We first considered the socialization of the large iron industry, the great forest domains, and the coal mines and the wholesale coal industry and designed a project to carry out the expansion of hydropower in common-interest forms. Thus, the polity was first to take over control of the two most important raw materials, iron and wood, and the two most important energy sources, coal and water power. But during summer 1919, it became increasingly clear that these projects faced insurmountable obstacles.

In their opposition to the expropriation of some branches of industry, the capitalists first found a powerful ally in the particularism of the provinces. The provincial governments of Styria and Carinthia demanded that the iron industry not be socialized by the state but distributed among the provinces. All provincial governments declared that each province should exercise sole control of its hydropower. The provinces, in reaction to the socialization of the forest domains, presented completely different plans; they began passing provincial laws to compensate for the abrogation of the peasants' easements upon the state forests through distributing land to them. That is, instead of socializing the forests, they distributed them to the peasants. This opposition of the provinces drew out the negotiations over socialization precisely at a time when conditions were most favorable for their success.

As a first step, we focused on the socialization of the iron industry, which would have to begin with the socialization of the Alpine Montangesellschaft. Conditions were favorable. The Prague Iron Industry Company had sold off its Alpine shares, and the company was now completely in the hands of German-Austrian capitalists. The stock prices were low; we could have inexpensively taken over the enterprise even after fully compensating the shareholders. But after we had already begun to set this in motion, we were thwarted by a counteraction made possible and promoted by a member of the government. Professor Schumpeter, the Minister of Finance of the first coalition government, had been a staunch supporter of socialization. In the first weeks of the Revolution, he had flirted with Bolshevism and then actively worked with the Socialization Commission in Berlin; there, as well as later on, during the period of Hungary's soviet dictatorship, he criticized the socialization policy of Social Democracy in Vienna as being insufficiently energetic and not radical enough. But very soon thereafter, he accomplished a complete about-face. He had established contact with the Viennese banker Richard Kola who at Schumpeter's behest undertook an operation to stabilize the German-Austrian krone and bought up foreign currencies for the Ministry of Finance. On Schumpeter's behalf Kola went to Zurich where he negotiated a major transaction with an Italian financial group for which he began to buy up shares of the Alpine Montangesellschaft. Schumpeter supported this action by his banker because Kola handed over the lire he received for the Alpine shares to the Treasury, which urgently needed foreign currencies to pay for food and coal. Schumpeter supported this although he knew that we had already targeted the socialization of the Alpine Montangesellschaft. He supported it without informing other members of government. We only learned of the whole transaction when it was too late to stop it. It unleashed a fierce conflict inside the coalition government in which Schumpeter sought and got the support of Vienna's Christian Social Party; the conflict ended with Schumpeter's exit when the second coalition government was elected. The end result of Schumpeter's action was that we were confronted with foreign capital in the Alpine Montangesellschaft. Now the Italian general who headed the inter-Allied Armistice Commission in Vienna emerged quite openly as the advocate of the Italian shareholders of the Alpine Montangesellschaft. When the German-Austrian government claimed some of the new shares issued by Alpine, by virtue of Clause 37 of the Law on Enterprises of Common Economic Interest, the Italian government coerced the sale of these shares to an Italian bank group. The socialization of the Alpine Montangesellschaft became impossible once it was in Italian hands. Our state was too weak internationally to dare expropriate foreign capitalists.

But our other socialization projects also came up against impediments that had their origin abroad. The socialization of the coal industry would have had to begin not with our coal mines, which only met a small part of our needs, but with the wholesale coal business. The organization of coal that had been created in wartime would have had to be taken over by an enterprise of common economic interest. Moreover, the state organization of coal was at the time in no position to meet coal requirements while private entrepreneurs through their individual business contacts in Czechoslovakia and in Upper Silesia could get coal illicitly to which the state could have no access. It was especially the commercial enterprises in which the Upper Silesian coal wholesalers themselves had interests that were indispensable for our coal supply. Under these conditions a monopolization of the coal trade by an enterprise of common economic interest could only have reduced our coal supply. Consequently, the idea had to be tabled.

The expansion of hydropower was impossible without foreign capital. At first we believed we could transfer the whole electricity service to an enterprise of common economic interest which would then form mixed-economy enterprises, with the participation of foreign capital, for the expansion and operation of the individual water works. However, all negotiations with foreign capitalists demonstrated that foreign capital itself regarded such socialization with suspicion. We therefore concluded that we could not socialize hydropower without endangering its expansion.

All these external impediments to socialization could be traced to a common cause. Since the lifting of the blockade our imports of foreign goods had greatly increased. But the disruption of our production made it impossible to export enough to be able to pay for the imported goods with the receipts from our exports. If we could not pay for imports through the export of our products, then we had to do so through selling off our means of production. It was unavoidable that German-Austrian shares and enterprises should be sold abroad and that foreign capital should penetrate our production. The debit in our balance of payments had to be covered through capital imports. Any expropriation of private capital would have to endanger them. We could not expect foreigners to buy our shares and enterprises and invest their capital in our industry if they had to fear expropriation.

Thus, indigenous capitalists who resisted the socialization of their means of production could correctly argue that they understood the real needs of the economy, which required the influx of foreign capital. This resistance became all the stronger the more obvious this real need became ever since the lifting of the blockade.

The need for capital imports was by no means an absolute impediment to any socialization of private industry. Had the powerful movement that emerged from the war carried out the socialization of individual branches of production in other countries, then the socialization of individual branches of production in German-Austria ought not to have impeded the necessary capital imports if it were accomplished in legal forms and with appropriate compensations and limited to a few predetermined branches of production—as we had planned—leaving all the others to the free movement of the market. But as soon as the Western powers had overcome the social crisis of the months of demobilization, and as soon as the Reichswehr in the German Reich had put down the revolutionary workers' movements, pushing the proletariat onto the defensive and thus removing socialization from the agenda there as well—in other words, as soon as capitalism was again consolidated in all of Western and Central Europe and had repelled the onslaught of socialism—any socialization of an individual branch of industry, even in due legal form and with full compensation for the owners, was denounced as "Bolshevism." Naturally then, the most dependent European state most reliant on foreign capital influx could no longer dare carry out more expropriations if it did not want to shut off this influx needed to cover its food, coal, and raw-material supplies. Therefore, in summer 1919 resistance to all attempts at socialization very quickly gained strength; as soon as Hungary's soviet dictatorship collapsed, it became obvious that there no longer was any prospect of enforcing socialization.

In his *Class Struggles in France*, Marx criticizes the illusions of the Parisian workers of 1848 who "thought they would be able to consummate a proletarian revolution within the national walls of France. . . . But French relations of production are conditioned by the foreign trade of France, by her position on the world market and the laws thereof."[11] If it is true that the world market imposed its laws even on the relations of production of France in 1848, how much more was this true of German-Austria in 1919, dependent as it was on foreign food and coal deliveries, on foreign credits and the influx of foreign capital. Within the all too restrictive and porous "national walls" of German-Austria, the social revolution certainly could not be consummated. But even so we had to fight for socialization here too as long as there was even the smallest hope that the Central European revolution, born of the war, could go beyond the framework of the bourgeois property order and proceed to the "expropriation of the expropriators." As soon as it was certain that capitalism was asserting itself and consolidating not just in the victor countries but also in the revolutionized Central European states, we had to suspend our struggle for the expropriation of private industry and limit our socialization to the construction of the common economy on the restricted basis of the remnants of the state war industries.

Our struggle for socialization was therefore not futile. It is a law of every revolution that it must set itself goals beyond what is immediately achievable in order to achieve what is currently practicable. Only the general attack, which the working class mounted against the capitalist system in pressing for the expropriation of capital, could have unsettled capitalism so severely that it had to make the most far-reaching concessions possible within the capitalist system. The massively reinforced power of the working class in industry, the revolutionizing of labor law and labor protection legislation, the new democratic labor statute embodied in the factory councils and office staff councils, the substitution of bureaucratic management by enterprises of common economic interest, such far-reaching interventions into the sovereignty of capital as the compulsory hiring of unemployed workers in factories, or Clauses 8 and 37 of the Law on Enterprises of Common Economic Interest—these are the real results of our fight for socialization. It is true that we could not break apart the capitalist system itself. At the same time as our national revolution, coming up against France's victorious imperialism, had to adopt a "Western orientation" and renounce the goal of annexation to Germany, our social revolution had to give up the goal of immediate expropriation of the expropriators. It was a bourgeois revolution that had been accomplished in the countries surrounding German-Austria; within the framework of the bourgeois revolution around us, the social revolution could not be accomplished in our small and weak country. But if our revolution could not break capital's domination of production, it nevertheless implanted the nuclei of the socialist order of production of the future, elements of a statute regulating production that realizes the self-determination of the working class in the process of production, which, as above all with the factory councils and the enterprises of common economic interest, only need to be developed in order gradually to rein in the domination of capital and eventually destroy it.

CHAPTER 12

THE STATE AND
THE WORKING CLASS

The Revolution had smashed the military power apparatus that had held down the working class. The working class became free; no armed force kept it in check. But at the same time the Revolution had broken up the old Austro-Hungarian economic area, plunging German-Austria into dire misery and onerous dependency on other countries. This was the twofold inner contradiction of the Austrian Revolution: the contradiction between the enormous political power of the working class and its terrible misery, and the contradiction between the working class's freedom at home and its oppressive dependency on capitalism abroad.

This contradiction could only be resolved by the self-restraint of the proletariat, only if the proletariat itself—based on its own understanding and will—imposed limitations on the exercise of its freedom and power. Failing to do so would have brought conflict with other countries, leading to famine, invasion, and the downfall of the newly won freedoms.

Through mass strikes, the railwaymen and workers in vital industries could have forced the state to give them everything they demanded. No power existed to compel them to fulfill their duties; there was no Technical Emergency Relief* ready to replace their labor power. No external force, only their own insight, could make them limit their demands to what the impoverished state could deliver without destroying the whole national economy.

In the barracks actual power was not in the hands of the officers but in the hands of the soldiers' councils. No coercive military body put the

* See Glossary.

Volkswehr at the service of the coalition government. As long as the soldiers' councils and Volkswehr members were convinced that the program of the coalition government was the only one possible and even necessary, the Volkswehr, filled as it was with revolutionary spirit and proletarian class consciousness, placed its arms at the service of the government.

Workers and soldiers could, at any given moment, have established a dictatorship of the proletariat. There was no power to prevent it. Only their own understanding that under the given international conditions a red terror would inevitably be followed by a white terror saved them from this temptation.

Every revolution has to defend its course against masses that, filled with revolutionary illusions and passions, rush forward beyond what is possible under the given social conditions and what can be demanded and achieved under the given historical conditions. But the coalition government of the German-Austrian Revolution had no coercive instrument to hold back the masses filled with revolutionary passion. The German-Austrian Revolution would have drowned in famine and invasion if the revolutionary masses had not themselves imposed limitations and been content with what was economically possible and what was achievable and defendable within the international power relations. The specific and most difficult problem of the Revolution was to persuade hungry and despairing masses agitated by all the emotions that war and revolution stirred up, not by using force to keep them down but by deploying intellectual means to get them to decide freely, based on their own knowledge, not to overstep the limits imposed on the Revolution by the country's economic misery and economic and military impotence.

This was the peculiarity of governance under the revolutionary regime: unlike all governments before and after it, it could not govern through force aimed at keeping the governed obedient but only by intellectual suasion, by appealing to the masses' intelligence and comprehension of the country's predicament, by appealing to their sense of responsibility.

If the government could appeal to the masses only through intellectual means, it could do this only through the large social organizations, acting in close cooperation with them, taking no important steps without their approval. Only the influence of the soldiers' councils on the militiamen assured that they would follow the orders of the State Secretary of the Armed Forces, and so he could not exercise his office other than in continuous consultation with the soldiers' councils. Only the influence of the trade unions and of the personnel representatives of the railwaymen, of the postmen, and of the telegraph and telephone employees guaranteed the maintenance of communications; thus, the Minister of Communications could not fulfill the functions of his office other than in the closest possible consultation with the trade unions and personnel representatives. If food and coal deliveries stalled, if the workers were to rebel here or there against the terrible economic deprivation, then it was only the workers' council that could pacify the excited masses; to fulfill his duties, therefore, the Minister of the Interior had no choice but to act in the closest possible consultation with the workers' councils. Similarly, the Ministry of Social Welfare and the Food Ministry could only be managed in the closest possible consultation with the trade unions and consumer cooperatives, respectively. Thus, the organizations gained decisive influence in the whole state administration. The obligatory maxim of government was to undertake no government action without consulting the organization of those directly affected by the action.

But this brought about a change in the functions of the organizations. If the organizations shared in the decisions regarding all-important activities of the government, then they had to assume responsibility for these before the masses. If in daily negotiations with the government, the organizations carried out what was possible and achievable, then it was incumbent on them to avert demands from the masses for the impossible and unachievable. If the government had become the executive organ of the organizations' will, then the organizations had to become organs through which the government governed the masses. In this way Social Democracy, the trade unions, the soldiers' councils, and the workers' councils became partners in government power and organs of government power at the same time.

The structure of Social Democracy and of the trade unions was completely transformed. The Revolution brought to them vast new sectors of the population. In 1913, Social Democracy had 91,000 members in the German districts of Inner Austria; in 1919 it had 332,391. In the same districts the trade unions had 253,137 members in 1913 and 772,146 in 1919. Two-thirds of the party and trade-union membership consisted of newly recruited comrades who only encountered the old cadre after the October Revolution. The indifferent who took no part in the labor movement before the war, the submissive whom factory feudalism had driven toward the yellow unions, the employees who kept apart from the workers before the war—they all streamed into the party and the trade unions. Members with no party and trade-union experience now filled the organizations.

The structural changes went hand in hand with changes in the functions of party and trade union. Before and during the war, our most important task was to revolutionize the masses: to pull the servile out of their inherited submissive faith in authority in the state and the factory, lead the timid to recognize the power that organization gives to the masses, and awaken a fighting spirit among the hesitant. During and after the Revolution, an entirely different task confronted us. Now the masses, whom the collapse of the old machinery of domination had filled with an exalted confidence in their own power, needed to learn to use this power prudently. We now had to prevent the newly won freedom of the masses who had been brutalized by four years of war from degenerating into unbridled violence, to prevent the masses' terrible deprivation from tempting them to strike out in blind, suicidal ways, to prevent them from being misled into converting the illusions produced by the Revolution into deeds that would have caused their ruin. Before the Revolution we had to be "agitators"; after it we had to be "brakemen." The new task was easy where we had to deal with our old cadre, disciplined and well schooled by decades-long struggles and with confidence in our leadership. It was incomparably more difficult where we had to deal with the newly recruited masses lacking all political and trade-union training.

The mechanism of government worked in this way: on all important government actions, the Social Democratic members of government worked out prior agreements with the leadership of the large proletarian organizations, with the top organs of the party, the trade unions, and the workers' and soldiers' councils. The Social Democratic members of government then had the task of pushing through in the government and the National Assembly what was agreed upon. But the leaders of the proletarian organizations had to gain the support of the masses for the government program they had approved with members of government and also move the masses to abandon demands that went beyond the program. The leaders of the proletarian organizations first had to have the understanding and approval of the delegates of the party, the trade unions, and the workers' and soldiers' councils. Then these delegates had the most difficult and important task of all: asserting the policy of the organizations in factory and barrack meetings before the masses themselves. At these meetings, wildly excited masses were confronted by a party delegate, a factory council, or a soldiers' council on the platform. The audience would be dissatisfied. They would demand more than the delegate could give them. They would cry out for forcible decisions. The delegate would speak of the economic plight of the Republic, of its dependency on foreign countries, of the superiority of the foreign capitalist powers and the danger of coming into conflict with them. In the hall there would be hunger, despair, passion; on the platform understanding of what is possible economically, awareness of the international limits of the Revolution, exhortation to prudence, and appeals to the sense of responsibility. It was a hard struggle, a struggle that made not only the highest intellectual demands on the delegates but also the highest moral demands. For the sake of the cause, they had to confront their own comrades fearlessly; to stand up under insults, complaints, at times even threats and maltreatment from the excited masses; and still, in arduous struggle against despair, carry out the policy adopted as the only practical one. Friedrich Adler, whose revolutionary deed had gained him the greatest popularity, said at this time: "Popularity is capital that should only be used in order to be consumed." This high moral principle motivated not merely a few dozen party and trade-union officials, but many thousands of modest delegates, factory councils, and workers' and soldiers' councils.

In factory and barrack meetings of this kind, the great temptation of Bolshevism was fended off and labor discipline gradually restored. In meetings like these, irresponsible strikes were averted and order restored when hunger and excitement led the masses to violence and excess. The history of the factory and barracks assemblies is the inner, intellectual history of the Austrian Revolution; for the bourgeoisie, which had hardly noticed this great process of intellectual self-mastery of the working class, this was the Revolution's secret history.

In the American Declaration of Independence of 1776, democracy was defined as a system of government based on the consent of the governed. Never and nowhere was democracy in this sense more completely realized than in this first phase of the German-Austrian Revolution. Its government, lacking all means of force against the governed, could govern only by painstakingly winning, daily and hourly, the consent of the governed. These methods were imposed on it by the very weakness of the state power that emerged from the Revolution. With these methods it had to try to govern under the most unfavorable conditions imaginable: at a time of extraordinarily great mass privations, at a time of extraordinarily great mass excitement, and at a time in which a large section of the masses were demoralized by four years of war. The attempt could only succeed at the cost of many heavy sacrifices, even many intellectual sacrifices. But it did succeed. That it did succeed is what, in human terms, constitutes the greatness of the German-Austrian Revolution.

It is important to examine more closely the letter and spirit of the methods of governance.

By means of elections, parliamentary democracy seeks to secure agreement between the governing and the governed. It considers this agreement secured if the whole population is called on every third or fourth year to elect the parliament, which then determines the composition of the government and controls its actions. The working class everywhere has learned that this belief is an illusion; that the power of the bourgeoisie over the press, the pulpit, and the electoral apparatus enables it to determine the outcome of elections such that governments chosen by universal suffrage become class governments of the bourgeoisie, governments by a minority. As a consequence, the whole revolutionary movement unleashed by the Great War has everywhere been characterized by the working class's struggle against mere parliamentary democracy. This struggle gives rise to the idea of the soviet state just as much as it does the British idea of the guild state. As fundamentally different as these ideas are, they both involve the proletariat's search for a means of more completely securing the agreement between the governing and the governed than that of mere parliamentary democracy.

In modern capitalist society, alongside political democracy, embodied in the democratic organization of the state and municipality, an industrial democracy is developing, which lives in the large democratically organized trade unions and workers' consumer societies, in the professional organizations of employees and officials, and in peasant cooperatives. Political democracy only recognizes people as citizens; it ignores their economic position, profession, or social function and summons all citizens without distinction to the ballot box, grouping them only according to geographical electoral districts. By contrast, industrial democracy groups people according to their occupations, their workplaces, and their function in the economy; it organizes them according to their social function into factory, professional, and industrial organizations. In the struggle against mere parliamentary democracy, the working class has everywhere, although in very different forms, counterposed to political democracy, which calls on the citizen without distinction to create the national will, the ideas of functional democracy, that is, the demand that the government be controlled by the citizens collected and organized according to occupation or work-place—in other words according to their social and economic function. While political democracy demands that the government rule in agreement with the parliament, elected every few years by all of the people, functional democracy demands that the government in each branch of its activity stay in constant touch with the organized totality of the citizens directly affected by the particular branch of government, organized according to their occupation or their workplaces and their social and economic function. A combination of political and functional democracy was the essence of the government practice that the power relations emerging from the Revolution imposed on the government of the Republic.

The bourgeoisie saw in this strong impact of functional democracy in the practice of government nothing other than the workings of illegal "parallel governments" or "creeping Bolshevism." In reality it meant not only an expansion of the idea of democracy as government with the consent of the governed; it was not only the legal form of the exercise and expansion of the power of the working class; it was not only the saving of the country from the danger of bloody catastrophe. It was more than this. It was the most powerful means of the self-education of the masses. It was the means of effecting a complete revolution in the relation of the masses to the state. It was the means of awakening the initiative of the masses and unleashing the most fruitful kinds of self-activity among them.

First, the constant efforts in the assemblies of party and trade-union delegates, in the workers' and soldiers' councils, in the factory and barrack assemblies, in which the agreement between the government and the governed had to be worked out day after day in hard struggle—all this had considerably broadened the horizon of the working masses. In these passionate discussions the masses had to gradually learn how economic laws explain currency depreciation and the higher cost of living, to understand the dependency of food supply and the labor market on international relations, and to see the Revolution in their own country against the perspective of international development. But the factory and barrack assemblies had not only to broaden the masses' intellectual horizon but also make their moral fiber more effective, leading them to subordinate their passions to sober reasoning, to use their power prudently and their freedom with a sense of responsibility. For only in this way was it possible to guide the people through a time of the severest economic privation and great external dangers without resorting to force or bloodshed.

All this changed the whole relations of the masses to the state. The masses saw that their organizations dominated the government. They saw that the government had to keep in constant touch with them through the proletarian organizations. The masses saw that they themselves could determine government policy through their delegates. They saw that the government could not control them by coercive means but could conduct state business only with the assent of the working class. For the masses, the Republic was not merely a political constitution in which the Emperor no longer had a place but a kind of state that subordinated its governance to the effective control of the proletarian organizations. Democracy was no longer merely government by officials elected by universal suffrage but the method of government, which had to be worked out for each individual legislative act by gaining the assent of the masses affected by it. The Republic at first could only bring the masses starvation rations, unemployment, deprivation, and misery, and it had to disappoint many optimistic hopes of its supporters. But it also gave the masses freedom—not the freedom of self-indulgence, but the freedom that consisted in removing the barriers to the action of the proletariat built by a force that could have opposed it; instead, the barriers were those erected by its own understanding, by its own sense of responsibility, by its own reasoned will as expressed in its delegate, factory, and barrack assemblies. This was the experience that filled the working class with republican patriotism, that enabled it to suffer severe privations without rebelling, make heavy sacrifices, and curb its own passions for the sake of the preservation and consolidation of the Republic.

In the end, the continuous internal struggle within the delegate, factory, and barrack assemblies became the driving force of the powerful intellectual movement in the masses. The collapse of imperial rule had shaken all the authorities in state and society. If the highest and most powerful authority of all had fallen, then every executive body in its office, every factory manager in his factory, even every housewife in her kitchen, saw their authority shaken. Bourgeois ladies indignantly, and gentlemen scornfully, recounted the story of a cook who called out to the lady of the house: "I'm not going to be told by you how to cook. We're living in a Republic now, and I can cook better than you." But scorn was now out of place, for the shattering of the subservient faith in the traditional authorities, the awakening of souls kept so long in a servile state to a consciousness of their own worth triggered the greatest intellectual development. The mass assemblies in which the most momentous decisions of state life were submitted to the consultation and resolutions of the masses powerfully reinforced their aroused self-confidence. The awakened intellectual energies of the masses cried for an outlet, and the Republic opened many new domains of work to them.

In the first months after the October Revolution, the masses' yearning for activity was satisfied by the economic activities of the workers' councils. But these activities, borne by the elementary mass movement, very often dilettantish in the choice of means, and filled with the illusion that they could negate elementary economic laws through sheer force, could not satisfy the masses for long. The workers very soon recognized that hunting down small-scale hoarders carrying a couple of kilos of potatoes home in their rucksacks did not mitigate misery and that the sealing of one district from others could only aggravate misery. This policing on the part of the workers' councils gradually became less important. On the other hand, the political significance of the workers' councils grew in spring 1919 at the time of resistance to Hungarian Bolshevism. They transformed themselves gradually from organs of revolutionary intervention in economic administration into organs of the political class struggle. When, in the same period, the factory councils came into existence, the yearning of the masses for more direct social and economic participation was amply and more purposefully fulfilled. In the factory councils, many thousands of workers performed helpful social and economic tasks for the workers of their plant; and since they had to do so in the closest cooperation with the workers of the plant and under the daily control of the factory assembly, the whole mass of workers were continually involved with the problems of this social and economic work.

Alongside the council movement, the democratization of administration also afforded new spheres of activity to satisfy the yearning of the masses for self-activity. The Revolution abolished the privileged franchise on which municipal representation had been based. Universal suffrage radically changed the composition of municipal representation. In 236 municipalities Social Democracy captured a majority of seats and in 103 municipalities half of the seats. As a whole, Social Democrats were elected in 1,050 municipalities. Hundreds of metal workers and carpenters, railway conductors and forestry workers, employees in industry, and public school teachers now took over the offices of mayors and municipal executives, which formerly had been occupied by landlords, lawyers, and merchants. A revolution took place in the council chambers of the cities and industrial villages: the class that had previously dominated the municipalities was dethroned, and a new class took control.

The working class had to take over administration of the municipalities under the most difficult conditions, as war and currency depreciation had wrecked municipal finances, and without ever having had an opportunity to learn how to conduct municipal business, because the privileged franchise had kept them far away from the council chambers. It is therefore not surprising that in the beginning many errors in the choice of leading people and in the conduct of business were made. But a vast area for the schooling, the self-education of the working class, was opened up with the conquest of the municipalities—a few blunders are not too high a price to pay for the schooling of a new, rising class in the exercise of government. For the first time it was possible for thousands of workers to learn the conduct of public administration, and since this had to occur under the constant control of the local party organizations, the worries of the municipal administration became the worries of the whole organized working class; not only the chosen functionaries but the whole mass of active comrades became familiar with and involved in the problems of local public administration. This then was another new sphere of activity that broadened the horizon of the masses; it too deepened their insight into the conditions and the responsibility of public administration.

All this self-activity of the masses rested on the eight-hour day, which afforded tens of thousands of workers the leisure that enabled them to take part in municipal and district government, in local school and public welfare committees, in municipal and district economic offices, in the apartment-request and apartment-assignment commissions. But the eight-hour day was also the basis of other forms of self-activity of the masses. The workers tried to use the leisure time they had won to immediately ease their economic privation. A garden-plot movement already began to appear during the war; the workers began to cultivate the soil surrounding the cities and industrial districts, planting vegetables and raising small animals. The eight-hour day gave this movement a new impetus; thousands used the new leisure time to work in their *Schrebergärten*.* As a result Vienna was gradually ringed by 60,000 garden plots. But the housing shortage continued. To cope with it the small gardeners began to build huts on their plots.

---

* *Schrebergarten* (singular): a small garden plot, often including a small cabin, typical of northern, central, and eastern European social democracies and then of eastern European countries under state socialism; in Britain, allotments.

Such isolated instances finally gave rise to the settlement movement. Settler cooperatives emerged that sought to reduce the high cost of apartment construction by having the settlers themselves use the time freed up by the eight-hour day to collaborate in the construction of their homes. Thus, out of the initiative of the masses there gradually grew a whole system of nonprofit housing construction. The settler cooperatives are building groups of one-family houses. The work is done partly by the settlers themselves, alongside their professional occupation, partly by the Grundstein, a production cooperative of construction workers founded by the construction workers' association. The building office of the Settlement, Apartment, and Building-Material Guild,* in which the settler cooperatives were united with the construction workers, provides the building plans and directs construction. The Common-economy Settlement and Building Material Agency, founded by the Vienna Municipality and the Central Confederation of Settlement Cooperatives,† supplies the construction material. The state and municipality covers possible wasted expenses.

The whole movement is noteworthy in many respects. Its origin in popular initiative indicates the creative power of the masses' desire for self-activity liberated by the Revolution. Its structure shows the coupling of diverse forms of cooperative and trade-union organization. Its basis in the labor power of the settlers themselves shows how the eight-hour day in the factory by no means limits total work to eight hours. While refusing to give capital more than eight hours of corvée, the worker takes it upon himself to work some additional hours in his own garden plot or on his settlement house. The organism of the worker cannot endure more than eight hours of eternal monotony in the factory, but he does not refuse other work done under other conditions requiring another set of muscles and nerves.

However, it was not only economic privation that provided mass initiative with its content and purpose. The intellectual excitement moving through the masses had to set its own intellectual goals. More than anything else it was the great enterprise of school reform that set more ambitious objectives for popular energy.

After the February elections, Otto Glöckel took charge of the Ministry of Education. To the bureaus composed of legally trained administrative officials, he immediately added a School Reform Department made up of experienced educators headed by Viktor Fadrus. They went to work

---

* Siedlungs- Wohnungs- und Baustoffgilde.
† Siedlungsgenossenschaften.

right away, setting themselves two tasks: the reorganization of schools and the restructuring of teaching methods.

The goal of the new school organization is the comprehensive school attended by all children from six to fourteen, irrespective of the class position of their parents: from the ages of six to ten the general elementary school, from eleven to fourteen a middle school for all. Differentiation occurs only afterward: continuing education and vocational schools on the one side and secondary schools with a humanist and scientific orientation on the other side. The first task was to put this plan to the practical test. To this end the old military educational institutions have been transformed into state educational institutions. It is an attempt at breaking the educational monopoly of the owning classes; at the age of ten especially gifted proletarian children are enrolled in these institutions and taken through to the higher education level. This is at the same time an attempt at testing the plan of a new school organization; the new types—the comprehensive middle school for those from ten to fourteen years of age and the new German Middle School—were first tested here. Finally, it also was a site for the study of new methods of instruction and education; the state educational institutions are at the same time experimental schools for innovative methods. The compulsory comprehensive middle school, first tested in practice in the state educational institutions, is then to be generally introduced. The Vienna City School Council took the first steps in this direction in the school year 1922–23.

Much more important than the new organization of education are the new instruction methods. Here the reform could take effect far more quickly. The curricula of our primary schools had still been based on provisions laid down in 1883. A new curriculum was drafted for the elementary school, first tested in 150 experimental classes and then universally adopted from 1920. An activity school instead of a learning school—that was the watchword. The children no longer have to learn by heart what the teacher recites to them. From their own observations, their own activity, their own work they have to generate knowledge. The division of the curriculum is no longer determined by the system of sciences but by the experience of the children. The shackles of the curriculum have been broken; instruction for language learning, arithmetic, and writing no longer occurs in separate courses. The children look around them on educational walks, and instruction is based on what has been observed in each walk. For example, the children may be taken to a railway station. Then, when they are back in school, they process what they have seen, above all drawing and modeling it. A school, which is to educate people not for the study but for the workshop, must train the eye and hand, not only the memory and the capacity for conceptualization. At the same time we write the names of objects that we draw and model; in this way we learn writing. From time to time we calculate: if there are thirty seats in a railway car, how many are there in the whole train? What does the trip to the next station cost? What would it cost if we all travelled together? In this way we learn to multiply. Where can the train take us to? Through which valleys, across which rivers? In this way we learn geography. Who has already travelled by train? Now write down the story of this trip. This becomes a composition exercise. How is it that the locomotive moves the train? This brings us to physics.

The new instructional methods put much greater demands on the abilities and knowledge of the teachers. The whole teaching staff has to retrain. The reform of instructional method was prepared in district teacher conferences; there the teachers organized themselves into task forces, which met every month to work out the work plan for the following months. Training courses were established for teachers. New intellectual life pulsated among teaching staff.

And this movement immediately became popular among the whole population. Parents' associations and councils are an essential element in the school reform system. They provide a continuous personal relationship between teachers and parents. The newly founded parents' associations enthusiastically went to work and soon had considerable effect. They collected large sums to supply schools with teaching supplies for activity instruction, with materials and tools, with books and pictures. And they soon went further. They paid teachers to do remedial instruction for the slower children or give attention to the instruction of particularly gifted children. They hired custodial and youth-welfare personnel. The members of the parents' associations began to keep an eye on school attendance; they went from house to house and exhorted neglectful parents to send their children to school.

All those for whom the old and the traditional were sacred regarded this revolution in the schools with mistrust and unease. When Glöckel abolished the obligation of teachers and students to take part in religious instruction, clericalism began openly to oppose educational reform. School reform became a subject of political contestation. This only made large sections of the working class more supportive.

Popular interest in educational questions had been roused, and this

now began to be felt in the workers' organizations. The *Kinderfreunde**
movement grew at a rapid pace. In Lower Austria, for example, the Kinderfreunde Association had 3,000 members in 1913; 3,881 in 1917; 18,432 in
1919; and 35,918 in 1920. In the period of greatest privations, it was above all
the care provision facilities of the Association, which supplied free meals
for children in its homes and crèches and in its recreational facilities and
vacation colonies, that attracted proletarian mothers to it. But as the interest of the masses in educational questions grew, the Association began to
transform itself from a care provision association into an educational organization. Naturally, this did not all go off without some dilettantish exper-
imentation. But all these attempts stimulated thousands of working-class
women to think about educational problems, and the proletarian youth
began to learn to free itself from the spell of old surviving traditions.

Thus, the awakened yearning of the masses for self-actuation opened
up ever new spheres of activity. Tens of thousands of people, whose
lives had previously been divided between eternally monotonous, de-
intellectualized, mechanical factory work and an animal existence in the
paltry hours of leisure with the family or at the inn, now found new spheres
of activity and a purpose in life in the party or trade-union organizations,
in cooperatives, in the factory councils and workers' councils, in municipal
representation and the manifold institutions of communal and municipal self-government, in the garden-plot and settlers movement, in parents'
associations, and in the Kinderfreunde. This social self-assertion of the
masses has produced a new type of human being.

In the days of upheaval, the revolutionary type was the homecoming
soldier, filled with wild passions by his terrible experiences, who believed
that with rifle and hand grenade he could overturn everything that existed.
He was joined by the revolutionary opportunist who from the overturn of
all that existed hoped to gain power, position, dignity, and income. But
very soon the leadership of the movement passed to a completely different
kind of person, of incomparably higher intellectual and moral quality: the
tens of thousands of party and trade-union delegates, members of workers',
factory, and soldiers' councils, who acted with a great sense of responsibility
and the capacity to channel into the most fruitful creativity the mass energy that threatened to destroy the Revolution itself through revolutionary
impetuosity. The rise of this intellectual élite of the working class from the
womb of the masses and the leadership and education of this mass by this

---

*Friends of Children.

intellectual élite of their own flesh and blood is the real accomplishment of the Revolution. For the transformation of state and social institutions is not an end in itself; the latter has meaning for the development of peoples only insofar as it involves the awakening, the inner transformation, and the upward movement of humanity.

The German-Austrians had been the dominant people of the Habsburg Monarchy. When the national revolution of the Czechs, Yugoslavs, and Poles broke up the Habsburg Monarchy, German-Austria was left in a state of terrible privation and impotence, which put insurmountable obstacles in the way of our Revolution. It was unable to achieve annexation to Germany. It could complete a social transformation only within very narrow limits. Forced to be moderate and self-restraining, it everywhere remained poor in terms of heroic deeds, dramatic episodes, or romantic battles. But it was just the privation and impotence of this Revolution that underlay its unique greatness. Precisely because privation and impotence prevented us from establishing a strong revolutionary power we could conquer hegemony among the masses only by intellectual means. Precisely because privation and impotence forced moderation on the Revolution, the self-conquest, the curbing of mass passions through the insight of the masses had to be accomplished through the most difficult intellectual struggles among the masses themselves.

This hegemony among the masses through purely intellectual means, this self-conquest of the masses through purely intellectual struggles, broadened their intellectual horizon, kindled their intellectual agility, and maximized their drive to self-actuation. The outer poverty and impotence of the Revolution thus became a cause of profound inner transformation. The tens of thousands who found a purpose in life beyond purely personal interest through responsible action in the organizations and in administration, the hundreds of thousands whose horizon was vastly broadened and whose feeling of personal co-responsibility for the fate of their class and their people was wakened, testify to the soul-rousing and soul-educating power of this Revolution. The many tired laboring animals dully living on in the eternal monotony of handed-down traditions became co-thinking, co-working, co-struggling personalities conscious of their co-responsibility. This revolutionizing of the intellectual life of the leading stratum of the masses is the greatest result of the Revolution—because all of the revolution in the state, the municipalities, in the barracks, the factories, and the schools are mere means serving the final end—the revolution in people's souls.

The whole history of class struggles of the proletariat is not only the history of the revolution in the conditions under which the working class lives but also the history of the development of the working class itself. At the beginning of this development, the worker in the factory was nothing but a tool in the hands of the factory owner, without a will of his own, and in his meager evening hours of leisure nothing but an exhausted, brutish animal. At the end of this development the worker matured into a many-sided personality, who, capable of governing his own life and labor, will no longer tolerate a master because he needs none. This development from laboring animal into a personality is the development toward socialism. The revolutionizing of state and social institutions is only significant for progress toward socialism to the extent that it comprises the evolution of the laboring animal into a personality.

Victor Adler, photo
by Albert Voisard,
Österreichische
Nationalbibliothek,
Vienna (Inventory Pf
736 : B (1))

Karl Renner, photo
by Albin Kobé, 1925,
Österreichische
Nationalbibliothek,
Vienna (Inventory
203.179 – D)

Otto Bauer ca. 1920,
Bildarchiv der Kommu-
nistischen Partei Österreichs (KPÖ)

Otto Bauer ca. 1930,
Bildarchiv der Kommu-
nistischen Partei Österreichs (KPÖ)

Friedrich Adler before the Special Court, May 1917, Verein für Geschichte der ArbeiterInnenbewegung, Vienna

Friedrich Adler, ca.
1918-20, Bildarchiv der
Kommunistischen Partei
Österreichs (KPÖ)

The remains of the Austro-Hungaran Army,
Bolzano Station, November 6, 1918,
Museo Storico Italiano della Guerra,
Rovereto

The remains of the Austro-Hungaran Army, Bolzano Station, November 6, 1918, Museo Storico Italiano della Guerra, Rovereto

Officers' Mess at the Piave Front, Heeresgeschichtliches Museum, Vienna

Waiters at the Officers' Mess, Piave Front, Heeresgeschichtliches Museum, Vienna

Proclamation of the Republic in front of the Parliament, November 12, 1918, Bildarchiv der KPÖ

Soldiers Councils with German and Austrian representatives of workers and soldiers councils in the palace of the Austrian Embassy in Petrograd, early 1919. Notes in English on back: front row sitting left to right: Dr. Machler of the German Soldiers' and Workers' Soviet; Dr. Eduard Fuchs, in the center; Mr. Duda, Chairman of the Austrian Soldiers' and Workers' Soviet; Mr. Maurice Laserson. Standing behind from left to right: Mr. Bruck of the secret police, and 9 members of both soldiers' and workers' soviets." Verein für Geschichte der ArbeiterInnenbewegung, Vienna

Julius Deutsch, 1930s, Vienna, Verein für Geschichte der ArbeiterInnenbewegung, Vienna

Recruiting for the new Volkswehr at the Deutschmeister Barracks in Vienna, November 4, 1918, Österreichische Nationalbibliothek, Vienna (Inventory S 646/83)

Nussdorf (Vienna), Volkswehr motor boat flotilla, 1919, Heeresgeschichtliches Museum, Vienna

Arbeiter!

Arbeitslose, Heimkehrer u. Invalide!

Wir Wiener Volkswehrmänner haben in den letzten Tagen durch unser Verhalten den Beweis erbracht, dass die Revolution in unseren Händen in guter Hut ist.

Darum wenden wir uns an Euch, Ihr Brüder im Proletariergewand, und **beschwören** Euch, die Sache der Revolution nicht durch gewissenlose Scheinradikale und reaktionäre Elemente gefährden zu lassen.

Jede Revolution treibt ihre Schmarotzer ans Licht.

Erkennen wir sie, lassen wir uns nicht von ihnen schädigen!

Es gilt, einmütig zusammenzuhalten!

Dazu rufen Euch die sozialdemokratischen und kommunistischen Volkswehrmänner Wiens auf!

Beherziget unseren Mahnruf!

Proletarier Wiens!

Duldet nicht die Provokation der Unbesonnenen!

Unterstützt uns Volkswehrmänner in der Abwehr gegen die Hyänen der Revolution!

Den Wühlern und Provokateuren ist die ernste Mahnung gegeben:

Die Geduld der Volkswehrmänner ist durch den aufreibenden Dienst der letzten Woche erschöpft.

Hütet Euch, den Bogen zu überspannen!

Der Vollzugsausschuss des Soldatenrates
der Volkswehr Wiens.

WORKERS!

Unemployed, Returnees, War-Wounded !
In recent days we of the Vienna People's Defense Force have demonstrated through our action that the Revolution is in good hands.
Therefore we are turning to you, our proletarian brothers, to implore
you not to let the cause of the Revolution be endangered by unprinci-
pled seeming radicals and reactionary elements.

Every revolution flushes out its parasites.

Let us detect them and prevent them from damaging us!
We need to stand together as one!

This is what
Vienna's Social Democratic and Communist Defense Militia
are calling on you to do!
Heed our warning!
Proletarians of Vienna!
Do not permit the provocation of reckless individuals!
Support us, the People's Defense Militia, in resisting
the hyenas of the Revolution!
We issue a serious warning to the agitators and provocateurs:
The patience of the People's Defense Militia has been exhausted by
last week's stressful events.
Beware of overstepping the mark!

The Executive Committee of the Soldiers' Council
of the Vienna Volkswehr

Placard, Executive Committee of the Soldiers' Council of the Vienna
Volkswehr, 1918, Österreichische Nationalbibliothek, Vienna (Inventory
PLA16304022)

Wien: 12 Heller.
Monatlich K 3.50 mit Zustellung ins Haus.

Illustrierte
Kronen Zeitung

20. Jahrgang
Nr. 7003.

Wien, Mittwoch den 2. Juli 1919.

Ausbreitung der Streiks in Deutschland.

Bilder aus der Reichskonferenz der Arbeiterräte. Arbeiterführer und die Häupter der Kommunisten.

Kronen-Zeitung, July 2, 1919, "The Reich Conference of the Workers' Councils – Labor Leaders and Communist Spokespeople"

"Breitner Taxes – therefore vote Social Democrat"—Every municipal apartment building boasted the inscription "built with funds from the building construction tax," referring to the wealth tax conceived by Hugo Breitner to finance housing construction.

Friedrich-Engels-Hof and swimming pool, Vienna, Twentieth District, 1920–30, Verein für Geschichte der ArbeiterInnenbewegung, Vienna

Municipal housing: Reumannhof, Vienna, Fifth District, view through the pergola, after 1926, Österreichische Nationalbibliothek, Vienna (Inventory L 31.144-C)

Above: Volkswehr in the courtyard of the Rossauer Barracks, battalion inspection, Vienna, December 1919, photographer Richard Hauffe, Österreichische Nationalbibliothek, Vienna (Inventory 224120-B). Below: Soldiers' Council, *Wiener Blatt*, 1918

Hörlgasse – Maria-Theresien-Strasse, *Das interessante Blatt*, June 1919

Demonstration against the Kapp Putsch, March 14, 1920 (the banner reads "Long live the international world revolution!"), Bildarchiv der KPÖ

Municipal housing: Reumannhof, Vienna, Fifth District, shop front side, after 1926, Österreichische Nationalbibliothek, Vienna (Inventory L 54.003-C)

The municipal housing project Karl-Marx-Hof, Vienna, Nineteenth District, 1987 (opened 1930), Verein für Geschichte der ArbeiterInnenbewegung, Vienna

Sandleiten Municipal Lending Library, Rosa-Luxemburg- Gasse, Ottakring, Vienna 1928–29. The wall text reads "[Books have] brought us into slavery–books will free us again," Verein für Geschichte der ArbeiterInnenbewegung, Vienna

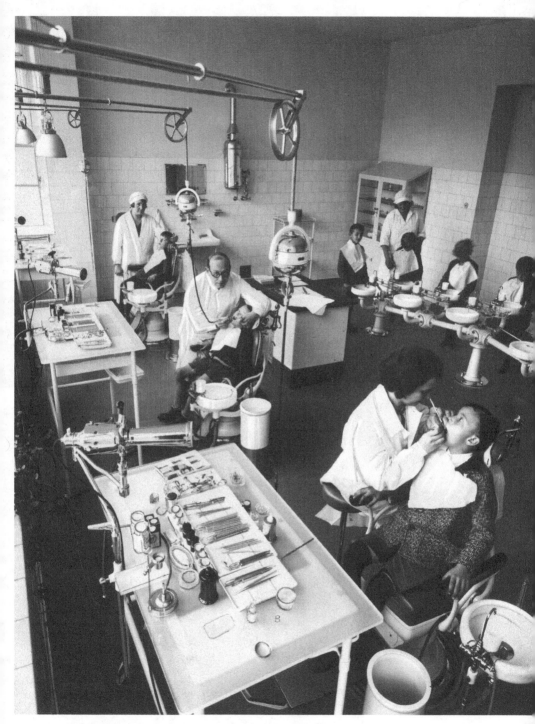

School dental clinic in the Karl-Marx-Hof, May 23, 1935, Verein für Geschichte der ArbeiterInnenbewegung, Vienna

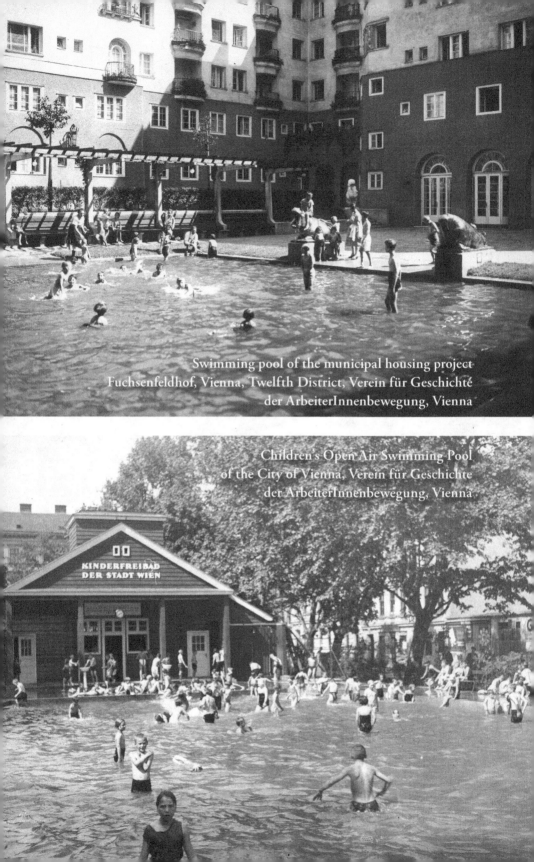

Swimming pool of the municipal housing project
Fuchsenfeldhof, Vienna, Twelfth District, Verein für Geschichte
der ArbeiterInnenbewegung, Vienna

Children's Open Air Swimming Pool
of the City of Vienna, Verein für Geschichte
der ArbeiterInnenbewegung, Vienna

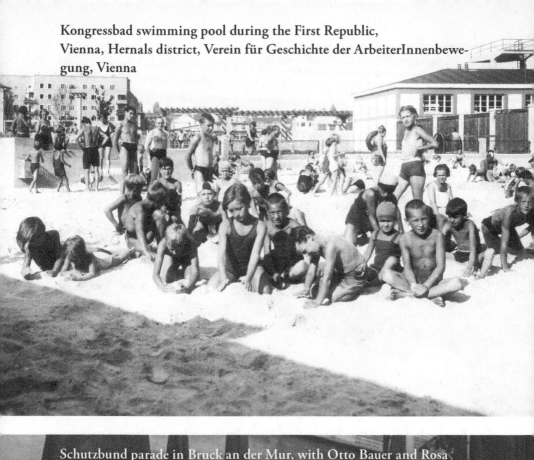

Kongressbad swimming pool during the First Republic, Vienna, Hernals district, Verein für Geschichte der ArbeiterInnenbewegung, Vienna

Schutzbund parade in Bruck an der Mur, with Otto Bauer and Rosa Jochmann, ca. 1930, Verein für Geschichte der ArbeiterInnenbewegung, Vienna

Friedrich Adler, Otto Bauer, Karl Kautsky (from left to right). Special Party Congress of the SDAP in Vienna's Arbeiterheim in Favoriten, October 14-16, 1933, Verein für Geschichte der ArbeiterInnenbewegung, Vienna

PART IV

THE EQUILIBRIUM OF CLASS FORCES

CHAPTER 13

ECONOMIC TRANSFORMATION AND SOCIAL REGROUPING

D uring the first months following the end of the war, international capitalism appeared to be severely shaken. In a bloody civil war, the Russian Soviet Republic beat back the attacks of the counterrevolutionary generals. The German Reich was dominated by the workers' and soldiers' councils; in a series of uprisings, Spartacus sought to push the German Revolution beyond the bounds of bourgeois democracy. In Munich and Budapest, dictatorships of the proletariat had been established. Even the victorious countries had not been untouched by the revolutionary wave. When the Entente powers protracted their own military demobilization during the peace negotiations, the agitation in their army camps led to a series of mutinies, and in the victorious countries too the workers, returned from the front, marched through the streets unemployed and embittered. It seemed as if the war would directly turn into world revolution.

But after only a few months, the waves of revolution receded. As early as spring 1919, the countries of the victorious powers entered a period of economic upturn. Industry quickly absorbed the unemployed. The demobilized soldiers found employment in the factories and their wages rapidly rose. The period of prosperity that followed the war overcame the crisis of demobilization. In the states whose victory had made them masters of the world, capitalism had quickly recovered from the social crisis provoked everywhere by the return of the masses from the army back into production,

294

without too much disruption. But capitalism also reconsolidated itself in defeated Central Europe. In Germany, the communist uprisings of December, January, and March had ended in heavy defeat; their only result was the establishment of the counterrevolutionary Reichswehr, which from then on held the proletariat in check. In Bavaria the communist dictatorship had collapsed in May, in Hungary in July; the counterrevolution was triumphant. In the east, the forces of the Soviet Republic were held in check by the armed intervention of the Entente. In late summer 1919 it already become evident that capitalism had survived the severe shock.

But the proletariat still did not feel beaten. The year 1920 brought a whole series of proletarian uprisings, but all of them ended in heavy defeat. In March the Kapp Putsch* provoked a massive revolt of the German proletariat, which mounted a general strike that saved the Republic. But wherever the proletariat tried to burst the limits of the bourgeois republic, it was repressed with bloodshed. In May the French workers rose up, but their mass strike ended in heavy defeat. In the summer months the victorious invasion of the Red Army in Poland kindled the hopes of the proletariat; broad sections of the workers hoped that the Red Army would overrun Poland, creating a bridge between the Russian and German revolutions, and carry socialism to Central Europe at the point of the bayonet. The heavy defeat of the Russians before Warsaw in August put an abrupt end to all these hopes. In September Italy reached the high point of its social crisis; the Italian workers took over the factories, while the state authorities did not dare protect capital's property. For a few days the means of production were in the hands of the proletariat, but then they were forced to give up their occupation. In December Czechoslovakia was shaken by a mass strike; it too collapsed without result. By the end of 1920 capitalism had everywhere pushed back the proletariat's offensive.

Meanwhile, the economic boom, which had begun in spring 1919, came to an abrupt end. Already by spring 1920 the industrial crisis had broken out in Japan and in America and in the summer in the victorious and neutral countries of Europe. In all countries with a stable and appreciating currency, unemployment rose and wages fell. The workers struck back against the pressure of sinking wages. The year 1921 brought a series of gigantic trade-union struggles, of which the lockout of the British miners was the most powerful. Occurring at a time of severe industrial depression, these wage struggles ended in defeats. In all countries affected by the crisis,

* See Glossary.

the demands for unemployment and strike pay emptied the coffers of the trade unions, and the fear of unemployment broke the fighting spirit of the working class. Repeatedly, the workers had to accept wage reductions without resistance. Their power in the factories was seriously weakened. If capitalism was on a victorious offensive in the west, in the east the power of the communist offensive collapsed. The Kronstadt Rebellion and mass walkouts by workers forced the Soviet government to change course. The "New Course" restored capitalism in Russia.

After the collapse of the March putsch in Germany, communism in Central Europe also had to call off its putsch tactics. Now the proletariat was everywhere pushed into the defensive.

Thus, the history of the years 1919 and 1920 is the history of the incremental reconsolidation of international capitalism, which had been weakened by the war. Under pressure of this international development, the power relations among the classes in German-Austria inevitably changed as well.

During the first months after the upheaval, the German-Austrian bourgeoisie had submitted to the hegemony of the working classes almost without resistance. At that time the social revolution in German-Austria seemed to be much more limited than in the other defeated countries. In November 1918 the workers' and soldiers' councils had taken over the government in Germany; in German-Austria the Revolution remained within the forms of parliamentary democracy. In the winter, bloody civil war continuously raged in the streets of Germany's major cities; German-Austria was spared street warfare. In spring 1919 the dictatorship of the proletariat was proclaimed in Hungary and in Bavaria; in German-Austria Social Democracy fended off the onslaught of communism. At that time the German-Austrian bourgeoisie felt fortunate that it was spared the worst, which had befallen the bourgeoisie of the other defeated countries, and it submitted without resistance to the hegemony of Social Democracy.

But already the first victories of international reaction in 1919 changed the mood of our bourgeoisie. In Germany, the Reichswehr was established, which suppressed the proletariat and held it in check; in Austria the socialist Volkswehr still fended off the reaction. In Germany, the Technical Emergency Relief prevented any shutdown of vital services or production; in Austria the state could still only manage the public enterprises in cooperation with the proletarian organizations because without them it could not guarantee the continuation of vitally important enterprises. In Germany, the dominance of the workers' and soldiers' councils was very soon followed by their dissolution; in Austria the workers' and soldiers' councils never exercised domination, but they remained a strong active power when workers' and soldiers' councils no longer existed in Germany. In Hungary and Bavaria, the communist dictatorship was followed by the bloody suppression of the proletariat; in Austria the self-restraint of the Social Democratic leadership kept the proletariat from defeat and its instruments of power intact.

In summer 1919, after the victories of the counterrevolution in Germany and Hungary, the Austrian bourgeoisie recognized that the Bolshevik terror in Germany and Hungary, so quickly followed as it was by its counterrevolutionary demise, was greatly preferable to the endless "terror" of the Social Democratic leadership, which had kept the Austrian proletariat from defeat. When in fall 1919 the exiled revolutionaries from Hungary, Bavaria, Yugoslavia, and Poland found asylum in Austria, the bourgeoisie saw that it was only in Austria that the power of the proletariat was still unbroken. At a time when the Austrian bourgeoisie could almost regard the White Army in Hungary and the Orgesch* in Bavaria as its reserve armies, which if needed it could call upon for help against the Austrian proletariat, the unbroken position of power of the Austrian proletariat seemed to it an intolerable anachronism. Now, after the defeat of the open Bolshevism in Hungary and in Bavaria, it was time to suppress "creeping Bolshevism" in Austria.

To the extent that international capitalism reconsolidated from 1919 to 1921, the self-confidence of Austria's bourgeoisie was also boosted. It finally dared again to resist the proletariat after the German and Hungarian revolutions suffered heavy defeats in 1919. It regained the confidence to try and govern alone after international reaction had repelled the proletariat's offensives. It went on the offensive after the proletariat in all Europe had been pushed into the defensive. In Austria, too, the history of the years from 1919 to 1922 is the history of the progressive growth of the self-confidence, power of resistance, and offensive strength of the bourgeoisie and the progressive rallying of all the owning classes against the proletariat.

The strengthening of bourgeois class consciousness was accelerated and reinforced by the economic and social upheavals brought about by the breakup of the former large economic area.

The most serious consequence of the disintegration of the Austro-Hungarian economic area was the revolution in the currency. The destruction of the old imperial community was followed by the dissolution of the

---

* See Glossary.

old currency community. On January 8, 1919, the Southern Slav government ordered the overstamping of the krone bills that circulated in the former Austro-Hungarian areas of Yugoslavia. On February 25, Czechoslovakia too decided to overstamp the krone bills. German-Austria answered this with the enactment of February 27 that provided for the overstamping of the krone notes there as well. With this, the old Austro-Hungarian currency community was dissolved; the Austro-Hungarian krone was replaced with the German-Austrian krone. The value of the Austrian krone was no longer determined by its purchasing power in Czechoslovakia, Yugoslavia, or Poland but by its far lower purchasing power in German-Austria, blockaded by all the neighboring states and suffering from the most serious shortage of goods. Whoever wanted to buy Czech coal or sugar, Galician petroleum or Transylvanian wood, Hungarian cattle, or Yugoslav grain now no longer needed Austrian krone bills but Czech or Yugoslav kronen, or the not overstamped krone bills at first still used in Poland, Hungary, and Romania.

Austrian kronen were only still needed by foreigners if they wanted to buy German-Austrian goods; but German-Austrian industry, disrupted as it was by coal and raw materials shortages, offered little for the foreigner to buy. Thus, demand for Austrian kronen had to significantly lower its exchange rate. The price drop of the Austrian krone at the time was thus the inevitable effect of the breakup of the Austro-Hungarian economic area, an inevitable effect of the fact that its value was no longer based on the fertile plains, the sources of coal and crude oil, and the industrial and port facilities of the large old economic area but only on the poverty of the German-Austrian mountainous regions.

The fall of the krone was accelerated by other circumstances. The flight of capital abroad had assumed major proportions during the war, but the Revolution stimulated even greater capital flight. Trembling at the danger of expropriation, the capitalists moved their assets to Switzerland; the strict prohibitions issued by the first two governments of the Republic were circumvented or violated. Capital flight was particularly great at the time of the onslaught of Hungarian Bolshevism. This naturally increased the supply of Austrian kronen abroad, and so their value fell even further. At the same time the Entente lifted the blockade of German-Austria. For four and a half years, German-Austria had been cut off from foreign countries. Now the consumers, starved for foreign goods for so long, voraciously pounced on the products that had suddenly become available again, and merchants rushed to replenish their long empty warehouses. The rush on foreign products caused the demand for foreign means of payment dramatically to explode, which put still more downward pressure on the exchange rate of the krone. A few weeks later the first draft of the peace conditions became known. The terribly harsh conditions destroyed all confidence in German-Austria's economic future. Foreign speculators now unloaded their krone bills, and Austrian capitalists sold their krone securities in order to buy foreign currencies and securities with the proceeds. The krone rate was shaken even more.

Thus, all effects of the great catastrophe conspired in this first phase of currency depreciation to depress the price of the krone. In the first years of the Republic, the period of working-class hegemony, currency depreciation was the direct effect of the great historic catastrophe itself; no financial-policy measures could stop it. It was the direct effect of the collapse of the old large economic area, the revolutionary upheaval in all of Central Europe, and the peace dictated by Entente imperialism. The result was that the krone lost nine-tenths of its value within a year. The krone's rate in Zurich, which in the first weeks after the collapse of the Monarchy held at 30 centimes, had by the end of 1919 sunk to 3 centimes.

Nor was this the end of currency depreciation. The violent depreciation of currency in the first years of the Republic had seriously damaged the national budget. While public expenditures rose with currency depreciation, state revenue could only be slowly increased at a time of complete stagnation of production and severe social crisis. The deficit therefore had to be covered by the issuance of paper money. In the degree that the volume of circulating bank notes swelled, their value sank. The krone rate thus continually fell. By the end of 1920 in Zurich it was at 1.05; by the end of 1921, it was at 0.11 centimes. While the currency depreciation in the first years of the Republic was the direct result of the dissolution of the old economic area, in the following period it was the result of the wrecked public budget, which necessitated a continuous increase of paper money.

But the currency depreciation was not only the consequence of the great historic catastrophe that befell Austria in 1918; it was at the same time an indispensable means for rebuilding the economic life that had been completely destroyed by this catastrophe. The elementary process of currency depreciation set capitalist production and exchange of commodities in motion again.

In summer 1919, the great boom of the Vienna stock exchange began. Day after day stock prices began to adapt to the falling currency value.

The capitalists tried to protect their capital from depreciation by investing it in currencies and stocks. Stock quotations rose extremely quickly. The enormous speculative profits attracted increasingly broader strata of the bourgeoisie, of officialdom, and of the employee stratum to stock exchange gambling. Yesterday's winnings at the stock exchange were squandered today in wild luxury consumption.

From the stock exchange the movement spread to trade. The stock exchange speculated on a continual fall of the krone; its price therefore sped downward faster than its own value and purchasing power fell. The disparity between the external value and the purchasing power of the krone was reflected in the far lower prices of Austrian goods at home than they had in the world market. Great profits could be made by selling Austrian goods abroad. It is true that they came up against many import and export restrictions by which the countries tried to protect their economies at a time of great privation. Unscrupulous profiteering, which knew how to get around the prohibitions in thousands of devious ways and manipulate the bureaucracy that had to apply these prohibitions, broke through these obstacles. The native profiteer was joined by the foreign profiteer. Due to the gross disproportion between the domestic and foreign value of the krone, any clerk from a country with strong currency could seem a rich man in Vienna, and anyone who bought up goods in Vienna with foreign money could reap enormous export profits. The period of the great "closeout sale" came in which foreign dealers bought up for a song the raw material stocks that the Republic inherited from the Army Administration and the household items and jewelry of the Viennese patricians impoverished by the currency depreciation. In grotesque images, Pierre Hamp has described how the "gold diggers" of all countries pounced on the pauperized nation.

In reality, this period of profiteering, however parasitic it seemed, prepared the way for the restoration of trade in Vienna. The great power of attraction Vienna exerted on foreign merchants due to the disparity between the purchasing power and the price of the krone, between its domestic and foreign worth, and between domestic and world market prices, made Vienna a major commercial center again. Yugoslav, Romanian, Polish, and Hungarian merchants returned to Vienna to buy not only Austrian products but also those of Czechoslovak industry. Vienna regained its old function as commercial intermediary between the industrial districts of the Sudeten lands and the agrarian districts of the Danube basin. And with commerce, trade and industry finally revived.

The first to feel the effect were the luxury trades, which boomed in the period of huge stock-exchange and racketeer profits and the influx of foreign merchants. But the industrial sector recovered more slowly. It is true that it too felt the great export premium due to the disparity between the domestic and foreign worth of the krone. But industry could not use the export boom as long as coal and raw-material shortages strangled its production. Only gradually, with the restoration of production in the neighboring countries, did coal and raw materials begin to flow somewhat more steadily into Austria. Austrian industry could obtain as much coal and raw materials as it needed once the industrial crisis struck the countries with strong currencies in the summer of 1920 and the market there for coal and raw materials shrank.

We imported 12 million double centners* of coal and coke in the second half of 1919, 40 million in 1920, and 58.4 million in 1921. Our cotton imports amounted to 26,511 centners in the second half of 1919 and to 126,464 and 260,511 in 1920 and 1921, respectively. The importation of all important industrial raw materials rose at similar rates. We were saved from the effects of the shrinkage of international markets by the currency depreciation, which kept the production costs of our industry far below the international level.

The shortage of coal and raw materials, which had prevented us from taking advantage of the international boom of 1919–20, was overcome precisely due to the international industrial crisis. Consequently, the period of economic boom came to Austrian industry only when it had already ended in the world market.

Only now could our industry fully utilize the export premium afforded by the disparity between domestic and world market prices. Our industry was able significantly to expand its foreign markets at a time when the world market was suffering from the international depression. Our exports are listed in the following table:

---

* A centner equals 50 kilograms and a double centner 100 kilograms.

Item	Second half of 1919	1920	1921
Paper and paper goods	310,688	957,056	1,144,300
Leather and leather goods	12,232	40,443	59,280
Furniture and furniture parts	24,052	91,914	90,966
Iron and iron goods	755,557	1,918,523	1,951,928
Machines and equipment	125,441	411,642	538,015
Electric machines and equipment	25,366	81,488	111,757
Vehicles	43,611	144,379	178,477
	2,081[a]	12,491[a]	13,411[a]
	13[b]	40[b]	38[b]
Precious metals and derived goods	3,937	1,878	4,926
Chemical intermediate and end products	155,624	471,086	510,540
Clothes and cleaning rags	4,043	12,189	5,121
Linens	263	3,273	4,814

Note. All items are measured in double centners except where noted.
a. By piece.
b. Metric tons.

Reinvigorated by this growth in exports, industry now could absorb the masses of unemployed. At 186,000 in May 1919, the unemployment figure had reached its high point. Now it fell rapidly. At the beginning of 1920, about 64,427 persons were drawing unemployment compensation; but in July, that number had dropped to 23,970, and at the end of the year it fell to 16,637. Throughout 1921 unemployment remained very low. Currency depreciation had been the means to reanimate industry and bring the masses of workers back to the production sites from which they had been snatched by the war and to get them used again to regular work.

Industrial prosperity enabled the working class to obtain higher wages. The export industries, which exchanged their products against foreign money, could raise krone wages to the degree that the krone's value dropped. The increased wages in the export industries drove up wages in other branches of industry, albeit not to the same extent. The rapid pace of currency depreciation required a rapid adjustment of wage rates to the changes in the value of money. One wage increase quickly followed another. The ongoing involvement of all workers and employees in movements for higher wages increased the trade unions' power of attraction. Already by 1922 more than one million workers and employees—that is, nearly one-sixth of the total population—were organized in the free trade unions.* With strong trade unions behind them, the working class could take full advantage of the industrial boom. The calculation of wage adjustments based on the official cost-of-living index figure became the means to automatically adjust wages each month to alterations in the krone's purchasing power and so avoid difficult struggles for improved wages. This wage payment method was proposed in November 1919 by Renner at a joint conference of the entrepreneurs' associations and the trade unions called by the government and introduced, though at first in a very incomplete form, into the collective contract of the metal industry and then gradually reinforced and extended to almost all larger branches of industry.

Thus, the standard of living of the working masses was gradually improved. Import statistics show the rise in mass consumption. Imports to Austria were as follows:

Item	Second half of 1919	1920	1921
Grains and flour[a]	2,359,571	6,131,404	7,560,558
Meat and draft cattle[b]	18,487	37,141	130,928
Cooking fats[a]	122,036	432,396	402,867
Tobacco[a]	7,845	66,084	113,777

a. In double centners.
b. By piece.

* The name adopted by the Social Democratic trade unions before the war to distinguish themselves from the Christian and German-National trade unions.

The health conditions of the working masses rapidly improved. In Vienna, the number of deaths dropped dramatically between 1918 and 1921:

Year	Total deaths	Deaths by tuberculosis
1918	51,497	11,531
1919	40,932	10,606
1920	34,197	7,464
1921	28,297	5,265

The improved nutrition of working-class youth can be seen in the measurements taken in the apprentice recreation homes of the Public Health Authority. The average body weight of apprentices increased between 1919 and 1921:

Age (years)	Weight (kilograms)	
	1919	1921
14–15	40.93	44.35
15–16	42.66	45.45
16–17	47.48	50.13

As the unemployed "home-comers" became regularly employed industrial workers, as work stoppages as a result of coal and raw-material shortages ceased, and as the nutrition of the working masses improved, the workers became more pacific. The stormy interludes in the factories and the streets, which had frightened the bourgeoisie in the first months after the upheaval, became rarer. In the factories labor intensity and discipline increased. In the state it was again possible to govern without fearing daily worker uprisings or needing daily consultations with the labor organizations. The revolutionary state of stress was overcome by the industrial boom.

As a result, private industrial entrepreneurs became more self-confident. They had been intimidated so long as their factories were in a state of chaos; they regained their self-confidence as soon as their factories were in full operation again. At the time of the major crisis, when the coal and raw-material shortage made full production impossible, they had not fought against the introduction of the eight-hour day, but now that it was preventing them from fully utilizing the boom they complained about "social-policy experiments." At the high point of the revolutionary convulsions, they had acquiesced in the new social-policy legislation without resistance; now they began to rebel against the "social-policy burdens." The industrialists began to mobilize all the owning classes against the position of power that the workers had achieved in the state.

But the currency depreciation not only restored trade, small-scale production and services, and large-scale industry; it also produced a major regrouping within the whole bourgeoisie. A new bourgeoisie arose and the old bourgeoisie drowned.

At first the currency depreciation favored those strata of the old entrepreneurial class whose firms had their offices in Vienna but their factories outside German-Austria, mostly in Czechoslovakia. These entrepreneurs drew their income in Czech kronen but spent it in Austrian kronen. They therefore benefitted from the great difference between the domestic and foreign value of the krone. Alongside them there was a new stratum of the bourgeoisie that derived great profits from this disparity. Great new fortunes were made from currency speculation and profiteering. The serious obstacles that legislation attempted to put in the way of currency speculation and profiteering could only be circumvented by particularly cunning and unscrupulous dealers. These were methods of "primitive accumulation" in Marx's sense, from whose application these new fortunes arose. Such methods were unfamiliar to capitalists used to the normal forms of operation in highly developed industrial environments. But they were all the more familiar to the traders from the agrarian countries of the east, where capital, living within the pores of a still precapitalist society, was accustomed to use the more brutal and corrupt methods of "primitive accumulation." The Galician Jews, whom the war had driven to Vienna in large numbers, and Hungarian dealers, who had sought refuge in Austria from the Revolution, represented a large contingent of those exploiting the boom in currency depreciation. They were joined by the still numerous "gold-diggers" from the countries with strong currencies, who came to Austria to take advantage of the "closeout sale" boom. Thus, a new bourgeoisie developed from the currency-depreciation boom, which for the most part was composed of elements of a very low cultural level from outside the country, who owed their success to their business acumen and moral unscrupulousness. What Engels had said in 1848 a few weeks before the Austrian March Revolution had become true: "it may be the really vile, really dirty, really Jewish bourgeois who buy up this venerable empire."[1]

The philistine luxurious lives of the new bourgeoisie, which had become rich on the misery of the country, embittered the broad masses. A wave of anti-Semitism broke out across the country.

The same process of currency depreciation that had created the new bourgeoisie impoverished the old bourgeoisie. The rentiers were the first to be hit. During the war, the overwhelmingly larger part of the bourgeoisie's mobile capital had assumed the form of war bonds. The Republic paid the interest on the war bonds in paper kronen. As the value of the paper kronen sank, the rentier class was expropriated. In 1920 the interest the state paid the rentiers represented one hundredth of its nominal value, and in 1922 only one ten-thousandth. The millionaire who had invested his wealth in war bonds had become a beggar.

With the rentiers, house owners were also expropriated. The Rent Protection Act[2] passed during the war was upheld. Rents, expressed in paper kronen, only rose slowly, while the value of paper kronen sank rapidly. The maintenance of rent protection was one of the most effective means of raising the masses' standard of living. The cost of renting an apartment soon absorbed only a very small fraction of wage income. The masses could satisfy their housing needs much better than before the war. *Bettgeher** and subtenants disappeared from workers' apartments. The fact that there was a housing shortage in Vienna, even though the population was considerably reduced as a result of losses in the war, the drop in the birth rate, and the great wave of emigration after the Revolution, proves that the masses of people in the workers' neighborhoods did not live in as crowded conditions as they had before the war. But this improvement in housing culture, one of the happiest results of the social upheaval, occurred at the cost of the building owners; the rent was confiscated to the benefit of the tenants. Thus, one of the largest sectors of the bourgeoisie was economically expropriated.

Higher officialdom too was squeezed by the currency depreciation. The state, the provinces, and the municipalities were struggling against the greatest financial difficulties and could only raise the stipends of their employees much more slowly than those of employees in industries working for export and in the banks and commercial enterprises advantaged by the currency depreciation boom. However, the salaries of the lowest categories of public employees, who even previously could afford to do little

---

* In contrast to subtenants, *Bettgeher* were people who rented beds without contracts from workers normally for single shifts and normally on a one-time basis. A bed could be shared successively by several people.

more than live, had to be raised to the degree that the purchasing power of money sank. This could be done only by cutting the salaries of the higher officials. Their salaries rose much more slowly than the value of money sank. From the end of 1915 through March 1920, the salaries of unmarried state officials of the eleventh rank were still raised by 215 percent. The salary of a Hofrat* in 1915 was 8.6 times higher than that of an official of the lowest rank, but in 1920 it was only 3.3 times higher.

The free professions were also affected by the currency movement. The impoverished people had to use their whole income to secure the most indispensable and urgent items for existence. They had to forego everything else. With the pauperization of the most numerous strata of the bourgeoisie, doctors, writers, and artists lost their clientele, and they too fell into a state of bitter privation.

While a new and alien bourgeoisie was making great fortunes from the country's misery, the wealth of the Old-Austrian bourgeoisie was liquidated by the currency depreciation. It was torn away from its accustomed bourgeois standard of living. Thousands who were rich before the war could now only live by selling their old furniture and jewelry and renting out their rooms to strangers. They could no longer afford housekeepers; books, the theater, and concerts became prohibitive luxuries.

The Old-Viennese patricians, the leading sections of the Austrian intelligentsia, and large parts of the middle and lower bourgeoisie were impoverished by the currency depreciation. They had been the actual ruling class of the Habsburg Monarchy, which they had supplied with its officials and officers. They had been the carriers of Austrian patriotism, of Old-Austrian traditions. For a century they had been the bearers of the specifically Austrian culture, of Viennese literature, of Viennese music, and Viennese theater. They were the real vanquished of the war. It was their Empire that had collapsed in October 1918. And with their Empire they lost their wealth.

Their economic fate determined their social and political ideology. In the last year of the war, they had yearned for peace. At that time they hated German imperialism, which was prolonging the war. Many of them hoped to save their Empire by separating from Germany, and through democracy and national autonomy within the Empire to pave the way to a separate peace. At that time their pacifism brought them close to Social Democracy.

* An honorary title bestowed on state officials with academic backgrounds and after a certain number of years in service.

And when democracy triumphed in October 1918, many of them were also filled with the spirit of the new times and ready to associate themselves with the rising power of the working class, calling themselves "intellectual workers." But after a few weeks their mood changed. The new times had impoverished and embittered them. Their resentment was turned against the two classes that had risen out of the catastrophe that had destroyed the old bourgeoisie: against the new bourgeoisie that had profited economically from the catastrophe, and against the working class, which the catastrophe had raised to political hegemony. They saw many Jews among the enriched profiteers and among the leaders of the workers. Anti-Semitism provided the glue for their twofold hatred.

Very soon their resentment at the workers became greater than their resentment at the profiteers. After all, the profiteer was in the last analysis simply a successful businessman; to their bourgeois way of thinking it seemed only natural that profits and wealth should arise from buying and selling. But every day their bourgeois prejudices collided with the new power and self-confidence of the workers. To the physician it seemed to be the end of the world that nurses and attendants should want to share in the management of the hospital. The chief clerk was angry at the changed attitude of his clerks, the housewife at the suddenly awakened self-confidence of her cook. But what they all especially resented was the changes in wages. The krone incomes of the rentier and the landlord stayed the same despite the depreciation of the krone; the krone incomes of the high official, the artist, the doctor, rose much more slowly than the value of the krone sank; but workers in the export industries favored by the currency depreciation could rapidly increase their income. The intellectuals could not see that the wage increases merely represented the adjustment of the money wage to the falling value of money; they could only see that the workers' wages rose quickly while their income did not do so at all or only much more slowly. The intellectuals did not see that the working class's standard of living, despite all wage raises, remained at a much lower level than it had been at before the war; they only saw that the workers' standard of living still gradually improved while theirs constantly sank deeper with the progression of the currency depreciation. The intellectuals did not understand that the upheaval in the distribution of income was the result of an elementary economic process, the inescapable effect of the great historic catastrophe of the war, of the dissolution of the old economic area, of the dictated peace. They took the wage increases, which were the consequence of the currency depreciation, for the cause of the currency depreciation and thus for the cause of the immiseration of the "middle class."

When the wages of artisans occasionally exceeded the income of the academically educated, they took this for the despotic workings of the new political power of the working class. That the laundress was better paid than the university assistant became the slogan of agitation. Class envy of the proletariat became the ruling passion of the declining strata of the bourgeoisie. It filled the broad strata of the middle and lower bourgeoisie with hatred for the Revolution, the working class, and Social Democracy.

It is interesting to follow the effect on Austrian literature of this rapid change of mood of the bourgeois intelligentsia. In the last years of the war and at the time of the upheaval, the rebellion of a significant section of the German-Austrian intelligentsia against the horrors and sordidness of the war found expression in a series of literary works. Towering above them all is Karl Kraus's play *The Last Days of Mankind*, in its gruesome truth and fullness the most powerful monument to the war. This rebellion against the war filled not a few young intellectuals with revolutionary emotions. As reserve officers, many of them sat in the midst of the noisy goings-on at the officers' mess, as depicted by Ernst Angel:

> *Outside, the Redeemer died a long festering death on barbed wire,*
> *Inside, the slinking orderly Judas offered up the roast.*

And in the midst of his comrades, the young poet waited hopefully for the imminent, avenging Revolution:

> *But you can already hear it, the doors burst open by disgust,*
> *Did you come finally to destroy us, son of sacrifice?*
> *Spewing revolt and fusel at us with foaming mouth.*
> *Lewd and threatening. Travesty of the future alliance.*
> *Tomorrow's hangmen. Magistrates of the Last Judgment.*

And when the Revolution had come, as

> *Thinkers of steel conspiring with thinkers of mind*
> *close the throat of machines become fat on victims,*

the poet greeted the Revolution with the most exuberant expectation:

> *Your rage versifies the future; and Eden sprouts from our sins,*
> *Humankind united and blooming, surrounded by gardens.*
> *Friendship mends strife, forges covenants,*

The dream of the prophets is dreamed into being.

But the terrible disillusion came all too soon: instead of the people's liberation in romantic, heroic struggle, there was the harsh class struggle whose form and content was determined by economic privation and powerlessness; instead of the league of humanity reconciling quarrels, there was the defenseless impotence of the vanquished and the brutal force of the victors; instead of the yearned for Eden, there was the country's economic catastrophe, the economic ruin of the class that had been the carrier of its intellectual life for a century. It could not empathize with the other, neighboring peoples whom the upheaval had liberated from their old chains while it put new chains on the German-Austrians, as the victims of this upheaval. That this Revolution had awakened the sleeping souls of the working masses in German-Austria and given a new, higher purpose in life to broad masses was not noticed by a single one of the poets and artists of our bourgeoisie; the tidings of the spiritual revolution occurring in the factories and workers' quarters did not penetrate to their writing desks, to their coffee houses. They only experienced the decline of their own class. They sought refuge in images of the past. When Old-Austria collapsed, they painted pictures of its past greatness; the baroque and Biedermeier periods reemerged for them. And their memory of times when their class was richer and happier always ended with words of lament; Felix Grafe provides an example:

> *Whither is this going? Who trampled on the dream?*
> *No crying brings it back, no prayer awakens it,*
> *The day and its abundance is dissipated.*
> *And where we once lay in the intoxication of beholding,*
> *Effusively breathing words and kisses:*
> *The fist of action horrendously slew us.*

In the terrible year of misery following the war, the intelligentsia believed it was seeing the complete demise of its Vienna, of the old, great Vienna. It was in this mood that Karl Hans Strobl wrote his fantasy novel *Gespenster im Sumpf* (Ghosts in the Bog). In it Vienna perishes in famine and civil war. The population has died out, the houses are falling apart, rats are living in the rubble. A handful of people are still moving about in the sea of rubble; they call themselves state secretaries, and one man, by the name of Laufer,* who calls himself chancellor, is the leader of the gang. Now and

---

* An allusion to Renner; both words can be translated as "runner."

then they are able to capture a rich American woman who is inquisitively touring the rubble of the moldering city and demand ransom money to free her; this they call a wealth levy. But at the edge of the city there are still brutish people living in burrows; they believe in a legend that powerful demons called factory councils had once been present in their midst. . .

Then, when Vienna's economic life began to revive, although the intelligentsia no longer saw the demise of their city, they still saw the demise of their class. For them and for the immiserated middle strata, there is no more future in the city. This is the mood in which Rudolf Hans Bartsch wrote *Ein Landstreicher* (Tramp): Back to the soil is where we need to go if we still want to live. We must become peasants—but "sublimated peasants, book-reading peasants, music-listening peasants." Disgusted by everything else that happened in the time of the Revolution, Bartsch nevertheless effusively celebrates the small-garden and settler movement as the beginning of the return to the soil.

It was against the rising profiteering on the one hand and the strengthened working class on the other that the hatred of the economically impoverished intelligentsia was directed. It was the bourgeois commonplace conception of what was happening, which Thaddäus Rittner shaped into a tale full of subtle irony in his novel *Geister in der Stadt* (Ghosts in the City). The city is dominated by "the muscles and the finances." Their servants, however, consist of artists and scholars; they form the "lowest layer of society." They strive to eat in the most unmannerly way possible and speak in the most uncultured way possible in order to be like their new masters. They bow deeply before every "street sweeper and tram conductor." It is the "victory of material over spirit." But suddenly a theater of phantoms appears in the city, which soon contaminates everyone. There all at once people begin to speak again of things other than money. The need for art and science emerges once again. And now the oppressed—the artists and scholars— can once again dare to present demands. Now they gradually regain the upper hand again. The time comes when once again manual workers feel oppressed and again conspire against the dominating intellectuals.

The cultured bourgeoisie sees its time as coming again. Certainly, the old rule throughout the broad Empire has been destroyed. Old wealth has been destroyed. But in narrower confines one can also build a new house. Franz Werfel gives form to the myth of this hope in his play *Bocksgesang* (The Song of the Ram). There the "unchristened," the half animal, which Gospodar Milić has kept in his stall, has broken its chains; and the sight of it has unleashed the revolt of the "landless." It is the unchristened, the unbridled, the animalistic-demonic in people that the Revolution has unleashed; and its content is the satanic mass, the cult of the animalistic-demonic. But the Janissaries come and crush the "landless." It is true that Gospodar's property has been destroyed; but liberated from the eternal fear of the unchristened, freed of the burden that comes with rule and possession, he goes about building himself a new house in order to live in it with his wife more poorly but more happily.

The same evolution of moods that is so clearly reflected in literature can also be observed in our scholarly production—most clearly, of course, in the field of economics. The extensive academic literature on socialization appeared in the first months after the Revolution. But after just another few months, the mood suddenly turned. Now literature appeared of an entirely different stamp. Books like Othmar Spann's *Der wahre Staat* (The True State) and Ludwig Mises's *Gemeinwirtschaft* (Socialism) are key representatives of this genre. The former wants to bring us back to Adam Müller, the latter to Bentham. The former to the romantic philosophy of the state, the latter to Manchester liberalism. Spann champions "work of the more noble strain," the work of artists and scholars; Mises in a far more sober way defends the freedom of "the owners of the means of production." Spann represents the flight of the bourgeois intelligentsia impoverished by the currency depreciation to the romantic ideal of a corporative state order; Mises represents the reawakened self-confidence of the entrepreneurs lifted up by the currency-depreciation boom, who demand the liberation of their entrepreneurial activity from all state and trade-union constraints. But common to both is the passionate rejection of socialism, the passionate hatred for the labor movement.

Although few in number, the bourgeois intelligentsia has a disproportionately large influence on society. This sector above all others shapes "public opinion." Public opinion began to turn against the power of the working class, against socialism. Large sections of the intelligentsia, of officialdom, of the employees, and of the petty bourgeoisie, which had been pulled along in autumn 1918 on the red tide, became deadly enemies of Social Democracy by summer 1919. For them the paramount task was to reinstate the domination of the bourgeoisie in state and society and gather together around this goal all forces hostile to the working class.

At the same time the mood of the peasantry fundamentally altered. Returned to his village, the "home-comer" quickly became a peasant again. In his village he suffered no privation. He had no lack of food. The currency depreciation allowed him to pay back his mortgages. It had made the land tax insignificant. His comfortable property soon made the peasant forget what he had experienced in the barracks and at the front, how his village was oppressed by the war economy's requisition system. The hostility of the mighty democratic movement to militarism, the bureaucracy, and war profiteering, which in the first months after the upheaval had surged through the villages, was of short duration. At that time the peasant too had contemplated a revolution in the relations of property. And the movement was not without its results. After the Resettlement Law of May 1919,[3] the peasant lands, which had since the 1870s fallen into the hands of the large landowners, were expropriated and used to create new peasant land and cottager settlements. Through several provincial laws, land easement* and hunting rights were revised. But very soon the master peasants† came to recognize that the revision of the relations of landed property could become dangerous to them. The Revolution had awakened the small people in the village. Universal suffrage increased their power in the townships. The struggle between the townships and the agrarian associations,‡ between the landless laborers§ and the half-free peasants¶ for ownership of the old common lands, for usufruct of forest and pasture commons came to life again. The Tenant Protection Regulation[4]** of August 5, 1919, which slowed the adjustment of rent to the currency depreciation and in so doing transferred a part of the ground rent to the lessees, was a victory for the small people over the big people in the village. The large-scale farmers began to defend themselves against the revision of the traditional relations of property. Now it became easy for the bourgeoisie to mobilize them against "socialization."

The movement that had swept through the villages after upheaval had a twofold character from the very beginning. But its democratic character quickly vanished, and its class character hostile to the working class appeared all the more strongly. The Revolution had indeed awakened the

---

* Servituten.
† Herrenbauern.
‡ Agrargemeinschaften.
§ Häusler.
¶ Rustikalisten. A Rustikalgut is the land held by the half-free peasant; Dominikalland is that held by the lord.
** Pächterschutzverordnung.

village proletariat. The rapid development and the overwhelming successes of the young trade unions of the land and forest workers frightened the peasants. At the same time the peasant saw the close connection between the movement of the land workers and that of the industrial proletariat. When the factory whistle blew after eight hours, the farm hand folded his arms too. At the village tavern the railway worker teased the farm laborer who worked more than eight hours. In the village there was a lack of labor power, while the state was paying support for the unemployed in the city. Everywhere the master peasant saw his interests opposed to those of the working class—in the struggle around the purchase prices of the state's Grain Market Agency,* the restoration of free trade, and the development of property taxes. Was the urban entrepreneur not his natural ally in the fight against the eight-hour day and unemployment compensation, the urban merchant his natural ally in the fight for free trade, and the urban capitalist his natural ally in the struggle against capital levies and property taxes? Now in the farmers' tavern too the watchword became: Social Democracy is the enemy!

Thus, a united front of the owning classes gradually developed against the working class. Banking capital, which demanded free currency trading; industrial and commercial enterprise, which defended itself against "social-reform burdens"; commercial capital, which fought for free trade; the nouveaux riches, who trembled at the threat of wealth levies; the declining strata of the bourgeoisie and intelligentsia, which were indignant at "high wages"; the peasants, who were frightened at the movement of the land workers—they all united against the working class. All inner antagonisms between the urban and village bourgeoisie now seemed insignificant in the face of the common conflict with the proletariat. The Jewish profiteer gladly contributed to the electoral campaigns of the bourgeois parties whose victory alone could protect him from high property taxes, the confiscation of his foreign currency, the heavy "burdens" of social policy, and state regulation of his business. What did he care if these parties fought Social Democracy with anti-Semitic arguments? What does the weapon matter with which you defeat the enemy? The best weapon is the one that defeats him! Anti-Semitism, arising as it has from the declining bourgeoisie's resentment of the new ascendant bourgeoisie, became the instrument of this new bourgeoisie itself—a populist weapon against Social Democracy.

The strengthening of the owning classes was a gradual process. It began

---

* Getreideverkehranstalt.

in summer 1919 with the victory of the counterrevolution in Hungary. It was accelerated in the second half of 1920, when the period of industrial prosperity overcame the revolutionary excitement of the working masses and reestablished the self-confidence of the entrepreneurial classes. It progressed further when the elections of October 1920 revealed the defection of broad sections of the middle strata from Social Democracy and the defeats of the international proletariat in 1920 and 1921 put the proletariat on the defensive everywhere. And so too in Austria the tide of revolution ebbed.

CHAPTER 14

THE STRUGGLE FOR
REPUBLICAN INSTITUTIONS

After the ratification of the Treaty of Saint-Germain, the coalition government formed in February 1919 resigned from office. On October 17, 1919, the second coalition government was formed. On its face there was no change of governmental system but only in the personal composition of the government. In reality, this government—already in its formation but most especially in its effect—made clear the shift in social power relations that had occurred since the counterrevolution in Hungary.

At the time the first coalition government was formed, the sharpest clash within the government was between the peasant and Viennese branches of the Christian Socials. This antagonism was overcome as the "home-comers" became peasants again, the peasant movement lost the strong democratic features it had in the time of upheaval, and it turned continuously more one-sidedly against the working class. The Viennese Klerikalen* gradually succeeded in bringing the peasant deputies under their leadership. The prelate Ignaz Seipel† became the de facto leader of the Christian Social Party. Thus, the Christian Social Party was far stronger in the second coalition than it was in the first. The first coalition was a class alliance of the workers with the peasants. The second was a banal party coalition of Social Democrats and Christian Socials.

Social Democracy now no longer shared the government with the rep-

---

* The Wiener Klerikalen were the wing of the Christian Social Partly (Christian Socials) under the direct influence of the Catholic hierarchy whose leading figure was Ignaz Seipel.
† See Introduction to this volume, Note 36.

resentatives of the peasantry but with the part of the bourgeoisie represented by the urban Christian Socials, which now once again commanded
the peasant vote. This bourgeoisie's self-confidence had already been greatly
strengthened ever since it stopped trembling at the likelihood of the proletarian revolution once the counterrevolution prevailed in Hungary and Bavaria. It narrowed the scope for action of the new government through the
coalition agreements concluded at the formation of the new government
and through the coalition committee under whose control the new government's actions were placed. All important governmental acts and bills had
from now on to be agreed in the Coalition Committee between the two
parties. In it they were of equal strength. The first Renner government had
been the organ of the working class's hegemony; in the second coalition
government, which Renner also headed as State Chancellor, a state of equilibrium existed between the forces of the classes represented in it.

There now followed a sterile war of position between the two coalition
parties. Each of them was strong enough to block the actions of the other,
but neither of them was strong enough to impose its will on the other.
The government's capacity to act and to legislate was paralyzed. The Peace
Treaty forced us to change the organization of our armed forces. After the
Peace Treaty had redrawn our territorial boundaries and blocked annexation to Germany, the Constituent National Assembly had to give the Republic its constitution. The currency depreciation required measures that
would put our shattered state finances in order; a decision had to be made
on the wealth levy put forward by the Social Democrats. But the coalesced
parties were unable to come together around any of these problems. The
machine of legislation stood still.

In only one instance were we able to overcome this state of paralysis.
To do so a powerful external stimulus was needed. On March 13, 1920
the march of the Döberitz troops on Berlin—the putsch attempt* by the
Reich-German counterrevolution—became known in Austria. The masses
saw the German Republic threatened and immediately understood that
the Austrian Republic was also in danger. Great excitement gripped the
factories and barracks. On the very next day the Volkswehr battalions and
crowds of workers demonstrated in the Ringstrasse against the counterrevolution. In the German Reich the proletariat rose up, summoned by the
government itself. It could not be foreseen where the general strike of the
German proletariat would lead, nor how far the excited masses of the Aus-

---

*The Kapp Putsch.

trian proletariat would be carried along with it. The Austrian bourgeoisie was intimidated. We used the crisis to break the resistance of the Christian Socials to the Defense Law proposed by Julius Deutsch—and they did give in. The Defense Law[1] was passed by the National Assembly in the days of the Kapp Putsch.

The outer parameters of the Defense Law were dictated by the Peace Treaty. The organization of the Volkswehr did not correspond to the provisions of the Peace Treaty. In its place a new army had to be created. Since the victory of the counterrevolution in Hungary, we felt a threat from the east; we needed a combat-ready army that could protect our borders against invasion by Hungarian troops and our republican constitution against the Habsburg counterrevolution based in Hungary. The fighting capacity of the army presupposed discipline. In October 1918 the officers' authority had collapsed. In the Volkswehr the officers were powerless. Real power lay in the hands of the soldiers' councils; it was only under their control that the officers could issue commands. It could not stay that way. If we wanted a combat-ready army, the command authority of the officers would have to be restored. But while the reestablishment of military discipline in our army was necessary, it was nevertheless dangerous. It is true that since the upheaval Deutsch had appointed many of the rank and file as officers; these "Volkswehr lieutenants" were now to pass over into the army. But the overwhelming majority of the officers still had to be taken from the officer corps of the old k.u.k. army. It was reactionary in its outlook, educated as it was in monarchical traditions. Had we surrendered the militiamen to the absolute power of such an officer corps, the new army would have become a blind instrument of the monarchists against the Republic, of the bourgeoisie lusting for violent counterrevolution against the proletariat. The Kapp Putsch in Germany had just shown how great this danger really was; there the Republic's army had actually risen against the Republic. The task was therefore to restore the authority of the officers and the discipline of the rank and file and at the same time create guarantees that authority and discipline could not be misused by transforming the army into a tool of political and social reaction. This was the extremely difficult problem that our Defense Law had to solve.

We did not restore the old military tribunals. The jurisdiction for military offences was transferred to the civil courts. The provisions of the military penal code were softened, but provisions were brought back into force that threatened violations of military discipline with severe punishment. We did not restore the power of superiors to inflict punishment with the degrading imprisonments and corporal punishment of the k.u.k. army. The power to inflict punishment was transferred to disciplinary commissions formed by the rank and file. But the punishments that these disciplinary commissions can impose—reducing salaries, expulsions from the army—are severe enough to enforce discipline in the new army. The Military Criminal Code Amendment and the Disciplinary Law solved one problem: restoring military discipline.

The Defense Law then had to solve the other problem: creating guarantees that the militiamen would remain free men who, disciplined in the daily carrying out of their military service, would nevertheless remain sufficiently self-confident to disobey orders if the commanders wanted to misuse them for reactionary purposes, for the counterrevolution. The new law therefore determined that the militiamen would remain in full enjoyment of all their rights as citizens; this provision enabled us to bring the militiamen together into a "Military Association,"* the trade union of those serving in the army, which not only looked after the material interests of the militiamen but also had to provide for their education in a republican and socialist spirit. For this purpose the Defense Law also introduced into the new army the soldiers' councils, with a different structure and more restricted powers. Delegates freely elected by the militiamen were inserted into every command center, not only as guardians of the rights and interests of the militiamen but also of the republican character of the army. How the men see fit to use these rights depends on the composition of the armed forces. This is why we took care to include provisions in the Defense Law that facilitated the recruitment of industrious, self-confident workers for the new army. To this end the Defense Law makes it possible for the militiamen to move up into the officer corps and stipulates that those who are not accepted into the officers schools should be given opportunities during their service for continuing professional training for their later life.

The Defense Law thus created a peculiar dualism that has no counterpart in any army in the world and that penetrates the whole structure of the Republic's army. It is the dualism between military discipline and civic freedom, between military hierarchy and trade-union organization, between the command authority of the superior officers and the right of the delegates to control it, between military and vocational training. It is undeniable that this dualism created difficulties inside the army. But it is indispensable if the authority of the officers taken over from the Imperial

---

* Millitärverband. See Glossary.

Army is not to turn the army into an instrument for the overthrow of the republican constitution and a violent crackdown on the working class. Only when the old Imperial officer corps is replaced by a new officer corps arising from the rank and file of the republican army itself, no longer socially and politically reactionary and no longer dominated by monarchical traditions, will we be able to forego the system of counterbalances to the command authority of the officer corps, this system of institutions through which the Defense Law attempts to avert the misuse of authority at the service of social and political reaction.

As soon as the Defense Law was passed, Deutsch set about organizing the new defense force—the Federal Army,* as it has been called since November 1920. Its rapid creation was a significant organizational achievement, chiefly due to the work of the head of the State Military Office, General Körner, one of the best officers of the Imperial Army, who has placed his great military prowess and his (in the best sense of the word) soldierly personality at the service of the Republic ever since the overthrow of the Monarchy. Recruiting the cadre of the Federal Army was the special concern of Social Democracy. We succeeded in bringing the best elements of the Volkswehr into it, uniting the overwhelming majority of militiamen within the Military Association and in placing the overwhelming majority of the soldiers' councils under our leadership.

The transition from the Volkswehr to the Federal Army did not occur without difficulties, however. On the one side, the militiamen, so accustomed to other conditions in the Volkswehr, often passionately rebelled at first against the restoration of the officers' authority. On the other side, the officers immediately tried to impede the activity of the soldiers' councils, which was based on the Defense Law, and to force the modus operandi of the military back into the old forms with which they were familiar from the Imperial Army and which were incompatible with the self-confidence of the republican militiamen. This led to frequent conflicts resulting, in the most extreme cases, in charges of mutiny and insubordination brought before courts; the harsh sentences reflecting the class hatred of the bourgeoisie for the militiamen, considered the linchpin of the proletariat's power, only aggravated the antagonisms within the Federal Army. However, all the difficulties of the transition period were gradually overcome and the institutions of the new defense constitution brought into regular operation, which as they became established were continually less disrupted by friction and conflict.

---

* Bundesheer.

The Volkswehr, which had arisen in the stormy days of the Revolution, had been an instrument of the proletariat's offensive. But as a revolutionary improvisation, it could only remain in existence during the revolutionary period. Without orderly routine, without military discipline, it could not be a permanent entity. The Federal Army, created at a time in which the tide of the Revolution had already receded, is quite a different thing. It emerged at a time in which the proletariat could not make new conquests but had to consolidate the essential achievements of the preceding revolutionary period and transform them into lasting institutions of the Republic. To a great extent this was successfully accomplished by the creation of the new Federal Army. The equilibrium between the authority of the officer corps and the organization of the rank and file through the Military Association and the delegates reflects the balance of class forces that existed in the period of the Federal Army's emergence. Although due to the restoraton of the command authority of the officer corps the Federal Army was no longer an instrument of the proletarian offensive, it was at the same time not an instrument for a monarchist counterrevolution—as occurred with the German Reichswehr in the days of the Kapp Putsch—thanks to the composition and organization of its rank and file and the rights with which they were endowed by the Defense Law. Because the weapons were in the hands of a class-conscious proletarian rank and file, the proletariat was protected from forcible suppression by an armed counterrevolution.

At a time of great danger, of the struggle for Burgenland, this military mechanism was made a reality for the first time and doubtless stood the test. The restoration of military discipline created an internal order and capacity to act, which proved effective in the occupation of Burgenland. The republican spirit and socialist convictions of the rank and file enormously increased their vigilance and combativeness in the fight against the bands of the Magyar counterrevolution.

During the great agitation caused by the Kapp Putsch, the bourgeois parties agreed to the Defense Law. But when the general strike of workers in the German Reich ended with no other result than the mere consolidation of the Republic, the Christian Socials regretted having been caught by surprise during the days of agitation. Now they regarded the Defense Law as a heavy defeat for the bourgeoisie. The antagonisms between the coalition parties became sharper. The war of position in the coalition cabinet and the Coalition Committee started up again. The opposition of the Christian Socials to all our demands was reinforced.

The more the bourgeoisie's opposition grew within the coalition, the greater was the rebellion of the working class against the coalition's policies. There was no strong opposition within the working class to the coalition policy as long as the government was an instrument of working class hegemony. But as soon as there was an equilibrium of class forces within the coalition and their mutual opposition made the coalition government unproductive, an increasing opposition to coalition policy quickly grew within the working class. Already in 1919 a group of party comrades came together within the Vienna workers' councils, which—in contrast to the Left of the war period—called itself the "New Left" and constituted itself inside the Vienna workers' councils as the Social Democratic Working Group of Revolutionary Workers' Councils, which published a weekly paper. This group categorically called for a council dictatorship and believed that the coalition policy indicated the party's departure from the principles of the class struggle; in their opposition to the party leadership they became close to the Communists, and this opposition within the party became important in spring and summer 1920.

This was the time when the military victories of the Russian Soviet Republic had awakened the passionate enthusiasm of the whole international proletariat. At the time of the Russo-Polish War, the workers' councils established control commissions, which oversaw rail traffic and had great success in combating illicit trading in weapons and munitions for Poland and Hungary. However, while the workers' councils were unanimous in this act of solidarity with the Russian Revolution, the general enthusiasm for the Russian Revolution caused a section of the workers' councils to throw itself into the arms of Bolshevik ideology. At this time the party split was gestating within the Independent Social Democratic Party of Germany, in France's Socialist Party, and in both social democratic parties of Czechoslovakia; large sections of these parties, which had already come under the spell of Bolshevism, demanded affiliation to the Moscow International. This wave of Bolshevism that coursed through all of Europe was bound to influence the thinking of broad strata of the Austrian working class. And this influence had to grow all the stronger as the Austrian working class felt its influence within the coalition weakening and the results of the battles it had carried out on the soil of democracy becoming sparser. And so the influence of the New Left grew. It gave expression to the opposition of the masses to the coalition policy, and its agitation fed and strengthened the masses' revolt against it.

In the workers' councils the Communists and the New Left organized in the Working Group operated as small but cohesive groups. The other workers' council members, who made up the overwhelming majority, were not organized into groups; each of them voted according to their personal conviction. The more discontented the masses became with the coalition policy, the more frequently the Communists and the Working Group won them over for their motions. In this way, as early as June 1920, at the third congress of the National Workers' Council,* the New Left commanded the majority of votes.

We could see that the coalition had become sterile because of the strong opposition of the bourgeoisie and that there were no more prospects for us to reach agreement with the Christian Socials over the big pressing questions of the Constitution, the wealth levy, and the management of next year's grain harvest. On the other hand, we could see that ever greater sections of the working class demanded the dissolution of the coalition. Long before the third congress of the National Workers' Council, we had decided to break up the coalition. But we could not allow ourselves to do so immediately. The party first had to stay in government for a short while in order to complete certain tasks that were important for the proletariat. Deutsch accelerated the creation of the new Federal Army and the dismantling of the old officer corps; Glöckel secured the most important measures of the school reform; and Hanusch speeded up the passage of a few more important laws and directives to supplement the social policy legislation of the first coalition government. Laws regulating mediation panels and collective bargaining, the establishment of the factory and office workers' Chambers of Labor,† special laws and directives on the employment contracts of housemaids and on the labor conditions of specific categories of workers (in the hospitality sector, in law offices), above all the law of March 24, 1920, which established the permanent institution of unemployment compensation in place of the provisional state unemployment support— these were the social policy achievements of the second coalition. As soon as these important achievements of the working class had been secured, we could give in to the pressure of the working masses and dissolve the coalition.

The dispute around the passage of the Defense Law provided the opportunity. On May 25 Deutsch had issued a decree that regulated the au-

---

* Reichsarbeiterrat.
† See Glossary.

thority of the soldiers' councils. This decree was fiercely contested by the bourgeois parties. At the meeting of the National Assembly on June 10, we saw ourselves confronting a coalition of the Christian Socials and the Pan-Germans, which was united in assailing Deutsch. In the course of the violent debates, Kunschak dared to threaten us with the dissolution of the coalition. We took him at his word. The Social Democratic members resigned from the government, and the workers received the news with great rejoicing.

We demanded that the bourgeois parties that had united against us on June 10 form a government alone. But they would not risk it and refused to form any government without our participation, and so the National Assembly was no longer capable of producing a government from its members. The parties therefore agreed to hold new elections and in the meantime to entrust the carrying out of government business to a government composed of all parties in proportion to their strength, the so-called proportional government, which was elected on July 7, 1920.

The effects of the break-up of the coalition were immediately visible. As long as the coalition existed, the disputed issues were settled between the coalition parties within the Coalition Committee; if agreement was reached in the Committee, then the coalition parties had to vote en bloc in the National Assembly. Thus, the Christian Socials could not combine their votes with those of the Pan-Germans against us. It was not the bourgeois majority that decided against the Social Democratic minority; rather, the decision was made through a compromise between the two equally strong parties within the Coalition Committee. But now there was no longer a coalition. All parties retained full freedom in the face of the proportional government. Each party could now vote as it liked. The Christian Socials and the Pan-Germans could combine their votes against us and vote us down. Now the fact that the National Assembly had a bourgeois majority became operative.

In fact, immediately after the dissolution of the coalition we were confronted by a bourgeois coalition. In this second coalition government we could not reach consensus on the nature of the wealth levy and the state regulation of the wheat supply; the bourgeois coalition now decided against us on both questions. On July 21, the National Assembly voted on the wealth levy.[2] The bourgeois majority voted down our motions. The version of the law it shaped fixed the levy so low and stretched out the payment installments over such a long period as to defeat the goal of the law,

which was to meet the state deficit in the long term at the cost of the owning classes and thus shut down the money-printing presses. The vote on
state regulation of the wheat supply took place on July 6.[3] The bourgeois
majority cancelled the strict control of wheat, and the law it passed against
us was the first decisive step toward the restoration of free trade. The two
most important principles of our economic policy—to cover the greatest
possible part of the state deficit at the cost of property and to maintain a
planned economy for food supply—had suffered defeats.

Our position was much stronger in the debate around the third of the
great contested issues, over which the second coalition government had
foundered: the question of the constitution. The Constituent National Assembly had been elected to give the Republic a constitution. None of the
parties wanted to stand for election without having fulfilled this task. But
the Constitution could only be passed with a two-thirds majority. On this
question the bourgeois majority could not outvote us. In the end, by August,
a compromise was arrived at on the basis of the draft worked out by Professor Hans Kelsen.* Immediately before the new elections of October 1, 1920,
the Constituent National Assembly approved the Federal Constitution.

Since the upheaval, class antagonisms had been expressed through
the struggles between the state, the provinces, and the municipalities. The
peasantry and the bourgeoisie of the rural towns represented the particularism of the provinces. The working class defended the unity of the state
as well as the local governance of the municipalities, the districts, and the
counties against this particularism. The Constitution could only produce
a compromise between these opposing forces. It could not take away from
the provinces what they had already conquered at the expense of the state
in the tumultuous days of November 1918. The state was therefore constituted as a federation of provinces. But the Constitution had to put an
end to a further anarchic proliferation of provincial particularism at the
expense of the federation and rein in the powers that the provinces had
usurped in such a way that the unity of the federation as an economic and
legal area would be secured and the coercion of minorities in the provinces
prevented. The Constitution accomplished this. It established the unity of
the currency, economic, and customs territory and compelled the provinces gradually to dismantle the barriers they had erected against one another and against Vienna. It protects the social and political minorities in
the provinces by prescribing the principles of the provincial constitutions,

---

* See the Introduction to this volume, p. 5f.

the principles of the provincial and municipal electoral law, and the legal equality of all state citizens with provincial citizens. It forecloses any further anarchic development of provincial sovereignty by granting the federal government the right to issue instructions to provincial governors and to veto provincial laws; it invests the Constitutional Court with the right to annul unconstitutional provincial laws and directives and to remove provincial governors from office who act unconstitutionally. Thus, the Constitution has given the provinces legal recognition but also legal restrictions and limited the powers that they usurped during the Revolution.

The regulation of the relation between the provinces and the local administration in the municipalities, the districts, and the counties was much more difficult than regulating the relation between the state and the provinces. In the former case it was not a matter of the legal regulation of a development that had already taken place but of the creation of legal institutions in the first place. The Revolution had replaced the bureaucratic authoritarian regime in the state and in the provinces with government by the people's deputies elected by representative bodies of the people. In the districts, however, bureaucratic authoritarian administration by the district commissioners had survived the Revolution. Subordinating these commissioners to the provincial governors would have meant subordinating the proletarian industrial districts to the bourgeois-agrarian majorities in the provincial Landtage.* We therefore could not permit any expansion of the legislative and administrative powers of the provinces without a simultaneous democratization of local administration and the unification of the villages into municipalities that are self-governing through either the district or county legislatures, both freely elected, to which the administrative authorities must be subordinated. Indeed, the Federal Constitution establishes the general principles of such a democratization of local government, but it left its implementation to later legislation. We therefore had to insist that those provisions of the Constitution governing the distribution of power between the federal state and the provinces would come into force only when a special constitutional law on the carrying out of democratic local administration in the districts or counties is enacted. Consequently, while the constitutional provisions that subordinate the provinces to the federal state came into force, those provisions that expanded the area of authority of the provinces remained preliminarily suspended. They still have not come into effect.

---

* See Glossary.

The most important innovation in the Constitution was the new legal status of Vienna. In May 1919, Social Democracy won a majority of seats in the City Council of Vienna, and from then on Jakob Reumann has been the mayor and head of the municipal administration. The Social Democratic majority had given the large municipality a new municipal constitution drafted by Robert Danneberg and implemented with skill and energy by Chief Executive Director Hartl; it introduced the ministerial system into municipal administration and placed the individual magistrate departments under the "administrative selectmen" elected by the city council, thereby replacing the bureaucratic magistracy with democratic self-government by people's deputies. At the same time, the Social Democratic majority, under the responsible and courageous leadership of Hugo Breitner—and a newly created municipal taxation system along with insistence that municipal public enterprises use their revenue to cover their operational expenses—had brought the city finances, which had been completely destroyed by the war, back on its feet, despite the ongoing currency depreciation. Thanks to this policy, the control of municipal administration in the great city, which contained nearly three-tenths of the entire federal population, became one of the most important pillars of the working class's power in the state. The next task was to free this important sphere of power from the constraints imposed on it by Vienna's inclusion in the province of Lower Austria, and thus subordination to the Lower Austrian provincial government and its legislation. The separation of Vienna from Lower Austria, the constituting of Vienna as an independent federal province, was made possible and prepared by the Federal Constitution and fully carried out in December 1921. With this, the mayor of Vienna acquired the rights of a provincial governor, the city senate the rights of a provincial government, and the city council the powers of a Landtag. The elevation of Vienna to the status of an independent federal province not only consolidated the working class's strongest bulwark within the federal state but also weakened the motivating force of the provincial rebellion against the federal state. As soon as every right that the provinces had contested at the cost of the federation was no longer a mere weapon of the bourgeois-agrarian provincial governments but had at the same time become a weapon of the proletarian provincial government in Vienna, a rapidly growing resistance to provincial particularism appeared within the bourgeoisie itself.

Thus, the debate over the Federal Constitution ended with a defeat for provincial particularism. In its formal structure and terminology, the federalist principle is meticulously retained, but in reality the Federal Constitution was an important step in overcoming the legal anarchy caused by the rebellion of the provinces since the days of the upheaval and at the same time meant a substantial weakening of the reactionary impulse of provincial particularism.

After the relations between the federation and the provinces, the next important task in shaping the Constitution was establishing the organs of the federal government. The German-Austrian Revolution had begun as a parliamentary revolution whose result was parliamentary rule. The president of the National Assembly fulfilled the functions of a head of state, the government was elected by the National Assembly, the Executive Committee of the National Assembly was directly involved in administrative decisions, and the National Assembly controlled the Army. It was the parliamentary form of political democracy in its most radical expression, and it was ferociously attacked by the bourgeois parties during the consultation process. They wanted to limit the powers of the National Council elected by popular vote in two ways: alongside the National Council they wanted a Federal Council* elected by the provincial parliaments having equal powers with the former; and they wanted both chambers to be counterbalanced by a Federal President with extensive powers. Every province—whether Vorarlberg (population 140,000) or Vienna (population 1,800,000)—was to send an equal number of representatives. In this way the Federal President and Federal Council, as organs of bourgeois class rule, were to constrict the powers of the democratic National Council. We succeeded in completely defeating this proposal. Although we voted for the installation of a Federal President and a Federal Council, the powers of both were so narrowly circumscribed that the rule of the parliament that had emerged from general suffrage, one of the results of the Revolution, remained undiminished. And the composition of the Federal Council was so disposed that the working class was represented in it just as fully as in the National Council, at times even more strongly.

A catalogue of human and civil rights could not be inserted into the Federal Constitution, because the parties could not agree about the relations of church to state and to school. Yet several particularly important "basic rights and rights of freedom" conquered by the Revolution were anchored in the Constitution as constitutional principles. Thus, the Constitution excluded all "privileges of birth, gender, social rank, class, and of creed." All public employees, including members of the Federal Army,

---

* See Glossary.

were ensured the full enjoyment of their political rights. The Constitution established universal and equal suffrage for all citizens, without distinction of gender, for all representative bodies of the federal state, the provinces, and the municipalities, and it prohibited any kind of electoral disenfranchisement. It enshrines as elements of the Constitution the decisions of the Provisional National Assembly on the abolition of censorship and of restrictions on the freedom of association and assembly and the laws on the banishment of the Habsburgs and the annulment of nobility. It abolishes the right of the government to declare a state of emergency.

With the Defense Law, the Federal Constitution is the most important result of this phase of development. These two laws gave the Republic its most important foundational institutions. Promulgated when the revolutionary tide was ebbing, both laws had the task of codifying the most essential achievements of the preceding revolutionary period, transforming them from improvisations into permanent institutions of the Republic. In this sense, both laws represent the legislative completion of the revolutionary period.

With these two laws the Constituent National Assembly had fulfilled its duty. On October 17, the first National Council was elected. The electoral results showed that the masses of workers remained unshakably in the camp of Social Democracy; the Communists garnered an insignificant number of votes. But the voting results also showed that the masses of officials, employees, petty bourgeois, and peasants who in 1919, under the influence of the war and Revolution, had voted Social Democratic, had now returned to the camp of the bourgeois parties. The number of Social Democratic votes decreased from 1,211,814 in 1919 to 1,022,606, in 1920, while the number of Christian Social votes rose in the same period from 1,068,382 to 1,204,912. The composition of parliament shifted substantially. The number of Christian Social seats rose from 63 to 82, the Pan-German from 24 to 26, while the number of Social Democratic seats declined from 69 to 66. We immediately accepted the consequences of this result. On October 22, the Social Democratic members of the proportional government resigned, and Social Democracy decided not to participate in the formation of a new government. On October 21, 1918, the Provisional National Assembly had constituted itself; on October 22, 1920 the Social Democratic ministers left the government. After being led for two years by Social Democracy, government power reverted to the bourgeoisie.

CHAPTER 15

THE STRUGGLE AGAINST
THE COUNTERREVOLUTION

On November 20, 1920, the Republic's first bourgeois government was elected. The Tyrolean Christian Social deputy, Dr. Michael Mayr, became the head of government as Federal Chancellor. The ministerial posts went to Christian Social deputies and nonparty bureaucrats. Although the Pan-Germans supported the Christian Social government, they did not send any representatives to it.

In the first years of the Republic, the working class would not have tolerated a bourgeois government for a single week. Now things were different. The onset of prosperity, which gave the workers regular employment and adequate nutrition, had dispelled the revolutionary tension in the masses. After the defeats of the working class in Hungary and Germany, the masses no longer pushed for a dictatorship of the proletariat. After the experiences with the second coalition government, and under the influence of the New Left's agitation against the coalition, the working class saw a purely bourgeois government as a lesser evil in comparison to a new coalition. And so the working class left the government of the Republic to the bourgeoisie and the peasantry.

Although the new government was bourgeois, it was nevertheless the government of a still very weak, fearful bourgeoisie, one whose self-confidence was only gradually reawakening. Thus, the government tried to avoid any serious conflict with the Social Democratic opposition in the National Council, all the more so that it could never be quite certain of the support of the Pan-Germans. It is true that the relations between the government and the proletarian organizations became more distant once representatives of the proletariat no longer belonged to the government, but they were by no means completely ruptured. The bourgeois government too could not administer the railways and state enterprises other than in agreement with the trade unions and personnel representatives; the influence of the trade unions on administration thus remained very great. A bourgeois war minister became head of the Federal Army; but as civilian commissioners appointed by the National Council alongside the Minister of the Armed Forces, Deutsch and Smitka could continue to strongly influence the administration of the army. During the second coalition the working class had seen how limited our power really was, even when our representatives sat in government; it now saw that it did not become powerless even if it left government to the bourgeoisie. Thus, the working class had little difficulty in adjusting to this bourgeois system of government.

During the coalition government, the government's initiative had kept legislation moving forward. This now stopped. The bourgeois government neither wanted nor could lead in a proletarian direction, but it did not dare lead in a bourgeois one. And so it did not lead at all. It did not govern; it merely administered state business.

Only in one area was the bourgeois government purposefully active. It gradually but systematically demolished the war economy, the state regulation of economic life. Already in the last years of the war, black marketeering had steadily grown, but after the collapse of military power the incomparably weaker republican government was no longer in a position to effectively enforce the wartime economic control measures against the passive resistance of the traders and the peasantry, the anarchy of the provincial governments, and the corruption of a not inconsiderable part of the poorly paid bureaucracy by the profiteers. This already undermined the whole system of state control of food and raw materials, but starting in 1920 still greater difficulties arose from the gradual revival of trade with foreign countries. Import and export bans, without which central control of the economy is impossible, now appeared as fetters on the further revival of commerce. While the law of July 6[1] had broken the state control of the wheat supply, now the bourgeois government, giving in to the pressure of commercial capital and the peasantry, repealed one wartime measure after the other and in this way gradually restored "free trade." In the process the state lost all control over the movement of prices, the fall in the purchasing power of the krone was accelerated, and state expenditures rapidly increased.

This was all the more disastrous because all efforts to raise the state's tax revenues had ceased after the transfer of government power to the bourgeoisie. The bourgeoisie had been incensed at the new property taxes that the second coalition government had introduced in the state and the Social Democratic municipal majority in the city of Vienna. The bourgeois parties had conducted their electoral campaigns in autumn 1920 under the slogan "against over-taxation." When they took over the government they could not further increase the property taxes, but they also did not dare to impose higher consumption taxes on the masses. Nothing therefore was done to decrease the state budget deficit and limit the proliferation of paper money. The whole financial policy of Finance Minister Grimm was focused on obtaining foreign loans. And because this effort failed, the value of money sank lower and lower.

But soon signs of discontent with the system of government appeared in the bourgeois camp itself. The bourgeoisie was disillusioned because despite its electoral victory, despite government power having passed into the hands of its parties, the power of the working class had remained very strong. In large sections of the bourgeoisie, the conviction grew that only a counterrevolutionary force could break the Austrian proletariat's strong position of power, and belief in the viability of the Austrian Republic was shaken in autumn 1920 and January 1921 by the rapidly progressing currency depreciation. The Austrian counterrevolutionaries, too weak on their own to dare strike out at the proletariat, began to place their hopes in both neighbor states in which the red terror of communism had paved the way for the white terror of counterrevolution: Hungary and Bavaria.

A strong movement for the restoration of the Habsburgs had developed in Hungary since the victory of the counterrevolution. Since then a twofold danger threatened us from Hungary. First the danger to our republican Constitution—the restoration of Habsburg in Hungary would have encouraged the counterrevolutionaries in Austria and ensured them of Hungary's military assistance for the restoration of the dynasty in Austria. Second, the danger for our borders—it was to be expected that the dictatorship of the counterrevolutionary officers in Hungary would not peaceably vacate the Burgenland, which the Peace Treaty of Saint-Germain had awarded to us, but would forcibly resist its transfer. For these two reasons we had to reckon with the possibility of a dangerous conflict with Hungary. At the time of the second coalition government, we had already taken steps to protect ourselves against this danger. The Hungarian menace had prompted us to strengthen the fighting capacity of our defense force through the Defense and Disciplinary Laws. It also impelled us to improve our relations with Czechoslovakia.

From the time of its origins, from the battles of the Czech Legions on the Volga and in Siberia, the Czech Revolution had a double-edged character. It was revolutionary against the Habsburgs but counterrevolutionary against the proletarian revolution. At the time of the revolution against the Habsburgs, the Czech movement was the strongest revolutionary force in Austria. At that time we did not oppose it but supported the Czechs' right of self-determination in order to seize this right for the German-Austrian people as well. After the upheaval, the counterrevolutionary character of the Czech Republic emerged. From then on we stood in vehement opposition to it; we had to defend proletarian German-Bohemia against Czech annexation and had to resist the pressure to send arms to the Czech Army against proletarian Hungary. But after the proletarian dictatorship was overthrown in Hungary and after the Peace Treaty decided German-Bohemia's fate, our relations with the Czech Republic changed once more. In the face of the menace of the counterrevolution emanating from Hungary, the Czech Republic was the strongest protector of the achievements of the Revolution of 1918 and was our natural ally against the menace of Habsburg restoration in Hungary and against the threatened Hungarian attack on Austria.

On January 9, 1920, during the second coalition government, Renner had gone to Prague to forge closer relations between Austria and Czechoslovakia. The result of his voyage was not only a series of treaties that consolidated our economic relations with Czechoslovakia and facilitated compliance with the Peace Treaty but also a political agreement between Renner and Beneš in which the two ministers pledged to support one another in repelling counterrevolutionary attempts. Renner assured the Czech Republic of Austria's "benevolent neutrality" in the event of a Czech-Hungarian war, and Beneš assured Austria support in the event of a Hungarian attack. These agreements caused passionate indignation not only in the Viennese monarchist wing of the Christian Social Party but also among the ruling powers in Hungary. The Hungarian and Austrian counterrevolutionaries now proceeded to cooperate very closely against us, above all against Renner's foreign policy, with Hungary's Vienna embassy organizing and financing the Christian Social campaign against Renner.

In the days of the proportional government, the antagonisms between Austria and Hungary were exacerbated. On June 20, 1920, the Amsterdam

International Trade Union Federation called a boycott against counter-revolutionary Hungary, which was suppressing and murdering the working class. Austria's railway workers, postmen, and telegraph and telephone employees fully carried out the boycott; for seven weeks all communication between Austria and Hungary was completely blocked. But what succeeded in Austria did not succeed in the other successor states; Hungary could maintain its communications with the outside world by way of Slovakia and Yugoslavia. The boycott thus had no effect on Horthy and had to be suspended on August 8. It had not only created conflicts between the Austrian and Hungarian governments but, since it blocked food supplies from Hungary to Austria for several weeks, it had also led to heated conflicts within the masses of workers for and against a foreign policy directed against Horthy's Hungary. These confrontations became particularly intense in the October 1920 electoral campaign.

When the Christian Social Party took over the government after the elections, it first tried to establish friendly relations with "Christian Hungary." But all these efforts failed because the price Hungary asked for rapprochement was Austria's abandonment of its claims to the Burgenland or at least to the greater part of it. This the Christian Social government could not accept without incurring fierce resistance not only from the Social Democrats and the Pan-Germans but also from part of its own supporters. Negotiations then could only end with new bellicose threats from Hungary, which finally compelled the Mayr government to return to the path that Renner had blazed. Mayr expressly maintained the political accords that Renner had concluded with Beneš.

These accords took on practical importance when Karl Habsburg suddenly turned up in Steinamanger* on March 26, 1921. We were directly confronted by the long predicted danger of the restoration of the Habsburg kingdom in Hungary. Once again, as in the days of the Kapp Putsch, a powerful movement ran through the working class. Federal Chancellor Mayr had not only personally been an adherent of annexation to Germany and for this reason a republican; he also knew the menacing power of the movement that had gripped the proletarian masses in Austria. In the most critical days he did not allow himself to be influenced by the monarchist wing of his party but was careful to act in agreement with Social Democracy. In the session of the National Council on April 1, which turned into an enormous rally for the Republic, Mayr declared that the govern-

* Szombathely in Hungarian.

ment would tell the Great Powers and the successor states that it had to regard the restoration of a Habsburg in Hungary as a threat to the peaceful development of the Austrian Republic. This declaration aligned Austria with Czechoslovakia, Yugoslavia, and Romania, which had declared the Habsburg restoration in Hungary to be a threat to European peace and, threatening blockade and military measures, demanded the expulsion of Karl Habsburg from Hungary. When he yielded to pressure from the Entente and Little Entente* and travelled from Steinamanger to Switzerland on April 4, the Mayr government granted him permission to travel through Austria only under conditions formulated by the Social Democratic Party and accepted by Mayr. As the prisoner of a detachment of the republican Federal Army commanded by a Social Democratic officer, and escorted by the Social Democratic deputies Sever and Adolf Müller,[2] Karl Habsburg was obliged to travel through Austria. In Bruck an der Mur it was only with considerable effort that the two Social Democratic deputies could get the train through the masses of demonstrating workers.

These incidents provoked great resentment among the reactionary sections of the bourgeoisie. Its monarchist traditions, its monarchist sensibility, had been deeply wounded. Its resentment turned against the Mayr government; the Christian Social provincial governments now began to rebel against the federal government. The bitter realization that the Vienna government, even after it had fallen into the hands of the bourgeoisie, was still under the powerful influence of the working class made the movement for secession from Vienna, for breaking the provinces loose from the federation, once again flare up among the bourgeoisie and the peasantry of the western provinces.

The international weakness of the Hungarian counterrevolution, the international difficulties standing in the way of a Habsburg restoration, was shown by the history of the Habsburg Putsch. The weaker Budapest proved to be, the stronger was Munich's power of attraction as the other center of counterrevolution for the Austrian counterrevolutionaries. Secession from Austria and union with Bavaria—this now appeared to the leaders of provincial particularism in the western federal provinces as the only way out, the only way of being saved from the Austrian Republic whose evolution went so contrary to their wishes.

There had long been very close ties between Bavarian reaction and the leading reactionary cliques in Tyrol and Salzburg. In the days of the

* See Glossary.

Kapp Putsch, Kahr had seized power in Bavaria and established the brutal reign of reaction in Bavaria, after which Bavaria became the admired model for Austrian reaction. The revolutionary ideal of annexation of German-Austria to the German Republic had been concretized by the Tyrolean and Salzburg peasant leaders as the reactionary objective of the annexation of Tyrol and Salzburg to reactionary Bavaria. The evolution of Bavarian particularism and its temporary support by French imperialism seemed to bring into the realm of possibility the unification of the Austrian Alpine provinces with Bavaria in the form of a clerical Baiuvaric kingdom. And as fantastic as this objective first seemed, the organization of the Heimwehr* had provided a fertile opportunity in 1920 for the practical activity of cooperation between Bavarian reaction and the reaction in the Alpine provinces.

The Heimwehren had emerged in the first months after the upheaval in Carinthia and Styria when they protected the border against Yugoslavia. At the time of the Hungarian and Bavarian council dictatorships the movement spread; in many villages the peasants had organized and armed against Bolshevism and against the wheat and livestock requisitioning by the workers' councils. But it was only in 1920 that the movement spread significantly and became centrally organized. The movement was strongest in Tyrol. There the units of the Heimatwehr were brought together under the command of the Christian Social Landesrat Steidle through the statutes established on May 15, 1920. The Tyrolean example was imitated in Salzburg. The arming of the Tyrolean and Salzburg Heimatwehr was facilitated by smuggling weapons from Bavaria; the Bavarian Orgesch protected its weapons and munitions from the grasp of the Entente's Disarmament Commissions by smuggling them into Tyrol and Salzburg. In June and October 1920, Tyrolean railway workers were able to confiscate such transports to the Tyrol; in October 1920 documents came into our hands that corroborated the reports of Bavarian arms smuggling to Salzburg. Later, the Heimatwehr completed their equipment by seizing and plundering state arsenals; in Tyrol they robbed the state arsenals in Kramsach, Höttinger-Au, and Hall. The Tyrolean and Salzburg Heimatwehren came into very close contact with the Bavarian Orgesch; at the end of July 1920 a meeting of Bavarian and Austrian Heimatwehr leaders took place in Munich at which the Tyrolean and Salzburg leaders declared, after a speech by Escherich, that they stood under the command of the Bavarian Orgesch.

---

* See Glossary.

On November 20, 1920, the railway workers prevented a joint demonstration of the Bavarian and Tyrolean Orgesch by stopping the trains.

The movement in Styria and Carinthia had a somewhat different character. The close ties with Bavaria and the political objective of annexation to Bavaria did not exist there. These Heimwehren had no goal other than to serve the bourgeoisie and peasantry against the working class. This made it all the more possible for them to win the financial support of big industrialists and the banks, and these provinces were the first in which these donors pledged regular contributions to the Heimwehr.

The arming of the reaction obliged the working class to arm itself in turn, and the workers' councils organized this defense. The activity of the workers' councils had fundamentally changed since the October 1920 elections. In the electoral campaign, the leaders of the New Left, Dr. Frey and Rothe, had run against Social Democracy; now there could be no more doubt that they were doing the business of the Communists. Consequently, the mass of comrades who had been under the influence of the "New Left" now separated from these leaders. The dispute over the policy of the coalition had ended after the elections when the Social Democrats left the government. From then on all Social Democratic members of the workers' councils organized themselves in groups that ran for elections united against the Communists. Dr. Frey and Rothe, who did not want to subject themselves to the group discipline of the Social Democratic workers' council groups, left the party and went over to the Communists; only a very small part of their former following went with them. In all workers' councils from then on a small Communist group confronted the large, organized Social Democratic majority with unified leadership and voting compactly. One result was that the political debates within the workers' councils lost their importance and interest. At the same time the workers' councils also lost their economic functions. With the dismantling of the war economy and the revival of "free trade," the diverse economic administrative bodies within which the representatives of the workers' councils had been active were gradually dissolved. With the decline of the Revolution, its organs gradually lost their sphere of activity. But the arming of the counterrevolution gave the workers' councils a new function once more. They soon set about creating and developing the Ordner organizations* as a defense against the reactionary Heimwehren, self-styled "self-protective associations," and "front-fighter organizations."

---

* See Glossary.

The Habsburg Putsch in March 1921 gave both parties added motivation to continue arming. The working class saw the Republic threatened, and so it stepped up the development of its Ordner organizations in readiness for any monarchist putsch attempt. On the other side, the Habsburg Putsch had accentuated the antagonisms inside the reactionary camp. For a moment the emergence of Karl Habsburg in Hungary had strengthened the optimism of the legitimist wing of Tyrol's Christian Socials, which, led by Aemilian Schöpfer and supported by the clergy and the urban Christian Socials, hoped for the return of the Habsburgs. But the pitiful outcome of the Habsburg Putsch had very quickly strengthened the supporters of annexation to Bavaria, who, led by Schraffl and supported by the peasant organizations and the Heimatwehren, saw their goal not in Habsburg restoration in Austria but in separation from Austria and annexation to reactionary Bavaria. After the end of the Karl Putsch, the adherents of the Bavarian orientation in Tyrol believed they were dealing a decisive blow against the adherents of the Habsburg orientation and that they could establish annexation to Bavaria as the unanimous will of the whole Tyrolean people. And they could mobilize the whole people by hiding the concrete goal of annexation to Bavaria behind the general slogan of annexation to Germany, which stirred Pan-Germans and Social Democrats as well. The Tyrolean State Parliament decided to hold a plebiscite on annexation to Germany on April 24, 1921.

With this decision, the sentiment for annexation to Germany was given a fresh impulse, but this movement was very different from the annexation mobilization of November 1918 and in 1919. The 1918 mobilization had arisen out of the spirit of the national revolution; the annexation movement of 1921 was of reactionary origin, even though through the revolutionary slogans of annexation it could mobilize the classes hostile to reaction. In 1918 the movement had been borne by Social Democracy, led by Vienna's government, with annexation to Germany as its goal; in 1921 the movement was led by the provincial governments of the alpine provinces, directed against Vienna's government, and its goal was the secession of the provinces from the federation and annexation of the individual provinces to Bavaria. In 1919 the Tyrolean provincial government had fought against annexation and caused considerable trouble for our struggle for it; in 1921 the very same Tyrolean provincial government placed itself at the head of the movement for annexation. In 1919, at a time when Great Britain, the United States, and Italy "wavered and discussed" for three months before

the Paris Peace Conference made its decision on annexation, the struggle
was a serious one; in 1921 in the face of the already ratified Peace Treaty, the
movement was without prospects.

Nevertheless, this movement too proved the great power of attraction
of the idea of annexation to Germany. On April 24, 146,468 men and
women, almost nine tenths of eligible voters, voted on annexation; 144,342
of them voted for annexation and only 1,794 voted against it. From Tyrol the movement spread to Salzburg where another plebiscite was held:
103,000 voted for and 800 against annexation. Meanwhile, France had
intervened; its government demanded the suspension of the plebiscites. It
threatened Austria: if it did not stop the plebiscites, France threatened to
withhold the anticipated foreign credits, the reparation commission would
demand reparations from Austria, and Burgenland would not be ceded.
Under pressure from France, Federal Chancellor Mayr had to demand that
the provinces call off the plebiscites. But since the Habsburg Putsch he had
lost influence on his party comrades. Despite Mayr's objection, Styria's
Landtag set a plebiscite on annexation for May 31. As a consequence of this
decision, the Mayr government resigned. No one could form a new government without guaranteeing that the provincial movement for annexation would not bring the government into serious conflict with France.
Eventually, Christian Socials and Pan-Germans came to an agreement to
refrain from plebiscites on annexation for six months; the movement for
annexation was only to restart if the promised foreign credits did not arrive
by the end of autumn 1921. On this understanding a new government was
formed on June 21 headed by Vienna's chief of police Johann Schober; it
was a cabinet of officials in which the Christian Social and Pan-German
parties were represented through only one deputy each.

The movement for annexation in the provinces ended in defeat, not
only in Styria, where the state parliament had had to revoke the decision to
hold a plebiscite, but also in Tyrol and Salzburg where the plebiscite did not
go beyond an ineffectual demonstration. The provinces thus learned that
strong external obstacles stood in the way of secession from the federation.
They had to see that they could not secede from the German-Austrian
Republic but had to live within it, and this facilitated the absorption of the
provinces into the federation.

The process of absorption was in turn facilitated by the direction of
economic development. One of the strongest incentives to provincial particularism in 1918 and 1919 had been the food shortage, and the struggle against

export of food and raw materials from the countryside was its most popular focus of activity; but when the food, coal, and raw-material shortages were gradually overcome, and since Austria after the outbreak of the international market-outlet crisis in 1920 could once again get as much food, coal, and raw materials as it could afford to pay for, this economic basis of provincial particularism gradually disappeared. In 1919, when Vienna's industry came to a standstill because of the coal and raw-material shortages, the Alpine provinces viewed Vienna as the "hydrocephalus," which took their food without anything in return. Since 1920 when Viennese industry and commerce were back in full swing again, Vienna was no longer a "hydrocephalus" but rather the great source of tax money from which the federation derived four-fifths of its tax revenue, and the exports of this big industrial and commercial city supplied the federation with foreign means of payment, which was the only thing that allowed it, even the Alpine provinces, to buy foreign wheat and coal. With this the economic basis of the secession movement gradually disappeared. The movement for annexation in spring 1921 was the last great rebellion of the provinces against the federation.

It was also the last flicker of the struggle for German unity. After the Peace Treaty, annexation could no longer be an immediately achievable goal of current politics but only a national ideal to be cultivated until such time as a radical revolution in the relations of power in Europe enables its realization—this had by now become evident even to the petty bourgeois philistines sitting around beer tables in provincial towns. And their enthusiasm for it quickly cooled. If the hopelessly ongoing depreciation of the Austrian krone had convinced them of Austria's unviability, then they did not see salvation in annexation when under pressure of the French-imposed reparation burdens the German mark hopelessly and continuously sank. Still in 1921, during the formation of the Schober government, the Pan-Germans had reserved the right to demand a continuation of the plebiscites on annexation if the Republic did not receive the anticipated foreign credits by autumn 1921. The foreign credits did not come, but by then there was no longer talk of annexation plebiscites.

Social Democracy supported the efforts of the Mayr governments to induce the provinces to renounce the plebiscites. We knew that under the given relations of power in Europe they would not result in annexation but only lead to a serious conflict with France. We helped the government to avert this conflict; we predicted that for the near future, the Republic would enter into serious crisis and that any conflict with the Great Powers could become very dangerous. The ratification of the Treaty of Trianon was imminent, and this made the question of the transfer of German-Western Hungary to Austria a practical one. This meant that we were about to face the most difficult and dangerous conflict with the Hungarian counterrevolution.

On July 26, 1921, the Peace Treaty of Trianon was ratified. An inter-Allied commission of the Entente headed by the Italian general Ferrario was to take over the Burgenland from Hungary and deliver it to Austria. Hungary openly prepared for armed resistance to the transfer.

Austrian Social Democracy had never demanded annexation but only the right of Burgenland to self-determination. In the peace negotiations in Saint-Germain, our delegation had not demanded the simple cession of German-Western Hungary to Austria; it asked for nothing other than that German-Western Hungary should itself decide, in a free plebiscite under neutral occupation and control, the state to which it wants to belong. The Entente, it is true, had responded to this demand by dividing German-Western Hungary into two. The draft Peace Treaty, which was handed to our peace delegation on July 20, 1919, promised Pressburg* to Czechoslovakia; to Hungary it promised Hungarian Altenburg,† Wieselburg, Güns,‡ and St. Gotthard; a few frontier municipalities to Yugoslavia; and only the remainder of Western Hungary to Austria. Our peace delegation protested against this decree by the Powers. On August 6, 1919, it responded to the Powers and their draft treaty, which wanted to give us a part of German-Western Hungary, that German-Austria did not wish for such a present; German-Austria wanted to acquire German-Western Hungary only if this were the will of the German-Western Hungarian population itself. The peace delegation wrote:

> The German-Austrian Republic holds that the principle of the right of peoples to self-determination should be scrupulously carried out. In order now, at the outset, to dispel suspicions of a measure taken against the will of the people, German-Austria allows itself to insist that, by means of a plebiscite carried out under the direction and oversight of the allied and associated main powers, the direct opinion of the inhabitants of Western Hungary be gathered as to the state into which they would like to be integrated.

---

* Old-Austrian name of Bratislava in present-day Slovakia.
† Old-Austrian name of Mosonmagyaróvár in present-day Hungary.
‡ Old-Austrian name of Kőszeg in present-day Hungary.

This demand was not only in accordance with democratic principles but also with Austria's interests. In the same note we requested that Carinthia, German-South Tyrol, the Böhmerwaldgau, and the Znaimer Kreis, which the Entente wanted to take from us, should decide its national affiliation through a free plebiscite; we had to support this request by asking for a plebiscite under the same conditions for Burgenland as well, although the Entente proposed to award it to us. Our request that the people of Burgenland should themselves decide on their state affiliation, moreover, reinforced our protest against the division of German-Western Hungary; we demanded that a plebiscite take place not only in the parts of Burgenland awarded to us but also in the whole German area of settlement in Western Hungary. The Entente refused these requests. In its note of September 2, 1919, it insisted on the borders already established in the July 20 draft. "Within these borders," the cover note of the final text of the Peace Treaty said, "the ethnic character and national sentiment of the inhabitants point to annexation to Austria too clearly for the Powers to consider it necessary to conduct a plebiscite."

When it became obvious in summer 1921 that Hungary was preparing for armed resistance to the transfer of Burgenland, Social Democracy once again demanded that Austria propose a peaceful resolution of the conflict through democratic principles. We considered it necessary that Austria show itself to be ready for a democratic solution in order, wherever possible, to avoid an armed conflict. For this reason, and to avoid armed conflict with Hungary, we proposed on August 13 to the Committee for External Affairs that Austria offer Hungary a solution in which both states would leave the decision on the future of Burgenland to the people of Burgenland. We proposed that Austria declare itself ready to recognize the decision made by the Burgenland's people through a plebiscite, if conducted not only in the parts of German-Western Hungary granted us by the Peace Treaty but also in the parts left to Hungary, and if this plebiscite were held only after the withdrawal of the Hungarian troops and authorities and with adequate guarantees for a fully free vote. But on August 13 the bourgeois parties could not decide to make a proposal of this kind to Hungary. Only on August 27 did the Committee for External Affairs accept a motion that the government declare itself ready, after the transfer of Burgenland to Austria, to negotiate with Hungary an "amicable solution to the border questions on the basis of the will expressed by the people of the Burgenland." But it was already too late. Hungary's military preparations in Burgenland were by now in full swing. In Ödenburg a company of Hungarian troops stood under the command of Major Osztenburg; the officers of the Prónay and Héjjas detachments led armed irregulars here,* mostly recruited from Székelys and some from Magyars who had fled from Translyvania and Slovakia.

We had been at pains to give Austrian policy a direction that could enable a peaceful and democratic solution of the dispute over the Burgenland. But we were aware that the prospects of winning over Hungary's officer dictatorship for such a solution would have been very poor even if Austria had early on shown itself ready to decide the conflict according to democratic principles. Therefore already by spring 1921 we had repeatedly urged that the Federal Army be expanded and equipped to be able to defend our freedom and borders in the looming conflict with Hungary.

But in this we came up against insuperable opposition. The governing Christian Social Party did not want an expansion of the Federal Army. Already by spring 1921, leading Christian Social deputies, above all Dr. Mataja, and leading Christian Social newspapers, above all the *Reichspost*, had urged that Austria not use the Federal Army at all in occupying the Burgenland. This agitation against the use of the Federal Army had originated from the clerical elements in Burgenland itself. The Ödenburg clerics were Magyarones†; despite their German nationality they preferred "Christian Hungary" to democratic Austria. At the time of Hungary's council dictatorship they had suffered greatly in the red terror and so they agitated against Austria with the claim that it was ruled by "creeping Bolshevism" and that the Austrian Federal Army was a Bolshevist Red Army. They cried out to the whole world that the Burgenland people would rebel against the invasion of this red army. This agitation of Ödenburg's Magyarones resonated with the Viennese clericals who believed that the Burgenland's people had been filled with a reactionary outlook from their experience of Hungary's council dictatorship and hoped to build on the Burgenland to form a bulwark of reaction within Austria. They feared that occupation of the Burgenland by the republican-proletarian Federal Army could interfere with this and preferred that it be occupied only by a constabulary. After its occupation they wanted to establish a contingent of troops there that would serve the purposes of the Burgenland and Viennese clericals who, in their agitation, succeeded in winning over the inter-Allied Generals Com-

---

* Generally known as the White Guard.
† See Glossary.

mission in Ödenburg. The Commission ordered that to occupy Burgenland, Austria only be permitted to use the gendarmerie, not the Federal Army. Despite our protests, the Austrian government complied with this order by the Entente generals, since that was its wish in the first place.

Thus on August 28, the gendarmerie (consisting of only 1,950 men in eleven columns) marched into the Burgenland. They immediately were confronted by the Magyar irregulars. The gendarmerie detachments were too few in number and too badly equipped to overcome the resistance of Horthy's bands. In the south the gendarmerie could not get through the Styrian border. In the north they could occupy a part of Burgenland but were tied down in small-scale warfare with the bands, causing many casualties. However, at this point the irregulars were still very weak. If the Federal Army had marched into the Burgenland on August 28, it would have had little difficulty in driving off the Magyar bands. But the gendarmerie was far too weak to do this; and the cheap success the irregulars had chalked up against them stirred up great enthusiasm in Hungary, which brought strong reinforcements to the irregulars in the following days. The number of irregulars now quickly grew, and they became bolder. Within a few days the situation of the gendarmerie detachment stationed in Agendorf* became very dangerous; on September 8 it had to be withdrawn across the Lower Austrian border. But already before this, on August 31, the Magyar irregulars had themselves attacked Old-Austrian territory—on August 31 a Magyar band had already overrun Hohenbrugg in Styria.

The danger was now very serious. A war between Hungary and Austria could arise from the confrontations between the bands and the gendarmerie. Hungary was mustering a strong contingent of regular troops on Burgenland's eastern border, and it seemed possible that it wanted to settle the dispute by force. In compliance with the Peace Treaty, Austria had been disarmed by the Entente; Hungary, whose Peace Treaty had also just come into force, had not been disarmed. With its military superiority, Hungary could in one stroke take possession of the Wiener Neustadt industrial district and directly threaten Vienna. This danger was all the more serious because we had to reckon with the possibility that the strong concentration of troops in Western Hungary might be used for a Habsburg restoration bid. Since Karl Habsburg's Easter Putsch, the antagonisms in Hungary between the legitimists and Horthy's supporters, who had rejected the King's immediate restoration, had been considerably aggravated. Already by the

---

* Old-Austrian name for Ágfalva in Hungary.

summer, the powers of the big and Little Entente feared that the legitimists would move Karl to repeat his March attempt. It was all the more plausible that the troops being amassed in Western Hungary might be used for this purpose, as Osztenburg, who was the commander in Ödenburg, was a well-known legitimist.

As late as August, we had advocated a peaceful democratic solution to the dispute over the Burgenland, to avoid an armed conflict if possible. Now that the conflict had broken out, we had only one mission—to deploy all our force in resisting the Hungarian counterrevolution. The civil commissionership in the Ministry of War, where Julius Deutsch and Johann Smitka served, and the soldiers' councils secured decisive influence over the military defense measures. The equipping of the Federal Army, neglected up to then, was rapidly completed. A part of the Federal Army took over the patrolling of the border, while the battalions from the western provinces were brought to Vienna to form a combat reserve. Social Democratic agitation reinforced the militiamen's conviction that in fighting Horthy's Hungary they were fulfilling their revolutionary duty to defend the Republic against the Monarchy and the achievements of the working class against the counterrevolution. The party called on the young workers to enter the Federal Army as long as the danger lasted, and thousands left their workplaces and did so. On September 5, the Federal Army had its baptism of blood. Near Kirchschlag the Second Battalion of the Fifth Infantry Regiment fended off an incursion of Magyar irregulars into Lower Austrian territory. Our army's casualties were two dead, fourteen wounded (five of whom subsequently died), and three prisoners (who were murdered by bandits). On September 23 and 24, the Third Battalion of the First Infantry Regiment faced heavy combat near Bruck an der Leitha; there too a Magyar attack on Lower Austrian territory was fought off with heavy casualties. For more than two months the weak forces of the Federal Army patrolled the 250 kilometers of frontier, repeatedly obliged to fight off surprise attacks by the bands. Forty soldiers of the Republic died and sixty-six were wounded.

With the Federal Army the Ordner organizations went into action as well. After the gendarmerie had been withdrawn from the Burgenland, the Magyar irregulars came close to Wiener Neustadt whose workers, deployed in their Ordner battalions, stood battle-ready day and night as long as the danger of an attack lasted. Liaison between the Federal Army and Ordner organizations was established; in the event of combat the Ordner battalions were placed under the command of the Federal Army. In the entire industrial district along the Southern Railway route, Ordner organizations were so equipped that in the case of a Hungarian advance toward Vienna they could attack the Hungarian troops in their flanks and rear and so bog down their reinforcements in guerrilla warfare.

In the meanwhile, the Powers had intervened in order to save the endangered peace. Italy did not want the Little Entente to become the arbiter between Austria and Hungary. Foreign Minister Torretta invited Austria and Hungary to negotiations at Venice, and England and France recommended that Schober accept the invitation. The negotiations began on October 11 and showed that the Italian government, which had always regarded Hungary as Italy's future ally against Yugoslavia, wanted to force a compromise favorable to Hungary. Torretta threatened a rejection of all loans to Austria if it did not submit to his proposals. Under this pressure Schober agreed to the Venice Protocol, in which the Hungarian government promised to remove its irregulars from the Burgenland while Austria agreed that a plebiscite should decide the state affiliation of the city of Ödenburg and its periphery.

A plebiscite in Ödenburg was in accordance with our basic outlook. But we had always insisted that Austria would only recognize a plebiscite if there were sufficient guarantees for a completely free vote. The Venice Protocol did not provide for them.

The Protocol had not yet been ratified when events took a new turn. Our prediction that the mustering of Hungarian troops in Western Hungary might facilitate a new Habsburg Putsch was confirmed.

On October 20, Karl and Zita Habsburg arrived by airplane in Ödenburg. Karl immediately declared that he was assuming the rights of a ruler in Hungary and appointed a government. A section of the troops concentrated in Western Hungary, with Lehár and Osztenburg at their head, put themselves in Karl's service and set out for Budapest. On October 22, Czechoslovakia declared it would regard Karl's restoration in Budapest as a casus belli. Yugoslavia and Romania joined in this declaration. On October 24, the Great Powers demanded Karl's dethroning and imprisonment. The Hungarian counterrevolution split. The legitimists believed that the moment was propitious for completing the counterrevolution with the restoration of the Kingdom, while Horthy's supporters rejected restoration in order to save the counterrevolutionary regime from imminent external attack. On October 24, Gömbös headed a battalion of hurriedly assembled students and threw himself against the royal troops near Budaörs. The Habsburg troops were beaten and Karl was taken prisoner. But the Little Entente was determined to prevent any such future attempts. It demanded that Hungary categorically depose the House of Habsburg. Since Hungary procrastinated, Czechoslovakia and Yugoslavia mobilized a part of their armies. Hungary had to submit. On November 5, the Hungarian National Assembly passed a law that rescinded Karl I's[3] sovereign rights and the Pragmatic Sanction, and restored the right of the Hungarian nation to freely elect its king, postponing this election to a later time. On November 10 in a note to the Conference of Ambassadors, the Hungarian government declared that Hungary would hold the election of the king only in agreement with the Great Powers and would comply with the prohibition on Habsburg restoration imposed by the Conference of Ambassadors on February 4, 1920 and April 3, 1921. Karl Habsburg was put on an English monitor and interned by the English on Madeira, where he died on April 1, 1922.

The Austrian government might have used the international crisis triggered by the Habsburg Putsch to secure the support of the Little Entente for the decision on Ödenburg. It did not do so. The appearance of Karl Habsburg in Ödenburg had awakened all legitimist hopes of the Christian Socials' monarchist wing. The mobilization of the Czech army had revived the anti-Czech hatred of the Pan-Germans. Both governing parties had only one wish: not to appear on the side of the Little Entente in this hour. Unnecessarily, after the Czech mobilization, their government hastened to pronounce a declaration of neutrality in Prague. Austria had refrained from using the crisis in order to strengthen its position against Hungary. By contrast, Horthy's standing and that of his government in relation to the Great Powers was significantly improved by his decided repulsion of the Habsburg Putsch. The results were immediately apparent. On November 9 the Paris Ambassadors' Conference called for the ratification of the Venice Protocol; if Austria refused, the Entente would declare itself "disinterested" in the Burgenland question. This pressure made all parties agree to ratify the protocol.

The Habsburg Putsch had dissolved the irregulars in the Burgenland. The legitimist troops had marched with Karl Habsburg against Budapest. Horthy's bands were withdrawn by the Hungarian government as soon as it was certain of the ratification of the Venice Protocol. From then on the inter-Allied Commission in Ödenburg called on Austria to occupy the Burgenland with the exception of the Ödenburg plebiscite area; and now it no longer objected to the use of the Federal Army. The Federal Army's entrance began on November 13. The Austrian troops no longer met with resistance. On December 4, the occupation of the province by our troops was complete. The plebiscite in Ödenburg was to take place, but it soon became very apparent that General Ferrario, the chair of the inter-Allied General Commission, had orders to conduct the plebiscite in such a way that Ödenburg would fall to the Hungarians. It is true that the Austrian National Council had only ratified the Venice Protocol after the Powers had promised that the Hungarian troops would be evacuated from Ödenburg, which would be occupied by Entente troops before the plebiscite. And in fact, on December 8 Entente troops arrived in Ödenburg and the Hungarian troops left on December 12. But the administration remained in the hands of the Hungarian authorities, the Magyar mayoral offices prepared the voting lists, and Magyar irregulars were allowed to terrorize the population in the plebiscite area. The Magyar authorities left thousands of eligible supporters of affiliation to Austria out of the voting lists and included thousands of Magyars who were not eligible to vote. It was only on December 5, 6, and 7 that the Austrian government's plebiscite commissioners received these voting lists; but before they could inspect and rectify even a tenth of them, General Ferrario declared the complaint procedures closed on December 12. The General Commission insisted that the vote had to take place on December 14, even though the establishment of proper voting lists was impossible by that date. On December 13, the Austrian government therefore decided to have nothing to do with the plebiscite and recalled its commissioners. The vote was held on the next day without the control of Austrian entities. The result made it clear that, given a genuinely free and uncompromised vote, the plebiscite area would have declared for Austria. Apart from the border district of Zinkendorf, which Austria had been prepared to cede to Hungary without a vote and which was nevertheless allowed to vote, 14,308 votes were cast for Hungary in the plebiscite area and 8,222 for Austria. Hungary had a majority only in the town of Ödenburg, while the surrounding villages had all voted for Austria. On the basis of this vote, the inter-allied General Commission assigned the entire plebiscite area to Hungary. Thus the Burgenland lost its capital and was split into two parts connected only by a narrow strip of land. Its administration as an independent federal province was consequently made very difficult.

The Burgenland people had seen that Social Democracy was the driving force in the struggle against Hungary during the whole period from August to December. Large sections of Burgenland's population now flooded into Social Democracy. Thus, in a province without a city or industry, we received 38.5 percent of votes in the first National Council and Landtag elections on June 18, 1922 and became the strongest party in Burgenland's Landtag and executive. Through the small peasants and rural workers, we had thus conquered a new and very important power base for the securing of the Republic's eastern borders against the Hungarian counterrevolution. The Burgenland crisis revealed the internal strength of the Republic. Once again the bourgeoisie learned how determined and ready for sacrifice the proletariat was in defense of the Republic and what insurmountable international obstacles stood in the way of Habsburg restoration.

If the experience of the German annexation plebiscites had taught the bourgeoisie that it could not flee from the Republic to reactionary Bavaria, the experience of the Burgenland crisis taught it that there was no hope of overthrowing the Republic with the help of reactionary Hungary.

Just as the year 1919 taught the proletariat that it could not establish its dictatorship but must contend for power only in the framework of the democratic Republic, so the year 1921 taught the bourgeoisie that it can neither disrupt nor overthrow the Republic but only contend for dominance within its framework. Both classes had learned that it was not the overthrow of the democratic republic but only the struggle for power within it that could be the content of class struggle.

CHAPTER 16

THE PEOPLE'S REPUBLIC

When socialism first set about arousing the working masses to class consciousness, schooling them in the class struggle, and leading them in the first great class struggles, it taught the workers to understand the state against which it had to fight as the class state of the bourgeoisie and the government of the state as the executive committee of the ruling classes. And it encouraged and inspired the workers through the pronouncement that the day of the revolution will come in which the state, an instrument of domination of the bourgeoisie for the suppression of the proletariat, will become an instrument of domination of the proletariat for defeating the bourgeoisie. It corresponded to the emotional needs of the young proletariat, which was just then awakening, organizing for the first time, and entering the struggle, and the needs of its schooling, that the state theory of socialism in its current, popular version recognized no other state than the class state: the present class state of the bourgeoisie as the state form of the capitalist social order, and the coming class state of the proletariat as the means to overcome it.

But a more subtle Marxist analyis had already recognized other forms of state. It knew that class struggles can sometimes give rise to situations in which, as Engels expressed it in his *Origins of the Family, Private Property and the State*, "the warring classes balance each other."[1] If no class is any longer in a position to defeat and suppress the others, then state power ceases to be an instrument for the domination by one class of the others. In this case state power takes on a life of its own in relation to the classes; it confronts the classes as an independent power and subordinates them all to itself. This, in Marx's and Engels's conception, was the origin of absolutist monarchy in the seventeenth and eighteenth centuries and of Bonapartism in the nineteenth.

The German-Austrian Revolution was one of these instances in which "the warring classes balance each other." From the outset, the equilibrium of class forces here was based on the relations of power between the big industrial district of Vienna, Lower Austria, and Upper Styria, on the one hand, which could not be governed against the workers, and the large agrarian area of the other provinces, on the other hand, which could not be governed against the peasants; it was from the very start founded on the contradiction between the strong power of the proletariat in the country and the complete impotence of the country in the face of the capitalist powers outside our borders. But in the first years of the Republic, owing to the powerful revolutionary tension in the masses, the relations of forces shifted in favor of the proletariat; though the proletariat could not establish its sole dominance, it still did achieve hegemony. But to the degree that the revolutionary excitement in the masses was dispelled—under pressure of the results of class struggles abroad and due to the effects of the revival of capitalist economic life in the country itself—the class forces reached a state of equilibrium.

But this state of equilibrium did not lead here, as so often before in history, to the independence of state power from the classes, not to the subjugation of all classes to absolutism or Bonapartism. Economically dependent as they were on foreign countries, militarily powerless against outside forces, threatened with foreign intervention and occupation, the classes could not bring their struggle to the point of a forcible decision. They had to work out new compromises on a daily basis. Thus, the equilibrium of class forces did not lead here to the subjugation of all classes to an autonomous state power but obliged all of them to share state power among themselves.

Until October 1920 this division of power among the classes was expressed in the coalition government, which brought the classes together to rule in common. After the October 1920 elections, it was expressed in the power-sharing between the bourgeois government and bourgeois parliamentary majority on the one side and, on the other, Social Democracy, resting on strong parliamentary power and especially strong extra-parliamentary power bases, which effectively influenced, controlled, and restricted the bourgeois government. It also found expression in the combination of parliamentary democracy, which handed government power to the bourgeoisie, and functional democracy, which made the most important acts of government dependent on the consent and cooperation of the proletarian organizations. Furthermore, this division of power was seen in the organization of the Federal Army, which curbed the power of command of the bourgeois-oriented officers corps through the socialist sensibility and organization of the militiamen and the force of its soldiers' councils, and in the power relations between the bourgeois paramilitary units and the proletarian Ordner organizations, which held each other in check.

Since October 1920, the Republic has been ruled by a bourgeois government and a bourgeois parliamentary majority. Nevertheless it is not a class state of the bourgeoisie, a bourgeois republic. The proletariat's strong power base in the Army, in the Ordner organizations, and in vital public transportation services imposes strict limits on the power of the bourgeois government, which does not dare to challenge the working class to a decisive power struggle. In governing it has no choice but to seek compromises on a daily basis with the representatives of the working class in parliament and with the proletarian organizations outside of it. In all of the major crises of this period—at the time of the Kapp Putsch, Karl Habsburg's Easter Putsch, and the Burgenland crisis—the working class was able to exert a powerful influence on the course pursued by the bourgeois government.

Despite the working class's strong power base, the Republic was not a class state of the proletariat; it was not a proletarian republic. The working class could not abolish the capitalist economic order on which the state rested. Although it could narrowly limit the bourgeoisie's political power, it could not take power itself. The whole economic development of the Republic, the abolition of the wartime economy, and the restoration of capitalist free trade meant first of all the restoration of the bourgeoisie's economic order.

Thus, the Republic was neither a bourgeois nor a proletarian republic; it was neither an instrument of the bourgeoisie's class domination over the proletariat nor an instrument of the class domination of the proletariat over the bourgeoisie. In this phase it was the result of a compromise between the classes, a result of the equilibrium of class forces. Just as the Republic in 1918 grew out of a social contract, a treaty for the formation of a state concluded between the three major parties, which represented the three major social classes, so it was only able to continue by means of daily compromises between the classes.

The Revolution of 1918 smashed the political and legal social privileges of the ruling classes. Some of the republics created by the Revolution of 1918 (for example, the Hungarian and Western Ukrainian republics) called themselves "people's republics" at that time, by which they meant to convey that, class privileges having been abolished, the people as a whole would henceforth take the reins of government in its own hands. But here the phrase "people's republic" merely expressed a petty bourgeois illusion. The abolition of the political and legal class privileges did not cancel the class antagonisms. Democracy does not overcome class struggle but helps it reach its full development. The constitutional order, which bases government and parliament on general popular elections, does not prevent general popular elections from delivering the government and parliament into the hands of a class, making it the instrument of its domination over the other classes. The parliamentary democracy of universal suffrage does not abolish class rule but bestows on it the blessing of the whole people.

It is not in the sense of petty bourgeois illusion but with a quite different meaning that we may call the Republic that existed in Austria from autumn 1919 to autumn 1922 a people's republic. It was not a bourgeois republic in which the bourgeoisie would have been able to command the proletariat, as it does in the French or American bourgeois republics. But it was not a proletarian republic, in which the proletariat would command the bourgeoisie, as it tried to do in the Russian or in the Hungarian proletarian republics. It was a republic in which no class was strong enough to command the other classes and in which therefore all classes had to share state power among themselves. In fact, all classes of the people shared in state power, and the efficacy of the state was the result of the forces of all classes of the people; this is why we may call this republic a people's republic.

The petty bourgeois illusion is that the people's republic is materialized by the people rising above the class antagonisms in its womb, that the individual classes of the people have renounced mutual struggle. In reality the people's republic arises from the class struggle precisely when it results in a state in which "the warring classes balance each other." The petty bourgeois illusion posits that the people's republic is secured by parliamentary democracy simply because the parliament and government do in fact result from elections in which the whole people take part. But in reality a people's republic is in no way guaranteed by the legal institutions of parliamentary democracy from which the sole rule of one class can just as easily result. It is not from the formal legal equality of democracy but only from the real equality of the power of the warring classes that the people's republic emerges. In Austria from 1919 to 1922 it was not the result of parliamentary democracy but of the functional democracy that corrected and curbed parliamentary democracy; it was the result of the extra-parliamentary power of the proletariat, which hindered the bourgeoisie's parliamentary majority from establishing its class rule. Petty bourgeois illusion sees the people's republic as a permanent transcendence of class antagonisms; in reality the people's republic is a provisional result of class struggles, of a temporary equilibrium between the forces of the warring classes.

In fact, such an equilibrium cannot satisfy any class for very long. Every class strives to go beyond a state of equilibrium with other classes to achieve a situation in which it dominates.

Always and everywhere, the bourgeoisie loves to present its class rule as the self-government of the whole people, and its republic, the bourgeois republic, as the true people's republic. But when a balance of class forces really does distribute state power among all classes, then the bourgeoisie passionately rebels against the people's republic. It never resigned itself to the people's republic in Austria from 1919 to 1922 and was filled with the worst sort of disaffection from the state during the whole period. Throughout these years it refused to make any sacrifices for restoring order to the country's shattered finances; it sabotaged the expansion of the Federal Army, which was indispensable for securing our eastern borders; it always urged the missions of the Great Powers to interfere in the internal affairs of the Republic, conspired against the Republic now with Budapest, now with Munich, and pinned its hopes either on Habsburg restoration or the secession of the provinces from the federation. And when its experiences with the Habsburg putsches and the annexation referendums forced it to momentarily accept the Republic, it demanded the transformation of the people's republic into a bourgeois republic, adopting with increasing vehemence the slogan of the "restoration of state authority" to really mean the authority of the bourgeois government.

Nor was the proletariat any more content with the balance between the political forces. The sentiment that swept through the masses in 1920 against the coalition policy was simply the expression of the working class's disappointment that it could not assert its hegemony, its unhappiness that in place of its hegemony a power equilibrium arose. Nevertheless the relation of the proletariat to the people's republic was radically different from that of the bourgeoisie. When the people's republic was threatened by the counterrevolution, the proletariat rose to protect it.

At the time of the struggles over the Burgenland, the relation of the classes to the people's republic was most strikingly revealed. In the weeks of danger a mighty wave of republican patriotism surged through the working masses. The proletariat demanded the rapid expansion of the Federal Army to protect the endangered border; the bourgeois government sabotaged the effort. Thousands of proletarians volunteered for army service; the bourgeois government hesitated to take them in. In the midst of the Burgenland crisis, Social Democracy published its financial plan; but the bourgeois government refused to impose the high taxes and ask for the kind of sacrifice from all classes that the proletariat proposed. The normal division of roles between government and opposition was completely inverted; in Austria the state necessities, which the government everywhere in the world has to enforce against the opposition, had to be enforced by the opposition against the resistance of the government!

The bourgeoisie could not get over the fact that it could no longer command the proletariat as it had up to 1918, that actual power in the state had to be shared with the proletariat; hence its disgruntled attitude toward the state. The proletariat felt it had made great progress in no longer being a mere object of legislation and administration, as it was up to 1918, conquering an essential share of actual power in the state; hence its republican enthusiasm. If power in the Republic was shared between all classes, the actual existence of the Republic was not guaranteed by the will of the governing bourgeoisie but only by the determination of the proletariat in opposition.

A Republic in which no class was strong enough to dominate the other classes and in which actual power had to be shared among all classes of the people—this Republic, led by a disgruntled bourgeoisie, which had to govern in a republican manner against its will and under the powerful control of the proletariat—this Republic, carried and secured by the proletariat's republican sensibility, its republican willingness to sacrifice, and its republican enthusiasm—this was the people's republic of Austria.

When all classes have a share in state power and all governing requires daily compromises between opposed class interests, the state machinery works slowly, cumbersomely, and with a great deal of friction. Nevertheless, the achievements of the two-year period of class equilibrium recounted here—the period from autumn 1919 to autumn 1921, that is, from the conclusion of the peace negotiations to the end of the Burgenland crisis—were not insignificant. Economically, it was characterized by the revival of industry and commerce, which on the one hand overcame the mass privations of the end of the war and considerably improved the working class's standard of living, but on the other hand abolished the state-run war economy and restored a purely capitalist economic order.

Socially, the period was characterized by the dissipation of the state of excitement of the period of demobilization, by the return of the unemployed masses to industry, and by the restoration of work discipline and the gradual rise in the intensity of labor in the production sites. The political achievement of this period was the consolidation of the Republic, which received its defense law in the period of the second coalition government and its federal constitution in the period of the proportional government. The Republic was reinforced at the time of the first two bourgeois governments when the experience of the two attempted Habsburg putsches had demonstrated the futility of a monarchist restoration, and the experience with the provinces' annexation movement the futility of secession. In the Burgenland crisis the Republic's definitive borders were established, it overcame the threat of a war with Hungary that had loomed for two years, and it came to recognize the power of the moral energy that was determined to defend the Republic. Thus, the loose cluster of divergent provinces remaining after the breakaway of the Slav nations from the Empire, and ravaged by revolutionary convulsions, gradually became a state.

However, although the Republic had been economically and politically consolidated its existence was nevertheless undermined by the breakdown of its finances. The Burgenland crisis had given fresh impetus to the depreciation of the krone. The ongoing, continually accelerated process of the currency depreciation threatened to throw the Republic into a currency catastrophe, which could become more dangerous to its existence than Prónay's bands and Osztenburg's battalions. After the resolution of the major political problems, all energy had to be directed toward fending off the looming economic danger. In the midst of the Burgenland crisis, Social Democracy had already formulated the watchword for this new struggle: On October 1, 1921 we had published our financial plan, and with it began the struggle against the impending economic catastrophe.

PART V

THE RESTORATION OF THE BOURGEOISIE

CHAPTER 17

THE CURRENCY
CATASTROPHE

The evolution of class struggles is determined by the development of economic conditions. From the founding of the Republic up to the Geneva protocols, the development of economic conditions was expressed in the depreciation of money. The process of currency depreciation went through a series of different phases in this period, and it is useful to draw distinctions between each of them.

The first phase of the process of currency depreciation comprised the period from the founding of the Republic to the conclusion of the peace negotiations in Saint-Germain. This phase was the direct effect of the war, the defeat, and the disruption of the old greater economic area, which followed the abolition of the currency union with the successor states and finally the depressive effects that the publication of the peace conditions produced.

The currency depreciation, itself the direct result of the great historical catastrophe, increased state expenditure but did not allow revenue to be increased at the same rate. The state nevertheless still had extraordinary resources for maintaining its economic functions. In particular, in this period the state obtained a large foreign credit; we succeeded in receiving from the Entente and from the United States a credit of $48 million, which was increased to $82 million during 1919. However, this was not given in cash but in the form of food sent us by the Allied powers. It thus could not be used for the systematic reconstruction of state finances but only for feeding our people, which could not be done from the revenues of our own industry, paralyzed as it was by the shortage of coal and raw materials.

Still, this credit covered a part of the state deficit. Another part was covered by an extraordinary source of income, the very significant revenue derived from the tax on war profits in the first year after the war,[1] which then made up more than 40 percent of total state revenue, a sixth more than all other direct taxes put together, and three times as much as all the indirect taxes, monopolies, and customs duties.

The financial policy of this first phase chiefly served financial purposes. While the state budget was largely based on property taxes, especially the tax on war profits, we kept indirect taxation very low. In addition, we dispensed foodstuffs supplied by foreign credits far below their cost price. Through both means food prices were kept low despite the depreciation of the krone. This enabled the working masses, who could not work due to the shortage of coal and raw materials, to survive the period of most severe privation. It also helped to relieve some of the social tensions of the period of the onslaught of Hungarian Bolshevism and prevented the class struggle from turning into civil war.

It was already obvious then that drastic measures were necessary to restore equilibrium to state finances. Our plan was first to impose a onetime heavy wealth levy to finance the budget deficit for some time and thus halt the money presses; the time in which the deficit would be covered by revenue from the wealth levy was to be used for raising the regular tax revenue and bringing order into state finances through savings. However, Schumpeter, the first coalition government's Minister of Finances, considered it impossible to carry out these profoundly interventionist measures at a time of such a deep trough in our economy, of the most extreme social crisis, and especially during the peace negotiations; for we did not yet know what the Peace Treaty would have in store for the standing of our state, our borders, our currency, and our foreign assets and foreign debts. We therefore contented ourselves with preparing the wealth levy by freezing and inventorying bank deposits while postponing its enactment to the period after the treaty. We were all the more resigned to this plan as we did not foresee how long the peace negotiations would last.

With the conclusion of the peace negotiations at Saint-Germain the second phase of the currency depreciation began. It lasted until the summer of 1921. The currency depreciation of this second phase was no longer the direct consequence of the abolition of the old economic sphere and of the dictated peace of Saint-Germain. The effect of these events had already been felt with the exchange rate of 3 centimes,* which the krone reached at the end of 1919. The continued currency depreciation in the second phase was rather the consequence of the broken down state finances, which necessitated a constantly increasing supply of paper money.

The extraordinary income from the tax on war profits dried up in 1919; only small residual amounts still came in. In 1920 there was far less foreign credit available than in 1919. In 1920 we still received from the United States $20 million worth of flour, from Switzerland and the Netherlands $10 million worth of foodstuffs on credit, from Argentina 5 million pesos, and from England no longer credits for the state but raw-material credits for our textile industry as well as seed potatoes for our agriculture. The foreign credits covered only a small part of our deficit. Now we had to set about putting the Republic's finances in order.

The whole first half of 1920 was taken up by the struggle to shape the wealth levy. It was one of the contentious issues that brought down the second coalition government, and it could only be finally settled during the proportional government, when the bourgeois majority decided the question against Social Democracy. It gave the wealth levy a form that thwarted the goal of covering the state budget deficit for a longer period and halting the printing of money. Nevertheless, the financial policy of the second coalition government and the proportional government, led by Finance Minister Dr. Reisch, was by no means ineffectual, but its results were not felt before the first half of 1921. This is when the big revenues from the wealth levy came in, and at the same time the tax law passed together with the wealth levy came into force. In 1921 the revenue from the wealth levy, translated into kronen at the exchange rate obtaining at the time of the receipts, amounted to one-third of total state revenue, about two-thirds more than the proceeds from total direct taxes, and about a fourth more than proceeds from indirect taxes, monopolies, and customs duties. Thanks to this large and extraordinary income, the gold value of state revenue in 1921 was almost one-fifth higher than in 1920, despite the ongoing currency depreciation.

It is true that after the elections of October 1920, the efforts to reduce the deficit through raising state revenue were no longer continued. The Mayr government, whose economic policy was led by Minister Dr. Grimm,

---

* In Swiss currency.

concentrated its efforts on obtaining new foreign credits. In fact, in March 1921 the allied Great Powers asked the League of Nations to review the conditions on which international credit could be extended to Austria. In 1921 the League's finance committee sent a delegation to Vienna to negotiate with the Austrian government the conditions of an international restructuring loan. Thus, the first half of 1921 was the most favorable period in the financial history of the Republic. As a result of the large revenues from the wealth levy, the deficit was relatively small; on the other hand, the negotiations with the League of Nations offered hope that Austria would receive a large credit within a short time. The currency depreciation was temporarily halted, and for some weeks the krone's exchange rate even rose.

The year 1920 saw the onset of the industrial prosperity that reached its peak in 1921. The large volume of exports brought the economy great quantities of foreign means of payment with which greater amounts of foreign foodstuffs and raw materials could be purchased and imported; as long as there was hope of international credit, foreign speculators bought krone bills; during this boom foreign speculators bought stock in Austrian enterprises. Thanks to this influx of capital, domestic consumption could grow beyond the limits set by domestic production. The lack of goods was overcome. Krone wages rose more quickly than the purchasing power of the krone fell—that is, real wages rose.

The turning point came in the summer of 1921 with the third phase of currency depreciation, which lasted until the Geneva loan negotiations in September 1922. In this phase the depreciation was substantially accelerated, threatening to completely destroy the value of paper money and cause the complete collapse of the economy and the state. Averting the currency depreciation became the exclusive goal of the class struggle. And this struggle ended with the cancellation of the equilibrium of class forces that had prevailed in Austria since the counterrevolution in Hungary and the Peace Treaty of Saint-Germain.

In the second half of 1921 the advance payments of the wealth levy had already been received and used up. Since the state could not expect further extraordinary revenue, its deficit grew. At the same time, hopes of a large loan, stirred up by the League of Nations' activity in the spring, were dashed; it became obvious that the League's operation was foundering on international difficulties. The two causes created a combined effect, and the tempo of currency depreciation quickened. It was further accelerated by the collapse of the German mark, which led German capital to quickly get rid of its krone assets. Its effects were aggravated by the fact that the Czech krone rapidly rose starting in August 1921 in all currency markets, which meant that Austria's purchases of coal and important foodstuffs quickly became exceedingly expensive.

Since the beginning of the war, prices increased at a quite uniform pace, doubling from year to year. If we index the cost of living in July 1914 at 1, then, according to information from the Central Statistical Commission, the figures each July were as follows:

1915	1.6
1916	3.4
1917	6.8
1918	11.7
1919	25.1
1920	51.5
1921	100.0

This shows that even the political upheaval did not essentially accelerate the tempo; each year brought a doubling of prices. Only in the second half of 1921 did prices increase markedly more quickly. The increases from then on, still indexed to July 1914, were as follows:

July 1921	100
October 1921	190
January 1922	664
July 1922	2,645

From July to October 1921 prices doubled in a single quarter—previously, they had taken a full year to double. From October to January prices tripled; in the years of the war and the Revolution that kind of increase occurred in a year and a half, but now only in three months. From January to July 1922 prices quadrupled; by contrast, this took two years in the war and Revolution period!

The influx of foreign capital ceased; foreign speculators stopped buying krone notes once the credit proposal collapsed, and so there was no longer any hope that the krone's exchange rate would increase; what is more, foreign speculators stopped buying Austrian stocks once they saw that the stock prices, measured in kronen, increased more slowly than the krone's value decreased; thus, the gold value of the stocks constantly dropped. The influx of foreign means of payment therefore shrank. But the need for foreign currency grew. The importers no longer risked using foreign commercial credit because the currency depreciation made such credits too risky. Everyone who had debts in foreign currency or as krone debts valorized according to the Peace Treaty rushed to cover them by accumulating foreign currencies. Since the krone rate rapidly sank, the capitalists hurried to transform all their stocks of kronen into foreign means of payment and assets. The "flight from the krone" increased the need for foreign means of payment. A rapidly growing portion of the foreign currency streaming into the country in the form of visible and invisible goods and security exports ended in the hands of capitalists stockpiling foreign currency and was hoarded unproductively by them. In the second phase of the currency depreciation, consumption could expand beyond the limits imposed by production thanks to the influx of foreign capital, but now it had to shrink to a level below the limits set by production since Austrian capital was extending credit to foreign national economies through its massive stockpiling of foreign securities. Consequently, the standard of living of the masses had to deteriorate.

The working class very soon felt the pressure on its standard of living. Certainly, industry was very busy, with unemployment at its lowest point in autumn 1921. But the working capital of industry had been destroyed by the currency depreciation. The rapid depreciation of the krone required the rapid expansion of industry's working capital, but it was increasingly difficult for industry to obtain the necessary capital, and so it was no longer in a position to raise wages as quickly as the purchasing power of money dropped. Real wages began to fall. The working class, accustomed for two years to a slow but steady improvement in its standard of living, was suddenly thrown back to the low level from which it had already emerged. The masses' resentment found expression in a spontaneous demonstration of Viennese workers on December 1, 1921, which ended in plundering and demolishing shops and luxury hotels in the city center.

For two years inflation had been a means of invigorating industry and raising the standard of living of the workers. Now its economic and social effects had changed; it plunged industry into a severe crisis of capital and depressed the masses' standard of living. Despite this, the government persisted in the passivity in which it had been stuck since the October 1920 elections. Social Democracy had to take the initiative in order to force a serious attempt to rein in the budget deficit and thus dam the source of the ongoing and destructive increase of paper money. On October 1, 1921 the Social Democratic Party, the trade unions, and the proletarian cooperatives published their joint financial program.

As at the time of the struggle around the wealth levy, our financial plan was based on our belief that an extraordinary measure had first to be enacted to provide the state with the means to cover its deficit for a long period without increasing the supply of paper money. For this purpose we wanted to use the foreign currencies and securities stockpiled by the capitalists. Our financial plan thus included a compulsory loan in foreign currencies, foreign bills of exchange, and foreign securities. If the state was at first to create the means to suspend the printing of money for a long time, this time had to be used to increase regular state revenue and reduce state expenditures. For a solid increase in state revenue, the financial plan proposed the expansion of property taxes and the constitution of compulsory industrial cartels as tax-farming institutions.* It attempted to reduce state expenditures through the progressive reduction of state food subsidies. The state had been delivering bread, flour, and fat to the population way below their cost prices. This food price reduction had been necessary in the first years of the Republic to prevent serious social upheavals. At the time it was not a cause of inflation since the state itself did not have to pay for the foodstuffs but was assigned them on credit by the US relief organizations. Things were completely different once the foreign food credits had dried up and the state therefore had to pay for food in cash but at the same time was compensated only a small part of the price by the consumers. Giving out food under its cost price had now become a source of inflation. Indeed it gradually became the principal source of inflation since the sales prices were raised much more slowly than the krone rate fell. In autumn 1921 state food subsidies were the biggest expenditure items in the state budget; any containment of the increase of paper money was impossible as long as the state was burdened with this expense. Thus, in our financial plan we declared ourselves ready to cooperate in the reduction of state food subsidies. But we tied this to certain conditions: the reduction was not to occur all at once but in steps; the real wages of workers, employees, and officials were not to be cut, and the law thus had to ensure them wage subsidies paid by the entrepreneurs not only for themselves but also for their wives and children equivalent to the cancelled state food subsidies.

The strong impression that our financial plan produced wrenched the bourgeois parties out of their finance policy passivity. Minister of Finance Grimm resigned; on October 7 Professor Gürtler, the leader of the Chris-

---

* Zwangsverbände der Industrie als Steuergesellschaften.

tian Social Party's peasant and democratic wing inclined toward cooperation with Social Democracy, was appointed Finance Minister. He adopted
a considerable part of our financial plan. In November and December he
launched a series of new property taxes, and in December he introduced the
reduction of the food subsidies while fully including in the law the guarantees for the real wages of workers on which we had insisted in our plan. It is
true that he could not decide in favor of a compulsory loan from holders of
foreign assets and currency, which we had demanded as the first and most
important measure. He hoped to accomplish the same goal through the
Law on Declaring Possession of Foreign Currency of December 21, 1921[2]
and avoid the compulsory requisition of foreign currency and assets. But
experience proved this half-measure to be ineffective. Schober's new foreign
policy went hand in hand with Gürtler's financial policy; both were equally
strongly influenced by Social Democratic conceptions. In the struggle for
the Burgenland, Schober had come into conflict with Hungary and consequently become closer to Czechoslovakia. In December, Federal President
Hainisch and Federal Chancellor Schober visited Lana in the Czech Republic. During the visit Schober and Beneš worked out a compact on December 16, 1921 in which the two republics pledged to faithfully implement the
Peace Treaty, support each other against all counterrevolutionary attempts,
and submit any disputes between them to an arbitration court. Czechoslovakia extended Austria a credit of 500 million Czech kronen and also promised
to support Austria's efforts to obtain credits in London and Paris.

In fact, the new financial policy, especially the reduction of the food
subsidies, had made a strong impression in London and Paris, and the
rapprochement with Czechoslovakia improved the foreign policy standing
of the Republic.

Now it really was possible to obtain credits again. England granted a
loan of £2 million, France promised 55 million francs, and Italy 70 million
lire. As soon as the English loan arrived, the krone stopped sinking. Had
the government used this stabilization of the krone rate to energetically
pursue the financial policy initiated in November and December it would
have done something important and lasting for the improvement of public
finances. But there were political obstacles in the way.

The Pan-Germans fervently opposed the Treaty of Lana, recalled their
representative Dr. Waber from the government, and went into opposition,
with the result that the government no longer had a majority capable of
acting. Social Democracy could not want the government to fall on account

of the understanding reached with Czechoslovakia, nor did it want an interruption of the financial policy that had just begun, which followed the direction set by our financial plan. Therefore, on March 16, 1922 the Social Democratic deputies adopted a resolution in which they declared their readiness to support the government, provided the contents of any further financial policy measures was agreed on with the Social Democratic deputies. But even having lost the votes of the Pan-Germans, the government still did not accept the Social Democrats' offer; it made no attempt to reach an understanding with us over the further direction of financial policy.

This behavior of the government was the result of the fierce opposition to Gürtler's financial policy from the capitalist camp. Already in November the stock exchange had gone on strike to demonstrate against his high Stock Exchange Entrance Fee.* In December a Tax on Banking Transactions[3] and the Law on Declaring Possession of Foreign Currency had enraged finance capital. The capitalist press screamed that the finance minister was under the dictate of Social Democracy. This cry was echoed in the clerical camp commanded by Seipel, which found it unbearable that Social Democracy could effectively influence the policy of the bourgeois government. Gürtler met with increasing opposition in his own party. Now he feared any agreement with Social Democracy since he was being daily accused of being under our dictate. But the concrete difficulties of reaching an understanding were also very great. After the reduction of the food subsidies, the deficit of the state enterprises was the biggest burden on the state budget. We therefore demanded that the next financial policy measure be the administrative and financial independence of the state enterprises under an independent administration organized on the example of the enterprises of common economic interest. The bourgeoisie saw in this demand a push toward "socialization." Seipel publicly repudiated our organizational plan before negotiations with Gürtler were possible.

When the government lost the support of the Pan-Germans and made no effort to accept the help offered by the Social Democrats, it ceased to have a majority capable of carrying out policy, and its financial policy came to a complete standstill. Meanwhile, the English loan had been quickly used up. To ease the crisis of capital, Gürtler had induced the Austro-Hungarian Bank† to take up bill brokering again on a wider scale. The discounting of large-sum bills of exchange supplied financial capital with huge resources,

---

* Börsenbesuchsabgabe: an entrance fee paid mainly for the traders' staff.
† See Glossary.

which increased its demand for foreign currency. The finance minister had to use as means of payment a portion of the English loan to prevent demand from driving up foreign-currency exchange rates. Thus, the banks used the paper bills that the state itself made available to them through the central bank in order to snatch the English-loaned money from the state within a few weeks. But as soon as people became aware that this currency was running out, the foreign currency rates began to rise again.

In short, the English loan was used up in a few weeks without it being put to use. Consequently, the expected loans from France, Italy, and Czechoslovakia were not forthcoming; after the experience with the English loan, these states could reasonably suppose that no credit would help Austria's financial policy. Had the Schober-Gürtler government, at the moment of the arrival of the English loan, continued to energetically pursue the policy that had been initiated under the influence of our financial plan in autumn 1921, it would have been possible to quickly obtain the French, Italian, and Czech credits, to stop the money printing presses and thus take the most decisive step toward putting the state's finances in order. In autumn 1922 this actually did occur with the help of the same loans that had first been made liquid at that time. In the spring this was impeded by the finance-policy passivity into which the government fell precisely at the moment the English loan arrived and by the serious mistake of the discount policy initiated precisely at this time. Thus, not only was the success of the measures adopted in November and December 1921 thwarted, not only the most favorable moment for the improvement of public finance missed, but the impression was also conveyed abroad that it was useless to grant loans to Austria without putting Austrian finances under strict controls. The fateful errors committed in February and March 1922 are largely responsible for the oppressive conditions provided by the Geneva protocols of October 1922.

Both bourgeois parties share responsibility for these disastrous errors, above all the Pan-Germans. Due to the Treaty of Lana, they withdrew their support for the government at precisely the moment when it needed a strong majority for carrying out the financial measures, which had become necessary and, with the arrival of the English loan, possible. The very same Pan-Germans, who did not want to subordinate their qualms about the Treaty of Lana to the needs for financial reconstruction, accepted, only a few months later and for the sake of financial reconstruction, the far more oppressive conditions of the Geneva protocols. But the culpability of the group of Christian Socials led by Seipel is still greater. The needed financial measures could indeed have been carried out even without the support of the Pan-Germans, since the Social Democrats had offered their support in the resolution of March 16. This offer went unanswered because Seipel, completely under the spell of the financial press, rejected any control of financial policy by the Social Democrats. Thus, the crucial opportunity had to be missed. Social Democracy, in offering its cooperation through the March 16 resolution, did everything within its power to prevent this momentous error. The behavior of both bourgeois parties made our offer ineffective.

As a consequence of these events, we came into the sharpest conflict with the government, which was no longer capable of an active financial policy. When Gürtler raised the customs surcharge without consulting us, we presented a motion in the Finance Committee to censure him. Since, for political reasons, the Pan-Germans voted with us, our motion was accepted on May 10. Gürtler resigned. Seipel, who had prevented cooperation with Social Democracy in March, now sought to construct a firm coalition of the bourgeois parties against Social Democracy. Schober's government resigned on May 24; on May 31 the Seipel government was elected. It was essentially different from the two earlier bourgeois governments. The Mayr government had been a Christian Social one, which always had to secure the support of the Pan-Germans on a case-by-case basis. The Schober government was a government of officials over which the Christian Socials and the Pan-Germans exerted control by each having one ministerial post. The Seipel government was created from a formal coalition compact of all bourgeois parties, composed of Christian Social and Pan-German deputies, and its aim from the very beginning was to forge a firmer alliance to stem the influence of Social Democracy, which had proved so strong at the time of the Burgenland crisis and in the initial stages of Gürtler's financial legislation. Despite even this we could still force the new government to act under our pressure.

The Seipel government took office at a time when the currency depreciation was advancing more quickly than ever before. In the first twelve days of June, the rate of the Swiss franc in Vienna rose from 2,151 to 4,110 kronen. In the second week of June, it was obvious that it was difficult to have even the necessary foreign currency to pay for the most urgent coal imports. There was a clear danger of coal supplies being held up even though the large banks had hoarded huge sums of foreign currency. On June 13, the steering committee of the Social Democratic deputies visited the Federal Chancellor and told him that Social Democracy could no longer assume responsibility for the behavior of the masses of workers driven to despair by the price increases if the government did not, within twenty-four hours, order the banks to make available to the state all the foreign currency they held. The threat worked.

On that very day, Seipel and his finance minister Ségur moved the banks to make available a part of their stores of foreign currencies for the founding of a new money-issuing central bank.* Ségur's financial plan, drafted in the following days, was based on this decision. But even if this financial plan came originally from Social Democratic initiative, the bourgeois government and its majority shaped it in such a way that we were obliged to fight against it. At any rate, the financial plan, passed in July by the bourgeois majority, fell apart in a few weeks. The founding of the bank of issue failed because of the refusal of the French and English management of the Länderbank and the Anglo Bank† to participate in putting up the capital stock. The compulsory loan, which was to cover the state deficit, was devalued by the ongoing depreciation of the krone, since the bourgeois majority had rejected our demand to valorize the bond debts. The tax laws could not even come into effect because the bourgeois majority had tied them within a legislative "package" to the founding of the bank of issue. The collapse of Ségur's financial plan undermined all confidence. In summer 1922 the currency depreciation became truly frenzied. From June 1 to August 25 in Vienna the Swiss franc quoted as follows:

June 1 .... 2,151 kronen
July 3 .... 3,948 kronen
July 14 .... 5,748 kronen
July 31 .... 8,013 kronen
August 11 .... 10,243 kronen
August 25 .... 15,993 kronen

Prices rose at a frightening rate. According to the Joint Commission, the cost of living rose from:

May 15 to June 14...................... by 71 percent
June 15 to July 14 .... by 41 percent
July 15 to August 14 .... by 124 percent
August 15 to September 14 .... by 91 percent

---

* The Austrian National Bank (Österreichische Nationalbank) replacing the Österreichisch-Ungarische Bank; see Glossary, "Bank, Austro-Hungarian and Austrian National."
† Two private banks founded before the war, the Länderbank owned by French and the Anglo Bank by British capital.

Prices were doubling every month; in the years of the war and Revolution, they had doubled every year.

In August the Foreign Exchange Board* was no longer able to muster the foreign means of payment to purchase the needed food, coal, and raw-material imports. Imports stalled. A complete collapse of the economy appeared imminent. The agitation among the working masses indicated that economic collapse would unleash the most violent social convulsions. In the border provinces, people feared that the neighboring states would exploit the impending social agitation for their own ends. The Burgenland feared the incursion of Magyar irregulars, and Carinthia feared the invasion of Yugoslav troops.

The government sought help abroad. It addressed an urgent plea to the representatives of the Entente powers assembled in London. On August 15, Lloyd George replied in the name of the Supreme Council: "The representatives of the Allied governments have come to the conclusion that it is impossible for them to hold out hope that their governments might grant Austria new financial aid. Nevertheless, they have all agreed to refer the question of Austria to the League of Nations for examination and report." Nobody in Austria had any hope in the League after the failure of its action in 1921. Lloyd George's answer therefore had to be understood as a curt refusal of any aid. Seipel answered on August 18 that with this rejection the financial problem had become a highly political one and that "the Central European problem"—that is, the problem of Austria's existence as an independent state—had been opened. This answer aggravated the sense of panic, because it meant that the government itself feared economic and social collapse within a very short space of time and the consequent dissolution of Austria and invasion of the border provinces by foreign troops. At the same time Seipel announced that he was going to Prague, Berlin, and Rome to personally discuss the Austrian problem with the statesmen of the countries most directly concerned. It was obvious that the government was ready to try anything to get aid from abroad, even sacrificing the independence of the Republic.

On August 23 a conference was convened of the Social Democratic Party, the trade unions, the cooperatives, the Chambers of Labor, and workers' councils. It came to the conclusion that the severe economic and political crisis required a complete change in our political policy. Since Oc-

---

* Devisenzentrale, a regulatory body founded in 1916 controlling the purchase and sale of foreign currencies.

tober 1920 we had refused any participation in the government. Now we declared our readiness to be part of the government under certain conditions.

Since October 1921, as the opposition, we had been attempting to impose on the bourgeois government a financial policy that could ward off the impending currency catastrophe. We had forced Gürtler into a financial policy along the lines of our own; but from the very start his policy had stalled. On Ségur we had forced the requisitioning of the banks' foreign currency stores, but he only used this for a financial plan that we were obliged to reject and which completely collapsed in a few weeks. Experience showed that it was not enough to impose policies on a hostile government from outside. If we wanted to save the Republic from imminent economic collapse, then we had to take financial policy into our own hands, enter government, and occupy the Ministry of Finance with a person from our own ranks.

However, it was not only the financial crisis but also the political crisis that forced us to enter the government. We saw the dangers of the political turn that had just been accomplished by Seipel with his declaration of August 18. We saw the dangers of Seipel's recent visits to Prague, Berlin, and Verona. Of this the manifesto of our August 23 conference said:

> The government is continuing [despite all disappointments, despite the shameless breaking of dozens of solemn promises on the part of the world capitalist powers] to seek aid abroad. It is doing so by dangerous means. If Mr. Seipel's methods could bring us any foreign loan at all then they could only impose intolerable conditions on it, that is, the cost would be the complete subjection of German-Austria to the control of foreign powers, the complete loss of the last vestiges of our state independence. We need to arm ourselves against this danger of bartering away our independence.[4]

Thus, everything pushed us in the direction of getting both financial policy and foreign policy under our direct control. How could we do this? We could not contemplate taking power by revolutionary means. Trust in Austrian paper money dwindled from day to day. A revolutionary uprising of the proletariat would have totally obliterated it. The exchange of paper kronen for foreign money and goods, which became more difficult with each passing day, would have thus become completely impossible. It would have completely ended any possibility of foreign supplies of foodstuffs, coal, and raw materials. A famine catastrophe, civil war, invasion, and counterrevolution at the point of foreign bayonets would have been the inevitable consequences. If we wanted to prevent the complete collapse of

monetary value, only one way was open: form an all-parties government*
together with the bourgeois parties and within it ensure our control over
financial and foreign policy. But we could not enter such a government
unconditionally. The August 23 manifesto stated:

> Only if the bourgeois parties finally recognize the danger of the com-
> plete collapse of our economy; only if they become conscious of the fact
> that if everything collapses even the possessing classes cannot save them-
> selves from bankruptcy; only if the fear of this catastrophe forces the
> possessing classes to make the necessary sacrifice, thus preparing them
> to meet our most important and urgent demands and give up their sabo-
> tage in the face of all the economic and social necessities—*then and only
> then* [comrades] is there a possibility of carrying out in agreement with
> the bourgeois parties what has to be carried out, *then and only then* could
> temporary cooperation with the bourgeois parties be a means for us of
> rescuing the Republic and the economy from the present severe danger.[5]

The resolutions of the August 23 conference were motivated by the
conviction that the political system prevailing in the Republic since autumn 1919, the system of equilibrium of class forces, had temporarily foundered on the task of restoring health to the state budget and putting an
end to the multiplication of paper money to avert the impending currency
catastrophe. This task was in reality very difficult. The Republic had inherited a state apparatus from the old Monarchy that was much too large and
costly for the small new state. Moreover, through the effects of the war,
the dissolution of the old greater economic area, of the Revolution, and of
provincial particularlism, the functioning of this apparatus had been disrupted, complicated, and made more expensive. Covering the costs of this
apparatus from tax revenue was all the more difficult as apartment-tenant
protection and the decay of the rentier class had dried up the most fertile of
the old sources of tax revenue, while the new wealth was hidden in forms
that easily evaded the grasp of the tax authorities.

There could be no solution of this difficult problem as long as the class
forces were in equilibrium. The resistance of the bourgeoisie and the peasantry was too strong for the proletariat to have succeeded in forcing a solution with socialist means, with ruthless encroachments on property rights.
The working class's resistance was too strong for the bourgeoisie to have

---

* Konzentrationsregierung.

been able to effect a solution at the cost of the proletariat, through ruthless reduction of the number of state employees and the ruthless expansion of the system of indirect taxation. Thus, the system of balanced class forces foundered on the currency catastrophe. The road ahead could pass either through the restoration of working-class hegemony or the restoration of the bourgeoisie.

Meanwhile, Seipel had set out for Prague, Berlin, and Verona. The bourgeoisie waited for the results of his journey. Had he returned empty-handed, the bourgeois government would have fallen; the bourgeoisie would have been obliged to submit to our conditions, and the bourgeois parties would have had to form a government with us within which Social Democracy would have been assured the leading, the decisive role. But if Seipel were to succeed in obtaining foreign loans at whatever cost, then the bourgeoisie, saved from the bitter necessity of capitulating to the working class, would have preferred to submit to foreign control rather than control by Austria's proletariat; the aid from foreign capital would consolidate the bourgeois government and therefore the bourgeoisie's control of the Republic. Thus, everything now depended on whether the bourgeoisie succeeded in getting the support of foreign capital. If it did not, then it would have to submit to the working class's hegemony. If it were able to get the effective support of international finance capital, it would have an opportunity, for the first time since the Revolution, to push back the powerful influence of the proletariat and with the help of foreign gold establish bourgeois class rule in the Republic.

CHAPTER 18

THE GENEVA PROTOCOLS

During the war, the Czech and Yugoslav émigrés had formed an alliance, which was the basis of the alliance of the two new states after the Revolution. The alliance of the two Slav states faced Hungary on the one side and Italy on the other; Hungary, seeking opportunities for a war of revenge against its two Slav neighbors; Italy, which contested with the Slavs for domination of the eastern Adriatic coast. Austria is the bridge between the two Slav states; in their common war against Hungary they could not do without Austrian means of transport. Austria is also the bridge between Italy and Hungary; in a common war against Yugoslavia, they would need to use Austrian transport routes.

The struggle over the Burgenland brought Austria closer to both Slav states. The Treaty of Lana was the result of this phase of development. But since the end of the Burgenland dispute, those tendencies in Austria were gaining strength that pushed for a shift away from the Slav group and rapprochement with Italy and Hungary.

These tendencies were found among the counterrevolutionary groups in Austrian society, which developed sympathy for Hungary when the counterrevolution raged there, and for Italy when Fascism was rapidly rising. They hated Czechoslovakia and Yugoslavia, in part because the power of the two Slav states stood in the way of Habsburg restoration, and in part because Czechoslovakia was holding three million Germans under foreign rule. Czernin was the spokesman for this tendency; he was the chief advocate of the idea that Austria had to seek protection in an Italian-Hungarian combination to establish internal "order" and reinforcement against the Slav neighbors to the north and south.

374

These counterrevolutionary tendencies found support in the foreign policy of Carinthian and Styrian provincial particularism. When economic collapse threatened Austria in August 1922, both of these provincial governments demanded an understanding with Italy, so that in the event of a catastrophe, it might protect Carinthia and Styria from the danger of a Yugoslav invasion.

Under the influence of these tendencies, Federal Chancellor Seipel set out to Prague, Berlin, and Verona on August 20, 1922. The meager official reports on the visits in Prague and Berlin did not disclose the purpose of the trip. Only at Verona was the secret revealed. Seipel offered Italy a currency and customs union with Austria. Italy was to include Austria in its currency community and thus save it from the threatened currency catastrophe. For this Austria was to merge into the Italian economic area, submitting economically and politically to Italy as a protectorate; a "greater Italy" would come into existence stretching to the Danube. Austria would be the bridge between Italy and Hungary, and this bridge between Yugoslavia and Czechoslovakia would fall within Italy's power.

The plan that Seipel proposed to the Italian minister Schanzer at Verona was incompatible with the interests of Yugoslavia and Czechoslovakia. Any attempt to carry it out would have involved Central Europe in embroilments highly dangerous to the peace. The Italian government hesitated. On August 15, the allied Supreme Council requested that the League of Nations examine Austria's economic situation. The Italian government directed Austria to the League. Only if the consultations in the Council of the League led to no result would Italy revert to Seipel's proposal.

Czechoslovakia and Yugoslavia had thus both gained time in which to carry out their countermove. The Czech foreign minister Beneš now took the initiative. His task was clear: on the one hand, he had to see to it that the League save Austria from the impending currency catastrophe, so that Austria would not throw itself into Italy's arms; on the other hand, the Powers had to place Austria under effective economic and political control so that its position between the two Slav states and also between Italy and Hungary could not be used as an object of dispute between the groups on either side. Beneš now endeavored to convince the English and French governments that peace in Central Europe was seriously endangered if Austria were to collapse and therefore be thrown into the arms of Italian imperialism. He now vigorously pursued a plan to enable a large international loan for Austria, guaranteed by the Powers, on condition that Austria be placed under the control of the League of Nations.

Seipel's gambit in Verona and Beneš's countermoves in Paris, London, and Geneva had completely altered the domestic situation in Austria. On August 23, Social Democracy declared its readiness to form a government with the bourgeois parties, which was to impede the imminent currency catastrophe. Three days later the situation had completely changed. Whether through Seipel's or Beneš's efforts, suddenly there was hope again of aid from abroad. The krone, which had reached its lowest point on August 25, stopped sinking. The bourgeoisie had hope again of escaping the currency catastrophe without having to capitulate to the proletariat; it was not prepared to submit to our conditions once it saw another way out. Returned from Verona, Seipel curtly rejected the forming of a new government. The representatives of the Austrian government travelled to Geneva; when the League of Nations met there, it could already be seen that Beneš's efforts had won over the English and French governments for the Czech plans.

The negotiations in Geneva lasted a few weeks. The conflict between Italy on the one side and England and France on the other, which had decided in favor of Beneš's plan, dragged on. Only on October 4 were the Geneva protocols signed by the representatives of England, France, Italy, Czechoslovakia, and Austria. Beneš's countermove against Verona was completely successful.

Seipel had played a bold game. He had staked everything on one card. The Austrian government itself had publicly declared before all Europe that Austria's complete collapse was inevitable if it did not immediately receive credits from abroad. If this aid were not forthcoming, such a declaration would have destroyed all confidence in Austria's ability to save itself, and it would have run the risk of truly heading toward the feared collapse. The Austrian government itself had offered Austria to Italian imperialism; if Italy had decided to take Austria at its word, our fate would have been to become an Italian colony. But reckless as Seipel's game was, he achieved his objective. When on August 15 the Great Powers asked the League of Nations to "examine the situation of Austria," this was barely more than a polite and indirect refusal of Austria's request for credit. Only under the pressure of the Czech countermove to the proposal Seipel made to the Italian government in Verona did the negotiations within the League concerning Austria become serious.

In the Geneva protocols for the reconstruction of Austria,[1] in fact, the Powers committed themselves to guaranteeing an Austrian loan of up to 650 million gold kronen: 130 million would be used to pay back the foreign credit extended to Austria in 1922, and 520² million would cover the Austrian deficit for a period of two years.

But Seipel's success came at a high price. He had offered Austria's economic and political independence for sale in Verona. Now he was taken at his word. Beneš's objective was to establish, instead of the Italian protectorate to which Seipel wanted to subject Austria, the common protectorate of the Entente Powers and of Czechoslovakia over Austria. This is what was implemented by the Geneva protocols.

The protocols first of all bind Austria to desist from any obligations that might endanger its independence in relation to any other state. With this provision Czechoslovakia has protected itself against annexation of Austria to Italy; but the same provision also excludes not only annexation of Austria to Germany but also any closer economic connection of Austria with Germany.

Second, the Geneva protocols subject Austria to dual control: control by a General Commissioner appointed by the League of Nations and control by a committee made up of representatives of the powers that guarantee the Austrian loan. The chair of this committee was to be named by the Italian government and the vice-chair by the Czech government. The Austrian government may not acquire any loan without the approval of the control committee and likewise requires approval by the General Commissioner before it can use the proceeds of the loan guaranteed by the Powers. The General Commissioner can specify the conditions under which he makes the loan installments available to the government. Since the government may no longer cover the deficit by inflation nor take up any further loan without the permission of the control committee, it cannot move the economy forward without the General Commissioner transferring the loan installments; the country is therefore completely at the mercy of the General Commissioner's whims.

Third, the Geneva protocols bind Austria to give the government unlimited power to carry out the reform and reorganization program to be agreed on by a delegation of the League of Nations and the General Commissioner, so that the government can apply the requisite measures for implementing this program without having to go to parliament for approval. In this way the counterweight of parliamentary power with respect to foreign control was to be removed.

On October 17, a delegation of the League of Nations' finance committee came to Vienna to hammer out the "programme of reforms and improvement" that Austria was to pledge to carry out within two years. The delegation was led by bankers. Its activity was determined by the idea that the reform and reorganization program had to win "the trust of foreign nations," that is, the trust of the foreign bankers who were to grant the credit guaranteed by the League. "Public credit," Marx said, "rests on confidence that the state will allow itself to be exploited by the wolves of finance."[3] If the reform and reorganization program was to attract loans from London, Paris, and Amsterdam, it had to present proof that the Austrian state was ready to be exploited by international high finance. It was the conceptions of the bankers who led the negotiations and a regard for the concerns of the bankers who were to grant the credits that determined the content of the "Reconstruction Law,"[4] in which the reform and reorganization program was laid down; its draft made it clear that the financial control of the League of Nations could be nothing other than control by international high finance. The Reconstruction Law wants to reorganize the Republic's finances through ruthless taxation of the masses on the one side, and the ruthless reduction of the number of civil servants on the other. The reorganization is to be carried out exclusively to the detriment of the broad masses of workers, employees, and officials, while the domestic possessing classes are meticulously spared. The most valuable property of the Republic is pawned and its independence surrendered.

At the beginning of Seipel's negotiations in Geneva, Social Democracy had clearly defined its position: no annexation to Italy and no control by the League of Nations beyond simply securing the interest payments for an international loan. But Seipel did not bother with this caveat in Geneva; he was convinced that Austria would not reject aid from abroad even with such oppressive conditions. He had no fear of foreign control over our whole public life. Convinced that parliament, left to its free will, would not be able to agree to the harsh measures needed to restore equilibrium to the state budget, he wished to place it under foreign control. In fact, he pinned his hopes on foreign control: the control of foreign capitalist governments over Austria was to free the Austrian bourgeoisie from control by Austria's proletariat. The Geneva negotiations were secret, and under cover of secrecy Seipel agreed to the conditions that completely abolished Austria's independence.

The Austrian people only learned of the results of the negotiations when they had already been concluded. On October 5 they first heard that the Chancellor had sold their sovereignty for 520 million gold kronen. And the dangers of this surrender of our independence became clear when the agreements with the League delegation were concretized in the Geneva protocols. We therefore had to wage a fierce battle against them and against the Reconstruction Law intended to enforce compliance with them.

But the campaign was conducted under the most unfavorable conditions. For four years the Austrian people had experienced the most frightening currency depreciation, followed by a state of panic in August when the total destruction of the value of paper money threatened to stop food supplies from abroad. But now suddenly everything changed. With the prospect of a large foreign loan, the krone rate stopped rising and prices began to fall. The panic disappeared. These positive effects of Geneva were visible to everyone. The ill effects predicted by the Social Democrats were at first nothing more than prophecies. The mood among the broad masses and extending deep into the ranks of the officials and employees was in favor of Geneva. We had to conduct our struggle against the mood of large sections of the population.

And in this struggle our goal had to be something other and much more than the mere dismissal of the Geneva protocols. We had lived through the August crisis. We knew that if the protocols were abandoned, there would at first be no prospects of foreign credits; then, if very energetic measures were not simultaneously enacted to ward off the currency collapse, there was the threat of a new fall of the krone and a new wave of price increases; there would be a new danger of foreign food supplies really ceasing, with Austria plunged into a famine catastrophe. Consequently, our position had to be that we would only impede ratification of the Geneva protocols if we could carry out finance policy measures that could fend off the threatened currency disaster.

This could have been possible: We could have demanded of the banks and stock exchange members a compulsory loan of 120 million gold kronen in foreign means of payment, and, further, through valorization of Ségur's compulsory loan, we could have increased its revenue by at least 60 million gold kronen; finally, we would have gold at our disposal from the liquidation of the Austro-Hungarian Bank in the sum of 35 million gold kronen. With these means we could have covered the state deficit for quite some time without having to print money; we could have stabilized the krone rate and so win time for the balancing of the regular revenues and expenditures of the state. It was thus economically feasible to prevent economic collapse even in the event of a repudiation of the Geneva protocols. But was it also politically possible? Were we in a position to bring down the Seipel government and replace it with one that would reject ratification of the Geneva protocols and at the same time take up the measures we demanded for financial self-help with sufficient energy and speed that the currency depreciation could really be averted?

The first precondition for this would have been to turn the popular mood against Geneva. We initiated a major propaganda drive launched at the October 14 party congress. This was followed by mass rallies and demonstrations. At bottom, this mass activity was a battle for the souls of the German-National intellectuals, officials, employees, and teachers. Only if we succeeded in mobilizing the national consciousness of the German-National electorate against Austria's submission to foreign rule could we hope to turn the Pan-Germans against Seipel, bring down his parliamentary majority, and so create conditions for a new course. But it was soon evident that our attempt had failed. The years of currency depreciation had hit the intelligentsia, officials and employees, and the mass of the German-National electorate the hardest. They were the ones now most ready to buy the stabilization of the krone at any price, even at the price of national independence. The German Reich was laboring under the tremendous burden of French reparation demands. The mark fell relentlessly. In this time of Germany's decline, the German-National intelligentsia in Austria lost faith in the ideal of annexation; it was ready to throw itself into the arms of the Entente to find relief from the currency depreciation. The national bourgeoisie no longer felt and thought in terms of nation; it only felt and thought in terms of being bourgeois. It preferred the stabilization of the krone paid by the proletariat under control of the Entente to its stabilization paid by the bourgeoisie under control of the proletariat. We soon realized that our struggle for national independence found no echo in the national camp and that our struggle against the Pan-Germans, who were surrendering national independence, now truly welded the Pan-Germans and Christian Socials together. With this all hope was lost of bringing down the government majority by democratic means and cancelling the Geneva protocols.

At the same time an event occurred outside Austria's borders that made our struggle against Geneva particularly dangerous. On October 29 the Fascist revolt in Italy compelled the liberal bourgeoisie to capitulate, and government power fell to the Fascists. This posed a grave threat to us. If our campaign against Geneva led to serious internal embroilments in Austria, then the nationalism that had just come to power in Italy could have recourse to Verona and, taking Austria at its word, implement the "greater Italy" that Fascism had promised the nationalist youth, by extending Italy's sphere of power to the Danube along the line of least resistance. As great as the dangers of the Geneva protocols were, the danger of a revival of Verona was now much greater after the victory of the white terror in Italy.

It was not only a matter of cancelling Geneva. We could only prevent its ratification if we could simultaneously form a government capable of energetic financial self-help. How could we achieve this? With democratic means? This was impossible because we could not win the Pan-Germans over to opposing Geneva in order to bring down the parliamentary majority, which was pledged to Geneva. With revolutionary means? That would mean unleashing a civil war in the face of the popular pro-Geneva mood, thus making the economic catastrophe, which had been imminent in August, inexorable, triggering the intervention of an Italy that had just turned Fascist—that is, it would have provoked dangers far worse than those of the Geneva protocols itself.

We therefore could not prevent the ratification of the Geneva protocols, and so the only thing left was to use the power of the mass movement we had unleashed to minimize the dangers of the protocols. This attempt was doubly successful. We were able to break the dictate of the Geneva protocols regarding one of its aspects. According to the protocols, parliament was to give the government full powers for two years for carrying out the "reforms and improvement programme." We succeeded in having these powers invested not in the government but in an "extraordinary cabinet council," that is, a committee of parliament itself. This effectively prevented the exclusion of parliamentary representation from the most important legislative acts. Then we put through a whole series of important changes to the "reforms and improvement programme" itself and the Reconstruction Law regulating its implementation. In this way a number of attacks on the working class's economic interests were averted. Only when the government and the delegation of the League's finance committee made these concessions could the National Council ratify the Geneva protocols on December 2.

The decision about the Geneva protocols was in the first place one involving the two historical tendencies whose struggle pervades the whole recent history of German-Austria: Austrianism and Germanism. When the Habsburg Empire collapsed, this old conflict was embodied in the dual government, which existed in German-Austria from October 30 to November 12, 1918: the antagonism between the Lammasch-Seipel government, the last Imperial government on the one hand, and the Staatsrat elected by the Provisional National Assembly, the first republican government, on the other hand. The Lammasch-Seipel government had been appointed by the Emperor in order to cover Andrássy's offer of a separate peace. Its guiding idea was that Austria should save itself from the catastrophe of the Central Powers by separating from Germany and throwing itself into the arms of the Entente and make itself eligible for accession to the Entente by satisfying the demands of the Slav nations within the Habsburg Empire. The Staatsrat embodied the opposite tendency; its leading idea was that after the disintegration of the Habsburg Empire, German-Austria must separate its destiny from that of the Habsburgs and seek its future in annexation to Germany. The contest between the two tendencies was decided on November 12, 1918: the Social Democratic working class and the German-National bourgeoisie overthrew the Lammasch-Seipel government and proclaimed the Republic and union with Germany. But the antagonism between Austrianism and Germanism persisted in the soul of German-Austrians. It appeared again at the time of the peace negotiations. Our peace delegation fought at Saint-Germain for annexation to Germany, but Austrianism did not want it. During the negotiations Lammasch defended the plan of transferring all of Austria's power, including the right to sanction all laws and state treaties and to name all higher officials and officers, to a commission to be appointed by the League of Nations, thereby making it eligible for loans for economic reconstruction. Both plans failed. Our campaign for annexation foundered on the Entente's resistance. At that time plans such as Lammasch drafted still unanimously rejected the national and republican desire for freedom of the German-Austrian people. And so Austria led an independent life, not as a part of the German Reich nor as a colony of the Entente. But among ever greater sections of the Austrian people, the hardships of this involuntary independence gradually wore down their national and republican desire for freedom.

By fall 1922, facing imminent currency collapse, the whole Austrian bourgeoisie was ripe for capitulation to the Entente. Now Seipel could fulfill Lammasch's legacy. In the Geneva protocols, German-Austria again renounced annexation to Germany. In the first renunciation it had grudgingly given in to the commandment of the all-powerful victors; in the second, in accepting the Geneva protocols it sold annexation out for ready cash: 520 million gold kronen. And since Austria could not maintain its economy alone, annexation to Germany was replaced with subjection to the supremacy of the Entente. Thus in changed form the Geneva protocols completed what Lammasch had defended during the peace negotiations in Saint-Germain. And so in the end the conception of the Lammasch-Seipel government prevailed over the conception of the Staatsrat. German-Austria separated from Germany and threw itself into the arms of the Entente in order to save its economy from collapse and its bourgeoisie from the Revolution. If in November 1918 the German-Nationals had stood by the side of the working class against Old-Austrianism, which had become pro-Entente, then in October 1922 they fought united with the Old-Austrians against the working class for surrendering our national sovereignty to the Entente. Within the soul of the bourgeoisie, Old-Austrianism had completely prevailed over Germanism. The whole bourgeoisie had turned from the ideas of November 12 to Lammasch's outlook—October 4, 1922 was Seipel's revenge for November 12, 1918. The national revolution of the German-Austrians was liquidated.

The Geneva protocols meant the liquidation of the national revolution and was also an important step on the way to the liquidation of the social revolution of 1918. At one fell swoop the protocols turned the power relations between the classes upside down. Dr. Zimmerman, the mayor of Rotterdam, was named as General Commissioner of the League. He came to Vienna to carry out the reforms and improvement program designed by the bankers of the League of Nations delegation and steer Austria's financial policy in such a way as to motivate the bankers of London, Paris, Amsterdam, and Zurich to grant credits. Austria's possessing classes heartily welcomed him; from the beginning he was besieged with representatives of the large banks and industry who tried to move him to intervene against the working class. He had to come into conflict with Austria's working class because the bankers' program collided with their interests. Thus the proletariat is facing not only the Austrian government but a foreign General Commissioner whose power over Austria is practically unlimited because at any moment he can make the continued existence of Austria's national economy impossible. The balance of power between the classes of Austrian society was essentially altered as soon as this new force was activated within it. It abolished the equilibrium of class forces. The equilibrium of class forces—which has so often in history led to state power existing independently of all classes, as under absolutism, which subordinated all classes—was now cancelled by state power fleeing into the protection of foreign countries, with the foreign rulers becoming lords over all classes.

Ever since October 3, 1918, all initiative in German-Austria had pro-ceeded from the working class, from Social Democracy. The bourgeoisie had always obstructed and hindered us, but the initiative had always been in our hands. Seipel's was the first action that had come from the initia-tive of the bourgeoisie. In Seipel they had for the first time found a far-sighted and energetic leader. The implementation of the Geneva protocols was their first great victory over the working class, and the stabilization of the krone rate since Geneva their first visible success. The bourgeoisie's self-confidence had been powerfully reinforced. The whole of the owning classes now really stood behind Seipel: the Christian Socials as well as the Pan-Germans, the big banks and large industries as well as the landowners and the small-scale craftspeople, the bishops along with the stock exchange, the Jewish capitalist press as well as the noisy anti-Semitic swastika groups. At the time of the Mayr and Schober governments, the antagonisms be-tween the bourgeois parties had strengthened the Social Democratic op-position in parliament; this is all over now. In parliament we are facing a tight majority with a unified leadership, a majority with a significantly strengthened self-consciousness, a majority whose government moreover has greatly expanded powers due to the Reconstruction Law. The working class's power in parliament has been perceptibly weakened.

The economic and social position of the working class has been weak-ened at the same time by the industrial crisis, which erupted with the sta-bilization of the krone rate. On August 25, the exchange rate reached its highest level. For a short while it was lowered by hope of a large foreign loan; then the krone rate stabilized. With this the tension between its do-mestic and foreign value, which up to then had supported the exports of Austrian industry and hindered imports of foreign products, disappeared. In the period of currency depreciation, Austrian industry consumed its capital, burdening itself with bank debts at exceedingly high interest rates, and had not renewed its plant. Now it was deprived of the benefit of a de-preciating currency and had to face the competition of foreign industry. At this point the international crisis in sales, which has been weighing on the whole world market since the summer of 1920, broke out in Austria as well. The crisis was exacerbated by two factors: on the one hand, by the precipi-tous fall of the mark under pressure of the reparations crisis in autumn 1922 and the occupation of the Ruhr in January 1923; on the other hand, by the cut-back of all state jobs and public contracts, measures which the lack of finances forced the government to take as soon as the printing of additional money was forbidden.

The number of those receiving unemployment compensation was, by month:

August 31,247
September 38,000
October.............................. 58,018
November 83,387
December 117,891
January 161,360
February 169,075

With unemployment, short-time work also became a mass phenomenon. According to a survey organized by the trade unions, at the end of December 1922 only 275,733 out of 620,573 organized workers had full employment; 206,257 had only part-time jobs; and 138,583 were unemployed. Under pressure of the industrial crisis, the system of wage indexing collapsed; the workers had to swallow painful pay cuts. Even the income of full-time workers fell significantly, while the food prices fell only a little in the autumn months and already began to rise again in winter; the part-time workers and unemployed plunged into severe misery. The standard of living of the working masses, which had tangibly improved from 1919 to 1921, now perceptibly worsened again. The fear of layoffs and worry for one's employment made the workers compliant in the face of the entrepreneurs; the power of the factory councils was perceptibly weakened. In order to avoid defeats in times of market stagnation, the trade unions had to try to sidestep difficult battles; and their power too was weakened by this. The workers saw themselves put on the defensive all along the line. While the implementation of the Geneva protocols powerfully reinforced the bourgeoisie, the working class's sense of its own power was shaken by the industrial crisis.

Analogously to the effect the crisis had on workers in private industry, the power of the employees in state offices and enterprises was weakened by the reduction of the federal civil service. The first demand of the foreign control to which the Geneva protocols had subjected Austria was the dismissal of a third of federal civil servants. By the end of 1922, as many as 25,000 officials had to be laid off; an additional 75,000 will have to leave the state service by mid-1924. Every single civil servant now fears dismissal and seeks to curry favor with his superiors to be spared this fate. The power of the trade unions and of office personnel representation has been weakened by individual fears of dismissal. At the same time counterrevolutionary and fascist tendencies have gained strength within the bourgeoisie. The victory of Fascism in Italy has everywhere strengthened the counterrevolutionary tendencies pushing for the violent overthrow of the working class and the establishment of a Caesarist dictatorship. In Bavaria, in particular, the National Socialist movement gained significant strength in autumn 1922. It then spread to Austria. Very great sums of money streaming in from Germany have enabled the swastika brandishers to organize raucous agitation that exploits popular hatred of the "nouveaux riches" to mount anti-Semitic pogroms and exploits the misery of the unemployed for counterrevolutionary aims; they are attempting to recruit and buy the declassed unemployed for their storm troops against the working class. Similar efforts were organized by different groups of former front combatants and Heimwehr groups. The working class answered by building up its Ordner organizations. But these organizations now have to realize that they are facing numerous opponents mostly consisting of past officers of high military caliber who are very well-equipped thanks to the abundant funds at their disposal. At the same time, entrepreneur associations and fascist organizations have tried to create a Technical Emergency Relief to serve in defeating strikes in vitally important enterprises.

The whole development has everywhere greatly strengthened the confidence of the bourgeois government. While it can always hide behind the authority of the General Commissioner of the League of Nations and has a more united and self-confident majority in the National Council than ever before, it has in addition far less to fear from the proletarian mass uprising outside parliament due to the increase in short-time work, unemployment, and cutbacks. With the restriction of parliamentary democracy due to the emergency powers that the Geneva protocols have given the government, functional democracy has also almost completely disappeared and the "authority of the state" has been restored. The government now dictates where it formerly had to reach agreement with personnel representatives and trade unions. This is no longer a weak, hesitant bourgeois government like those of Mayr and Schober. It is the power-conscious government of the owning classes, which intends to use the weakening of the working class to restore the class rule of the owning classes and reconstruct the Republic as the bourgeoisie's instrument of domination.

Reaction is clearly expressed in the financial policy introduced by the Geneva protocols. While the finance policy of 1919 and 1920 had shifted the source of state revenue policy from consumption taxes to property taxes, now the implementation of the "Reconstruction Law" has shifted it back from property taxes to consumption taxes and duties. We see the same tendency at work in the domain of social policy; there is no longer talk of its extension; the working class will have to tenaciously defend what has already been won. We see the same tendency in the sphere of school policy; the provinces' finances are being reorganized at the cost of elementary schools, and in the provinces (but not in Vienna) sixty and seventy children are being crammed into one class, thus destroying the new educational methods. The new tendency is above all seen in the government's systematic offensive against the three most important pillars of working-class power: the municipalities dominated by the working class, the transport and communication services dominated by the trade unions, and the power of the proletariat in the defense force. The class struggle of the bourgeoisie against the proletariat is taking the form of a dogged small-scale war of the bourgeois federal government against the proletarian domination of the municipality of Vienna, the constant struggle waged by the administrations of the transport and communications agencies against the power of the personnel representatives of the railway workers, the postmen, and the telegraph and telephone employees, and the constant offensive of the Federal Army commands directed against the powers of the soldiers' councils and against the civil rights of the militiamen. It is there that reaction is strongest. The government is trying as quickly as possible to push out of the Army the soldiers taken over from the Volkswehr who have been educated through the war and the Revolution; it is trying to wear down the young militiamen who first enlisted in 1921 and 1922 by systematically favoring those who are submissive and systematically bullying the undesirables until they become passive tools of the reactionary officer corps.

And so bourgeois rule has returned—with the surrender of national independence, the subjection to the dictate of foreign control, with the economic crisis, wage pressure, short-term jobs and unemployment, with a frightening deterioration of the working masses' standard of living, the slashing of tens of thousands of official and teacher jobs, the immiseration of small businesses crushed by the crisis, and the closing of schools and scientific institutes.

But its restoration is not yet complete. The working class is temporarily weakened but not yet conquered. A million workers and employees are still united within trade unions. The working class still commands the capital city, which contains nearly three-tenths of Austria's people. The proletariat can still stop the vital transport and communication services whenever it wants to. The Federal Army has still not become a usable tool for the violent suppression of the proletariat. The bourgeoisie still does not have a two-thirds majority in parliament and thus cannot change the rules of procedure, which provide the proletarian minority with the weapon of obstruction, nor revise the Constitution, which sets limits on the power of the majority. Only if the bourgeoisie manages to wrest all of these instruments from the proletariat will its restoration really be completed and the Republic, which the working class founded, really become a bourgeois republic.

CHAPTER 19

THE ACHIEVEMENTS OF THE REVOLUTION AND THE TASKS OF SOCIAL DEMOCRACY

The war plunged all of Europe into a revolutionary crisis, but it took only a few weeks to overcome the crisis of military demobilization in the Western European Entente states. In Germany, Hungary, France, and Italy, the proletariat already suffered a series of heavy defeats in 1919 and 1920. Since 1921 the international proletariat has been thrown on the defensive. For economic and social reasons, the bourgeoisie's international offensive has been especially fierce and violent. For economic reasons: Europe's impoverishment through war, the need to raise the deeply depressed rate of accumulation, the difficulty of competition in a world market affected by severe industrial crisis and made despondent by the breakdown of currencies—all this drives wage pressure and the dismantling of worker protections. For social reasons: the bourgeoisie, frightened by the intensity of the revolutionary onrush of 1918 and 1919, no longer feels secure enough to content itself with the methods of rule that sufficed before the war. In all states east of the Rhine—Austria being the only exception—it has armed itself with the weapons of emergency law; restrictions on freedom of association, assembly, and of the press; and the use of jury courts. In many of these states—and Austria is among them—the bourgeoisie has recourse to the weapons of violent fascist organizations. Thus, in all of Europe the revolutionary crisis of 1918–19 has been followed by heavy backlash.

But the 1918–19 revolutionary crisis did not solve any of the problems arising from the war. The imperialist governments of the victorious powers have not solved the Franco-German reparations problem, incorporated the Soviet Republic into the European state system, or established a stable peace in the territories of the formerly Russian "border peoples" and the Austrian "successor states"; nor have they suppressed the revolutionary ferment between the Bosphorus and the Tigris and between the Nile and the Ganges. Although US capitalism seems to have already overcome the serious postwar industrial crisis, the recovery of European capitalism is hampered by political crises and unrest. Economic pressure and political crises are aggravating the social unrest and driving toward new social convulsions.

It thus appears that the present phase is only a *transitional period* between two revolutionary processes: between the severe revolutionary convulsions Europe experienced in 1918–19 and the new severe military, revolutionary, or counterrevolutionary convulsions to which the still unsolved problems posed by the war are leading.

The developments within the territories once ruled by the Habsburg Monarchy correspond to this general European development. Here too the revolutionary process has for now been interrupted. In Czechoslovakia, in Yugoslavia, and in Poland, where the revolution has remained a purely national one, it already reached its endpoint in 1918 with the establishment of the new national states. Within the span of one year, Hungary underwent the tragedy of its revolutions and counterrevolution. The Geneva protocols cut short the revolutionary process in German-Austria. It would appear that the national revolution has been liquidated by Geneva and the social revolution ended with the formation of a strong, self-confident bourgeois regime protected by the capitalist governments united in the League of Nations. In reality, however, all the problems introduced by the Revolution of 1918 remain unsolved.

The ideas of the national Revolution of 1918 were falsified and mutilated by imperialism. Although it granted the Czechs, the Poles, and the Yugoslavs the national statehood for which they had striven, imperialism, in building these states, did not implement the right to self-determination of the peoples; instead it created new conditions of domination. It drew the boundaries of the new states in such a way that the national problems that had blown up the Habsburg Monarchy have arisen again in the new states. Czechoslovakia can only rule the subjugated Germans, Slovaks, Magyars, and Ruthenians by force. Once the development of class antagonisms within the dominant Czech people explodes or weakens its united front against the oppressed nations, this domination will no longer be able to masquerade as parliamentary majority rule. The Czechoslovak Republic would then have to enter into a severe state crisis. The Kingdom of the Serbs, Croats, and Slovenes has not realized the Yugoslav ideal of a federation of Southern Slav peoples but rather subjugated them to a Greater Serbian military monarchy. The antagonism between Yugoslavism and Great Serbianism lives on in the struggle around the constitution, in the rebellion of the Croats and Slovenes against Great Serbian centralization, and it reinforces reactionary Croat and Slovene ethnic particularism, impeding the consolidation of the Yugoslav state.

The counterrevolutionary forces that have seized power in Italy and Hungary are lying in wait for any escalation of the internal crises of the Czech and South Slav states. Every collision between Serbia and Croatia will offer the Italian Fascisti an opportunity to realize their plans for domination of the Adriatic and encourage the Magyar officer caste, which is pinning its hopes on Magyar irredentism in Slovakia and in Transylvania, and in the Banat on Slovak and Croatian ethnic particularism. The fear both Slav states have of Italian imperialism and Magyar revanchism is keeping the whole area of the former Danube Monarchy in a state of latent warlike tension. Moreover, any collision between these states would have to throw German-Austria into severe new convulsions and stir up all the old national and social problems of the Revolution of 1918. Thus, on the territory of the Austro-Hungarian Monarchy the revolutionary transformation process appears only to be interrupted and not completed. Here too the period of reaction we are experiencing is probably only a transitional period between two revolutionary processes.

Nobody can foresee how long this transition will last. It is certainly possible that it will soon come to an abrupt end. But it is just as possible that it will last many years, and for this we must be prepared and seek to understand the nature, problems, and tasks of the period.

The overwhelming majority of the German-Austrian bourgeoisie— whose traditions are overwhelmingly Old-Austrian and Habsburg—had to be forced to accept the Republic in 1918. To them the young Republic appeared an instrument of the proletariat's strong and menacing power; it could never win the love of the bourgeoisie. As soon as the Revolution's setback gave the bourgeoisie new hope, it at first looked to a Habsburg restoration, which for it meant the defeat of the proletariat: it meant the restoration of the greater Empire and the hope of winning back its lost market and trade areas and sphere of domination. But the experience of the two Habsburg coups in 1921 taught the bourgeoisie that Habsburg restoration is impossible as long as the power of Czechoslovakia and Yugoslavia remains unbroken. The bourgeoisie had to accommodate to the Republic. Not overthrowing the Republic but conquering it and upsetting the equilibrium of class forces, replacing it with the rule of the bourgeoisie and turning the people's republic into a bourgeois republic—this is the only goal the bourgeoisie can have in the transitional period.

Too weak to achieve this objective alone, it threw itself into the arms of the foreign capitalist governments. The object of the Geneva protocols is not to overthrow the Republic but to restructure its finances. But at the same time it is changing the Republic's social content. Under the cloak of this restructuring of the Republic, it is accomplishing the restoration of the bourgeoisie.

The Christian Social Party together with the much smaller Pan-German Party constitute the parliamentary majority and have formed the government. These are the parties whose base is among the upper and middle peasantry led by the Catholic clergy and among the urban petty bourgeoisie. Unlike the Czech and Polish petty bourgeoisie, these classes do not have democratic, revolutionary traditions; in 1918 they stood in the camp of the Habsburg counterrevolution, and their hearts are still there. For them the Republic is nothing but a fact they are forced to accept, which for the time being they cannot escape. Their republicanism is their fear of the Czechs. A virile love of freedom, without which democracy is impossible, is foreign to them; as the rulers of democracy they only feel secure operating behind the controlling organs of foreign countries. Their economic policy is determined by the overwhelming power of the landowners in their midst and their social policy by the anger the peasant feels at the assertiveness of his farmhands and the anger of the petty bourgeois at the rebelliousness of his journeymen, and their cultural policy by the dull narrow-mindedness of the Alpine village tavern. They are under the command of Roman clericalism; they get their instructions from the Cardinal Archbishop. Having willingly subordinated themselves to foreign control, they have lost their nationalism; they find a pathetic substitute for it in an anti-Semitism that, seeing as their government is dependent on large Jewish banks, cannot touch Jewish capital but has to act itself out instead in the hubbub against Jewish scholars and students. The political domination of this reactionary petty bourgeoisie constitutes the bourgeois republic in Austria.

But the parliamentary rule of the petty bourgeoisie is always and everywhere just a mask for the economic domination of finance capital; all petty bourgeois democracies become bankocracies. When the petty bourgeois parties hold down the working class and shift the burden of the state budget on them, dismantle worker protection legislation, transform the Federal Army into an effective instrument for keeping the working class down, and create a Technical Emergency Relief, they are only doing what finance, industrial, and commercial capital needs. As sincerely as they hate the Jewish bourgeois, they nevertheless do his business whether they want to or not. The beneficiaries of the suppression of the proletariat cannot be the native bourgeoisie pauperized by the currency depreciation; the beneficiaries are the nouveaux riches who have risen in the period of currency depreciation. The economic domination of this "really vile, really dirty, really Jewish bourgeois"[1]—that is the bourgeois republic in Austria.

But even these nouveaux riches only dominate a part of our machinery of production and circulation. To a great extent, and increasingly from month to month, foreign capital has penetrated into our banks and industrial enterprises. In many cases the Austrian chief executives are merely the sheriffs for foreign capitalists. And since Geneva this economic relation of domination corresponds to the political; in many relationships the Austrian government is merely the executive organ of the foreign General Commissioner. The actual and final beneficiary of the suppression of the Austrian proletariat will be foreign finance capital, whose economic and political command in Austria is becoming continually greater. Domination by foreign capital, exercised through the economic domination of Austrian war profiteers and racketeers, whose businesses are controlled by foreign capital, and through the political domination of the reactionary Austrian petty bourgeoisie, which willingly gives itself over to the dictate of the foreign General Commissioner—this is the final meaning of the bourgeois republic in Austria.

But it is by no means fully achieved. For more than four years the Austrian bourgeoisie and proletariat have waged a war of position in which one class may have pushed back the other for a time but neither of the two classes could dislodge the other from its important positions of power. Thus, the working class in Austria still has positions and instruments of power that are obstacles to absolute bourgeois rule; in order to establish its class rule, the bourgeoisie must try to wrest these positions and instruments of power from the proletariat.

It is conceivable that the bourgeoisie will attempt this through a violent coup. And certainly the official and legal reactionary forces since Geneva have made it possible for the unofficial, illegal reactionary forces—the swastika brandishers, former front combatants, and Heimwehren, which are arming themselves for a violent coup—to become much stronger. The working class must therefore remain armed to fend off a violent attack, and if it is adequately armed then the bourgeoisie will scarcely be able to risk a violent attack. The bourgeoisie cannot wish for open civil war, since this would completely destroy Austria's credibility abroad and sabotage the Geneva plan based on foreign loans, which would destroy the whole basis of the bourgeoisie's dominion. Moreover, the bourgeoisie will all the more refrain from taking this path, which is very dangerous for it, because it does not need to. For if state power remains for a few years in the hands of a bourgeois government provided extraordinary powers by the Geneva protocols, supported and reinforced by a General Commissioner of the League of Nations who has dictatorial power over state finances, then through systematic work the government can break down the proletariat's positions of power within a few years, without having to smash them violently.

This especially applies to our position of power in the Federal Army. The militiamen who have been schooled by their experience in the war and the Revolution are leaving the army when their term of service ends. By favoring the submissive and bullying the self-confident, it is very easy for the commandants to tame the young recruits taking the place of the militiamen, and through the manner in which they select soldiers to be trained as officers it is also easy for them to favor the bourgeois-minded. In this way, a systematically operating Minister of Defense can, within a few years, without creating too big a stir, without provoking very broad struggles, transform the Federal Army into a trustworthy instrument for defeating and suppressing the proletariat. Similarly, a strong bourgeois government can systematically strengthen the bourgeois paramilitary forces and weaken the proletarian ones; it can gradually push back the influence of the office personnel representatives and the trade unions in federal enterprises and agencies and equip a Technical Emergency Relief to resist strikes in vital services; it can systematically impair the finances of the municipality of Vienna, thus creating a dilemma for the Social Democratic city government and so undermine the domination of the working class in what is by far the largest federal state; by peaceful means it can conquer a two-thirds majority in the National Council and so change the National Council's rules of procedure that parliamentary opposition will be confined to ineffective criticism. Thus, within a few years a strong bourgeois government can gradually break apart the most important power bases of the proletariat. It if succeeds in this, then there no longer will be a counterforce to resist the threefold domination of the bourgeoisie—the political domination of the reactionary petty bourgeoisie, the economic domination of war-profiteering and racketeer capital, and the foreign domination of international high finance. At that point the Republic will have become a pure bourgeois republic.

It is self-evident that the proletariat must arm itself against this transformation of the Republic, founded and sustained by the working class, into an instrument of the bourgeoisie's class rule. But what political system can the proletariat oppose to the system that has developed since Geneva? Even at the point of greatest revolutionary tension in 1918–19, the German-Austrian working class could not establish its exclusive domination. It is much less in a position to do so today, at a time in which the proletariat of all Europe has been pushed into the defensive. In November 1918 the proletariat had usurped armed power while the bourgeoisie, surprised by events and deeply shaken morally, was unarmed. Since that time the bourgeoisie has had four years to arm itself. The establishment of the sole rule of the working class—whether this is in the form of a soviet dictatorship or that of a "workers' government" based only on a parliamentary minority, according to the communist recipe—could today only be the result of a complete victory of the proletariat in a bloody civil war. Any civil war today—surrounded as we are by Horthy's Hungary, the Yugoslavia of reactionary Greater Serbianism, the Fascists' Italy, and the Bavaria of the Orgesch—could only end with the military intervention of foreign forces. Already in September 1922, during the Geneva negotiations, the representatives of the capitalist powers raised the question of whether they should make the occupation of Austria by an international police force into a condition for granting loans. The more foreign loans flow into Austria and foreign capital invests in Austria, the more certain it is that the capitalist governments would decide on armed intervention—that is, the violent suppression of the Austrian proletariat—in the event of a civil war in Austria. Victory in a civil war, which would be the only way to establish a dictatorship of the proletariat or a "workers' government" on the communist model, is thus impossible in the present period. During the whole transitional period, a dictatorship of the proletariat is just as impossible and unachievable as a restoration of the Monarchy. Just as the bourgeoisie cannot set itself the goal of a Habsburg counterrevolution but only a bourgeois republic in the transitional period, so the proletariat cannot establish its dictatorship but only a people's republic in the transitional period.

The class rule of the bourgeoisie or the restoration of the equilibrium of class forces, the sole rule of the bourgeoisie or the sharing of actual power in the state between the bourgeoisie and the proletariat, a bourgeois republic or a people's republic—this is the issue around which struggle is waged in the transitional period, the period of the proletarian defensive.

The belief that the Geneva protocols will heal the ailing Austrian economy united all strata of the bourgeoisie and peasantry under reactionary command. It obstructed any rebellion of national self-consciousness against the foreign domination of international finance capital. It is allowing the bourgeois government to tend to the business of reaction under the pretext of healing the economy. If the belief in Geneva made possible the bourgeoisie's advance, then disenchantment with Geneva will make the proletariat's defense effective.

Up to 1918 the unity of the Austro-Hungarian economic sphere, encircled by tariff walls, assured Austrian industry its markets and Viennese commerce and banks a dominant position in an Empire of fifty million inhabitants. The revolution of the Yugoslavs, the Czechs, and the Poles broke apart this economic sphere. Seven-eighths of our old economic area have since then been closed off to our products through high tariffs. In seven-eighths of the area, in which foreign competition had been previously held at bay by high tariffs, we now have to compete with foreign industries whose production sites are located nearer to the coal deposits and the sea than ours and whose productive machinery is more up to standard.

This is the problem of the German-Austrian economy: Will our industry still exist with the loss of seven-eighths of its tariff-protected market? Will our commerce and banking still be able to assert itself after the loss of its dominant position in the old greater economic area? Will we therefore still be able to feed the masses of our urban population whose previous existence was based on industry, trade, and banking?

The currency depreciation veiled this problem: it gave an exceptional export advantage to industry; the tension between the internal and external value of the krone gave commerce extraordinary opportunities; the fluctuations of the foreign-exchange rate gave the banks a fruitful field of activity. It was only with currency stabilization that the real problem of the German-Austrian economy has been revealed. Only now will we see which branches of our industry, our commerce, and our banking are really viable after the loss of their old dominant position in a large tariff-protected economic area and which ones are condemned to shrink and degenerate. It will only now become apparent to what extent our industry's unfavorable situation and conditions of production can be compensated by lower wages for workers and employees and a lower standard of living for the masses, that is, by cultural regression, and whether industry can stand up to free competition—no longer modified by tariffs as it was up to autumn 1918 or by the currency depreciation, as it was up to autumn 1922, with industries working under more favorable conditions of production. Only now will we see what part of our urban population will no longer be able to find jobs and a livelihood in their homeland due to industrial regression and what portion of our workers and employees will only be able to find jobs and a livelihood in our industry at the price of accepting a lower standard of living, that is, staying at a lower cultural level than the workers and employees of other countries producing under better conditions. The problem of our national economy—the extent to which we are able to occupy our working masses at all, and the extent to which we can do so under tolerable conditions, in other words the extent to which we are condemned to industrial and cultural regression—is not only *not* being solved by the Geneva protocols, that is, by merely putting our finances and our currency in order, but is being laid bare for the first time.

The cause of our national economy's sickness is the fact that an industrial organism adapted to an economic area with fifty million inhabitants has been crammed into an economic area with six million inhabitants. The currency depreciation was only a symptom of this sickness. But the masses, having suffered for four long years from its consequences, took the symptom for the sickness itself. They willingly submitted to the painful operation to remove the symptom, believing this would cure the illness. They are now gradually discovering that Geneva is not a cure for the disease but only one of its symptoms, that it is only substituting some phenomenal forms of the illness in the place of another, that is, unemployment, wage depression, and industrial and cultural regression in the place of currency depreciation. As disillusionment with the effects of the operation spreads, a rebellion against the operation and methods of operation is growing. There is a growing resistance of the masses to the restructuring methods, which mend state finances at the cost of the economy, shift all the burdens of the reconstruction onto the broad popular masses while anxiously sparing the owning classes, and elevate every wish of international high finance to the status of an inviolable law for us. We will see a growing resistance of national self-consciousness to foreign domination—suppressed for the sake of financial reconstruction—as well as cultural resistance (repressed for the same reason) to the rule of the reactionary, clerical petty bourgeoisie.

The immediate task that Social Democracy has to confront in the transitional period is to make this growing dissatisfaction politically effective; to gather together the masses of white-collar employees and small tradesmen affected by the economic crisis, the officials threatened by the reduction of the public sector, the intellectuals rebelling against foreign domination, and to rally all of them around the working class on whom the full brunt of the blow has fallen; to facilitate the growth of public opinion opposed to reaction. And through these means it must aim at unsettling and finally overthrowing the bourgeois government, reconquering effective control of the working class over administration, thus preventing the bourgeois government from using its power for the gradual, systematic dismantling of the proletariat's key instruments of power.

If the bourgeoisie is trying to gradually chip away at the proletariat's instruments of power rather than smashing them by force, then this struggle has to be conducted not with the weapons of civil war but on the soil of democracy, with the weapons of democracy. The task in this battle is thus not to bash heads but to win minds. Above all, we need to bring the proletariat's organizations through the industrial crisis unweakened and unshaken. It is in times of crisis that the strength of proletarian organizations proves itself in the unshakable conviction, great capacity for self-sacrifice, and indomitable tenacity of its members. And then we must bring the small peasants and landless laborers and the white-collar employees and officials together in our front. We will be able to win them over more easily the more clearly we define the immediate objective of struggle. We will win over many who in their hopes for Geneva have thrown themselves into the arms of reaction if we are able to make it clear to them that we are not fighting against the bringing of order into state finances but the misuse of this process to erect the political rule of reaction and the economic rule of the bankocracy; if to the restoration of the bourgeoisie we oppose the ideas of the people's republic, which have appeal precisely for these middle strata and in which no class dominates the others but all classes have a proportionate share in state power.

Elections are one of the democratic instruments for translating the potential energy of the popular masses coming together in this way against the restoration of the bourgeoisie. If in the next National Council elections the reaction succeeds in winning just a few seats from us, they will have a two-thirds majority in parliament. Then they can change the procedural rules of the National Council in such a way that we can no longer obstruct their unhampered rule. Then they will have gained the time they need to systematically chip away at our most important power bases outside parliament. Conversely, if we gain seats at the cost of the bourgeois majority, then the reactionary government will be unsustainable; it will then collapse and there will be no more threat to our extra-parliamentary bases, which still obstruct the complete restoration of the bourgeoisie.

If the reactionary regime can be toppled, then perhaps we will again face the problem of whether we can and should make our parliamentary and extra-parliamentary power fully effective through participation in the government. It is by no means certain that this question will present itself. The experience of the two years from October 1920 to October 1922 has shown that in the face of weak bourgeois governments, a strong proletariat can maintain an equilibrium of class forces without having to directly participate in government. But at a time when the self-confidence of the bourgeoisie, its parties, and its government is considerably strengthened, when the government has become significantly stronger for being propped up by the foreign General Commissioner and thanks to the extraordinary powers it has gained through the Geneva protocols, a situation can arise in which we cannot overthrow the regime of bourgeois restoration if we are not prepared to replace it by a coalition government with our participation, a situation in which we cannot prevent the gradual chipping away at the proletariat's most important power bases if we do not achieve direct participation in government power and direct control of the state administration.

Not only the experiences of the Russian, German, and Czech revolutions but also our own experience in 1920 have clearly demonstrated the serious dangers of a coalition between Social Democracy and the bourgeois parties. These dangers would be much greater at a time when the freedom of movement of the government is constrained by international financial control, in which the possibilities for Social Democracy to act in the government would be significantly limited by the reinforced power consciousness of the bourgeoisie, in which the industrial crisis and mass unemployment would pose especially difficult tasks for a government in which Social Democrats participated. On the other hand, the experiences of August and September 1922, the time of the negotiations in Verona and Geneva, have shown what a huge source of power access to government power can be even in the face of a strong proletariat, how the bourgeoisie, when it has sole possession of government power, can use it to suddenly confront the proletariat with faits accomplis that shift power relations substantially in its favor, which the proletariat cannot undo. Social Democracy can therefore neither strive for a coalition government under any circumstances nor reject one under any circumstances. It is the concrete historical situation giving rise to such a coalition government and the specific historical conditions under which it is formed and functions that determines whether coalition government can be an appropriate and effective instrument in the class struggle.

The first coalition government in 1919 was the political instrument by means of which the working class exercised its hegemony. As soon as the backlash to the international revolution set in, as soon as economic upheaval and social restructuring in Austria unsettled even this hegemony, the coalition government was at first paralyzed by the class antagonisms at its core and finally blown apart by the sharpening of these antagonisms.

Since October 1920, government power has remained in the hands of the bourgeoisie. From 1920 to 1922, the bourgeoisie repeatedly offered us a new coalition. We always refused it for two good reasons.

The leading problem at that time was the currency depreciation. We could not enter government without having a possibility of putting a stop to the currency depreciation with *our own* means. *Our* means for stabilizing the krone were the requisitioning of foreign currency stocks, a compulsory loan adjusted for inflation, requisitioning of bonus shares, and compulsory industrial cartels as tax-farming institutions.* But we could not undertake such energetic interventions into property rights in the whole time from the summer of 1920 to the summer of 1922 even in a coalition government; the bourgeoisie's resistance had already become too strong. Thus coalition government was not a usable instrument to accomplish the positive task that needed to be accomplished at that time.

Coalition government at that point thus could only be a means to defend the power bases already conquered by the working class. But for this purpose we did not need a coalition. In the face of this period's weak bourgeois governments, we could defend the working class's power bases without having to participate in government.

---

* Zwangsverbände der Industrie als Steuergesellschaften.

In August 1922, for the first time, the currency catastrophe created a situation that gave the bourgeoisie no choice but to submit to our finance-policy demands. Only in this moment could the entry of Social Democracy into the government serve a positive purpose and acquire a positive meaning. We declared we were ready to form an all-parties government. But at the very last minute the bourgeoisie succeeded in obtaining the help of foreign capital and thus escaped the need to capitulate to our finance-policy demands.

Since then, the leading group of the bourgeoisie represented by Seipel has emphatically and bluntly rejected any coalition with Social Democracy. It wants to remain in sole possession of government power, which has been greatly strengthened by the Geneva protocols, because only by so doing can it gradually and systematically erode the power bases of the working class and finally completely defeat it with the help of heavily armed paramilitary organizations, an upgraded Technical Emergency Relief, and an army that has become reactionary.

In this essentially changed situation, the next task of the working class is to overthrow this regime of bourgeois restoration; after doing so it may become necessary to replace it with a coalition government of Social Democracy with one or the other bourgeois party. This would be a completely different kind of coalition government than that of 1919. While the 1919 coalition government, a government at the point of highest revolutionary tension, was an instrument of the working class's hegemony, a new coalition government, that of the transitional period, would only be an instrument for the proletariat's defense, an instrument of the working class to retain its endangered extra-parliamentary power bases and prevent the degeneration of the people's republic into a bourgeois republic. If we could maintain the equilibrium of class forces from 1920 to 1922 without having to participate in government, there may now be a situation in which we have to take direct part in a government strengthened by the Geneva protocols if we want to prevent the absolute class rule of the bourgeoisie.

But even in the significantly changed situation due to the effects of the Geneva protocols, Social Democracy should not unconditionally enter government at any given moment. Our entry into a coalition government must now also be tied to two preconditions.

Social Democracy can only participate in government as the delegate, as the trustee of the proletariat; it cannot govern against the will of the proletariat over the proletariat. If it has government power, it may only lead the masses of the proletariat by moral/intellectual means,[2] not keep it down by force. Therefore the first condition for Social Democracy's participation in a coalition government is that the overwhelming majority of the working class wants it. In 1920 we had to leave the government because the broad masses of workers were disillusioned and rejected it. Now too we may enter government only if the broad masses of workers are convinced that we cannot leave the now greatly strengthened power of government to the bourgeoisie alone unless we want to see our most important instruments of power systematically undermined and gradually dismantled. We can thus only enter a coalition government now if the great majority of the working class understands that it is, if not an instrument for the hegemony of the working class, an instrument for the restoration of the equilibrium of class forces, that even if it does not establish essential new achievements but only maintains and salvages the endangered achievements of the past revolutionary period, it can be an indispensable tool in the working class's defensive struggle.

Social Democracy can only participate in a coalition government if participation brings not the mere appearance of power but real power. If the coalition government were only the result of an accidental combination, then it would give us the mere appearance of power. For as long as the bourgeoisie is in a position to govern the Republic without us and against us, they will not buy our government participation with significant concessions, by conceding real power. Only if the coalition government is the final result of our energetic struggle against the bourgeoisie's government, only if this struggle has filled broad sections of the bourgeoisie with the conviction that it is no longer able to govern the state without us and against us, or at least that it cannot do so without the greatest difficulties and running the most serious risks—only then will the bourgeoisie have to purchase our government participation with significant concessions, by conceding real power. And only then, and not before, will a coalition government be an effective means for the working class's defensive struggle.

Consequently, the second condition of our entry in a coalition government is that such a government is not a mere parliamentary combination but the end result of an energetically, passionately, and tenaciously conducted class struggle, not the result of a parliamentary intrigue but the expression of a real shift in the relations of class power, not a mere configuration of parties but the expression of the restored equilibrium of class forces. Only under these conditions does a coalition government express the result of the class struggle rather than its forswearing; only under these conditions is it a means to carrying it out and stabilizing its results rather than suspending it, and only under these conditions is it the expression of the real temporary relation of forces between the contending classes rather than an illusory resolution of class antagonisms.

At present these conditions for Social Democracy's entry into a coalition government do not exist. They may perhaps be created in the course of the evolution that has set in since the Geneva protocols, perhaps by the progressive shattering of the illusions fomented by it, through the continuous rebellion of ever broader sections of the population against the economic and finance policy of the regime of bourgeois restoration—but certainly not without our resolute struggle against this regime.

The Communists unconditionally reject any participation by a workers' party in a coalition government with bourgeois parties. But if we reject any coalition government at a time in which exclusive rule by the working class is impossible, then we would be voluntarily submitting to the exclusive reign of the bourgeoisie, giving the bourgeoisie carte blanche to systematically undermine and gradually crush the working class's most important power bases. By contrast, to many constituencies of bourgeois democracy a grouping of all parties in a common government appears to be a worthwhile goal in all circumstances, under all conditions. However, if Social Democrats enter a coalition or an all-parties government without exercising real power and being really able to serve the working class, it would only undermine the trust the working masses have in Social Democracy and destroy the class organization of the proletariat on which its power depends. We cannot allow ourselves to carry out a coalition policy such as Czech, and occasionally German, Social Democracy has done—a politics in which coalition only means the subordination of Social Democracy to a de facto bourgeois system of rule. However, we have to understand that maintaining the most important power bases of the proletariat can depend on whether we are able to create a situation at the right time—that is, before the bourgeoisie seizes these power bases—in which the bourgeoisie is forced to concede a share of real power to us and give back the power bases they are threatening.

The struggle we must wage is for class power. The realization of class interests depends on class power; in particular it depends on the proportion in which the different classes will have to pay the costs of financial restructuring. But it is not about power and interests alone. As in every great class struggle, this struggle for class power and class interests involves a struggle between two different types of state, social, cultural, and intellectual life represented by the contending classes.

As long as the state has no violent means of defeating proletarian mass movements, it must repeatedly seek the consent of the masses, their voluntary agreement based on their own sense of things. It can only do so by exercising moral/intellectual leadership, which it no longer needs as soon as it has access to violent means of repressing and defeating the masses. The violent means then substitute for moral/intellectual leadership. As long as the state can only lead the masses by consensus, it needs the mediation of organizations; this function makes the organizations into state organs and co-rulers at the same time. As soon as the state can hold down the masses by violent means, it no longer needs the mediation of the organizations. The initiatives for developing a functional democracy spawned by the Revolution then atrophy; the state falls back to the level of a purely parliamentary democracy. As long as the state does not possess violent means for repressing the proletariat, democracy is the real self-government of the totality of the people. As soon as the state has sufficient means for repressing the proletariat, the bourgeoisie can rule the proletariat unimpeded if the elections give it a majority in the Republic's parliament; democracy is then transformed into a mere form of the bourgeoisie's class rule. This is what the struggle is about: it is a struggle between the *moral/intellectual and violent means of governance*; between *functional* and merely *parliamentary* democracy as methods of governance; between democracy as the real self-government of the *totality of the people* and democracy as a mere form of *class rule*.

The whole attitude of the working masses toward the state depends on the result of this struggle. Up to the Revolution of 1918, the state was a foreign, hostile force in relation to the working masses. With the Revolution of 1918, the working class suddenly became the pillar of the state idea. The will to maintain and protect the Republic was the powerful motivation behind the self-discipline, the self-mastery of the working masses in the times of famine and upheaval of 1919 and 1920. Republican enthusiasm raised the working class to the level of champion of the Republic's defense in the 1921 Burgenland crisis. The resolve to save the Republic was the source of the proletariat's self-sacrifice in the finance-policy struggles of 1922.

And with its relationship to the state, the working class's relationship to the nation has also changed. Up to the Revolution of 1918, the working class was the mortal enemy of national policy whose content was the maintenance of the rule of the German-Austrian bourgeoisie and bureaucracy over the other nations of the Habsburg Monarchy. Through the Revolution of 1918 the working class became the pillar of national policy whose content could now only be the right to self-determination of the German-Austrian people. The working class was the vehicle of this national idea in the struggle for annexation to Germany in 1918 and 1919, in the struggle for the Burgenland in 1921, in the struggle against German-Austria's subjugation under the foreign domination of international financial control in 1922.

But precisely with this subjugation, a devolution set in. If the state is transformed again into a class organization of the owning classes that forcibly represses the working class, then the working masses become alienated again from the state and begin to see it as a foreign and hostile force. If the nation is reorganized as the organization of the owning class's domination, then the forcibly repressed working class inevitably comes into sharp conflict with the idea of nation. The question, as seen from the point of view of the working class, of whether it should co-rule, co-lead the state, or be ruled by the bourgeoisie (which rules the state and constitutes itself as the nation) is tantamount to the question, seen from the point of view of the state and the nation, of whether state and nation morally/intellectually integrate the working masses, upon whose labor all state organization and all national cultural life rest, or state and nation are reduced again to a collection of organizations of the owning classes that forcibly dominates the working masses—who once again become mere subjects of the state, mere serfs of the nation—and therefore forgo the ideological integration of the broad working masses.

This is the problem in terms of state, nation, and culture posed by the transitional period in which we are living. But if our first task is to clearly determine possible and achievable objectives in this period and to adjust our methods of struggle to its conditions, then despite all of this we must still remain aware that the goals of the transitional period are temporary, transitional goals; that the slogans of the transitional period are only transitional ones; that our tasks will become essentially different and larger once the transitional period comes to an end, when the currently interrupted revolutionary process sets in once again; that the unstable equilibrium of Europe's state and economic order that emerged from the war can be annulled sooner than we imagine by events that introduce a new revolutionary period.

During the current transitional period, our national existence is circumscribed by the Treaty of Saint-Germain and the Geneva protocols. At this time we can only defend the remains of our national independence within these limitations and not beyond them. But if new revolutionary convulsions in Europe tear up the peace treaties of Versailles, Saint-Germain, and Riga and crack open the state systems based on them, if the internal structure of the Czechoslovak Republic and the Yugoslav Kingdom falls into severe crisis and the permanent latent danger of war in the whole area of the Habsburg Empire once again becomes acute, then the problem of our national existence will appear again in the way it did in 1918. Since the Geneva protocols do not solve the problem of our independent national existence, since the mere putting in order of our state finances not only does not resolve the question of our economic existence but poses it for the first time, the Austrian economy, which arose under the conditions of an Empire of fifty million people, will in any European crisis attempt to burst the bounds of the all too narrow framework of the smaller Austrian economic area. In any European crisis we will again face the problem of 1918: supranational federation of the Danubian peoples or national unity of the Germans; restoration of the Habsburg Monarchy or annexation to the German Republic.

In the transitional period the people's republic, in which no class dominates the other but power is shared among all classes in the nation, is the only possible, the only achievable goal of our struggles. But the people's republic is not the annulment of class antagonisms, not the end of class struggles, for class antagonisms cannot be annulled as long as the capitalist social order exists, and class struggles cannot end as long as the people remain divided in classes with mutually antagonistic interests and ideals. The people's republic is nothing but an expression of the temporary equilibrium between class forces—an equilibrium that is continuously in danger of being upturned by the class struggles that continue to be conducted within it. However, when major new convulsions in Europe push the class war between capital and labor toward a major new decisive battle, then the equilibrium of class forces will be transcended in Austria as well; then here too the choice will only be between the counterrevolution of the bourgeoisie and the revolution of the proletariat, between capitalism and socialism.

We must avoid two equally disastrous errors: that of the Communists who would assign the working class in the transitional period tasks that will only be solvable in a new revolutionary period, thus confusing the present with the future; and that of the petty bourgeois democrats who take the people's republic (which is only a transitional form of a transitional period) to be the arrival point of a development beyond which no new revolutionary periods can lead, thus confounding the future with the present.

Humanity had to pass from feudalism to capitalism through a series of successive revolutionary processes, each of which created transitional forms of state and social life and which in turn were only overcome by the following revolutionary process and supplanted by higher transitional forms, until eventually the path from the pure feudal state of the thirteenth century to the pure capitalist state of the nineteenth century was plotted. And so humanity will have to pass through a long series of revolutionary processes on its path from capitalism to socialism, working its way through a long chain of state and social transitional forms.

The 1918 Revolution was a revolutionary process of this kind, one of many that must follow one another. The revolution that destroyed the old Habsburg Empire was not our revolution, not the revolution of the German-Austrian proletariat, but the revolution of the Czech, the Yugoslav, and the Polish bourgeoisie. However, the Austrian proletariat used this revolution to destroy the authoritarian absolutist state on its own soil and to enormously expand its power in the state, in the provinces and the municipalities, in the barracks, the offices and schools, in the factory, the workshop, and the manors.

The result was the people's republic, a transitional phase of social life still based on the capitalist economic order but which keeps capitalist economic life under the control of a state no longer ruled solely by the ruling classes of capitalist society; a transitional phase of state life in which the state is no longer dominated by the bourgeoisie alone and cannot yet be dominated by the proletariat alone, in which the state is no longer an instrument of the bourgeoisie for repressing the proletariat and still not an instrument of the proletariat for overcoming the bourgeoisie's economic domination.

The Revolution of 1918 has come to an end. For the present, the task of the working class is limited to defending the achievements of this revolution against bourgeois reaction, to restoring and holding on to the transitional phase of state that it produced. But as soon as the problems unsolved by the 1918 Revolution, and still crying out for a solution, introduce a new revolutionary process, the state and social transitional phase that emerged from that Revolution will be disrupted and a new revolution will stormily lead to the next and higher transitional phase. Thus, the working class has to pass through a chain of revolutions and after each revolutionary phase defend the transitional form of state and social life that emerges from it against backlashes until a new period of revolutionary turbulence enables it to further develop the transitional form that arose from the previous form to reach a new, higher transitional form.

In this way the working class must keep climbing to new, always higher forms of state and social life, continually new phases in the world-historical process of the transformation of capitalist society into socialist society, until the goal is finally reached: socialist society. In this revolutionary process the idea of the people's republic that was produced by the 1918 revolution is realized and completed. For if the people's republic today can only be the expression of a temporary equilibrium between the forces of the contending classes that must be continually transcended by class struggle, then it only has its consummation in socialist society, which transcends the private ownership of the means of production and the division of society into classes, and thus class antagonism and class struggle, and in so doing arrives at the human community that is no longer torn into antagonistic classes.

WORKS CONSULTED BY BAUER

Details have been completed and published English translations cited.

Part I: War and Revolution

Chapter 1: The Southern Slavs and the War

Leopold von Ranke, *Die serbische Revolution—aus serbischen Papieren und Mitteilungen*, 2d ed. Berlin: Duncker & Humblot, 1844.

Stojan Novaković, *Die Wiedergeburt des serbischen Staates (1804–1813)*. Sarajevo: Institut für Balkanforschung, 1912.

R. W. Seton-Watson, *Die südslawische Frage im Habsburgerreich*. Berlin: Meyer & Jessen, 1913.

———. *The Southern Slav Question and the Habsburg Monarchy*. London: Constable, 1911. [Classic Reprint Series, 2015]

L[eo] v[on] Südland (pseudonym of Ivo Pilar), *Die südslawische Frage und der Weltkrieg. Übersichtliche Darstellung des Gesamt-Problems*. Vienna: Manzsche K.u.K Hof-, Verlags- und Universitätsbuchhandlung, 1918.

Hermann Wendel, *Aus dem südslawischen Risorgimento*. Gotha: Perthes, 1921.

Josef [Josip] Šuman, "Die Slowenen," in *Die Völker Österreich-Ungarns. Ethnographische und culturhistorische Schilderungen*, Zehnter Band and Erste Hälfte. Vienna: Prohaska, 1881.

August Dimitz, *Geschichte Krains von der ältesten Zeit bis auf das Jahr 1813: mit besonderer Rücksicht auf Culturentwicklung*. 4 volumes. Laibach [Ljubljana]: Kleinmayr & Bamberg, 1874–76.

Vladan Georgevic, *Das Ende der Obrenovitch. Beträge zur Geschichte Serbiens 1897–1900*. Leipzig: G. C. Röder, 1905.

Berthold Molden, *Alois Graf Aehrenthal. 6 Jahre äußere Politik Oesterreich-Ungarns*. Stuttgart: Deutsche Verl.-Anst., 1917.

Franz Conrad Von Hötzendorf, *Feldmarschall Conrad. Aus Meiner Dienstzeit. 1906–1918*. Vienna: Rikola-Verlag, 1921.

Otto Bauer, *Der Balkankrieg und die Deutsche Weltpolitik*. Berlin: Vorwärts, 1912.

Karl Kautsky, *Serbien und Belgien in der Geschichte. Historische Studien zur Frage der Nationa-*

litäten und der Kriegsziele. Stuttgart: Dietz, 1917.

Ferdo Šišić, *Dokumenti o postanku kraljevine Srba, Hrvata i Slovenaca 1914–1919*. Zagreb: Maticka hrvatska, 1920.

Franko Potočnjak, *Iz emigracije, Zagreb: Tiskara narodnin novina*. Zagreb: Tiskara narodnin novina, 1926.

Jovan N. Tomić, *Jugoslavija u emigraciji: pisma i beleške iz 1917*. Belgrade: Moderna Stampar. Vuk Karadžić, 1921.

Milan P. Djordjević, Србија и Југословени за време рата *1914–1918* [Srbija i jugosloveni za vreme rata 1914–1918]. Belgrade: Sveslovenska Knižara, 1922.

Chapter 2: The Czechs and the Empire

Otto Bauer, *Die Nationalitätenfrage und die Sozialdemokratie, in Marx-Studien. Blätter zur Theorie und Politik des Wissenschaftlichen Sozialismus,* Max Adler and Rudolf Hilferding, eds. Vienna: Verlag Wiener Volksbuchhandlung, 1924.

———. *The Question of Nationalities and Social Democracy,* trans. Joseph O'Donnell. Minneapolis: University of Minnesota Press, 2000.

Zdeněk Václav Tobolka, *Česká politika za světové války*. Prague: Tiskem Československého kompasu, 1922.

Karel Velemínsky, ed., *Masaryk osvoboditel: Sborník*. Prague: Sbornik, 1922. (Earlier edition published 1920)

Diplomatické dokumenty o čekoslovenském statú. Paris, 1918.

Ján Papánek, *La Tchécoslovaquie: Histoire juridique et politique de sa création*. Prague: Čin/ Orbis, 1923.

František Šteidler Vl, *Československé hnuti na Rusi*. Prague: Památnik Odboje, 1921.

Jaroslav Papoušek, *Zborov*. Prague: Čin, 1921.

(General) Jaroslav Červinka, *Cestou našeho odboje: Příspěvek k historii vývoje formací československého vojska na Rusi v roce 1914–1918*. Prague: F. Ždárský, 1920.

Vincenc Červinka, *Naši na Sibiři: Kapitoly vlastní a cizí*. Prague: Pražská akciová tiskárna, 1920.

Kratochvil Jaroslav, *Cesta revoluce: československé legie v Rusku*. Prague: Čin, 1922.

Radola Gajda, *Moja paměti*. Prague: Vesmír, 1920.

Nikolai Podvoisky, *Prawda o tschechoslowakach* [Правда о Чехословакии], Moscow, 1918.

Josef Logaj, *Československé legie v Italii (1915–1918)*. Prague: Památnik odboje, 1922.

Urteilsbegründung des k.k. Landwehrdivisionsgerichtes Wien gegen Kramář, Rašín und Genossen vom 3. Juni 1916 [Opinion of the Imperial Royal Landwehr Court in Vienna Against Kramář, Rašín, and Comrades, June 3, 1916].

Anklageschrift des k.k. Militärgerichts in Wien gegen Hajek, Dušek, Soukup und Genossen vom 2. August 1916 [Imperial Royal Military Tribunal, Indictment Brought Against Hajek, Dušek, Soukup, and Comrades, August 2, 1916].

Chapter 3: The Poles and the Central Powers

Wilhelm Feldman, *Geschichte der politischen Ideen in Polen seit dessen Teilungen (1795–1914)*. Munich: R. Oldenbourg, 1917.

Ludwig Bernhard, *Die Polenfrage. Der Nationalitätenkampf der Polen in Preußen*. Leipzig: Duncker & Humblot, 1910.

Rosa Luxemburg, *Die industrielle Entwicklung Polens*. Leipzig: Duncker & Humblot, 1898.

Michał Bobrzyński, *Wskrzeszenie Państwa Polskiego: szkic historyczny, T. 1: 1914–1918*. Kraków: Krakowska Spółka Wydawn, 1920.

Ignacy Juliusz Rosner, *W krytycznej chwili*. Vienna: Vernay, 1915.

Jędrzej Moraczewski, *Zarys sprawy polskiej w obecnej wojnie: rozmyślania polityczne na obecną porę*. Lausanne, 1915.

Ignacy Daszyński, *Cztery lata wojny: Szkice z dziejów polityki Polskiej Partyi Socyalno-Demokratycznej Galicyi i Śląska*. Kraków: Z. Klemensiewicz, 1918.

Anonymous, *Józef Pilsudski*. Warsaw, 1918.

Ottokar Graf Czernin von Chudenewitz, *Im Weltkriege*. Berlin and Vienna: Ullstein, 1919.

Edmund Glaise-Horstenau, *Die Zeit der Friedensschlüsse*, vol. 5 of *Der österreich-ungarische Krieg*, Max Schwarte, ed. Leipzig: Barth, 1922.

Chapter 4: German-Austria in the War

Karl Renner, *Österreichs Erneuerung. Politische-programmatische Aufsätze*. Vienna: Brand, 1916.

———. "Marxismus, Krieg und Internationale," in *Linke und Nation. Klassische Texte zu einer brisanten Frage*, Stefan Bollinger, ed. Vienna: Promedia-Verlag, 2009, 126–32.

———. *Das Selbstbestimmungsrecht der Nationen in besonderer Anwendung auf Österreich*. Leipzig: Deuticke, 1918.

Friedrich Adler, *Die Erneuerung der Internationale. Aufsätze aus der Kriegszeit*, Robert Danneberg, ed. Vienna: Ignaz Brand, 1918.

———. *Friedrich Adler vor dem Ausnahmegericht: Die Verhandlungen vor dem §-14-Gericht am 18. und 19. Mai 1917 nach dem stenographischen Protokoll*. Berlin: Paul Cassirer, 1919.

Denkschrift über die Rechts- und Arbeitsverhältnisse in den österreichischen Kriegsleistungsbetrieben (minutes of the "workers' day"). Vienna, 1916.

Gewerkschaftskommission Deutschösterreichs an den Gewerkschaftskongreß 1919, *Bericht Der Gewerkschaftskommission Deutschösterreichs an den Gewerkschaftskongreß … Protokolle der Verhandlungen vom VIII. österreichischen Gewerkschaftskongreß 1919*. Vienna: Verlag der Kammer für Arbeiter und Angestellte in Wien, 1919.

Klub der sozialdemokratischen Abgeordneten, ed., *Die Tätigkeit des Klubs der deutschen sozialdemokratischen Abgeordneten im österreichischen Reichsrat*, vol. 5. Vienna: Verlag der Wiener Volksbuchhandlung, 1917.

Protokoll der Verhandlungen des Parteitages der deutschen sozialdemokratischen Arbeiterpartei in Österreich. Vienna, 1917.

Edmund Glaise-Horstenau, "Österreich-Ungarns Politik in den Kriegsjahren 1914–1917," in

Der österreich-ungarische Krieg, vol. 5, Max Schwarte, ed. Leipzig: Barth, 1922.

Ottokar Graf Czernin von Chudenewitz, *Im Weltkriege*. Berlin and Vienna: Ullstein, 1919.

Otfried Nippold, "Heinrich Lammasch als Völkerrechtsgelehrter und Friedenspolitiker," in *Henrich Lammasch. Seine Aufzeichnungen, sein Wirken und seine Politik*, Heinrich Lammasch, Marga Lammasch, and Hans Sperl, eds. Vienna: Deuticke, 1922.

Um Friede, Freiheit und Recht! Der Jännerausstand des innerösterreichischen Proletariats. Vienna: Wiener Volksbuchhandlung Ignaz Brand, 1918.

"Ein Natonalitätenprogramm der 'Linken,'" *Der Kampf* XI, 4 (April 1918), 269–74.

Ongoing discussion of the Nationalities Program of the left throughout 1918 in *Der Kampf.*

Part II: The Overthrow

Chapter 5: The Formation of the National States

Karl Friedrich Nowak, *Der Sturz der Mittelmächte*. Munich: G. D. W. Callwey, 1921.

———. *The Collapse of Central Europe*. London: K. Paul, 1924.

Hugo Kerchnawe, *Der Zusammenbruch der österreichisch-ungarischen Wehrmacht im Herbst 1918*. Munich: J. F. Lehmanns Verlag, 1921.

Josef Redlich, "Heinrich Lammasch als Ministerpräsident," in *Henrich Lammasch. Seine Aufzeichnungen, sein Wirken und seine Politik*, Heinrich Lammasch, Marga Lammasch, and Hans Sperl, eds. Vienna and Leipzig: Deuticke, 1922.

Carl Friedrich Nowak, *Chaos*. Munich: Verlag für Kulturpolitik, 1923.

Graf Julius Andrássy, *Diplomatie und Weltkrieg*. Vienna: Ullstein, 1920.

Stenographische Protokolle über die Sitzungen der Provisorischen Nationalversammlung für Deutschösterreich, 1918 und 1919. I. Band: 1. (Eröffnungs-) bis 18. Sitzung. Vienna: Deutschösterreichische Staatsdruckerei, 1919.

Alois Rašín, "Převrat z 28. Října 1918," in *Maffie: tajná činnost několika českých vlastenců za války světové* (reprinted from the *Národní Listy* of 28. X. 1919). Prague: Nákladem "Národa," 1919, 5–23.

[Josef] Scheiner, "Vojenský převrat v Praze," in *Maffie: tajná činnost několika českých vlastenců za války světové*. Prague: Nákladem "Národa," 1919, 28–39. (Reprinted from the *Národní Listy* of October 28, 1919.)

Frant[išek] Soukup and Al[ois] Rašín, "Národní výbor a 28. Říjen," in *Národní shromáždění v prvním roce republiky—Ročenka Národního shromáždění československého* 1, v. Praze: Předsednictvo Národního shromáždění, 1919, 18–47.

Walther Tschuppik, *Die tschechische Revolution*. Leipzig: Tal, 1920.

Ferdo Šišić, *Dokumenti o postanku kraljevine Srba, Hrvata i Slovenaca 1914–1919*. Zagreb: Maticka hrvatska, 1920.

Chapter 6: The Dissolution of the Empire

Oszkár Jászi, *Magyariens Schuld, Ungarns Sühne: Revolution und Gegenrevolution in Ungarn.*

Munich: Verl. für Kulturpolitik, 1923.

Lajos Hatvany, *Das verwundete Land*. Leipzig: Tal, 1921.

Béla Szántó, *Klassenkämpfe und Diktatur des Proletariats in Ungarn*. Berlin: Schwarz, 1920.

Carl Friedrich Nowak, *Der Weg zur Katastrophe*. Berlin: Reiss, 1919.

Karl Friedrich Nowak, *Der Sturz der Mittelmächte*. Munich: G. D. W. Callwey, 1921.

———. *The Collapse of Central Europe*. London: K. Paul, 1924.

August von Cramon, *Unser österreichisch-ungarischer Bundesgenosse im Weltkriege. Erinnerungen aus meiner vierjährigen Tätigkeit als Bevollmächtigter Deutscher General beim k.u.k. Armeeoberkommando*. Berlin: Siegfried Mittler, 1920.

Hugo Kerchnawe, *Der Zusammenbruch der österreichisch-ungarischen Wehrmacht im Herbst 1918*. Munich: J. F. Lehmanns Verlag, 1921.

Ernst Horsetzky, *Die vier letzten Kriegswochen (24. Oktober bis 21. November 1918)*. Vienna: Harbauer, 1920.

Edmund Glaise-Horstenau, "Der Zusammenbruch," in *Der österreichisch-ungarische Krieg*, vol. 5, Max Schwarte, ed. Leipzig: Barth, 1922.

Carl Friedrich Nowak, *Chaos*. Munich: Verlag für Kulturpolitik, 1923.

"Berichte der Kommission zur Erhebung militärischer Pflichtverletzungen im Kriege" [Reports of the Inquiry Commission on Breaches of Military Duty During the War], in *Beilagen zu den stenographischen Protokollen der Konstituierenden Nationalversammlung der Republik Österreich, 1920*, vol. VI (containing Supplements 918–1034). Vienna: Österreichische Staatsdruckerei, 1920, Beilage 974.

Fritz Rager, *Warum hat Österreich-Ungarn den Krieg verloren?* Vienna: Vorwärts, 1920.

Chapter 7: The German-Austrian Republic

Julius Deutsch, *Aus Österreichs Revolution. Militärpolitische Erinnerungen*. Vienna: Wiener Volksbuchhandlung, 1920.

Otto Bauer, *Die Offiziere und die Republik. Ein Vortrag über die Wehrpolitik der Sozialdemokratie*. Vienna: Wiener Volksbuchhandlung, 1921.

———. "Der deutschösterreichische Staat," *Arbeiter-Zeitung*, October 13, 1918; "Selbstbestimmungsrecht und Wirtschaftsgebiet," *Arbeiter-Zeitung*, October 15, 1918; "Deutschland und wir," *Arbeiter-Zeitung*, October 16, 1918; "Das neue Europa," *Arbeiter-Zeitung*, October 17, 1918.

Friedrich Adler, *Nach zwei Jahren. Reden gehalten im November 1918*. Vienna: Brand, 1918.

Hans Kelsen, *Die Verfassungsgesetze der Republik Deutschösterreich: mit einer historischen Übersicht und kritischen Erläuterungen*, 1. Teil. Vienna: Deuticke, 1920.

———. Matthias Jestaedt, ed., *Hans-Kelsen-Werke*, vol. 5: *Veröffentlichte Schriften 1919–1920*. Tübingen: Mohr Siebeck, 2011.

Robert Freißler, *Vom Zerfall Österreichs bis zum tschechoslowakischen Staate. Eine historisch-politische Studie mit besonderer Berücksichtigung der Verhältnisse in Schlesien, Nordmähren und Ostböhmen*. Sopot: Hela-Verlag, 1921.

Rudolf Granichstädten-Czerva, *Tirol und die Revolution*. Innsbruck: Tirolia, 1920.

Chapter 8: National and Social Revolution

Josef Redlich, *Das österreichische Staats- und Reichsproblem: Geschichtliche Darstellung der inneren Politik der Habsburgischen Monarchie von 1848 bis zum Untergang des Reiches: 1: Der dynastische Reichsgedanke und die Entfaltung des Problems bis zur Verkündigung der Reichsverfassung von 1861, 1: Darstellung*. Leipzig: Der Neue-Geist-Verl., 1920.

Friedrich Freiherr von Wieser, *Österreichs Ende*. Männer und Völker No. 23. Berlin: Ullstein, 1919.

Karl Kautsky, *Habsburgs Glück und Ende*. Berlin: Cassirer, 1918.

Karl Marx, *Herr Vogt* (1860), in Karl Marx and Frederick Engels, *Collected Works*, vol. 17. New York: International, 1981, 21–327.

Friedrich Engels, *The Role of Force in History*, in Karl Marx and Frederick Engels, *Collected Works*, vol. 26. New York: International, 1990, 453–511.

Friedrich Schulze (pseudonym of Otto Bauer), "Marx oder Radetzky?" *Der Kampf* XI, 6 (June 1918), 361–83.

Part III: The Hegemony of the Working Class

Chapter 9: Revolutionary and Counterrevolutionary Forces

Staatsamt für Land- und Forstwirtschaft, ed. *Anbaufläche und Ernteergebnisse in der Republik Österreich im Jahre 1918*. Vienna: Österreichische Staatsdruckerei, 1919.

Staatsamt für Volksernährung, ed., *Der Bedarf Deutschösterreichs an wichtigeren Nahrungs- und Futtermitteln*. Vienna, 1919.

Niederösterreichische Handels- und Gewerbekammer, ed., *Bericht der Niederösterreichischen Handels- und Gewerbekammer über die Jahre 1914 bis 1918*. Vienna, 1920.

Berichte der Staatsregierung in der Sitzung der Provisorischen Nationalversammlung am 4. December 1918.

Zentral-Gewerbe-Inspektorat, ed., *Bericht der Gewerbeinspektoren über ihre Amtstätigkeit im Jahre 1919*. Vienna: Verlag des Zentral-Gewerbe-Inspektorates, 1920.

August Böhm, "Die sanitäre Lage der Stadt Wien." *Statistische Monatsschrift* II, 3 (1920), 14–17.

Paul [Pál] Pal Szende, *Die Krise der mitteleuropäischen Revolution*. Tübingen: Mohr, 1921.

Julius Braunthal, *Die Arbeiterräte in Deutschösterreich. Die Beratungen und Beschlüsse der II. Reichskonferenz. Das Organisationsstatut*. Vienna: Verlag der Wiener Volksbuchhandlung Ignaz Brand & Co., 1919.

Alexander Täubler, "Wesen und Mission der Räte." *Der Kampf* XII, 10 (June 7, 1919), 349–54.

Discussion of workers' councils at the 1919 party congress. *Protocoll der Verhandlungen des Parteitages der Sozialdemokratischen Arbeiterpartei Deutschösterreichs. Abgehalten in Wien vom 31. Oktober bis zum 3. November 1919*. Vienna: Verlag Wiener Volksbuchhandlung Brand, 1920.

Stenographisches Protokoll der Vereinigten Kommission für Kriegswirtschaft. Vienna, 1917.

Ludwig Mises, "Die politischen Beziehungen Wiens zu den Ländern." *Gesellschaft oesterreichischer Volkswirte Jahrbuch 1920.* Vienna: Fromme, 1920.

Die Wahlen für die Konstituierende Nationalversammlung [etc.], Beiträge zur Statistik der Republik Österreich I. Vienna, 1919.

Hans Kelsen, *Die Verfassung der Republik Deutschösterreich*, 3. Teil. Vienna: Deuticke, 1919.

Matthias Jestaedt, ed., *Hans-Kelsen-Werke*, vol. 5: *Veröffentlichte Schriften 1919–1920.* Tübingen: Mohr Siebeck, 2011.

Otto Bauer, *Protocoll der Verhandlungen des Parteitages der Sozialdemokratischen Arbeiterpartei Deutschösterreichs–abgehalten in Wien vom 5. bis zum 7. November 1920.* Vienna: "Vorwärts," 1920. [intervention concerning the government coalition]

Chapter 10: Between Imperialism and Bolshevism

André Tardieu, *La paix.* Paris: Payot, 1921.

Robert Lansing, *The Peace Negotiations: A Personal Narrative.* Boston: Houghton Mifflin, 1921.

Francesco Nitti, *Das friedlose Europa.* Frankfurt a.M.: Societäts-Dr., 1921.

———. *The Wreck of Europe.* Indianapolis, IN: Bobbs-Merrill, 1922.

John Maynard Keynes, *The Economic Consequences of the Peace* (Chapter III, The Conference). New York: Harcourt, Brace, and Howe, 1919.

Edvard Beneš and Karel Kramář, *Národní Shromáždění v prvním roce Republiky* [Report on the Peace Negotiations]. Prague 1919.

"Bericht über die Friedensverhandlungen." *Beilagen zu den stenographischen Protokollen der Konstituierenden Nationalversammlung der Republik Österreich, 1919*, vol. II, Beilage 379. Vienna: Österreichische Staatsdruckerei, 1919.

Otto Bauer, *Acht Monate auswärtiger Politik: Rede, Gehalten am 29. Juli 1919.* Vienna: Verlag Wiener Volksbuchhandlung, 1919.

Robert Freißler, *Vom Zerfall Österreichs bis zum tschechoslowakischen Staate. Eine historisch-politische Studie mit besonderer Berücksichtigung der Verhältnisse in Schlesien, Nordmähren und Ostböhmen.* Sopot, Berlin: Hela-Verlag, 1921.

Martin Wutte, *Kärntens Freiheitskampf.* Klagenfurt: Kleinmayr, 1922.

Ludwig Hülgerth, "Der Kärntner Freiheitskampf 1918–1919. Auf Grund amtlicher Schriftstücke und persönlicher Erinnerungen dargestellt vom Oberstleutnant Ludwig Hülgerth." *Carinthia. Mitteilungen des Geschichtsvereines für Kärnten* 111, 1–3 (1921), 11–28.

Endor, *Mémoire du Conseil d'État du Vorarlberg à la Societé des Nations.* Berne, 1920.

anonymous, *Enstehung und Zumsammenbruch der ungarischen Rätediktatur.* Sozialistische Bücherei 14. Vienna: Verlag Wiener Volksbuchhandlung, 1919.

Oszkár Jászi, *Magyariens Schuld, Ungarns Sühne: Revolution und Gegenrevolution in Ungarn.* Munich: Verl. für Kulturpolitik, 1923.

Béla Szántó, *Klassenkämpfe und die Diktatur des Proletariats in Ungarn*, with preface by Karl Radek. Vienna: Neue Erde, 1920.

Ernst Bettelheim, *Zur Krise der kommunistischen Partei Ungarns.* Vienna: Author, 1922.

Julius Braunthal, *Die Arbeiterräte in Deutschösterreich. Die Beratungen und Beschlüsse der II. Reichskonferenz. Das Organisationsstatut*. Vienna: Verlag der Wiener Volksbuchhandlung Ignaz Brand & Co., 1919.

———. *Kommunisten und Sozialdemokraten*, Sozialistische Bücherei No. 16. Vienna: Verlag Wiener Volksbuchhandlung, 1920.

Julius Deutsch, *Aus Österreichs Revolution. Militärpolitische Erinnerungen*. Vienna: Wiener Volksbuchhandlung, 1920.

"Dokumente zur Geschichte des 15. Junis." *Der Kampf* XII, 27 (October 4, 1919), 645–49.

Karl Radek, "Die Lehren eines Putschversuches." *Kommunistische Internationale II, 9*; also published as an appendix to Paul Levi, *Unser Weg. Wider dem Putschismus* (1921), and in *Die Rote Fahne* October 28–30, 1919 under the pseudonym Arnold Struthahn as "Die Krise in der deutschösterreichischen Kommunistischen Partei."

Chapter 11: The Revolution in the Factories

Julius Braunthal, *Die Sozialpolitik der Republik*. 12. November. No. 3. Vienna: Verlag Wiener Volksbuchhandlung, 1919.

Karl Pribram, "Die Sozialpolitik im neuen Österreich." *Archiv für Sozialwissenschaft und Sozialpolitik, Archiv für Sozialwissenschaft und Sozialpolitik*, 48 (1921).

Der erste Betriebsrätekongreß der Arbeiter und Angestellten der Metallindustrie: Protokoll der Verhandlungen. Vienna, 1921.

Zentral-Gewerbe-Inspektorat, ed., *Berichte der Gewerbeinspektoren über ihre Amtstätigkeit*. Vienna: Verlag des Zentral-Gewerbe-Inspektorate, 1920, 1921.

Jean Odon Niox Château, *Les conseils d'Entreprise et le contrôle ouvrier en Autriche*. Paris: Presses universitaires de France, 1923.

Otto Bauer, *Der Weg zum Sozialismus*. Vienna: Brand, 1919.

———. *Die Sozialisierungsaktion im ersten Jahre der Republik*. 12. November. No. 5. Vienna: Verlag Wiener Volksbuchhandlung, 1919.

Wilhelm Ellenbogen, *Sozialisierung in Österreich*. Vienna: Verlag Wiener Volksbuchhandlung, 1921.

———. *Die Fortschritte der Gemeinwirtschaft in Österreich*, Sozialistischer Aufbau. Schriften des Zentralverbandes für Gemeinwirtschaft No. 1. Vienna: Verlag Wiener Volksbuchhandlung, 1922.

Inge Debes, *Socialisering i Østerrike*. Socialisering No. 1 (utarbeidet etter opdrag fra den av Socialdepartementet nedsatte socialiseringskomite). Kristiania: Steenske Forlag, 1920.

Chapter 12: The State and the Working Class

Bericht der Parteivertretung der Sozialdemokratischen Arbeiterpartei Deutschösterreichs an den ausserordentlichen Parteitag in Wien, 1919. Vienna: Verlag des Sozialdemokratischen Parteisekretariats, 1920.

Bericht der Parteivertretung der Sozialdemokratischen Arbeiterpartei Deutschösterreichs an den ausserordentlichen Parteitag in Wien, November 1920. Vienna: Verlag des Sozialdemokratischen Parteisekretariats, 1920.

"Stärke und Leistungsfähigkeit der Gewerkschaften Deutschösterreichs im Jahre 1919." *Die*

Gewerkschaft, 1920.

On the settlement movement:
Otto Neurath, *Gildensozialismus, Klassenkampf, Vollsozialisierung*, Appendix: "Siedlungs-, Wohnungs- und Baugilde Österreichs." Dresden: Kaden & Company, 1922.
Wilhelm Ellenbogen, *Die Fortschritte der Gemeinwirtschaft in Österreich*. Sozialistischer Aufbau. Schriften des Zentralverbandes für Gemeinwirtschaft No. 1. Vienna: Verlag Wiener Volksbuchhandlung, 1922.

Otto Glöckel, *Ausführungen über den Stand der Schulreform in der Sitzung des Ausschusses für Erziehung und Unterricht*, April 22, July 23, and October 22, 1919, and February 12 and July 15, 1920. Vienna: Österreichische Staatsdruckerei.
———. *Schulreform und Volksbildung in der Republik*. Vienna: Verlag Wiener·Volksbuchhandlung Ignaz Brand, 1919.
Eduard Burger, "Bilanz der Glöckelschen Schulreform." *Monatshefte für pädagogische Reform*, 1920, 237ff.
Reinhold Lehmann, "Deutschösterreich bei Aufbau und Abbau." *Die Deutsche Schule* 26 (1922), 161–70.
Volkserziehung–Zeitschrift des Unterrichtsamtes. 1919 ff.

Part IV: The Period of Class Power Equilibrium

Chapter 13: Economic Transformation and Social Regrouping

Leon Trotsky, *Die neue Etappe. Die Weltlage und unsere Aufgaben*. Hamburg: Verlag der Kommunistischen Internationale, 1921.
———. *The First Five Years of the Communist International*, 2d ed., vol. I. New York: Pathfinder, 2009.

Friedrich Steiner, ed., *Die Währungsgesetzgebung der Sukzessionsstaaten Österreich-Ungarns. Eine Sammlung einschlägiger Gesetze, Verordnungen und behördlicher Verfügungen von 1892 bis 1920*. Vienna: Verband österreichischer Banken und Bankiers, 1921 (reprint Forgotten Books, 2018).
Moriz Dub, *Katastrophenhausse und Geldentwertung*. Finanz- und Volkswirtschaftliche Zeitfragen 65. Stuttgart: Ferdinand Enke, 1920.
Peter Hamp (pseudonym of Henri Bourillon). *Die Goldsucher von Wien. Eine Begebenheit unter Schiebern*. Basel: Rhein-Verlag, 1922.
Statistische Übersichten über den auswärtigen Handel. Vienna, 1920–22.
Unemployment statistics in *Amtliche Nachrichten des Bundesministeriums für soziale Verwaltung*.
Mortality statistics in *Statistischer Wochenbericht des Wiener Magistrats*.
Viktor Lebzelter, "Größe und Gewicht der Wiener Arbeiterjugend." *Mitteilungen des Volksgesundheitsamtes im Ministerium für Soziale Verwaltung—Organ des Obersten Sanitätsrates, der Landessanitätsräte, der Niederösterreichischen und Tiroler Ärztekammer*, 1922, 399–401.

Friedrich Engels, "Der Anfang des Endes in Österreich." *Der Kampf* VI, 9 (1913), 393–97 (from *Deutsche Brüsseler-Zeitung* 8, 27 January 1848).

Arnold Madlé, "Die Besoldungsverhältnisse der österreichischen Staatsbeamten 1914 bis 1920." *Statistische Monatsschrift* 3. Folge, II. Jahrgang (1920), Supplement.

Karl Kraus, *Die letzten Tage der Menschheit. Tragödie in fünf Akten*. Vienna: Verlag Die Fackel, 1919.

———. *The Last Days of Mankind*. New Haven and London: Yale University Press, 2015.

Emil Alphons Rheinhardt, ed., *Die Botschaft: Neue Gedichte aus Österreich*. Vienna: Strache, 1920.

Karl Hans Strobl, *Gespenster im Sumpf: Ein phantastischer Wiener Roman*. Leipzig: Staackmann, 1920.

Rudolf Hans Bartsch, *Ein Landstreicher. Roman*. Vienna: Rikola-Verlag, 1921.

Thaddäus Rittner, *Geister in der Stadt. Roman*. Vienna: Rikola-Verlag, 1921.

Franz Werfel, *Bockgesang. In fünf Akten*. Munich: K. Wolff, 1921.

Othmar Spann, *Der wahre Staat: Vorlesungen über Abbruch und Neubau der Gesellschaft*. Leipzig: Quelle, 1921.

Ludwig von Mises, *Die Gemeinwirtschaft: Untersuchungen über den Sozialismus*. Jena: Fischer, 1922.

Albert Schäfer, *Sozialdemokratie und Landvolk*. Vienna: Verlag Wiener Volksbuchhandlung, 1920.

Chapter 14: *The Struggle for Republican Institutions*

Die Tätigkeit des Verbandes der sozialdemokratischen Abgeordneten in der Konstituierenden Nationalversammlung der Republik Deutschösterreich, 13. Heft der Gesamtausgabe (October 1919–July 1920). Vienna: Verlag Wiener Volksbuchhandlung, 1920.

Julius Deutsch, *Aus Österreichs Revolution. Militärpolitische Erinnerungen*. Vienna: Wiener Volksbuchhandlung, 1920.

Otto Leichter, "Die neue 'Linke,'" *Der Kampf* XII, 14 (July 5, 1919), 434–42.

Otto Bauer, "Die alte und neue Linke," *Der Kampf* XIII, 7 (July 1920), 249–60.

Franz Rothe, "Die Arbeitsgemeinschaft revolutionärer Sozialdemokraten Deutschösterreichs," *Der Kampf* XIII, 9 (September 1920), 326–35.

Friedrich Adler, Report to the Party Congress of the Social Democratic Workers' Party of German-Austria: "Die Partei, die Arbeiterräte und die Internationale," *Protokoll der Verhandlungen des Parteitages der sozialdemokratischen Arbeiterpartei Deutschösterreichs. Abgehalten in Wien vom 5. bis zum 7. November 1920*. Vienna: Verlag der Wiener Volksbuchhandlung, 1920, 178–84.

Hans Kelsen, *Die Verfassungsgesetze der Republik Deutschösterreich: Mit einer historischen Übersicht und kritischen Erläuterungen, 5. Teil: Die Bundesverfassung*. Vienna: Deuticke, 1922.

Robert Danneberg and Carl Leuthner, *Verfassung und Sozialdemokratie. Reden der Abgeordneten Robert Danneberg und Karl Leuthner [...] Anhang: 1. Das Bundes-Verfassungsgesetz. 2. Das Verfassungsgesetz betreffend den Übergang zur bundesstaatlichen Verfassung*. Vienna:

Wiener Volksbuchhandlung der Vorwärts, 1920.

"Statistik der Nationalratswahlen des Jahres 1920." *Beiträge zur Statistik der Republik*. Österreich 11 (1921).

Chapter 15: The Struggle against the Counterrevolution

Österreichisches Jahrbuch 1921.

Berichte der Parteivertretung der Sozialdemokratischen Arbeiterpartei Deutschösterreichs an die Parteitage 1921 und 1922.

Julius Deutsch, *Die Fascistengefahr*. Vienna: Verlag Wiener Volksbuchhandlung, 1923.

Otto Bauer, *Die Aufgaben der deutschen Sozialdemokratie in der tschechoslowakischen Republik*. Teplitz [Teplice]-Schönau: Druck- und Verlags-Anstalt, 1920.

République Tchécoslovaque—Ministère des Affaires Etrangères. *Documents diplomatiques concernant les tentatives de restauration des Habsbourg sur le trône de Hongrie*. Prague: Politika, 1922.

Carl Werkmann, *Der Tote auf Madeira*. Munich: Verlag für Kulturpolitik, 1923.

Victor Miltschinsky, *Das Verbrechen von Ödenburg*. Vienna: "Literaria," 1922.

Chapter 16: The People's Republic

Otto Bauer, Report to the Party Congress of the Social Democratic Workers' Party of German-Austria: "Die politische Lage und die Aufgaben der Sozialemokratie," *Protokoll der Verhandlungen des Parteitages der sozialdemokratischen Arbeiterpartei Deutschösterreichs. Abgehalten in Wien vom 5. bis zum 7. November 1920*. Vienna: Verlag der Wiener Volksbuchhandlung, 1920, 136–46.

Part V: The Restoration of the Bourgeoisie

Chapter 17: The Currency Catastrophe

Richard Schüller, "Wirtschaftliche Bestimmungen des Friedensvertrages von Saint-Germain." *Zeitschrift für Volkswirtschaft und Sozialpolitik*, Neue Folge 1 (1921), 34–43.

Gustav Stolper, *Deutschösterreich Als Sozial- und Wirtschafsproblem*. Munich: Drei Masken Verl, 1921.

Paul Grünwald-Ehren, "Grundzüge der Finanzpolitik der Nachfolgestaaten der österreich-ungarischen Monarchie." *Zeitschrift für Volkswirtschaft und Sozialpolitik*, Neue Folge 2 (1922), 428–88.

Hélène Bauer, "Theoretisches zur österreichischen Handelsbilanz," *Der Kampf* XVI, 1 (January 1923), 22–31.

Die Tätigkeit des Verbandes der Sozialdemokratischen Abgeordneten im Nationalrat der Republik Deutschösterreich (August 1921–September 1922), vol. 16 of the Gesamtausgabe, Vienna: Verlag der Wiener Volksbuchhandlung, 1922.

Mitteilungen des Bundesamtes für Statistik, Vienna, 1922.

Chapter 18: The Geneva Protocols

Société des Nations, *Reconstruction de l'Autriche, Accords préparé par la Société des Nations et signés à Genève le 4 octobre 1922 avec les Documents et Déclarations publiques y relatifs. C. 716, M. 428*, 1922.

Rapport de la Délégation provisoire de la Société des Nations à Vienne, soumis au Conseil le 1er février 1923 (contenant le résumé de la situation au 15 décembre 1922) (C./S. C. A. 17).

Karl Renner and Karl Seitz, *Die Schmach von Genf und die Republik: Reden der Abgeordneten Renner und Seitz in der Sitzung des Nationalrates am 12. Oktober 1922*. Vienna: Verlag Wiener Volksbuchhandlung, 1922.

Otto Bauer, *Der Genfer Knechtungsvertrag und die Sozialdemokratie. Rede*. Vienna: Verlag Wiener Volksbuchhandlung, 1922.

Robert Danneberg, *Der Finanzplan der Regierung Seipel. Wiederaufbau? Rede*. Vienna: Verlag Wiener Volksbuchhandlung, 1922.

Gustav Stolper, "Der Weg zur Rettung," "Die falsche Alternative," and "Die Genfer Protokolle," *Österreichischer Volkswirt*, August to October 1922.

Franz Schumacher, "Lammasch in St. Germain," in *Henrich Lammasch. Seine Aufzeichnungen, sein Wirken und seine Politik*, Heinrich Lammasch, Marga Lammasch, and Hans Sperl, eds. Vienna: Deuticke, 1922.

Anton Proksch [article unsigned], "Kurzarbeit und Arbeitslosigkeit," *Arbeit und Wirtschaft* 1921, no. 4, 128–33.

GLOSSARY

Agendorf: Old-Austrian name for Ágfalva in Hungary.

Agram: Old-Austrian name for Zagreb.

Altenburg: Old-Austrian name for Mosonomagyaróvár in present-day Hungary.

Aussig: Old-Austrian name for Ústí nad Labem in North Bohemia in the Czech Republic.

Austro-Hungarian Compromise: see Dualism.

Ban, banate: A noble title in South Slav areas, used under the Habsburgs for chief government officials. The frontier province governed by a ban was known as a banate.

Banat: Historic region in southeastern Europe, covering parts of contemporary Romania, Serbia, and a small corner of Hungary.

Bank, Austro-Hungarian and Austrian National: Founded in 1867 in the wake of the Austro-Hungarian Compromise, the Österreichisch-Ungarische Bank was established as the common central bank of the Dual Monarchy. It was only dissolved in 1922. Founded on July 24, 1922, the Österreichische Nationalbank replaced the Austro-Hungarian Bank.

Bey: A provincial governor in the Ottoman Empire.

Bohemian Crown, Right of: In the Bohemian territories of the Habsburg Monarchy in the late nineteenth century the idea of the historic rights of the Bohemian Crown was based on the concept of the continuous legal existence of the Bohemian Kingdom within the Habsburg Monarchy as mandated by the Bohemian Diet in 1831 and formulated by František Palacký in 1836 in the first volume of his *History of Bohemia.*

Böhmerwaldgau: Bohemian Forest Region.

Brünn: Old-Austrian name of Brno in the present-day Czech Republic.

Carniola: A duchy that became a Habsburg crownland in the fourteenth century. It is now almost entirely contained within Slovenia; a small part lies in Italy.

Český svaz: "Czech Union" or the Club of Czech Deputies in the Chamber of Deputies of the Austrian Parliament.

Chambers of Labor: The Kammer für Arbeiter und Angestellte, legally founded in 1920, are the statutorily established workforce representative institutions on the level of the federal states. Like the Chambers of Commerce they have the right to review legislative bills. Their task is to investigate and document social conditions. From the outset they have acted in close consultation with the trade unions, which were established as associations.

Christian Socials: Christian Social Party (in German: Christsozialen).

Cisleithania: "This side of the River Leitha." After Austria-Hungary was reconstructed as a Double Monarchy in 1867 in the framework of a state reform (the "Ausgleich" or Compromise) giving far-reaching autonomy to the Kingdom of Hungary, the northern and western parts of the Empire, which consisted of crownlands inhabited by German-speaking and Slav populations, were designated Cisleithania in contradistinction to Hungary (Transleithania), whose western border was defined by the river Leitha. After 1867, the Kingdom of Hungary, the Kingdom of Croatia, the Kingdom of Slavonia, and the Principality of Transylvania constituted Hungarian and no longer Austrian crownlands.

Curia parliament: The electoral system under which the Haus der Abgeordneten (Chamber of Deputies 1861–1918) operated until 1906. (The members of the Reichsrat's upper house, the Herrenhaus (House of Lords), were of course not elected.) It included 203 members elected by the provincial diets through census suffrage; Hungary and the Lombard-Venetian territories were not represented. Voters were divided into four *curiae* (Kurien), that is, status and wealth categories. The provincial diets elected the deputies they would send by taking account of these curiae. In 1873, direct election of the deputies (at that point numbering 353) was introduced, but the curia system was retained. Taaffe's 1882 reform set the minimum tax rate as a condition for voter eligibility. Badeni's 1896 constitutional reform, through further reduction of the minimum tax rate, added a fifth curia (a general male voter class based on a minimum of six months residency in one place). Beck's constitutional revision of 1906 abolished the curia parliament (not least due to the influence of the 1905 Russian Revolution) and introduced general, equal, direct, and secret suffrage for men (with the Chamber of Deputies now counting 516 members). For the Vienna Municipal Council, curia suffrage continued to exist until 1919.

Dahia: The leaders of the auxiliary Janissary troops in the Ottoman Empire.

Dualism: The system, also known as the Dual Monarchy, established by the Austro-Hungarian Compromise of 1867 and lasting until 1918, dividing the Austrian Empire into Austrian and Hungarian crownlands, united by a common foreign policy, a common army for international deployment, and whose monarchs were the same person: both Emperor of Austria and King of Hungary. Each half maintained its own parliament and domestic institutions. See Trialism.

Enterprises of common economic interest: See Gemeinwirtschaftliche Anstalten.

Federal Council: See National Council.

Fiume: Italian and Old-Austrian name of Rijeka in Croatia.

Five-gulden men: During his second term as prime minister of Austria, the conservative Eduard Taaffe introduced an electoral reform enacted in 1882, which broadened suffrage with the aim of breaking the Liberal hegemony in the lower chamber. The reduction of the tax base to five gulden required for men over age twenty-four to vote—although still divided into four *curiae* (see Curia parliament)—permitted the development of mass parties, thus benefitting Karl Lueger's right-wing populist party, but also the Social Democrats.

Gemeinde, Bezirk, Kreis, Land: The term *Kreis* refers to the units of the state structure prior to the Compromise of 1867. However, the Kreise continued to live on as the territorial units of judicial and military administration, similar to wards or counties in the United States or Britain. In fact, today's thirty-nine Wahlkreise (election districts) correspond to the old Kreise. Bezirk (district) was the lowest level of state administration, which replaced the Kreise; there were ninety-five (today seventy-nine) of them. *Gemeinde* are communes or municipalities. *Land/Länder* is the designation for the former German-speaking provinces of the Austrian Empire, which became the federal states of the First and Second Republics.

In the early Republic, in connection with the workers' councils, the Kreis level came into play when the movement was too weak at the district level; in that case the local councils were pooled together into a Kreis council.

Gemeinwirtschaftliche Anstalte: Enterprises of common economic interest. *Gemeinwirtschaftliche Anstalt* has no exact English equivalent. It refers to the public sector embracing public services as well as nationalized/socialized enterprises. In Austria *Gemeinwirtschaft* also applies to cooperatives, trade-union-owned housing enterprises, and so on. It covers non-profit economic entities.

After the end of the war and the collapse of the Empire, numerous military factories and enterprises producing war machinery passed into the possession of the Austrian state. Factories and material were in danger of being very cheaply acquired by private investors. In July 1919 the Constituent National Assembly passed the Law on Enterprises of Common Economic Interest establishing a special public-law status for these enterprises. The Social Democratic leadership—whose most important socialization project, the Alpine Montangesellschaft, failed due to domestic and foreign resistance—tried economically, in the framework of the market economy, to strengthen the enterprises of common economic interest through cooperation with district entities, especially the Municipality of Vienna, the consumer cooperatives, the trade unions, and with the Workers' Bank. At the same time, it experimented with forms of economic democracy. In this context the most important enterprises were Österreichische Werke, Fischamender Werke, Steirisches Fahrzeugwerk, Wiener Holzwerke, the Austrian Central Medical Dispensary (Heilmittelstelle), and others.

Their importance in the economy declined sharply during the course of the First Republic. In 1936 they were liquidated by the corporatist dictatorship for political and ideological reasons.

Gemischtwirtschaftliche Anstalte: Mixed-economy enterprises are forms that admit the participation of private capital in enterprises with elements of enterprises of common economic interest.

German-Nationals: (Deutschnationalen) The term indicates the German-National tendency, the German-National Movement, and the various associated parties representing the German-National outlook in the Austrian Empire from the late nineteenth century. In 1891 the Vereinigte Deutsche Linke formed itself into the Deutsche Nationalpartei, which lasted only until 1896 when it became the Deutsche Volkspartei. In 1907, for the first time, this and other similar groups, among them that of Georg Henirich Ritter von Schonerer, came together in a loose association, to become in 1910 the Deutscher Nationalverband. By the end of the war they had broken up into seventeen different groups. In 1919 the Grossdeutsche Volkspartei was formed.

Greater-German: See Pan-German.

Grosswardein: The Old-Austrian name for Oradea in present-day Romania.

Güns: Old-Austrian name of Kőszeg in present-day Hungary.

Heimwehr (Heimatwehr): (Heimatwehr in Tyrol) Home Guard. Reactionary, local paramilitary units.

Honvéd: Honvédség—Royal Hungarian Landwehr (the armed forces proper to Hungary within Austro-Hungary).

Illyrianism, Illyrian movement: The mid-nineteenth movement for unification of Slovenia, Croatia, and Dalmatia inspired by the liberal values instilled by the short-lived French-established Provinces of Illyria, 1809–13.

Isonzo: Soča in Slovenian. A river in western Slovenia and northeastern Italy, important here because of the Battles of the Isonzo, a series of twelve major battles between Austria-Hungary and Italy from June 1915 to November 1917.

Jugoslavenski Odbor: The Yugoslav Committee established in London on May 1, 1915 and led by Ante Trumbić.

Kaaden: Old-Austrian name for Kadaň in Northern Bohemia, present-day Czech Republic.

Kapp Putsch: Also known as the Kapp-Lüttwitz Putsch after its leaders Wolfgang Kapp and Walter von Lüttwitz, an attempted coup on March 13, 1920, supported by sections of the Reichswehr, in reaction to the German Revolution.

Karwin: Old-Austrian name for Karviná in the present-day Czech Republic.

Komitadji: Rebel bands operating in the Balkans during the final years of the Ottoman Empire.

Kreis: See Gemeinde.

k.u.k.: Kaiserlich und königlich, that is, imperial *and* royal. Before the Austro-Hungarian Compromise of 1867, the designation was "k.k." "And" indicated the Dualist structure, and thus the relative autonomy of the Hungarian crownlands when referring to the institutions jointly administered by both halves: the military and foreign affairs institutions. The personal union remained in effect, that is, the Emperor of Austria was also King of Hungary. The Emperor was referred to as "His Imperial *and* Royal Majesty." Within the Austrian crownlands, k.k. continued to be used.

Kuruc: Armed anti-Habsburg peasant rebels in late seventeenth-century Hungary.

Laibach: Old-Austrian name for Ljubjlana.

Landsturm: A reserve and local defense force, divided, from 1867, into a k.k. (Cisleithanian) and a Royal Hungarian Landsturm (Honvéd).

Landtag: Provincial diet before the Revolution; the parliament of each federal state in the First and Second Republics.

Lemberg: Old-Austrian name of Lviv in present-day Ukraine (Lwów in Polish).

Little Entente: The Little Entente was an alliance formed in 1920 and 1921 between Czechoslovakia, Romania, and the Kingdom of Serbs, Croats, and Slovenes for common defense against Hungarian revanchism and a Habsburg restoration.

Maffie: An illegal, conspiratorial secret organization and the main component of the internal Czech resistance in 1914–18 against Habsburg rule. It advocated the founding of an independent Czechoslovakia and cooperated closely with other groups abroad.

Magyarones: Movement of Burgenland and Croatian nobility whose outlook favored a Greater Hungary.

Marburg: Old-Austrian name for Maribor in present-day Slovenia.

Mármaroszigeth: Hungarian name of Sighetu Marmaţiei in Romania.

Militarist faction (Militärpartei): The militaristic group around the Emperor; the militarist faction in and outside government.

Military Association: The *Militärverband*, the trade union established with the new Defense Law of March 18, 1920 that brought together the rank-and-file soldiers and noncommissioned officers of the New Federal Army, as well as parts of the officer corps close to Social Democracy. These consisted almost exclusively of the core cadre of the Volkswehr. After 1923, when discharged from the Army, they typically passed into the Republikanischer Schutzbund.

Mixed-economy enterprises: See Gemischtwirtschaftliche Anstalte.

Naczelny Komitet Narodowy: Pro-Austrian Supreme National Committee (NKN) in Galician Poland, 1914–17.

Narodni Svet: The National Council established in Laibach (Ljubljana) on August 16, 1918.

Národní Výbor: The National Committee established in Prague on July 13, 1918.

Narodno Vijeće: The South Slav National Council established October 6, 1918 in Zagreb.

National Assembly, Provisional and Constituent: The Provisional National Assembly (Provisorische Nationalversammlung—October 21, 1918 to February 16, 1919) consisted of the members of the Austrian Chamber of Deputies who represented German-speaking areas, some of which Austria lost through the Treaty of Saint-Germain. It was replaced by the Constituent National Assembly (Konstituierende Nationalversammlung) on March 4, 1919, which enacted the Austrian Constitution and was replaced on November 10, 1920 by the present-day National Council (Nationalrat) and Federal Council (Bundesrat).

National Council: (Nationalrat) the Austrian parliament established by the Constitution of October 1, 1920. The other house of parliament is the Federal Council (Bundesrat), chamber of the federal states with far fewer powers.

National obstruction: Filibustering in the Austrian Parliament on the part of the various nationalities.

Nikolsburg: Present-day Mikulov in the Czech Republic.

Ödenburg: Present-day Sopron in Hungary.

Ordnerorganisationen, Ordnerbataillonen: "Steward organisations," self-defense units organized by the workers' councils.

Orgesch: From Organisation Escherich, Bavarian paramilitary group (1920–21) founded by Georg Escherich, which established links with the Austrian right-wing militia, the Heimatwehr. It was disbanded by the Entente powers. In 1928 Escherich founded the paramilitary Heimatschutz.

Ostrau: Old-Austrian name of Ostrava in the present-day Czech Republic.

Pan-German and Greater-German (grossdeutsch and alldeutsch): See Friedrich Adler's distinction in Chapter 4. *Pan-German* (grossdeutsch) refers to the cultural and linguistic dimension, *Greater-German* (alldeutsch) to the imperialist and expansionist tendency of the German élites.

Paragraph 14 (December Constitution, 1867): Legislation applicable in emergencies, providing for the suspension of trials by jury and other civil liberties. Paragraph 14 includes the *Diktaturparagraph*, which, during the obstruction (see National obstruction), empowered the Emperor with the right of emergency rule, including the suspension of civil liberties.

Pola: Old-Austrian and Italian name for Pula in Croatia.

Pragmatic Sanction: An edict issued in 1713 by Karl VI (Holy Roman Emperor) to ensure that the Habsburg crownlands could be inherited by a daughter.

Pressburg: Old-Austrian name for Bratislava.

(Bad) Radkersburg: A spa town in Austria. Its Sloveninan name is Radgona.

Rayah: The name given to the non-Muslim subjects of a Muslim ruler.

Reczpospolita: Traditional Polish term indicating the Polish state or commonwealth.

Red Guard (Rote Garde): A militia unit founded in October 1918 by Egon Erwin Kisch and others. Although not a unit of the to-be-founded German-Austrian Communist Party, there was much overlap between the two organizations. They were incorporated by Julius Deutsch into the new Volkswehr but remained a locus of left-wing agitation and dissidence within it.

Reichsrat: The Austrian (Cisleithanian) Imperial Parliament—consisting of the Herrenhaus (House of Lords) and an elected Abgeordnetenhaus (Chamber of Deputies).

Reval: Name of Tallinn before Estonian indpenedence in 1918.

Ruthenians: After 1843, the term used for the Rusyns and Ukrainians within the Austrian Empire. Untill 1918 the term was largely synonymous with the Ukrainians of Galicia.

Sabor: Croatian parliament.

Saint-Germain, Treaty of: The treaty between the Entente powers and German-Austria.

St. Gotthard: Szentgotthárd in present-day Hungary.

Salurner Klause: In Italian, Chiusa di Salomo or Stretta di Salomo.

Schrebergarten (pl. Schrebergärten): Small garden plots, often including a cabin, typical of northern, central, and eastern European social democracies and then the eastern European countries under state socialism; in Britain, allotments.

Schutzbund: Republikanischer Schutzbund (Republican Protective League)—the Social Democratic's militia formed in 1923–24.

SDAPDÖ: Sozialdemokratische Arbeiterpartei Deutschösterreichs (Social Democratic Workers' Party of German-Austria), the name of the Social Democratic Party from 1918 to 1934.

Serbian Vojvodina: As an Austrian crownland, it was known as the Voivodeship of Serbia and Banat of Temesvarr. From 1876 under the Kingdom of Hungary, the region was split between Bács-Bodrog, Torontál, and Temes counties.

Sipahi, Sipahis: One of two types of light cavalry of the Ottoman army. There were the fief-holding provincial "timarli sipahi" (making up most of the army) and the regular palace troops, the "kapikulu sipahi." The Sipahi were in rivalry with the Janissaries, the elite corps of the Sultan.

Skupština: The Serb parliament.

Sokols (Sokol, Polish): Gymnastics organizations founded in the Czech lands of the Austrian Empire in 1862, which then spread to other Slav nations.

Staatsrat: The Council of State (October 30, 1918–March 15, 1919) succeeded the Reichsrat, or Cisleithanian parliament. It was the executive organ, essentially the cabinet consisting of the state secretaries and the state chancellor, of the Provisional National Assembly.

Stańczyks (Stańczyci): In Poland, from 1869, the political faction adopting the ideas of the *Teka Stańczyk* (Stańczyk's Portfolio) pamphlet and other writings advocating economic development but not political independence, especially from the Austrian Empire.

Steinamanger: Old-Austrian name for Szombathely in present-day Hungary.

Sternberg: Old-Austrian name for Šternberk in the Olomouc region of Moravia (Sudetenland) in what is now the Czech Republic.

Szlachta: Legally privileged Polish noble class from the time of the Kingdom of Poland and Grand Duchy of Lithuania.

Technical Emergency Relief: In Germany, a so-called Technische Nothilfe was established in 1919 by members of the Technical Department of the paramilitary proto-fascist Freikorps. With its stated purpose the protection and maintenance of vital services and industries, it was a strike-breaking unit that hired scabs to undermine workers' strikes.

Theiss: The German name of the river Tisza in Hungary.

Trialism: The idea—advocated, among others, by Franz Ferdinand—of a unification of the South Slav countries of the Monarchy with Serbia and Montenegro to become a state under the scepter of the Habsburgs, which would join Austria and Hungary as a third component on an equal level.

Trianon, Treaty of: The treaty between the Entente powers and Hungary.

Versailles, Treaty of: The treaty between the Entente powers and Germany.

Vojvodina: See Serbian Vojvodina.

Völkermarkt: A town in Carinthia, Austria. Its Slovene name is Velikovec.

Volkswehr: People's Guard or People's Defense Force, the popular militia, arising out of a network of Social Democratic soldiers stationed in Vienna organized by Julius Deutsch in the last months of the First World War. Before the Treaty of Saint-Germain prohibited it, and before the establishment of the Federal Army, it had functioned as the country's de facto army. The new militia of the Social Democratic Workers' Party, the Republikanischer Schutzbund (Republican Protective League) was founded in 1923–24 and led by Deutsch.

Wend, Wendenland, windisch: Terms originally referring to Sorbs and Sorb lands but which became customary in the Austrian Empire to refer to Slavs and Slav lands, and almost exclusively to Slovenes and Slovene areas. *Windische Mark* indicates *slovenska krajina* (Windic March or Slovene March), which approximately corresponds to Dolenjska or Lower Carniola in present-day Slovenia.

Wieselburg (Komitat Wieselburg, Gespanschaft Wieselburg): Old-Austrian name for Moson vármegye in what is now Slovakia.

Woyt: In Polish, *wójt;* in German, *Vogt.* Rural district or village headman and judge in Russian Poland.

Young Czechs: Young Czech faction of the Czech National Party; after 1874 it was known as the Young Czech Party (National Liberal Party).

Yugoslav Committee: See *Jugoslavenski Odbor.*

Znaimer Kreis: Old-Austrian name for the Znojmo District in Southern Moravia in what is now the Czech Republic.

INDEX OF PERSONS

Domes, Franz (1863–1930), Social Democratic trade-unionist and politician.

Dowbor-Muśnicki, Józef (1867–1937), Polish general in the Russian army; he headed a Polish corps that fought the Central Powers and then the Red Army.

Eberl, Franz (1876–?), factory inspector in Vorarlberg.

Ehrenhofer, Walther Edmund (1872–1928), Vienna factory inspector.

Eisler, Arnold (1879–1947), Social Democratic member of the Styrian parliament, alternatve member of the Federal Constitutional Court and lawyer for the state of Styria and Vienna's streetcar system.

Eldersch, Matthias (1869–1931), state secretary for the interior and education (October 17, 1919–July 7, 1920).

Ellenbogen, Wilhelm (1863–1951), physician and Social Democratic politician, member of the Chamber of Deputies (1901–18), the Constituent National Assembly and then of the National Council (1919–34), he was part of the party's inner leadership circle. Forced to emigrate to the US in 1938, his attempted return after 1945 came up against the resistance of the Austrian Social Democratic Party.

Engels, Friedrich (1820–95).

Escherisch, Georg (1879–1941), founder of the Bavarian right-wing paramilitary organization Orgesch.

Fadrus, Viktor (1884–1968), Austrian school-system reformer.

Fejérváry, Baron Géza (1833–1914), prime minister of Hungary (June 18, 1905–April 8, 1906).

Ferdinand I of Austria (1793–1875), Emperor of Austria (1835–48).

Ferdinand I of Bulgaria (1861–1948), king of Bulgaria (1908–18).

Ferrario, Carlo Antonio (1867–1958), Italian general heading the Entente's Inter-Allied Commission administering the Burgenland.

Fink, Jodok (1853–1929), Christian Social Party leader and Vice Chancellor in 1919 of the first Renner coalition government.

Foch, Ferdinand (1851–1929), French general and Supreme Allied Commander in the First World War.

Franchet d'Espèrey, Louis (1856–1942), French general in the First World War.

Franz Ferdinand, Archduke of Austria (1863–1914), heir to the throne.

Franz Joseph I (1830–1916, reign 1848–1916), Emperor of Austria and King of Hungary.

Frey, Josef (dates unknown), chair of the executive committee of the Viennese Soldiers' Council of the Viennese Volkswehr in 1919 and leading figure in the "New Left"—see Franz Rothe. Frey joined the Austrian Communist Party in 1921 and was expelled in 1927, subsequently becoming a key figure of the Trotskyist movement.

Gaj, Ljudevit (1809–1872), the key Croatian figure in the pan-Slavic Illyrian movement.

Gessmann, Albert (1852–1920), co-founder, with Karl Lueger, of the Christian Social Party, minister in the Beck cabinet.

Glaise-Horstenau, Edmund (1882–1946) military historian, National Socialist, and Vice-Chancellor in the Seyss-Inquart cabinet.

Glöckel, Otto (1874–1935), Social Democratic politician and the key figure in Vienna's 1920s school reform.

Goldscheid, Rudolf (1870–1931), Austrian sociologist, philosopher, and novelist.

Gömbös, Gyula (1886–1936), right-wing anti-communist and anti-Habsburg founder of a paramilitary unit; prime minister of Hungary from October 1, 1932 to his death on October 6, 1936.

Grafe, Felix (born Felix Löwy, 1888–1942), an Austrian expressionist poet and translator active in Munich and Vienna.

Grey, Edward (Viscount) (1862–1933), British Liberal politician and Foreign Secretary from 1905 to 1916.

Grimm, Ferdinand (1869–1948) was a financial advisor to the Habsburgs and tutor in finance to Emperor Karl. In 1918–19 he was Under Secretary for Finance and then Minister of Finance from November 20, 1920 to October 7, 1921. From 1921 he was President of the Credit Institute for Public Works and Enterprises. He played a role in Ignaz Seipel's work of reconstruction.

Grünberg, Carl (1861–1940), a professor of political economy at the University of Vienna who taught Bauer, Hilferding, and Renner. He was the founding director, in 1924, of the Institute for Social Research in Frankfurt a.M.

Guinet, Major Alphonse (dates unknown), the French military representative to the Czech Legion.

Gürtler, Alfred (1875–1933), Christian Social politician, advisor to Renner at Saint-Germain, and finance minister in both Schober governments.

Hadik, Count János (1863–1933), prime minister of Hungary for one day on October 30, 1918.

Hadji Mustafa Pasha (1733–1801), Ottoman commander who lived in what is now Serbia.

Hainisch, Michael (1858–1940), independent, first federal president of Austria (1920–28).

Haller, József (1873–1960), Polish lieutenant general and commander in the Polish Legions.

Hamp, Pierre (pseudonym of Henri Bourrillon, 1876–1962), author of hyperrealist novels about the world of work and the condition of the working classes.

Hanusch, Ferdinand (1866–1923), Vice Chancellor (July 7–October 22, 1920), social affairs minister. Under his aegis key features of Austria's social system were established: a public healthcare system, statutory paid leave, a minimum wage set through collective bargaining, a forty-eight-hour work week, the prohibition of child labor, unemployment insurance, and the six-week maternity leave.

Hartl, Karl (1878–1941), became chief magistrate of the city of Vienna in 1919 and director of the office of regional government in 1920, in which capacities he helped craft the legal basis for democratizing municipal government.

Hartmann, Ludo Moritz (1865–1924), Austrian Social Democratic politician and historian.

Hauck, (Karl?), Vienna factory inspector.

Hoffmann, Max (1869–1927), German general and chief of staff at the Eastern Front.

Hofmann, a comrade of Leo Deutsch, Braunthal, and Schuhbauer in the confrontation with communist influence in the Volkswehr; no other details are known.

Hohenwart, Count Karl Sigmund von (1824–1899), prime minister of Austria (February 7, 1871–October 20, 1871).

Hoover, Herbert (1874–1964), thirty-first president of the United States, after the First World War he led the American Relief Administration providing food to Central and Eastern Europe.

Horthy, Miklós (1868–1957), admiral and regent of Hungary from 1920 to 1944.

Hötzendorff, Baron Franz Conrad von (1852–1925), chief of staff of the Austro-Hungarian Army (1906–11 and 1912–16).

Hueber, Anton (1861–1935), leading Social Democratic trade unionist in Austria-Hungary and during the First Republic.

Hülgerth, Ludwig (1875–1939), named on November 12, 1918 commander-in-chief in Carinthia, where he organized local defense and built up the Volkswehr. In 1934 he became governor of Carinthia and in 1936 Vice-Chancellor under Schuschnigg.

Hussarek of Heinlein, Baron Max (1865–1935), next-to-last Prime Minister of Austria for three months of 1918.

Jellačić von Bužim, Count Josip (1801–59), Croatian lieutenant field marshal, Ban of Croatia (1848–59).

Joseph II (1741–90), Holy Roman Emperor, from 1780 to 1790 sole ruler of the Habsburg lands.

Joseph August, Archduke of Austria (1872–1962), Hungarian head of state for seventeen days in August 1919.

Juriga, Ferdiš (1874–1950), Slovak priest and politician.

Justh, Gyula (1850–1917), speaker of Hungary's Chamber of Deputies (1905–9).

Kahr, Gustav von (1862–1934), a Protestant monarchist and Prime Minister of Bavaria (March 16, 1920–September 12, 1921), who played an important part in suppressing the Munich soviet. Though a promoter of anti-Semitic policies he banned the NSDAP and helped prevent the 1923 Hitler-Ludendorff putsch in return for which he was murdered in Dachau in 1934.

Kállay, Béni (1839–1903), Hungarian consul-general at Belgrade (1869–72) and finance minister of Austria-Hungary (1882–1903).

Kara Djordje ("Black George"), sobriquet of Djordje Petrović (1768–1817), leader of the First Serbian Uprising (1804–17).

Karadjordjević, Petar (1844–1921), Peter I, King of Serbia (1903–18).

Karadžić, Vuk (1787–1864), philologist and the major reformer of the Serbian language.

Karl I (1887–1922), Emperor of Austria and King of Hungary; Emperor from November 1916 to his formal dethronement and exile in April 1919. In November 1918 he "renounced participation" in government affairs but did not abdicate. Hungary's National Assembly rescinded his right to the throne on November 5, 1921.

Karl Stephan, Archduke of Austria (1869–1933).

Károlyi, Count Mihály (1875–1955), leader of the First Hungarian Republic (1918–1919), prime minister briefly in November 1918 and president (November 1918–March 1919).

Kelsen, Hans (1881–1973), a leading representative of the school of legal positivism, founder of the pure theory of law, and an important scholar of international law and sanctions, was charged with the task of working out a constitution for the new state. It was ratified by the Constituent National Assembly in 1920 as the Federal Constitutional Law (Bundesverfassungsgesetz) and is essentially still in effect today.

Kestřanek, Paul (1856–1929), the last imperial military commander in Prague.

Khuen-Héderváry, Count Károly (1849–1918), Ban of the Kingdom of Croatia and Slavonia (from 1883); Prime Minister of Hungary (1903 and 1910–12).

Koerber, Ernest von (1850–1919), prime minister of Austria (1900–1904).

Köhler, Richard, active in the Soldiers' Councils and Volkswehr.

Kola, Richard (1872–1939), banker, writer, and journalist, often consulted on financial matters by Renner, Seipel, Schumpeter, and Steinwender.

Kolchak, Alexander Vasilyevich (1874–1920), Imperial Russian Admiral; from 1918 to 1920 he was recognized by the White movement as its leader.

Kollár, Ján (1793–1852), Slovak polymath and key proponent of Pan-Slavism.

Koritschoner, Franz (1892–1941), a leader of the January 1918 strike in Austria-Hungary, then member of the Austrian Communist Party; in 1926 he lived in the Soviet Union, working for Profintern, subsequently joining the CPSU. A victim of the Stalinist purges, he was extradited to Germany and murdered in Auschwitz.

Körner, Theodor (1873–1957). Born into a military family, Körner served as an officer in the Imperial Army on the Italian front and was centrally involved in the formation of the Federal Army in 1920. He was promoted to the rank of general in 1924. A Social Democrat, he became a member of parliament in 1924. Imprisoned under the Austro-fascist regime and under the Nazis, he was elected mayor of Vienna (1945–51) after the war and was the first elected president of Austria's Second Republic (1951–57).

Korošec, Anton (1872–1940), conservative Slovenian Roman Catholic priest. From 1907 to 1918 he served as a deputy (People's Party) to the Austrian parliament and (from October 29 to December 1, 1918) as president of the National Council of the State of Slovenes, Croats, and Serbs.

Kossuth, Ferenc (1841–1914), Hungarian economist and civil engineer involved in railroad construction in England and Italy and bridges on the Nile. In 1898 he became leader of the "obstructionists" (Independence Party). His father was Lajos Kossuth.

Kossuth, Lajos (1802–94), president of the Kingdom of Hungary during the revolution of 1848–49 and the iconic figure of Hungarian revolutionary republicanism.

Kramář, Karel (1860–1937), conservative member of the Young Czechs and deputy to the Austrian Parliament (1891–1915), he headed the Czechoslovak National Committee in Prague in 1918 and was the first prime minister of the new state.

Kraus, Karl (1874–1936), Austrian satirist, journalist, essayist, playwright, and poet best known internationally for his play *The Last Days of Mankind.*

Krek, Janez Evangelist (1865–1917), Slovene Christian Social politician and priest.

Kristóffy, József (1857–1928), Hungary's minister of the interior (June 18, 1905–April 8, 1906).

Kun, Béla (1886–1938), commissar of foreign affairs and de facto leader of the Hungarian Soviet Republic.

Kunschak, Leopold (1871–1953), Christian Social Party trade unionist, member of the Constituent National Assembly, chair of the Christian Social Party's leadership (1920–21), and one of the most important figures in the Freiheitsbund, a conservative though democratically oriented Christian trade union association opposed both to the leftist Schutzbund and the rightist Heimwehr.

Lammasch, Heinrich (1853–1929), Austria's last prime minister (October and November 1918) and the only non-noble to have served in that office, he opposed the alliance with Germany and supported the peace movement and, from 1917, advocated a separate peace with France. His appointment by the Emperor was a consequence of the failure of

Foreign Minister Czernin's policies; he was assigned the task of handing over state business to the new German-Austrian Staatsrat under Karl Renner.

Lansing, Robert (1864–1928), US Secretary of State (1915–1920).

Lasalle, Ferdinand (1825–64), the leading figure of the early German social democratic movement.

Lederer, Emil (1882–1939), German economist and sociologist.

Lehár, Anton (Antal) (1876–1962), Hungarian officer who supported the Habsburg attempts in 1921 to retake the Hungarian throne; he was the brother of composer Franz Lehár.

Levicki (full name and dates unknown), one of the two representatives of the Ukrainian Rada negotiating at Brest-Litovsk.

Linder, Béla (1876–1962), Secretary of War in Károlyi's government and a committed pacifist; Linder presided over the complete demobilization of Hungary's armed forces demanded by Wilson. He was subsequently military attaché in Vienna of the Hungarian Soviet government.

Ludendorff, Erich (1865–1937), German general who played a key role in the First World War; he was prominent in right-wing nationalist circles and a participant in the Kapp Putsch.

Lueger, Karl (1844–1910), founder of the Christian Social Party and mayor of Vienna (1897–1910) when he presided over much of the modern urban public-works development of the city. On the national level he was a proponent of federalism in place of Dualism, and anti-Semitism was a component of his populism within the city.

Luxemburg, Rosa (1871–1919), a leader of Social Democracy of the Kingdom of Poland and Lithuania, of the German Social Democratic Party, and co-founder, in Germany, of the Independent Social Democratic Party and the Communist Party of Germany.

Mackensen, August von (1849–1945), German field marshal who played a major role in the First World War.

Maister (Majstr) Rudolf (1874–1934), Slovene military officer and poet.

Marek, Alfred (1880–1941), a decorated officer of the Austro-Hungarian Army, subsequently active in the Volkswehr and Federal Army where he was in charge of weapon stores. However, in 1927 he violated the task entrusted to him and funneled large stores of arms to the ruling bourgeois parties.

Marx, Karl (1818–83).

Masaryk, Tomáš Garrigue (1850–1937), the leading figure of the Czechoslovak independence movement and first president (1918–35) of Czechoslovakia.

Mataja, Heinrich (1877–1937), member of the Christian Social Party, minister of the interior (October 30, 1918–March 15, 1919) and foreign minister (November 20, 1924–January 14, 1926).

Maximilian, Prince of Baden (1867–1929), a German general in the First World War and Chancellor at the end of the war; in October he invited two Social Democrats to participate in his cabinet, then unilaterally proclaimed Kaiser Wilhelm's abdication and appointed the Social Democrat Friedrich Ebert his successor, paving the way for the establishment of the Republic.

Mazzini, Giuseppe (1805–72), leading figure of the Italian Risorgimento.

Paskevich, Count Ivan Fyodorovich (1782–1856), Russian military leader who crushed the 1831 Polish November Uprising; Namestnik of the Kingdom of Poland (viceroy) from 1831 to 1855.

Pattai, Robert (1846–1920), Austrian Christian Social Party politician.

Pavlů, Bohdan (1883–1938), Slovak literary critic and Czechoslovak diplomat, active in the Czechoslovak Legions in Russia, which he represented in Siberia.

Pešeren, France (1800–49), Slovene poet.

Petschek (first name and dates not known), mentioned as one of the German-Czech representatives to the Austrian Parliament of the generation of Pacák, Prade, and Prášek.

Piłsudski, Józef (1867–1935), Polish chief of state (1918–22) and First Marshal (from 1920).

Plumb, Glenn E. (1866–1922), author of a plan for cooperative ownership of US railways.

Poincaré, Raymond (1860–1934), President of France (1913–20).

Potiorek, Oskar (1853–1933), governor of Bosnia and Herzogovina (1911–14) and commander of the Austro-Hungarian forces in the Serbian Campaign (1914–15).

Potocki, Andrzej (1908), governor general of Galicia (1903–8).

Prade, Heinrich (1853–1927), Czech member of the Austrian Chamber of Deputies (Deutsche Volkspartei) from 1885 and minister in the Beck government.

Prášek, Karel (1868–1932), Czech politician of the Independent Agrarian Party, member of the Austrian Parliament (1901–18), then of the Revolutionary National Committee (Národní Výbor) and president of the Czechoslovak Senate (1920–24).

Preuss, Hugo (1860–1925), German constitutional scholar who drafted the constitution of the Weimar Republic at the request of Friedrich Ebert.

Prochaska, Oskar, Austro-Hungarian consul in Prizren (1906–12).

Prónay, Pál (1874–1947 or 1948), the figure most closely associated with the atrocities of Hungary's white terror.

Rašín, Alois (1867–1923), a conservative liberal and Czechosloviakia's first minister of finance.

Rauch, Pavao (1865–1933), ban of Croatia-Slavonia (1908–10).

Redlich, Josef (1869–1936), a liberal jurist and finance minister in the Lammasch government.

Reisch, Richard (1866–1938), minister of finance in the third Renner government and in the Mayr government (October 17, 1919–November 20, 1920).

Renner, Karl (1870–1950), major theorist and leader of the Austrian Social Democratic Party, he led the first governments of the German-Austrian Republic, the First Republic, and, in 1945, the Second Republic.

Reumann, Jakob (1853–1925) was the first chair of the Social Democratic Party on its founding (1888–89) as well as the first Social Democratic mayor of Vienna (May 21, 1919–November 13, 1923). He was a key figure in the initiation of many "Red Vienna" social reforms: the construction of municipal housing, along with the healthcare, education, and vacation systems.

Ried (first name not known) (Oberbaurat), Chief Government Building Supervisor (Oberbaurat) in Vienna (1919–?).

Rittner, Tadeusz (1873–1921), an Austrian dramatist who wrote in both German and Polish.

Rothe, Franz (dates unknown), a member of the SDAP's "New Left" in 1919; he then moved to the Social Democratic Project Group of Revolutionary Workers' Councils (SARA), which included Josef Frey. In 1920 he entered the Austrian Communist Party.

Sankey, John (1866–1948), British Labour politician and Lord High Chancellor (1929–35).

Sarkotić von Lovćen, Baron Stephan (Stjepan) (1858–1939), Austro-Hungarian lieutenant field marshal and military governor of Bosnia Herzegovina during the First World War.

Schanzer, Carlo (1865–1953), prime minister of Italy in 1922.

Schober, Johann (1874–1932), Vienna's chief of police from 1918 until his death, interrupted by two brief periods as federal chancellor.

Schönburg-Hartenstein, Prince Alois (1858–1944), a colonel general appointed by Emperor Karl in 1918 to maintain domestic security, in which capacity he persecuted strike leaders and military deserters.

Schönerer, Georg (Ritter von) (1842–1921), the most radical Austrian Pan-German of the late nineteenth and early twentieth centuries, an extreme anti-Semite and fierce opponent of Roman Catholicism, and from 1879 to the end of the century, the leader of the Deutschnationalen and then the Alldeutsche Vereinigung.

Schöpfer, Aemilian (1858–1936), Catholic priest, co-founder and leader of the Christian Social Party in Tyrol, and acting governor of Tyrol (1916–17).

Schraffl, Josef (1855–1922), the leading Christian Social political figure in Tyrol in the first two decades of the twentieth century. A supporter of the Republic, he was the leader of the Tyrolean Farmers' League and was primarily concerned with agricultural modernization.

Schuhbauer, Theodor (dates unknown). An ally of Julius Deutsch's in the Volkswehr, Schuhbauer later headed the Wiener Gemeindewache and played a leading role in the Republican Schutzbund.

Schumpeter, Joseph (1883–1950), Austrian political economist, first coalition government's minister of finance, later professor at Harvard University.

Schwiedland, Eugen (1863–1936), political economist, worked with the new Republic's Socialization Committee.

Segre, Roberto (1872–1936), general heading Italy's military commission in Vienna in charge of monitoring compliance with the terms of the Armistice.

Ségur-Cabanac, August (1881–1931), Christian Social Party, federal finance minister (May 31, 1922–November 14, 1922).

Seidler von Feuchtenegg, Ernst (1862–1931), prime minister of Austria (June 23, 1917–July 27, 1918).

Seipel, Ignaz (1876–1932), Austrian prelate, leading figure of the Christian Social Party, twice Federal Chancellor, three times Minister of Foreign Affairs.

Seitz, Karl (1869–1950), Social Democratic president of the Constituent National Assembly (1919–20) and mayor of Vienna (1923–34). After Victor Adler's death (November 11, 1918), he served as party chairman, a position he held until after the refounding of the Austrian Social Democratic Party in 1945.

Seliger, Josef (1870–1920), a Sudeten-German Social Democratic member of the Austrian Parliament, then member of the Provisional National Assembly of German-Austria (1918–19).

Selim III (1761–1808), Sultan of the Ottoman Empire (1789–1807).

Semyonov, Grigory Mihailovich (1890–1946), leader of the White movement in Transbaikal (1917–20), then ataman of the Baikal Cossacks.

Sever, Albert (1867–1942), Social Democrat, native of Zagreb, the first democratically elected premier of the province (and then federal state) of Lower Austria.

Sevrjuk (dates and first name unknown), one of the two representatives of the Ukrainian Rada negotiating at Brest-Litovsk.

Siczynski, Myrosław (1887–1979), Ukrainan philosophy student at the University of Galicia in Lemberg (Lwow, Lviv), and member of the Ukrainian Social Democratic Party, who assassinated governor general of Galicia Andrzej Potocki in 1908.

Sixtus of Bourbon-Parma, Prince (1886–1934), served as a Belgian officer in the First World War.

Skałon, Gieorgij (1847–1914), Russian general and governor general of Warsaw (1905–14).

Skoropadskyi, Pavlo (1873–1945), Russian Imperial Army general; after the Ukrainian People's Republic was overthrown in 1918 he was briefly named Hetman of Ukraine, in which capacity he collaborated with the German Army.

Słowacki, Juliusz (1809–49), one of Poland's leading Romantic poets.

Smitka, Johann (1863–1944), first an officer of the Viennese garment workers' sick fund, he later became a Social Democratic parliamentarian (1907–30).

Smuts, Jan (1870–1950), prime minister of the Union of South African (1919–24, 1939–48) and member of the British Imperial War Cabinet (1917–19).

Šnjarić, Luka (1851–1930), General of the Infantry and last Austro-Hungarian commandant in Croatia.

Spann, Othmar (1878–1950), Austrian philosopher, sociologist, and economist whose anti-liberal and anti-socialist views in the end positioned him between Austro-fascism and National Socialism (he joined the Nazi Party in 1930), but whose unorthodoxy led to his being barred from teaching (1938–45).

Štefánik, Milan Rastislav (1880–1919), Slovak general in the French Army, member of the Czechoslovak National Council, and key participant in Czechoslovak independence.

Steidle, Richard (1881–1940), leader of the Heimwehr in Tyrol. Due to his clashes with the National Socialists he was brought to Buchenwald concentration camp where he died.

Steinwender, Otto (1847–1921), head of the Deutsche Volkspartei, Carinthian parliamentarian, and state secretary of finance in the second Renner government (1918–19).

Stöckler, Josef (1866–1936), Lower Austrian Christian Social Party parliamentarian, founder of the Lower Austrian Farmers' League, State Secretary for Agriculture (October 1918–July 1920), and Federal President (December 1930–May 1931).

Stolypin, Pyotr (1862–1911), Russian minister of the interior and prime minister from 1906 to his death by assassination.

Stremayr, Karl (Ritter von) (1823–1904), Prime Minister of Cisleithania for several months in 1879. In the next year, as both Minister of Justice and Minister of Culture and Education, he was the primary author of reform legislation allowing more use of the Czech language in the local administrations of Bohemia and Moravia.

Strobl, Karl Hans (1877–1946). A prolific writer of horror stories, he became increasingly anti-Semitic after the First World War and later dedicated himself to writing Nazi propaganda.

Stürgkh, Karl von (1859–1916), prime minister of Austria from 1905 to his assassination by

Weiss (Armand?—no details are known), a close ally of Julius Deutsch in the Volkswehr.

Wekerle, Sándor (1848–1921), first non-noble to hold office in Hungary; he was prime minister three times: 1892–94, 1906–10, and 1917–18.

Werfel, Franz (1890–1945), major Austrian novelist and playwright whose best known works are his novels *The Forty Days of Musa Dagh* and *Song of Bernadette*.

Wiedenhofer, Josef (1873–1924), Austrian Social Democrat; after a period as secretary of the Austrian Metalworkers' Association, he was a member of the Constituent National Assembly and then of the National Council until his death.

Wilson, Woodrow (1856–1924), twenty-eighth president of the United States (1913–24).

Windischgrätz, Prince Alfred (1787–1862), military commander who crushed the 1848–49 uprisings in Prague and Vienna and, in part, in Hungary.

Wutte, Viktor, (1881–1962), Styrian industrialist and politician, member of the Constituent National Assembly (for the Grossdeutsche Partei).

Wyspiański, Stanisław (1869–1907), Polish playwright, painter, and poet.

Zerdik, Johann (1878–1961), Christian Social politician; State Secretary for Trade, Commerce, Industry and Construction (March 15, 1919–June 24, 1920); and State Secretary for Public Works (October 30, 1918–March 15, 1919).

Żeromski, Stefan (1864–1925), Polish novelist and dramatist.

Zimmerman, Alfred Rudolf (1869–1937), mayor of Rotterdam (1906–23), then, in the service of the League of Nations, charged with enforcing the Geneva Protocols by controlling Austria's state finances, a mission that ended in 1926.

NOTES

Introduction: Otto Bauer and Austro-Marxism

1. Otto Bauer, *Zwischen zwei Weltkriegen. Die Krise der Weltwirtschaft, der Demokratie und des Sozialismus* (Bratislava: Prager, 1936), 92.
2. Michael Krätke, "Austromarxismus und Kritische Theorie" in *Handbuch Kritische Theorie*, Alex Demirovic and Tatjana Freytag, eds. (Wiesbaden: 2018), cited from https://www.researchgate.net/publication/327008956_Austromarxismus_und_Kritische_Theorie and https://www.academia.edu/37333262/Austromarxismus_und_Kritische_Theorie_Vorpublikation.
3. It is a great defect in the reception history of Austro-Marxism that the significant theoreticians Hélène Bauer, Therese Schlesinger, Marie Jahoda, and Käthe Leichter have been insufficiently acknowledged for the important role they played in establishing Austro-Marxism as a scientific school. Regrettably, in enumerating the significant representatives of Austro-Marxism Bauer neglected to point to these important women theorists, including his spouse Hélène Bauer.
4. Otto Bauer, "Austromarxismus," *Arbeiter-Zeitung*, vol. 40, No. 301 (November 3, 1927), 1 (reprinted in Sandkühler and De la Vega, eds., *Austromarxismus,* 49): "The first time we heard the word was a couple of years before the war from the lips of an American socialist, L. Boudin."
5. "Peoples which have never had a history of their own, which from the time when they achieved the first, most elementary stage of civilisation already came under foreign sway, or which were forced to attain the first stage of civilisation only by means of a foreign yoke, are not viable and will never be able to achieve any kind of independence." Friedrich Engels, "Democratic Pan-Slavism" (*Neue Rheinische Zeitung* Nos. 222 and 223, February 15 and 16, 1849), in Karl Marx and Frederick Engels, *Collected Works*, vol. 8 (New York: International Publishers, 1977), 367.
6. Jakub S. Beneš, *Workers and Nationalism: Czech and German Social Democracy in Habsburg Austria, 1890–1918* (Oxford: Oxford University Press, 2017), 63.
7. Beneš, *Workers and Nationalism*, 95.
8. Karl Renner, *Das Selbstbestimmungsrecht der Nationen in besonderer Anwendung auf Österreich* (Leipzig: F. Deuticke, 1918), 74.
9. Beneš, *Workers and Nationalism*, 240.
10. Beneš, *Workers and Nationalism*, 184.
11. See for example Josef Strasser, *Der Arbeiter und Nation* (Reichenberg: Runge & Co., 1912).

443

12. See Hans Mommsen, *Die Sozialdemokratie und die Nationalitätenfrage im Habsburgischen Vielvölkerstaat, Bd. 1: Das Ringen um die supranationale Integration der zisleithanischen Arbeiterbewegung: 1867–1907* (Wien: Europa Verlag, 1963), 389ff.

13. Otto Bauer, *Die Nationalitätenfrage und die Sozialdemokratie* (Vienna: Verlag Wiener Volksbuchhandlung, 1924), 113; Otto Bauer, *The Question of Nationalities and Social Democracy*, trans. Joseph O'Donnell (Minneapolis: University of Minnesota Press, 2000), 7.

14. See Eric J. Hobsbawm, *Nations and Nationalism Since 1780: Programme, Myth, Reality*, 2d ed. (Cambridge: Cambridge University Press, 1992), 8–10.

15. Bauer, *Die Nationalitätenfrage*, xvi; Bauer, *The Question of Nationalities*, 10, 12.

16. "Das Nationalitätenprogramm der Linken," in Otto Bauer, *Werkausgabe*, vol. 8 (Vienna: Europaverlag, 1980), 844.

17. Otto Bauer, "Österreichs Ende," *Der Kampf*, V (1938), 4, in Otto Bauer, *Werkausgabe*, vol. 9 (Vienna: Europaverlag, 1980).

18. Otto Bauer, *Der Weg zum Sozialismus* (Vienna: Verlag Wiener Volksbuchhandlung, 1921), 2.

19. Bauer, *Der Weg zum Sozialismus*, 35.

20. Bauer, *Der Weg zum Sozialismus*, 31.

21. Bauer, *Der Weg zum Sozialismus*, 27.

22. Bauer, *Der Weg zum Sozialismus*, 4.

23. The Communist Party of Austria (KPÖ) was founded on November 3, 1918, by a small group of intellectuals. The considerably more influential Radical Left, which formed Social Democracy's militant anti-war wing and played a leading role in the January 1918 strike, at first remained distant from the newly founded party, since it still hoped for a left turn in its own party. At any rate, it associated itself with the KPÖ in the next months. At the high point of the revolutionary surge and after the proclamation of the council government in Hungary, the party's membership rapidly grew to 40,000. Nevertheless, the Communists represented only a minority of the socialist movement, and the party isolated itself through unrealistic and sectarian tactics. After the defeat of the Bavarian (May 1919) and Hungarian (August 1919) soviets the KPÖ's influence and membership rapidly declined. The KPÖ only gained mass impact after the May 26, 1933 banning of the KPÖ and the military defeat of February 1934 when thousands of Social Democrats, disillusioned by their party leadership, joined the KPÖ. After Anschluss to Nazi Germany in March 1938, the KPÖ constituted the main force of Austria's anti-fascist resistance within the country, in the concentration camps, and among émigrés.

24. Hans Hautmann, *Die verlorene Räterepublik. Am Beispiel der Kommunistischen Partei Deutschösterreichs* (Vienna: Europa Verlag, 1971), 14.

25. Otto Bauer, *Bolschewismus oder Sozialdemokratie* (Vienna: Verlag Wiener Volksbuchhandlung, 1920), 4.

26. Bauer, *Bolschewismus*, 84.

27. Bauer, *Bolschewismus*, 88.

28. Bauer, *Bolschewismus*, 110ff.

29. Bauer, *Bolschewismus*, 113 (emphasis in original).

30. At the initiative of the Social Democratic chancellor, Karl Renner, in 1919, Hans Kelsen (1881–1973), a leading representative of the school of legal positivism, founder of the pure theory of law, and an important scholar of international law and sanctions, was charged with the task of working out a constitution for the new state. It was ratified by the Constituent National Assembly in 1920 as the Federal Constitutional Law (Bundesverfassungsgesetz) and is essentially still in effect today.

It was not only against Bauer that Kelsen defended his idea of a democratic—that is, socially neutral—constitution. At the end of his essay "Democracy and Socialism" (a response to Friedrich von Hayek's 1944 book The Road to Serfdom), he wrote: "The results of the foregoing analysis is that the attempts at showing an essential connection between freedom and property, as all other attempts at establishing a closer relationship of democracy with capitalism than with socialism, or even the exclusive compatibility of democracy with capitalism, have failed. Hence our thesis stands that democracy as a political system is not necessarily attached to a definite economic system" ("Democracy and Socialism," The Law School of the University of Chicago: Conference on Jurisprudence and Politics, April 30, 1954, 63–87). He presents the same argument in The Political Theory of Bolshevism: it is not the claimed socialist character of Soviet society that is the object of his critique but the sole reign of the Communist Party designated as the dictatorship of the proletariat. "The political form of democracy is compatible with a capitalist as well as with a socialist economic system as its content. And the same is true with respect to the political form of autocracy. . . . To identify socialism with democracy amounts to the attempt to substitute the one for the other." Kelsen, The Political Theory of Bolshevism. A Critical Analysis (Berkeley: University of California Press, 1948), 48.

31. Hans Kelsen, "Marx oder Lasalle. Wandlungen der politischen Theorie des Marxismus" (1924), in Demokratie und Sozialismus. Ausgewählte Aufsätze, Norbert Leser, ed. (Vienna: Verlag der Wiener Volksbuchhandlung, 1967), 139.

32. Kelsen, "Marx oder Lasalle," 139.

33. Kelsen, "Marx oder Lasalle," 145.

34. Kelsen, "Marx oder Lasalle," 149.

35. Kelsen, "Marx oder Lasalle," 160.

36. Otto Bauer, "Das Gleichgewicht der Klassenkräfte," in Austromarxismus. Texte zu "Ideologie and Klassenkamp," Hans-Jörg Sandkühler and Rafael de la Vega, eds. (Vienna: Europa Verlag, 1970), 94ff.

37. Karl Renner, Wege der Verwirklichung. Betrachtungen über politische Demokratie, Wirtschaftsdemokratie und Sozialismus, insbesondere über die Aufgaben der Genossenschaften und der Gewerkschaften (Berlin: Dietz, 1929), 35.

38. Renner, Wege der Verwirklchung, 35 (emphasis in original).

39. Renner, Wege der Verwirklichung, 136.

40. Krätke, "Austromarxismus und Kritische Theorie."

41. Otto Bauer, Sozialdemokratie, Religion und Kirche (Vienna: Verlag Wiener Volksbuchhandlung, 1927).

42. Sozialdemokratische Arbeiterpartei Deutschösterreichs, "Das Linzer Programm" (November 3, 1926), in Sandkühler and De la Vega, Austromarxismus, 385 (emphasis in original).

43. See Otto Bauer's speech at the Party Congress of the SDAPDÖ 1932, quoted in Norbert Leser, *Zwischen Reformismus und Bolschewismus*, 459.

44. See Joseph Buttinger, *Am Beispiel Österreichs. Ein geschichtlicher Beitrag zur Krise der sozialistischen Bewegung* (Cologne: Verlag für Politik und Wirtschaft, 1953).

45. Josef Hindels, *Erinnerungen eines linken Sozialisten* (Vienna: Dokumentationsarchiv des österreichischen Widerstands, 1996), 33.

46. Bruno Kreisky, Zwischen den Zeiten, Erinmerungen aus fünf Jahrzehnten (Vienna: Siedler/Kremayr & Scheriau, 1986), 203.

47. Otto Bauer, *Der Aufstand der österreichischen Arbeiter. Seine Ursachen und seine Wirkung* (Vienna: Verlag Wiener Volksbuchhandlung, 1947), 30.

48. Bruno Kreisky, *Zwischen den Zeiten, Erinnerungen aus fünf Jahrzehnten* (Vienna: Siedler/Kremayr & Scheriau, 1986), 203. The hatred of many Social Democrats for the Christian Social Party and the Austro-fascist regime was so great that there was something almost tantamount to sympathy for the Nazis when they murdered Dollfuss in July 1934.

49. Kreisky, *Zwischen den Zeiten*, 93.

50. Norbert Leser, *Zwischen Reformismus und Bolschewismus. Der Austromarxismus als Theorie und Praxis* (1968), 484.

51. See Kreisky, *Zwischen den Zeiten*, 195. Ignaz Seipel (1876–1932) was an Austrian prelate, leading figure of the Christian Social Party, and twice Federal Chancellor of Austria (May 1922–November 20, 1924; October 20, 1926–May 4, 1929). He was Minister of Foreign Affairs from October 20, 1926 to May 4, 1929 and from September 30, 1930 to December 4, 1930. Bauer wrote a notably respectful obituary in the *Arbeiter-Zeitung*, in which he said: "He who is a fighter will not deny personal respect to a born fighter of the enemy camp": "Ignaz Seipel," *Arbeiter-Zeitung*, August 3, 1932, in Otto Bauer, *Aus seinem Lebenswerk. Mit einem Lebensbild Otto Bauer von Julius Braunthal* (Vienna: Verlag Wiener Volksbuchhandlung, 1961), 240.

52. Raimund Löw, Siegfried Mattl, and Alfred Pfabigan, *Der Austromarxismus—eine Autopsie. Drei Studien* (Frankfurt a.M.: isp-Verlag, 1986), 37.

53. Ernst Wimmer, "Otto Bauers zwei Seiten (Zum 100. Geburtstag Otto Bauers)," *Weg und Ziel*, no. 9, 1981, 323ff.

54. See Otto Bauer, *Das Budgetsanierungsgesetz: Vortrag, gehalten am 9. Oktober 1931 vor den Vertrauensmännern der Postgewerkschaft* (Vienna: Verlag der Postgewerkschaft, 1931).

55. Fritz Weber, *Der kalte Krieg in der SPÖ. Koalitionswächter, Pragmatiker und revolutionäre Sozialisten 1945–1950*, Vol. 25 of Österreichische Texte zur Gesellschaftskritik (Vienna: Verlag für Gesellschaftskritik, 1986), 4.

56. See Ulrike Weber-Felber, "Gewerkschaftspolitik der Weltwirtschaftskrise. Die freien Gewerkschaften und das Problem der Arbeitsbeschaffung," in *February 1934 Ursachen Fakten Folgen*, Erich Fröschl and Helge Zoitl, eds. (Vienna: Verlag der Wiener Volksbuchhandlung, 1984), 130ff.

57. Leser, *Zwischen Reformismus und Bolschewismus*.

58. Karl Renner, "Ist der Marxismus Ideologie oder Wissenschaft?," *Der Kampf*, 21, 6 (June 1928), 255. Renner is referring to Bauer, whom he characterizes as a chaplain unable to lead an army.

59. Julius Braunthal, *Otto Bauer. Eine Auswahl aus seinem Lebenswerk*, 83.

60. Otto Bauer, *Der Aufstand der österreichischen Arbeiter. Seine Ursachen und seine Wirkung,* Verlag Wiener Volksbuchhandlung (Vienna: Verlag Wiener Volksbuchhandlung, 1947).

61. Otto Bauer, *Die illegale Partei* (Frankfurt a.M., 1971), 62.

62. Otto Bauer, *Kapitalismus und Sozialismus nach dem Weltkrieg Erster Band: Rationalisierung—Fehlrationalisierung* (Vienna, 1931).

63. Bauer, *Zwischen zwei Weltkriegen?,* 126.

64. Bauer, *Zwischen zwei Weltkriegen?,* 344.

65. Bauer, *Zwischen zwei Weltkriegen?,* 252.

66. Bauer, *Zwischen zwei Weltkriegen?,* 253.

67. Bauer, *Zwischen zwei Weltkriegen?,* 319.

68. Josef Hindels, Preface to Otto Bauer, *Zwischen zwei Weltkriegen?,* reprint edition (Vienna: Verband Sozialistischer Studenten Österreichs, 1975), 4.

69. Krätke, "Austromarxismus und Kritische Theorie," 2.

70. Gerd Storm and Franz Walter, *Weimarer Linkssozialismus und Austromarxismus* (Berlin: Verlag Europäische Perspektiven, 1984), 31.

71. See Storm and Walter, *Weimarer Linkssozialismus und Austromarxismus,* 66, 71ff.

72. Weber, *Der kalte Krieg in der SPÖ,* iii.

73. Weber, *Der kalte Krieg in der SPÖ,* 2.

74. Cited from Georg Klaus and Manfred Buhr, eds., *Marxistisch-Leninistisches Wörterbuch der Philosophie,* vol. 1 (Hamburg: Rowohlt Taschenbuch Verlag, 1972), 157.

75. Herbert Steiner, *Am Beispiel Otto Bauers—Die Oktoberrevolution und der Austromarxismus,* special issue of *Weg und Ziel,* 1967, 91.

76. Hans-Jörg Sandkühler and Rafael de la Vega, eds., *Austromarxismus* (Vienna: Europäische Verlagsanstalt, 1970), 13.

77. Detlev Albers, ed., *Otto Bauer und der "dritte" Weg. Die Wiederentdeckung des Austromarxismus durch Linkssozialisten und Eurokommunisten* (Frankfurt: Campus Verlag, 1979); Detlev Albers and International Union of Socialist Youth, eds., *Perspektiven der Euro-Linken* (Frankfurt: Campus Verlag, 1981).

78. Walter Baier, Lisbeth N. Trallori, and Derek Weber, eds., *Otto Bauer und der Austromarxismus. Integraler Sozialismus und die heutige Linke* (Berlin: Dietz, 2008).

79. Publication forthcoming

80. Karl Marx, *A Contribution to the Critique of Political Economy,* Part I, in Karl Marx and Frederick Engels, *Collected Works,* vol. 29 (New York: International Publishers, 1987), 263.

81. Krätke, "Austromarxismus und Kritische Theorie."

Part I: War and Revolution

Chapter 1: The Southern Slavs and the War

1. The Mürzsteg Agreement, proposed by the Russian and Austro-Hungarian empires to the Ottoman Empire and signed on October 2, 1903, consisted of a series of reforms to be monitored by several European powers in the area roughly corresponding to present-day North Macedonia, northern Greece, and Kosovo. As such it was the first interna-

tionally monitored agreement in European history.

2. From 1437 to 1439, and from 1526 to 1918 without interruption, the head of the house of Habsburg was at the same time King of Hungary. The Austro-Hungarian Compromise of 1867 established Hungary as an autonomous state with its own parliament. Thus, the relationship between Austria and Hungary was formally limited to a personal union, that is, the Emperor of Austria and King of Hungary were the same person. Institutionally, this was expressed by military and foreign affairs being administered jointly, and these institutions were designated "k.u.k" (kaiserlich und königlich), that is, "Imperial and Royal" to project the idea of relative independence. The state institutions relating only to the Austrian crownlands continued to be designated "k.k." (Imperial Royal). Thus, a governor's office in Tyrol, for example, was designated "k.k."

Chapter 2: The Czechs and the Empire

1. Also known in German as the Kleine Internationale. The self-designation of Austria's Social Democratic Workers' Party, which contained six national parties. The crisis of the Austrian "Little International" anticipated the downfall of the Second International.
2. Bauer mistakenly gives 1870 as the date.
3. It is not known which Romanov grand duke was being considered.

Chapter 4: German-Austria in the War

1. The 1899 Nationalities Program of Brünn (Brno) was internationalist-Austrian; the national parties constituting Austrian Social Democracy agreed on a compromise solution to national conflicts in the state. Maintaining Austria, at least Cisleithania, by transforming it into the "Democratic Federal State of Autonomous Nationalities" became the political objective of the party. Only after 1907 did this compromise collapse (and with it the unity of the party).
2. *Die Nationalitätenfrage und die Sozialdemokratie* (Vienna: Brand, 1907; see English translation: Minneapolis: University of Minnesota Press, 2000).
3. Prime minister of Cisleithania for a matter of weeks in October–November 1918, Heinrich Lammasch was the Austrian Empire's last prime minister and only non-noble to have served in that office. He was an early advocate of a league of nations and served as an arbitrator in the Hague Arbitration Tribunal. Before the outbreak of World War I, he warned Austria against rapprochement with the German Empire, favoring an agreement with the Entente powers. During the war he participated in the international peace movement. After the failure of Foreign Minister Czernin's policies, the Emperor appointed Lammasch Prime Minister on October 27, 1918.
4. That is, Renner had reasoned that, since national autonomy could not be based on the crownlands, whose populations were mixed, administration had to be decentralized down to the level that would yield, largely, ethnically homogeneous units.
5. *Protokoll der Verhandlungen des Parteitages der Deutschen sozialdemokratischen Arbeiterpartei in Österreich abgehalten in Wien vom 19. bis 24. Oktober 1917* (Vienna: Wiener Volksbuchhandlung, 1919), 116–19 (within report by Gabriele Proft).
6. "Ein Natonalitätenprogramm der, 'Linken,'" *Der Kampf. Sozialdemokratische Monats-*

schrift 11, 4 (April 1918), 271–74.

7. *Der Kampf* 11, 4 (April 1918), 271–73.

8. *Der Kampf,* 11, 4 (April 1918), 272.

Part II: The Overthrow

Chapter 5: The Formation of the National States

1. "Die deutsche Sozialdemokratie und das Selbstbestimmungsrecht der Nationen," *Arbeiter-Zeitung*, October 4, 1918, 1 (Bauer's emphases).

2. *Stenographische Protokolle über die Sitzungen der Provisorischen Nationalversammlung für Deutschösterreich, 1918 und 1919. I. Band: 1. (Eröffnungs-) bis 18. Sitzung* (Vienna: Deutschösterreichische Staatsdruckerei, 1919), 3; reprinted in "Die deutsche National-versammlung," *Arbeiter-Zeitung*, October 22, 1918, 3 (emphasis in original).

3. The word used in the *Protokolle* and the publication of the text in the *Arbeiter-Zeitung* is "inneren," that is, "internal" or "domestic," while Bauer has "neuen" (new).

4. *Stenographische Protokolle über die Sitzungen der Provisorischen Nationalversammlung für Deutschösterreich, 1918 und 1919. Beilagen* (Vienna: Deutschösterreichische Staats-druckerei, 1919) Beilage I: "Kundgebung der Nationalversammlung der deutschen Ab-geordneten," 1 (Bauer's emphases); reprinted in "Die deutsche Nationalversammlung," *Arbeiter-Zeitung*, October 22, 1918.

5. *Stenographische Protokolle über die Sitzungen der Provisorischen Nationalversammlung für Deutschösterreich, 1918 und 1919. I. Band: 1. (Eröffnungs-) bis 18. Sitzung* (Vienna: Deutschösterreichische Staatsdruckerei, 1919), 7; and in "Die deutsche Nationalver-sammlung," *Arbeiter-Zeitung*, October 22, 1918, 2–3.

6. James Brown Scott, *Official Statements of War Aims and Peace Proposals, December 1916 to November 1918* (Washington, DC: Carnegie Endowment for International Peace, 1921), 428–29.

7. Scott, *Official Statements of War Aims and Peace Proposals,* 436.

8. "Proclamation of the State of Slovenes, Croats and Serbs," in *Yugoslavia Through Documents: From Its Creation to Its Dissolution*, Snežana Trifunovska, ed. (Dordrecht: Marinus Nijhoff, 1994), 147–48.

9. On October 16, in an effort to retain the state as a federation, Emperor Karl issued a manifesto calling on the nationalities to create their own national councils. The Provi-sional National Assembly for German-Austria (also informally known as the Viennese National Assembly) was the first parliament of the state of German-Austria. It was active during and after the disintegration of the Austro-Hungarian Monarchy from October 21, 1918 to February 16, 1919.

10. *Stenographische Protokolle über die Sitzungen der Provisorischen Nationalversammlung für Deutschösterreich, 1918 und 1919. I. Band: 1. (Eröffnungs-) bis 18. Sitzung* (Vienna: Deutschösterreichische Staatsdruckerei, 1919), 61.

11. *Stenographische Protokolle*, 61. See Glossary, "Staatsrat."

12. *Stenographische Protokolle*, 62–63.

Chapter 6: The Dissolution of the Empire

1. The progressive, civic, social science journal *Twentieth Century* (1900–19) was published by the Budapest Sociological Society from 1901 onwards.

Chapter 7: The German-Austrian Republic

1. After organizing the Volkswehr, Julius Deutsch (1884–1968) established the Republikanischer Schutzbund (Republican Protective League), a Social Democratic militia in response to the Christian Social Heimwehren/Heimatwehren. After its defeat in February 1934 and the establishment of the corporatist Austro-fascist state, Deutsch fled to Brünn. He fought on the side of the Spanish Republic in Spain's Civil War and then moved to Paris; he later fled from Paris to the United States, returning to Vienna after the war.
2. "Deutsche Arbeiter-Marseillaise." Written to the tune of the Marseillaise by Jacob Ardorf in 1864 for the Allgemeiner Deutscher Arbeiterverein.
3. Viktor Wutte and Arnold Eisner. See Johannes Sachslehner, *1918: Die Stunden des Untergangs* (Vienna, Graz and Klagenfurt: Verlagsgruppe Styria, 2013). The two Wirtschaftskommissäre (economic commissioners) were de facto the Landverweser (provincial administrators); that is, Wutte and Eisler and their Wohlfahrtsausschuss (Welfare Committee) took over the entire administration of Styria.
4. As the historical period shifts from Habsburg Austria to the German-Austrian and then Austrian Republic, the word "Provinzen" for the precursors to today's Austrian federal states ("Bundesländer") was replaced by "Länder." For the previous period, "Länder" tends to refer to the old lands of the German Confederation.

Chapter 8: National and Social Revolution

1. Karl Marx, "Herr Vogt," in Karl Marx and Frederick Engels, Collected Works, vol. 17 (New York: International Publishers, 1981), 145
2. Friedrich Engels, "The Role of Force in History," in Karl Marx and Friedrich Engels, *Collected Works*, vol. 26 (New York: International Publishers, 1990), 466.

Part III: The Hegemony of the Working Class

Chapter 9: Revolutionary and Counterrevolutionary Forces

1. It is true that the local workers cooperated in preventing the delivery of food to Vienna; however, they did requisition much of it for themselves.
2. Bauer intends *formal* democracy here.
3. "Gesetz vom 12. November 1918 über die Staats- und Regierungsform von Deutschösterreich," *Staatsgesetzblatt für den Staat Deutschösterreich*, Jahrgang 1918 (Vienna: Aus der deutschösterreichischen Staatsdruckerei, 1918), 4–5 (StGBl. 5/1918).
4. Actually, two laws are involved here, one on popular representation and the other on the governance of the state: "Gesetz vom 14. März 1919 über die Volksvertretung" and "Gesetz vom 14. März 1919 über die Staatsregierung," *Staatsgesetzblatt für den Staat*

Deutschösterreich, Jahrgang 1919 (Vienna: Aus der deutschösterreichischen Staatsdruckerei, 1919), 405–10 (StGBl. 179–80/1919).

Chapter 10: Between Imperialism and Bolshevism

1. Ernst Bettelheim, *Zur Krise der kommunistischen Partei Ungarns* (Vienna: Author,
   1922), 13–14.

2. Until the definitive establishment of the Austrian Republic and its parliament, it
   was still natural to use the inherited term Reich to indicate German-Austria—all
   the more so that unlike the German Republic (Deutsche Republik, Weimarer Republik) the word Reich is part of the actual name of the country/republic itself:
   Österreich.

3. In both conferences the Social Democratic majority of the workers' councils, after
   some hesitation, accepted the participation of the Communists. The Preamble to the
   organizational statute established in the first Reich conference (held March 1–2) stipulated: "The aim and task of the workers' councils is to give expression to the will of
   the entire working population of all workplaces and professions. . . . Eligible for election are all who see their goal in the overcoming of the capitalist mode of production
   and understand class struggle to be the means of emancipating working people" (in
   Hans Hautmann, *Die verlorene Räterepublik. Am Beispiel der Kommunistischen Partei
   Deutschösterreichs,* 2d ed. [Vienna: Europa Verlag, 1971], 135). On the one side, this
   recognition gave a boost to the Communists; on the other side, it was advantageous
   for the Social Democrats in that they could conduct their debate with their left critics
   in the framework of the workers' councils, which, despite everything, they controlled
   by dint of their overwhelming majority.

4. Theodor Schuhbauer later headed the Wiener Gemeindewache (municipal security
   guards) and was to play a leading role in the Republican Schutzbund.

5. Karl Radek, later member of the Comintern's Executive Committee but already in
   1919 a key figure in the RCP's foreign policy, condemned Bettelheim's actions as
   infantile putschism, claiming he had no authority to represent the Comintern, nor
   did the Comintern even know who he was. See Arnold Struthahn (pseudonym of
   Karl Radek), "Die Krise in der deutsch-österreichischen Kommunistischen Partei,"
   Die Rote Fahne. Zentralorgan der Kommunistischen Partei Deutschösterreichs, October
   28, 29, and 30, 1919.

6. Bauer's representation of the Holy Thursday confrontations and the Communist Party
   putsch does not stand up to critical examination. Between March and July the domestic
   political crisis reached its climax. A fifth of the population had to look for work on a
   daily basis and due to wildly increasing prices could not afford basic food. The pen-
   sion claims of war invalids had still not been regularized. On April 17, assemblies and
   demonstrations of returning soldiers, the unemployed, and war invalids were called
   for which the Communist Party of German-Austria (KPDÖ) declared it did not take
   responsibility. In the afternoon several thousand people assembled in front of the Parliament. After fruitless negotiations stones were thrown at the building, at which point the
   mounted police made use of firearms. Two points of the building were set on fire. The
   situation only calmed down due to the intervention of the Volkswehr, which included

the Communist-influenced Volkswehr Battalion 41.

The leadership of the new Hungarian Soviet Republic naturally had a great interest in alleviating its own military predicament through a Communist takeover in Vienna, above all in order to get hold of the arsenal of weapons left over from the Monarchy that were stored in Vienna. For this purpose an emissary, Ernst Bettelheim, was sent to Vienna who passed himself off as the representative of the Communist International, took over leadership of the party, and prepared for a seizure of power by the Communist Party. However unrealistic this plan might have been, an opportunity appeared to exist when the Allied Military Commission in Vienna demanded the decommissioning of the left-oriented Volkswehr. On the appointed date, June 15, the Communist Party called the Revolutionary Soldiers Committee and Volkswehr Battalion 41 to an armed demonstration. However, two days previously, the Social Democratic leadership managed to get the Allies to preliminarily rescind the demobilization order. At the same time the Vienna Workers Council declared itself against a coup.

This changed the attitude of the KPDÖ. On June 14, a majority of its Executive resolved to distance the party from the erection of a council dictatorship and to call for a peaceful demonstration. Despite this, 130 Communist functionaries were arrested during the night who had clearly come together to implement the new orientation. On the following morning several thousand demonstrators assembled. When they heard of the arrest of their leaders, they made their way to the police jail to secure their release. En route there were clashes during which the police opened fire resulting in twelve dead and eighty seriously injured people.

Even the Social Democratic Secretary of the Interior Mathias Eldersch testified to the Provisional National Assembly in July that he "could not claim with any certainty that on June 15 the Communists intended to violently enforce the calling of a council republic." *Stenographische Protokolle über die Sitzungen der konstituierenden Nationalversammlung der Republik Österreich. 1919. Erster Band. 1. bis 46. Sitzung* (Vienna: Österreichische Staatsdruckerei, 1919), 627—cited in Hans Hautmann, *Die verlorene Räterepublik* (Vienna, 1971), 183.

7.   Robert Lansing, *The Peace Negotiations: A Personal Narrative* (Boston: Houghton Mifflin, 1921). Lansing speaks of his memorandum and its enumeration of "essentials" for a stable peace (192; 171 of the London, Constable, edition).

8.   Lansing, *The Peace Negotiations,* 195 (Constable edition, 173). Earlier in this work (99; Constable, 88), Lansing voices his criticism of Wilson's and the Supreme Council's policy toward Austria as a violation of the right to self-determination, specifically as regards South Tyrol and an article on unification in the August 1919 German constitution.

9.   As given in Francesco Nitti, *The Wreck of Europe* (Indianapolis, IN: Bobbs-Merrill, 1922), 91–101.

10. John Maynard Keynes, *The Economic Consequences of the Peace* (New York: Harcourt, Brace, and Howe, 1919), 48 (emphasis in original).

Chapter 11: The Revolution in the Factories

1.   In the original edition the name is misspelled as "Ammon."

2. "Gesetz vom 19. Dezember 1918 über die Einführung des achtstündigen Arbeitstages in fabrikmäßig betriebenen Gewerbeunternehmungen," *Staatsgesetzblatt für den Staat Deutschösterreich*, Jahrgang 1918, 221–2.

3. "Gesetz vom 17. Dezember 1919 über den achtstündigen Arbeitstag," *Staatsgesetzblatt für die Republik Österreich*, Jahrgang 1919 (Vienna: Österreichische Staatsdruckerei, 1919), 1327–29 (StGBl. 138/1918).

4. "Gesetz vom 30. Juli 1919 über den Urlaub von Arbeitern (Arbeiterurlaubsgesetz)," *Staatsgesetzblatt für den Staat Deutschösterreich*, Jahrgang 1919 (Vienna: Österreichische Staatsdruckerei, 1919), 994–96 (StGBl. 581/1919).

5. A committee established in the British Parliament in 1916. See Reconstruction Committee, "Interim Report on Joint Standing Councils," printed in full in Bulletin of the United States Bureau of Labor Statistics, No. 255 (Washington, DC, 1919). See also Earl J. Miller, "Workmen's Representation in Industrial Government," *University of Illinois Studies in the Social Sciences*, vol. 10, nos. 3 and 4 (1922): 405–588.

6. "Gesetz vom 15. Mai 1919, betreffend die Errichtung von Betriebsräten," *Staatsgesetzblatt für den Staat Deutschösterreich*, Jahrgang 1919 (Vienna: Österreichische Staatsdruckerei, 1919), 651–65 (StGBl. 283/1919).

7. See Vladimir Lenin, "Report to the All-Russia Congress of Representatives of Financial Departments of Soviets, May 18, 1918" and "Letter Addressed to the Conference of Representatives of Enterprises to be Nationalised, May 18, 1918" in Lenin, Collected Works, vol. 27, 383–89.

8. The original edition has "Plum."

9. Sidney and Beatrice Webb, *A Constitution for the Socialist Commonwealth of Great Britain* (London: Longmans, Green & Co., 1920).

10. "Gesetz vom 29. Juli 1919 über gemeinwirtschaftliche Unternehmungen," *Staatsgesetzblatt für den Staat Deutschösterreich* (Vienna: Österreichische Staatsdruckerei, 1919), 961–68 (StGBl. 389/1919).

11. Karl Marx, *The Class Struggles in France, 1848 to 1850*, in Karl Marx and Friedrich Engels, *Collected Works*, vol. 10 (New York: International Publishers, 1978), 56.

Part IV: The Period of Class Power Equilibrium

Chapter 13: Economic Transformation and Social Regrouping

1. Friedrich Engels, "The Beginning of the End in Austria," in Karl Marx and Friedrich Engels, *Collected Works*, vol. 6 (New York: International Publishers, 1978), 535.

    Bauer's writings are not free from the occasional use of the derogatory, anti-Jewish language widespread in nineteenth-century Europe, which casts "the Jew" in the economic role of the dealer and money-lender within the disintegrating natural economy. In the socialist movement this goes back to remarks by Karl Marx and Friedrich Engels, in particular to their early writings.

    Otto Bauer, who himself came from an assimilated Jewish family, could imagine no future for Jews other than assimilation (see *The Question of Nationalities and Social Democracy*, 291ff). This is all the stranger in that more than a million non-assimilated

Jews in the Austrian crownlands of Galicia and Bukovina lived in closed settlement areas carrying on a rich cultural and social life.

Despite the distance assimilated Jewish intellectuals like Bauer frequently felt from a Jewish way of life, specifically in the eastern part of the Monarchy, he regularly paid a synagogue tax as an expression of solidarity, as he put it, with the community discriminated against and threatened by anti-Semitism.

After Bauer moved his residence from Brno to Paris in 1938 due to Austria's annexation by Hitler's Germany, he regarded his main duty to be "to rescue the life of individuals regardless of their party or movement or anything else" (letter from Hélène Bauer, cited from Julius Braunthal, *Otto Bauer. Eine Auswahl aus senem Lebenswerk*, 100). His last article, "I Appeal to the Conscience of the World," appeared on the day he died (July 5, 1938) in the London daily *News Chronicle* and is dedicated to the fate of Jews threatened with extermination due to fascist barbarism. "I know, also, how small is the prospect that help for the victims will be forthcoming. Nevertheless, it is the simple duty of all of us not to tire in our efforts to bring help to the latest victims of Fascism and to appeal again and again to the conscience of the world."

2. "Verordnung des Justizministers im Einvernehmen mit dem Minister für öffentliche Arbeiten und dem Minister des Innern vom 19. Februar 1917 über die Geschäftsführung der Mietämter und der Bezirksgerichte in Angelegenheiten des Mieterschutzes," *Reichsgesetzblatt für die im Reichsrate vertretenen Königreiche und Länder* (Vienna: Aus der k.k. Hof- und Staatsdruckerei, 1917), 133–5 (RGBl. 53/1917).

3. "Gesetz vom 31. Mai 1919 über die Wiederbesiedlung gelegter Bauerngüter und Häusleranwesen (Wiederbesiedlungsgesetz)," *Staatsgesetzblatt für die Republik Österreich*, Jahrgang 1919 (Vienna: Aus der Österreichischen Staatsdruckerei, 1919), 739–44 (StGBl. 310/1919). The name of the state before October 23, 1919, was *Deutschösterreich*; after that it was *Republik Österreich*. The former appears in the title of the individual facsimiles containing laws prior to that date in 1919, while the latter appears in the title page of the complete annual edition published at the end of the year.

4. "Vollzugsanweisung der Staatsämter für Justiz und für Land- und Forstwirtschaft vom 5. August 1919 über den Schutz der Kleinpächter," *Staatsgesetzblatt für den Staat Deutschösterreich*, Jahrgang 1919 (Vienna: Aus der Österreichischen Staatsdruckerei, 1919), 1003–5 (StGBl. 403/1919).

Chapter 14: The Struggle for Republican Institutions

1. "Wehrgesetz vom 18. März 1920," *Staatsgesetzblatt für die Republik Österreich*, Jahrgang 1920 (Vienna: Aus der Österreichischen Staatsdruckerei, 1920), 232–40 (StGBl. 122/1920).

2. "Gesetz vom 21. Juli 1920 über die einmalige große Vermögensabgabe," *Staatsgesetzblatt für die Republik Österreich*, Jahrgang 1920 (Vienna: Aus der Österreichischen Staatsdruckerei, 1920), 1509–35.

3. The law is dated July 13: "Gesetz vom 13. Juli 1920, betreffend die Änderung einiger Bestimmungen des Gesetzes vom 3. Juli 1919, St. G. Bl. Nr. 345, über die Regelung

des Verkehres mit Getreide und Mahlprodukten im Wirtschaftsjahre 1920/21," *Staatsgesetzblatt für die Republik Österreich*, Jahrgang 1920 (Vienna: Aus der Österreichischen Staatsdruckerei, 1920), 1308–10.

Chapter 15: *The Struggle against the Counterrevolution*

1. Bauer mistakenly has July 6 instead of July 13.
2. Actually, Müller only became a Nationalrat deputy in 1923.
3. "Karl IV" in Bauer's text.

Chapter 16: *The People's Republic*

1. Karl Marx and Frederick Engels, *Collected Works*, vol. 26 (New York: International Publishers, 1990), 271: "By way of exception, however, periods occur in which the warring classes balance each other so closely that the state authority, as ostensible mediator, acquires, for the moment, a certain degree of independence of both. Such was the absolute monarchy of the seventeenth and eighteenth centuries, which held the balance between the nobility and burghers; such was the Bonapartism of the First, and especially of the Second French Empire, which played off the proletariat against the bourgeoisie and the bourgeoisie against the proletariat. The latest performance of this kind, in which ruler and ruled appear equally ridiculous, is the new German Empire of the Bismarck nation: here capitalists and workers are balanced against each other and equally cheated for the benefit of the impoverished Prussian backwoods Junkers."

Part V: The Restoration of the Bourgeoisie

Chapter 17: *The Currency Catastrophe*

1. In 1916 a progressive tax (with rates from 5 percent to 45 percent) was levied on higher company earnings since the outbreak of the war and individual excess income using the time frame of January 1, 1913 to July 31, 1914.
2. "Bundesgesetz vom 21. Dezember 1921 über die Anmeldung der Bestände an ausländischen Zahlungsmitteln (Valutenanmeldungsgesetz)," *Bundesgesetzblatt für die Republik Österreich*, Jahrgang 1921 (Vienna: Aus der Österreichischen Staatsdruckerei, 1921, 2147–49 [BGBl. 705/1921]).
3. "Bundesgesetz vom 20. Dezember 1921 über die Besteuerung des Geldumsatzes der Kreditunternehmungen (Bankenumsatzsteuergesetz)," *Bundesgesetzblatt für die Republik Österreich*, Jahrgang 1921 (Vienna: Aus der Österreichischen Staatsdruckerei, 1921, 2180–83 [BGBl 720/1921]),
4. *Arbeiter-Zeitung*, XXXIV, 232 (August 24, 1922), 1; the bracketed text from *Arbeiter-Zeitung* was omitted by Bauer.
5. *Arbeiter-Zeitung*, XXXIV, 232 (August 24, 1922), 2 (emphasis in original, not in Bauer); the bracketed text from *Arbieter-Zeitung* was omitted by Bauer.

Chapter 18: The Geneva Protocols

1. League of Nations, *The Restoration of Austria: Agreements Arranged by the League of Nations and Signed at Geneva on October 4th, 1922 with the Relevant Documents and Public Statements,* no date or place of publication; French and German texts: *Bundesgesetzblatt für die Republik Österreich,* Jahrgang 1922, Vienna: Aus der Österreichischen Staatsdruckerei, 1922, 1659–72 (BGBl. 842/1922).
2. Bauer mistakenly gives the figure 530.
3. Karl Marx, *The Class Struggles in France 1848 to 1850,* vol. 10, Karl Marx and Frederick Engels, *Collected Works* (New York: International Publishers, 1978), 59. Note: In the original German, Marx's wording is "durch die Juden der Finanz," which Bauer quotes.
4. "Bundesgesetz vom 27. November 1922 über die zur Aufrichtung der Staats- und Volkswirtschaft der Republik Österreich zu treffenden Maßnahmen (Wiederaufbaugesetz)," *Bundesgesetzblatt für die Republik Österreich,* Jahrgang 1922 (Vienna: Aus der Österreichischen Staatsdruckerei, 1922, 1673–82 [BGB 843/1922]).

Chapter 19: The Achievements of the Revolution and the Tasks of Social Democracy

1. Friedrich Engels, "The Beginning of the End in Austria," in Karl Marx and Frederick Engels, *Collected Works,* vol. 6, 535.
2. *Geistig* is the word used, which here indicates rule through cultural consensus. Bauer's concept is equivalent to the Gramscian idea of hegemony.

INDEX